Book Publishing With InDesign CC

Using Desktop Publishing Power
To Self-Publish Your Book

Book Publishing

With InDesign CC

Using Desktop Publishing Power
To Self-Publish Your Book

David Bergsland

Publishing globally online

Written and published in April, 2016
© David Bergsland • All Rights Reserved

ISBN-13: 978-1530967353

ISBN-10: 153096735X

Produced by Radiqx Press
314 Van Brunt Street
Mankato, Minnesota 56001
http://radiqx.com • info@radiqx.com

Please let me know if there is anyway I can help you in your publishing endeavors.

I dedicate this to my Lord & King

Acknowledgments

In a work which covers the past 40 years, the people who have helped are far too many to list. Michael Perry, Tom Clarke, Christ Hyde, and T.J. Allen have been of help. The groups at Christian Indie Authors, Indie Christian Authors, and Iron Sharpens Iron have helped a lot. It's been a wonderful experience for this old curmudgeon.

It been quite a voyage since I started to teach all this stuff in 1991. It's hard to believe how much I've learned and how often I've been humbled since I started doing this full-time in 2009. The growth pains and the stretching have been exhilarating.

Contents

Who's this book for?

Very specific people indeed:

- Authors and publishers who have come to realize that they need a better, faster, and more efficient publishing workflow.

- They also have come to believe that, for excellence in publishing, professional tools are required.

- They are willing to learn the new concepts and techniques to accomplish these goals.

This book is an enjoyable retail read masquerading as a textbook, or maybe it's the other way around. If I were still teaching my digital publishing degree, I would use it for the textbook of a 6-credit, two-semester course. There is a lot of material here. However, it is designed to be fun and engrossing to read over a period of several weeks or longer.

What is required?

- A willingness to learn

- A commitment to do what is necessary

- A willingness to spend the time required

- A basic knowledge of using InDesign CC: starting a new document, saving it to a specific folder, file management, basic tool usage, and all the rest of basic computer literacy. Sandee Cohen's *Visual Quickstart* book will enable this.

- A decision to pay for what is needed

This last one is the killer for many: You must be willing to spend $20 a month for InDesign CC. Many of you already have the full Creative Cloud with all of its applications. This costs around $50 a month.

You also must have fast internet access:

We won't specify it. But in our experience, this means a cable modem. There are other options, of course. But you need to be able to comfortably upload and download things in the gigabyte+ range.

With that covered, enjoy the book!

PART ONE:

The
Self-Publishing
Industry

CHAPTER ONE

Welcome to my world

I want to say some brief words of welcome as you start through this new book. You will discover that what I am doing is working creatively within InDesign to produce completed books almost as a fine art exercise while maintaining excellence and easily meeting production needs.

What I want to share with you is a method, an attitude, a service to the reader which is enabled by the typographic power of InDesign. I am discussing one-person do-it-yourself publishing, direct communication from author to reader.

Using the new 21st century paradigm of self-publishing

One of the wonderful things about the new publishing paradigm is the control we get as artists, authors, designers, and publishers over the entire package. A modern book is released in multiple sizes, versions, and formats. The content and design remain fluid as we shape the book while we learn and grow.

We can easily adjust content, layout, and presentation of our books after they are released in response to emails, beta readers, FaceBook friends, tweets, comments on our blog posts, pluses on our Google+ post comments, and the whole host of online social networking.

Who is this book written for?

The focus of this book is very sharp. It is for people who are producing books and booklets, non-fiction in specific—beginning with very limited capital and few personnel resources. The good news is that you can start with an able computer, the software I mention, and a vision. Money is not required to start, and little is required as you grow. It will take quite a bit of work, but not more than normal for a project with the scope of a book.

I'm sharing techniques for the new wave of author/publishers who are not (and do not intend to be) large publishing houses. It is designed to help those of you without the resources and connections nor inclination to intrigue the large, mass-market media houses with their incredible capital requirements and insane marketing needs that look more like addicted gambling than actual communication through book production—authors writing and publishers delivering to small niches.

Many new skills are required. One of the trials of the new paradigm is the incredible amount of knowledge and the various skills necessary to do all of this. The good news is that Adobe's Creative Cloud enables you to use these skills and gain the knowledge necessary quite easily for a small monthly fee. It is the only software available which gives you the power you need to publish creatively and professionally in one package.

My extensive background

I have been uniquely positioned to take advantage of the new workflow. I began as a fine artist in the 1960s and early 1970s. I learned typesetting and graphic design at the hands of a masterful art director in the late 1970s. I spent a decade as an art director myself within a large commercial printer in Albuquerque, New Mexico.

I began teaching these materials in 1991. Within a couple of years, a large traditional publisher was asking me to convert my handouts to a textbook on the new digital printing. I used that opportunity to develop the first all-digital printing and design curriculum in the country (as far as I can tell). I wrote a book a year for them on typography, FreeHand, Illustrator, Photoshop, and finally InDesign. *Publishing with InDesign* was one of the first books on the new software that would eventually take over the industry.

Becoming a teaching pastor as well as church administrator for my wife's church in Albuquerque in 1993 enabled me to use my skills in a whole new way. Materials for Bible studies, spiritual dramas, and worship services were a new joy for me.

While all of this was going on, in 1996, I took all my coursework online. I became involved with the distance learning initiative at my community college. I continued to write new instructional materials. I was supplying them to my students on the class Website as downloadable PDFs.

Then I found Lulu in 2002 and my world changed. With Lulu, then Createspace, then Scribd, then Zazzle, then Kindle, and then ePUBs with the iBookstore, Nook-Press, and Kobo Writing Life, I could get my writing out to my students very efficiently. Writing books became a real joy to me as InDesign kept getting better and better. More and more I was doing everything in InDesign except the photos. It is a great workflow I highly recommend.

I've been able to use all my experience, from fine artist to writer, graphic designer to publisher, as a synergistic whole which is immensely fun and deeply satisfying. This book serves as a reference book for graphic designers and/or authors converting to book production. It's one of the most complete typographic references for book design, among many other things.

Book design knowledge is rare among designers today.

You need to read or browse all the materials so that you can talk the same language as your suppliers and understand their needs. If you are working with someone else, it will take many sharing sessions. They are not you and they will not put the book together the way you would. You are using them because of their expertise in areas where you are lacking. Respect their advice. Support each other in this process.

This book is organized into seven major parts

There is no way around it. Creating a book and publishing it is a major project. There are seven major areas you need to have covered. Obviously, you can use these parts as references for that portion of your book.

- **Part One:** A basic overview of self-publishing

- **Part Two:** Writing the copy

- **Part Three:** Adding the graphics

How to make a graphic in InDesign. How to convert them in Photoshop for use in ebooks. What formats should be used and why.

- **Part Four:** Layout: designing the book

Here you get the information you need to use fonts professionally. This covers why and how typesetting (what we do in InDesign) differs from typewriting (what you do in Word and Scrivener).

Here is the conceptual knowledge on how to set up a functional default set of paragraph and character styles, plus an intro to object styles. You'll modify these for your use.

- **Part Five:** The various ebook versions

Here are design tips and techniques for converting your printed book to a downloadable PDF and various ePUBs: fixed layout [FXL] and Reflowable—ready to upload to iBooks, Kobo, NookBooks, Smashwords, and Draft2Digital. Included is a simple conversion process for your Kindle version.

- **Part Six:** Uploading to the various suppliers

Information and advice about the companies used in early 2016 for on-demand publishing for free or very close to it.

- **Part Seven:** Christian Marketing

Specific help for Christian authors to help your readers discover your book. This advice is quite different than what you will normally find. I'm no real marketing help to non-believers, though the techniques work for you, too.

CHAPTER TWO

The New Publisher

Here we are—late in the second decade of the new millennium and we now have a new type of publishing which truly helps individual authors and publishers. The new changes are almost designed for those of us who feel called to share our vision with our trainees, students, and sheep. The new methodologies work better for teachers and leaders in small unique niches than anyone else.

But who cares about books?

Actually, we do. Authors, as a group, are voracious readers. Part of the reason we write is to share the magic we found in books. Many of us start out our personal publishing efforts as bloggers these days—short, pithy writing offering a conversation with those we serve. These writings are easily compiled into books and ebooks. Even though the writing style will need a large transformation, blog post content is largely written and needs only copyediting to make it work in a book.

On the other hand, in a world gone mad for the flashy immediacy (and minimal content) of video, why should we worry about books anyway? The key lies in the parenthetical phrase above *"and minimal content"*. We all know the difference between reading the book and seeing the movie. With an excellent novel, you enter an entire world, directed by the wordsmithing of the author. With an excellent movie you are handed a very intense (but brief & limited) slice of the life of that world you entered in the book.

But even this misses the entire point of a good non-fiction book. The depth of knowledge, subtle word definitions, language studies, historical insights, maps, and all the rest provided by a book could only be handled [if it's even possible] by a very lengthy, ridiculously expensive movie. And these exceedingly lengthy explanatory movies are simply a waste of resources to produce for a relatively nonexistent audience. A four page, explanatory handout for an awards presentation banquet becomes a fifteen minute to an hour video. That would be a major production requiring many new skills and large expenses—and there is often subtle information available in the printed materials that simply cannot be translated into moving visuals.

Though it is true that videos might get us better numbers when we offer a class, it is also true that the students learn a more simple version of data and knowledge from videos than they do from books, writing, and research. Lectures and teachings are converted to books relatively easily. It is easy to add reference materials. Illustrations and graphics are commonly developed by the author for the oral presentation, and often they are ready to use.

Even so, things have radically changed. As a writer, most of my research and reference materials are now online. To be forced to return to printed reference works would really slow me down and I would miss many opportunities to cross reference and discover new insights.

The core is still the book.

Publishing is a huge industry. In 2012, the content creation industry in the US was 504 billion dollars. The largest segment of that was publishing books at $151 billion. Movies were second at $133 billion. But that does not tell the tale. Movies produced in 2015 were 9734 [by far the most ever]. The most recent figures for books show 2,200,000 new books a year. There's no comparison.

Books have been the major source of knowledge ever since our culture was torn apart by this new technology at the beginning of the Renaissance. Readily available books completely transformed our civilization.

The new digital production techniques have stirred the pot. Smartphones seem to have taken over the world. Now that they have screens of 6 inches or more, they are large enough to use for reading and statistics are showing that it is finally happening, especially for novels.

Of course, for the more complex non-fiction books, teaching materials, or any written material where you need people to be able to follow along page by page, a fixed layout is necessary. That still probably requires a tablet, laptop, or a desktop computer. We'll cover how to do all of this as we go through the book.

How have things changed?

The entire definition of a book has been revised: many of the materials in this piece you are reading did not appear as a book (in the traditional sense) at first. These paragraphs were first released as the first posting of a new series on my blog, *The Skilled Workman*, in April of 2011. There was a link to a free downloadable PDF version of these lengthy blog postings at Scribd. The intention was a fully developed book after I was given the complete vision to share. I ended up with six of these postings, as I recall. The book which resulted from this process was a synergistic improvement to the process. The first edition of *Writing In InDesign* was released in print through Createspace to Amazon at the end of July, 2011.

But a whole host of new options came into play as soon as this first part was posted on my blog. With the new Publish Online option in InDesign CC (2015) I could have simply offered it online for comments, and for early beta readers. But in 2011, I made a downloadable PDF for Scribd. I tweeted about it. I shared it on FaceBook. But if I thought it would help, I could have easily released a Kindle book, an ePUB, and several other ebook variations. I could have also offered it as a printed booklet. The new paradigm of publishing enables me to easily offer a book or booklet in a wide variety of formatted options to attract and communicate with various types of readers.

Most of these options are free. All they take is a little bit of effort on my part. But the final results are much better than what could be done in the old paradigm. The capabilities change weekly. In the summer of 2012, Kobo Writing Life was added to put ePUBs on Kobo. Since then, Draft2Digital appears offering listings to Kindle, iBooks, Nook, Scribd, and Kobo. Tomely from Australia appeared a few years ago. Gumroad offers an archive to download with DRM-free copies of the PDF, an ePUB with embedded fonts, and a Kindle version. We'll talk later about why the embedded font ePUBs matter. But now as mentioned, I can simply Publish Online for my beta readers to get feedback.

Desktop publishing has reached its potential

I clearly remember how excited I was in the early 1990s when I realized that the work I had been doing (designing printing materials) with a team of forty highly skilled people and millions of dollars of equipment could now be done by a single person working at their desk.

That is even more true today when for a small monthly payment, I can have the top professional software for publishing in print, ebook, and video. There is no better software for these processes than InDesign, Illustrator, Photoshop, Acrobat, and Premier Pro. I suspect, CC has all I need for doing audio books also, but I choose to let a man help me and we share the revenue.

It is true that I have taken things a little further than most by designing my own fonts, doing all my own illustrations, and so on. However, the concept is clear and the freedom to communicate in words from your computer is exhilarating. Books, blogs, ebooks, brochures, emails, and much more can be directed to your readers to help communicate the message you have been given.

A teacher/trainer/prophet/leader can now have a world-wide influence from his or her office. We are no longer limited by locale. The author can help the people he or she is called to serve no matter where they live. More than that, it can be done professionally and compellingly without the immense barriers erected by traditional publishing. Global publishing is increasingly part of what we do—from our computer in our home.

Here are some of the things that have changed in publishing since the 1990s:

- **Printing is now just an option:** The multi-million dollar printing presses have simply become an output option. The same is true of the expensive bindery equipment. All of the front end design and preproduction processes are given to us as software to be loaded into our computer and used in our office.

  It's all part of InDesign and Photoshop: They are now part of the creative process leading to many different types of fulfillment. The art department and prepress department of the printing companies are long gone as are the $100,000 copy cameras, the $500,000 scanners and color separators, the extremely skilled (& expensive) typesetters, layout specialists, camera operators, film assemblers, and all the rest. We, the document creators, now control all of that.

- **No expensive proofs:** Before the digital revolution a true proof, an actual copy of the finished product, cost hundreds or even thousands of dollars. Now we can simply have a single copy of our book printed—usually for ten dollars or less. Plus we can print proofs of individual pages for pennies. The various ebook formats are used as their own proofs and revised as necessary.

- **Lengthy lead times are eliminated:** I can remember the shock when my first book was published. It took so long to actually get it into print. It was common, back then, to spend a year writing a book and then another year or more to get it actually printed and released. This is the old paradigm.

  Now I write fully formatted [more about why, in a bit]. So, as soon as the book is finished, I can give it to the proofer, and it can be released within a day or two after the copyediting changes are received.

- **No minimum orders:** In traditional publishing, just setting up the plates to be printed cost at least $50 a page and usually closer to $100. Plus you had to run a couple hundred copies through the press to get the first usable copy. Additionally, there was no real way to bind a single book on a practical level. As a result you could easily spend a thousand dollars to get the first copy of each sheet of paper (which usually held four to thirty two pages of a book) and less than fifty dollars to get the next 2,000 copies as they were printed at 10,000 to 50,000 copies an hour. You no longer need to print hundreds or thousands of documents to get the cost per unit price down to the place you can afford. **You can print a single book.**

- **Not limited to brick and mortar bookstores:** This is why they are all dying. You can publish what you need when you need it. You can service a very small niche effectively and profitably. You can use the mammoth online bookstores to distribute your documents and books—as well as email and your own Websites. You can even serialize your new book in your blog—getting reader feedback as you go. All you need to do is give your readers a link to the finished book in Lulu or Amazon for them to get a copy.

- **Not limited to print:** You can offer your book in the iBookstore in iTunes, NookBooks at Barnes & Noble, the Kindle store on Amazon, on Kobo, Scribd, Lulu, and many more ebook venues.

- **Changes and corrections are normally free:** You are no longer dependent on your copyediting budget to get a professional book. You can upload a new version of the ebooks with typo fixes without interrupting the availability of the book.

  Once a book is released with an ISBN, you can still change everything except the size and binding of the book. **But even if you want to change the ISBN**, all you need to do is publish the book as a new book or a new edition. You can leave the old book for sale if you like, building separate readerships for similar content.

- **Targeted editions are no problem:** You can make specialized versions for various movements, denominations, synagogues, churches, areas, countries, and/or targeted audiences with little effort required. Normally, all you need is a new cover, possibly a change in the header/footer info on the master pages, and the copyright info.

- **Existing pieces from multiple books and documents can be assembled for special programs:** you can take your work and make it into a custom curriculum or special presentation at the conference or service to which you are called to share your work.

- **In addition, you can have live hyperlinks in all the ebooks:** This makes marketing your books more powerful because you can have links to your Website/blog, other books you have written, groups you are a member of, and more.

- **Plus, the ebooks all support video, and audio:** You are only limited by how much you want to learn. The software is no longer a limitation.

That's what this book is: It's a targeted version of my basic digital publishing writings directed at authors and self-publishers. There are many things here that would not appeal to non-writers or that they could not comprehend. It is a natural extension of my life and work as an illustrator, typographer, art director, font designer, author, teacher, and publisher.

Who benefits from this material?

As mentioned before, this book is for authors and publishers who are concerned about design quality, production efficiency, and production speed. Some of the people who will find these materials of great use are:

- **Writers who blog professionally:** I find that writing in or saving posts into InDesign enables me to keep my blog postings in folders on my hard drive where I can easily assemble them as books, booklets, and marketing materials.

- **Authors who write two or more books a year:** Publishing your work can be a huge waste of time. By doing your production work in InDesign, once the book is completed, it can be released in less than two days.

- **Authors who supplement their income by formatting and releasing books for others:** Many authors are now offering their production services to authors like themselves who do not want to take the time to learn to format and publish. This also helps keep up your InDesign skills while you are working on your books.

- **Publishers serving the new authors:** There are quite a few authors who do not want to have anything to do with formatting books. Publishers like myself can now offer publishing for these people while offering huge royalties of 40-60%.

Word processing was for the editors

If you work in Word, Scrivener, or any of the rest of the word processors, you are still stuck in the old paradigm. This is a world dominated by the editors. The new paradigm is a radical change.

What I am proposing is a workflow controlled by the authors

Now that traditional publishers expect you to do your own marketing, there is little reason to pay them 85%-95% of the royalties—as found in traditional author/publisher contracts. *It's a brand new world.* The author should be receiving from 40% to 95% of the income generated by the sale of the books. The only place that is not true is for audio books. But even so, you can receive good royalties if you narrate and produce those books yourself. However, this book will not help you there.

CHAPTER THREE

Developing the copy

There are many options. Most of you are accustomed to the very restrictive world of writing in a word processor. There's nothing wrong with that, but I will propose a better way in a bit. At present, most books are written in Word or Scrivener because the editors demand it. Pieces are added from blogs, Google Docs, Pages, Web pages, and so on.

The problem with this is the limits it puts on your book production. Word processors and HTML can produce decent quality novels as Kindle books and rudimentary ePUBs, as long as they are not illustrated. But fixed layout ePUBs, downloadable PDFs, Kindle's Textbooks, and the like are very clumsy to do in a word processor. There are simply too many things which cannot be done.

If you choose to use this type of professional editor, for your content that is up to you. It's a good workflow for raw copy. You can easily move your edited copy into an InDesign document to finish the production.

For proofing, a print layout works much better as beta readers can talk to you about the problem they see on page 189, for example. Being able to refer to page numbers is one great advantage of proofing with PDFs.

I prefer editors who will proof and edit by annotating a PDF. That works better for me. But that is just personal taste. What I am suggesting may very well cause you to rethink your writing process. For now, let me repeat, using word processors, blogs, and HTML editors makes things much more difficult.

Some of you will say that you prefer using Scrivener for the freedom it gives in adding bits and pieces to build a coherent whole. I can understand that—to a certain extent. But actually writing in Scrivener is an extremely clumsy process, because you formatting as you go is quite difficult.

The reason is that no word processor works fluently with styles. Paragraph, character, table, and object styles, applied by keyboard shortcut as you write give you power to communicate clearly with your readers—as you write.

But enough of that for now. Let me give you my rationale for writing in InDesign. You can certainly continue to write in a word processor or HTML editor, adding the pieces to InDesign when you are ready to put the book together. But that will become very slow and frustrating as you learn InDesign and what it can do.

Writing within InDesign

Here I am again recommending a road less traveled by—not unusual in my life and work. Before you get defensive about your workflow, let me tell you my reasonings. I fully recognize that most people write in Word, another word processor, or an HTML editor. As mentioned already, what these people do not realize [in many cases] is that this simple fact starts their book under a great handicap. Many of the effective typographic tools for communication are simply missing, If they are publishing their own book, Word simply does not provide many of the best tools for communicating clearly and easily with their readers.

But InDesign is too hard to learn!

No, it's not. That is only true if you try to use it occasionally. If you are using InDesign on a daily basis, you will quickly find that it is Word or Scrivener which are too hard to learn. I can use Word or Scrivener very fluently. I choose not to use them only because it is far too difficult to write in either of them. But then, what I want is to see the book as you will see it—as I am writing it.

This is not as much of an advantage if you are writing novels. But then consider this: I just received a MOBI (a Kindle book) obviously done in Word. I had reading troubles on the first page. The map is sideways. Maps are always a problem done in Word or any word processor. Word does not support CMYK or most vector formats. So, maps in Kindle books are usually low-resolution monsters, hard to read, and very ugly.

What are the advantages of writing in InDesign?

- **You can work fully formatted:** This enables you to see what the readers will see. The graphics will be in position so you can see them as the reader will see them. The page breaks will show, as will the margins, and all the rest of the page layout. You apply page breaks from with your paragraph styles.

- **You can use professional graphics:** Even if you are using Photoshop (as you will be for photos), you can place them as PSDs rather than damaging them by saving them in one of the Web formats.

  But more than that, the whole world of professional vector graphics, placed as EPSs, PDFs, or even .ai files is now possible.

  For your ebooks, you can import animations, videos, and audio files. These also work for downloadable PDFs.

- **If you are writing in InDesign, your InDesign skills are continuously improving:** This is the best way for you to make InDesign a tool which can be fluently used to create your books. It will raise you production abilities to levels you did not know existed.

- **If you are writing more technical books and training manuals, the lists and tables can be wonderful:** Most people have no idea what can be done with lists, tables, and similar typographic tools. I did a book for a man a while back who had 2-4 types of lists on each of three levels of indent—for a total of over a dozen different list styles.

This type of writing has many typographic needs which are absolutely horrible if done in a word processor. This simple list you are reading now with the custom bullet and the automatic run-in head is very difficult in Word. This paragraph uses a style with no bullet, but has the same indent, so it can be used to add paragraphs under a bullet before returning to the list.

I'm sure I could come up with a couple more reasons. But, by now you should be able to see some of the advantages to writing in InDesign. As mentioned, you can still write in the word processor of your choice. InDesign can import the .doc or .docx, bringing in all the styles you were using in Word. But normally, styles are not used in Word. This is a huge problem once you begin the conversion to an ePUB or Kindle book.

Books are not entirely about words

Of course as a writer this may not make much sense to you. But please hear me out. For years I have taught graphic designers that the content is all that matters. Now I am teaching writers that presentation and layout are a big part of your book. For designers, this has been a major fight because many never read the copy they design into books and printed materials. Now I am dealing with writers who do not see the need for typography and layout skills. In the publishing world there is a real disconnect between the writers and the book designers. They are treated as two entirely separate skill sets. It is better for them to merge, as much as possible.

Most designers do not deal well with words

Graphic designers [and this includes most book designers] are visual people, focused on how things look. One of my major concerns as I started to write books in the mid-1990s was my experience in my classes using published textbooks only as bad examples which provided poor communication. As a pastor, commercially available Bible studies were just as bad. They were extremely difficult to use because the layout caused massive turn-offs to the readers—and confused the heck out of them. The examples are endless.

My pursuit of functional, reader-centered books has been fraught with trials. I was constantly bumping up against standardized procedures of traditional publishers which really made their books hard to read or use effectively. This focus on the reader is so far outside the norm in publishing today that there is no room at all for an author who even cares about these things (except in this new paradigm of on-demand self-publishing.

Let's talk about some simple examples of this lack of concern for the reader

❧ **Illustrations listed by number with no connection to the copy talking about what is illustrated:** Most traditional non-fiction publishers require this typographic horror. In many cases, authors are not allowed to even pick out the images because they are not considered professional enough to understand what is required of an graphic.

But the results are illustrations, maps, charts, and photos listed by number which are often not on the same page (or even the same chapter) as the content they illustrate.

Why bother to even have them? Few readers will find them or take the time to look for them. The result is frustrated readership and readers who simply quit reading in disgust.

For fiction, it is equally bad to have an illustration or map which cannot be easily referenced by the reader. In my novels I add maps, and relevant portions of the main map, where they are needed in the copy to help the reader understand what is going on a little better. Always remember, the goal is to assist the reader to find the message of the book.

❧ **Heads and subheads generated by designers:** In many cases over the years I spent as a graphic designer, I wrote all the subheads, developed all the lists, wrote all the captions, and even wrote most of the headlines.

I developed them out of a need to help direct the reader through the copy I was formatting. The author commonly had no clue that they were desirable or necessary. I wrote them as a service to the reader.

As a writer, you must be aware of these issues and realize that they are a primary method of clearing up communication with the reader. Heads, subheads, list design, and all the rest are key elements of your support of easy understanding by the reader.

Page layout determined by fashion and visual concerns: Often fonts are chosen because they look good, hip, and fashionable. Layouts are determined by fashion. Columns, margins, sidebars and the like are chosen to stimulate visual interest and provoke excitement instead of being chosen to communicate the content effectively, clearly, and accessibly. Clarity and accuracy are rarely considered.

The most glaring example of this is seen in the books where content is broken up into small pieces—supposedly to help people with short attention spans. My wife and I recently bought a book on creationism that is virtually unreadable. The gorgeous, fancy illustrations push the copy into bits and pieces that randomly appear out of the visual clutter of the pages' backgrounds. My wife gave up on it. She asked me to give her a report—which I did.

But it goes much further than that. Here's a quote from Wikipedia about the normal traditional editorial process (please force yourself to read it, I realize it is difficult to read):

"*(Once)* a decision is taken to publish a work, and the technical legal issues resolved, the author may be asked to improve the quality of the work through rewriting or smaller changes, and the staff will edit the work.

Publishers may maintain a house style, and staff will copy edit to ensure that the work matches the style and grammatical requirements of each market. Editors often choose or refine titles and headlines. Editing may also involve structural changes and requests for more information."

Notice a couple of things. First, there is no hint that the publisher understands your niche. Second, there is nothing here about serving the readers. The readers' needs are not part of the process. It's all about sales and the marketing decisions of the publisher. Textbooks and study books are the worst examples of editorial damage.

In most cases they will not even talk to you as an author unless you can convince them that you have a large enough following to guarantee enough sales to cover the costs. Once you've passed that hurdle, they will normally insist that you fit your content into their style—even if that style hinders your book and may even offend your readers.

I had a book on InDesign published by a major publisher which was formatted in software which was incapable of showing what InDesign could do. It was a disaster in sales and in simple readability. I could only use it as a bad example in my classes.

Let's take a brief look at this world of traditional publishing—that relic of the information age which came before the digital desktop on-demand world in which we live. In general, these traditionalists are extremely confused by what is taking place in the self-publishing world.

Traditional publishing

The traditional model is completely bound up [or broken up] into areas of expertise that are gathered together in an assembly line production style for the finished product. This works relatively well for mass-market content where the audience is understood by everyone in the process. The list of people with whom you, as an author, are required to interact in this scenario is incredible. You will work with several types of editors (editor-in-chief, acqui-

sition editors, copyeditors), proofers, marketers, illustrators, art departments, production departments, assistants,
preflightists, IT specialists, and the list goes on. I won't
even mention the dreaded bean-counters and legal eagles.
These meetings and interactions are often delegated by
authors with clout to agents, publicists and the like. Yet,
they only give you around a ten percent royalty, your book
has a three to six month shelf life at most, and you are
still responsible for almost all the marketing.

The basic large company process

1. **Manuscript submission**: with an agent required
   who gets 15% of your royalties off the top.

2. **Editor (-in-Chief?)**: Acceptance of project
   and contract signing: setting up royalties,
   rights, advances, and so on; Fitting
   project into publisher's production
   plans and series developments

3. **Acquisition editors**: Setting up the work team,
   with veto authority over both concept and
   content (often expecting you to change your
   concept to meet their perceived need) though
   they often do not understand the niche.

4. **Marketing team**: determines focus, market,
   demographics to change your concept or focus)

5. **Technical editors**: make sure that
   technical details are accurate and
   instructions actually work

6. **Copyeditors**: fix grammar, rearrange
   copy, regulate consistency; often having
   full veto authority over content.

7. **Illustrators**: Fix up rough sketches from
   authors, converting them to professional
   graphics—drawn by people who often don't
   understand either the content or the audience

8. **Peer review**: manuscript is sent to peers
   in the field to determine relevance and
   acceptability. These peers are determined by
   the examination of their existing customers
   through the marketing department. They are
   often tangential to your area of expertise.

9. Art department: determines layout, typography, sets up digital workflow to conform to the publisher's current standards with no say by the author. They commonly emphasize unimportant content while ignoring the truly important.

10. Cover designer: Authors are rarely consulted and never allowed to do the cover. In the six traditional books I wrote in the 90s, I never even had choices. I found out about the cover when I had to add it to the digital files (in the early to mid-1990s they didn't know how to do digital files).

11. Page layout: a production job within the art department after manuscript approval. This is normally completely outside the author's control—"the realm of professional design".

12. Proofers: typos and typographic errors which must be "fixed" in the copy even if the author knows they are converting standard niche usage into actual content error.

13. Print-ready file production: Magic done by pros to the bafflement of the author (as far as they are concerned). *The only humor in my situation is that I was writing about digital print production way before the publisher implemented it in their company. So, I made more money formating the books than I did from royalties.*

14. Production proof: author often does not even see this

15. Production: outside author's control

16. Packaging: outside author's control

17. Marketing: formerly outside author's control. Now, the author is expected to do it all.

18. **Once the book is published you rarely hear from the publisher again:** except to get the yearly royalty checks. What they do is completely outside your knowledge or control.

This process is long and expensive

It's all about money. Books must support this huge bureaucratic infrastructure. Production costs run from tens of thousands of dollars on up to millions per book. If you cannot count on selling thousands or millions of books, they cannot afford to publish your work. It commonly takes a year after the manuscript is completed to produce the book. For time-sensitive work, this does not work well. The need can be fulfilled and gone before this type of traditionally published book reaches the marketplace. The book you are reading will now be updated every six months or so when InDesign releases a new version.

These specialists commonly do not understand your content

I have had copyeditors flag something that was standard industry usage because he/she did not speak the industry lingo. They had no idea what a separation is for an image, or a signature is for a book, or that leading is a specific measurement (and speaks of the metal slugs not a verb acted out by a person). Imagine finding editors and proofers for a book on a capella choir music, Hebrew word studies, corn genetics, liturgical dance, how occult practices have entered modern religion, contemporary futurism, newly invented technology, or whatever your niche is. It's not going to happen.

But you can write a book to your niche that will help your readers, sell well, and help support the work in which you are involved. You know your niche and you understand your readers much better than the publishing houses do. It will take some real effort on your part and quite a bit of work. But you can do it.

Niche writers to limited markets

Here we begin to see the modern reality of publishing. The change is of the same type as we saw with the conversion in television from three, then four, gargantuan mass-market networks to the current reality of thousands of channels on cable and satellite. The same thing has happened in magazines where there are now over 10,000 magazines in the US alone. There are now millions of active blogs. We are currently publishing over two million different book titles per year. Obviously things have changed a little.

In a typical niche, the overhead of traditional publishing is not good stewardship

Many of the new books are developed for very small niches when dealing with a global scale of things. Let's take this book you are reading on publishing books with InDesign. Statistics are hard to find. In the USA, the labor department says there are nearly 300,000 graphic designers but only 26,000 desktop publishers. They say that there are a little over 150,000 authors who are about 70% self-employed. Smashwords works with 18,000 writers. Lulu claims to have worked with over a million creators. But there are no stats on number of InDesign users, number of authors using InDesign, or anything like that. When I start looking for keyword searches on Google in this area, I am left with the notion that there may be a few thousand people doing this. That's my niche.

How does the publishing world handle a niche this small? It doesn't.

So, what is a writer to do? You do not have many options unless you have enough money to pay for all the services of a traditional publisher. One thing is certain, you do not want to go cheap and hire someone without references. Most pros will edit a sample to see if their style matches your need. Above all, you do not want someone who will beat your Word doc into submission and get it acceptable for an upload. If you are paying a pro to format your book, make sure he or she is using professional tools. The only two professional tools are InDesign and QuarkXPress [though Quark users are quite difficult to find any more]. Everyone has different figures as far as cost is concerned but these are some rough and probably minimal cost figures if you go traditional:

- **Copyeditor:** $300-1000
- **Book formatter:** $250-1500
- **Proofer:** $250-500
- **ISBN:** $100-$250 per book unless you buy a large block

- **Cover designer:** $100-1000 (or much more)
- **Printer:** $2000 or much more
- **Press release:** $500
- **Book review:** $1000
- **Marketing package:** $2,000 to $10,000
- **Books to give away:** $1000
- **Website:** $2000 plus $50 to $100 a month for ISP, Web access, site maintenance, et
- **& on & on & on**

So, what do you do if you do not have ten to fifteen thousand dollars with which to gamble? I've been challenged on the Book Designer blog with figures more like $2,000-$4,000 total. Guy Kawasaki puts the figure at about $4K. But that's still a lot of money (and marketing costs are not included). I'm expecting to sell 500-1,000 copies with a gross profit of well under $5,000. I'd be a fool to spend it all up front.

You must learn to produce your own books.

For the past two decades, I have taught digital publishing skills. During that time I have written and published books, both traditionally and on-demand. I have taught skills to present digital content transparently, effectively, and gracefully.

But Word [and word processors in general] cannot do this—except for very simple books like novels and essays without graphics. There are skills and capabilities that are necessary which are simply not available in Office.

It is true, that ePUBs and Kindle books cannot do many of these things either without the fixed layout options. But you will find it is very important to start with print quality which you can then dumb down to ereader levels. Going from the bottom is much more difficult. Believe me. A Word file crunched into a Kindle book is about the lowest place you can start on the quality scale.

What you need for print quality & fixed layout ebooks

- **Typography:** The skill to use fonts, paragraph styling, and page layout to invisibly communicate content: point size, leading, small caps, ligatures, oldstyle figures, lining figures, ems, ens, discretionary hyphens, tracking, kerning, and much more.

  All of these things are controlled with styles: paragraph, character, table, and object. For this you need a professional page layout program. Many of the necessary adjustments cannot be done in a word processor.

- **High resolution images:** You want vector graphics if possible. InDesign makes superior vector graphics. We'll talk about this in Part Three. Printing requires 300 dpi minimum for photos and bitmapped images. You'll need Photoshop for the high resolution images.

  For example, covers must be created at printing quality to enable all the various sizes required by Apple, Amazon, B&N, and so on. Kindle is currently requesting 1593 x 2500 pixels for the JPEGs uploaded for your Kindle books. That is more than to 5" x 8" at 300 dpi.

- **PostScript (or PDF):** This is a page description language that is required by book printers. You must be able to create and proof in PDF. This requires InDesign, Photoshop, and Acrobat Pro. PDFs produced by Word and Scrivener have serious problems sooner or later. All printing companies now require a PDF to print from. If you give them anything less, they make their own PDF and you have no control over what results from that conversion.

- **Page layout:** A thorough understanding of columns, margins, alignments, indents, gutters, lists, tables, headlines, subheads, sidebars, running heads, drop caps, and much more is required. Just a simple sidebar with a text wrap around the overlapping portions of copy is impossible in a word processor if you want that sidebar anchored to the relevant text.

I'll do my best to remember to define all these terms as I go. Some of you already know quite a bit of this—if you've been using InDesign before. But, to produce a professional book of excellent quality these things must be taken into account.

InDesign gives you layout power

Until you've tried it, you will find it hard to imagine the power of professional page layout. You can see the page as it develops and adjust things to help the reader understand your points. You really can help the reader comprehend your message. That's what excellent book design is all about.

You can use a subhead for clarity, a kicker as a small lead-in style to emphasize a header, lists to recapture the reader's attention with their rhythmic order, a sidebar for peripheral information to entertain the good readers, a table for overly complex lists, and much more.

Even more important, you can add graphics and illustration in the midst of the content which talks about that artwork. Charts, graphics, closeups, diagrams, and info-graphics can be an immense help to your readers. This is where page layout apps like InDesign truly shine. Photoshop is part of the package. Plus, InDesign can produce graphics faster and often better than specialized illustration apps like Illustrator.

You will be able see on the page, as you write or format, how clearly the content is being communicated—or not. It helps you change your content into something which communicates clearly and easily to your readers. It lets you see boring areas and fix them as you write. It provides the control you need to speak to your specific niche—emphasizing unique niche concepts as you go. You can also see when you've gone too far and lapsed into mere busyness and clutter.

Basically working in a page layout program gives you tools that word processors have a hard time even imagining—which could not be accomplished in that glorified typewriter even if you perceived the need. You will learn to communicate much more clearly. I focus on the readers and on what I can do to help you. I try to put myself in your shoes and answer your questions using both the content and the layout.

There is one problem with this book where you can help. Obviously, it is difficult for me as a daily InDesign user for well over fifteen years (plus a decade of PageMaker and Quark use before that) to put myself completely in your shoes. I can easily forget the many questions I asked as I started out (plus InDesign and the Adobe engineering team have provided answers to most of those original questions with updates providing these features to the application itself). If I miss something, email me so I can add it into the next update (which I will produce as soon as I find it necessary to do so). I'll do my best to answer you immediately. Use david@radiqx.com, @davidbergsland on Twitter, or radiqxpress on FaceBook.

When you're done, it's ready to print!

By working fully formatted, your InDesign document is the complete book—though you will need a separate document for the cover. If you print on-demand, it can be available to your readers in a couple weeks or less (even tomorrow, depending on the suppliers you use). If you produce an ePUB or downloadable PDF, they can have it to read this afternoon. A Kindle book might take another hour or so. All from the same content. In many cases, you can do it at very little cost to you—other than charges to see a printed proof.

As an example, I released a book over the weekend.

(Actually, this happened in April 2012.) It was a short book called, *Basic Book Typography*. In it I took out the typographic teachings from the original *Writing In InDesign* book (and several others) to make a more directed version for a wider audience. I did this while I was waiting for the general release of CS6 on April 23, 2012. The typography book avoided any of the version-specific areas. I finished editing and proofing on Thursday. I finished the conversion to Kindle on Friday. I uploaded the printed book to Createspace on Friday. I uploaded the Kindle version Friday. The files were approved by Createspace on Saturday and I approved them.

On Monday I made the changes necessary to convert the formatting to a version that would work better for ePUBs—which are required by everyone other than Kindle. Tody I just upload the reflowable ePUB to Draft2Digital. The fixed layout ePUBs and Kindle's textbook version are uploaded individually to iBooks, Kobo, and Kindle. By Monday night I was getting Amazon to repair some of the linkages for the printed and Kindle versions. Today the final step would be the DRM-free archives made for Gumroad. These packages enable readers to read the book on a huge variety of ereaders and apps.

Next I'd normally go get a new page set up on my Website/blog, post release notices, share with FaceBook, Google+, & Linked-In, and start tweeting about the new book. As the books become available I go to the online bookstores to make sure I didn't make any mistakes during the upload process.

This type of rapid release cycle is now normal

It will become second nature to you after you do it a few times. It is really fun as well. Once the book is nearly ready for release, I can begin to ramp up my marketing efforts. I'll write some friends who might find the book to be relevant and be willing to read and review it.

I'll cover the current options of the various suppliers available now at the time of release for this edition. You'll find this information in Part Six. For updates, you should follow my blog, FaceBook postings, and twitter feeds. This winter, Smashwords finally accepts ePUBs with embedded fonts. That means everyone does as of 2016.

The conversion process for ePUBs continues to mature as the industry stabilizes on standards. But there are not even ereaders for many of the new, proposed ideas for standards. As a result, this area will be changing a lot in the near future. But currently, there is no tool that is nearly as good as InDesign CC for the entire process.

CHAPTER FOUR

Reality orientation

But let's face it, teenagers and young adults don't normally have the foresight to do something like this—in most cases. By the time you are considering doing something like what we are discussing, you are commonly well on the way to maturity. It takes experience [and a minimal level of maturity] to produce anything worth sharing. It also takes time to learn how to write, how to communicate clearly, how to convert the vision you've been given, adding the nuts and bolts required to work in reality. This is grown-up work (no matter what your actual physical age is).

Plus, there is a lot to learn: typography, page layout, printing limitations, ebook limitations, and much more. BUT! You can do it simply, line upon line, precept upon precept, as you grow into the publisher you need to be. *How long will it take?* That depends on how seriously you take the assignments. I used to teach this stuff in two intense semesters to people starting from scratch who were not interested in writing. Most just wanted to draw. As a writer this will come more easily.

You can be up and running in a week or so, competent in a matter of months, and producing excellent work within a year.

But you will need to work at it and practice. In this new publishing paradigm, we can publish blog postings, white papers, books, booklets, essays, teachings, Bible studies, prophecies, forecasts, guides, brochures, and more. Of course, this assumes that you are writing on your computer. That is required, of course. If so, you already have a computer and some software. The question is whether or not it can do what you need it to do. Some upgrades may be necessary, though you'll be surprised at how little is actually required.

Let's start with the computer. The main thing is that ebooks are so new that current software is required. This requires a relatively new computer. What I am listing as minimums are based on the assumption that you will be using the Adobe Creative Cloud. This is especially true for ebooks. For print, CS6 works fine or even earlier versions.

Computer minimums [Spring of 2016]

You really need a Mac: but I won't argue about it. You'll need a 64-bit Intel CPU or better, a monitor at least 1600 pixels wide [2000 pixels or more is better], 8 GB or more of RAM [but you really need 16 GB with CC], Mac OSX.9 or better, a 500 GB hard drive or better, and safe backup storage. You'll need a full keyboard with a numerical keypad and the editing keys will help. If you have a laptop with all its limitations, you'll want a wired USB or Bluetooth keyboard with a full set of function keys, editing keys, and a numerical keypad.

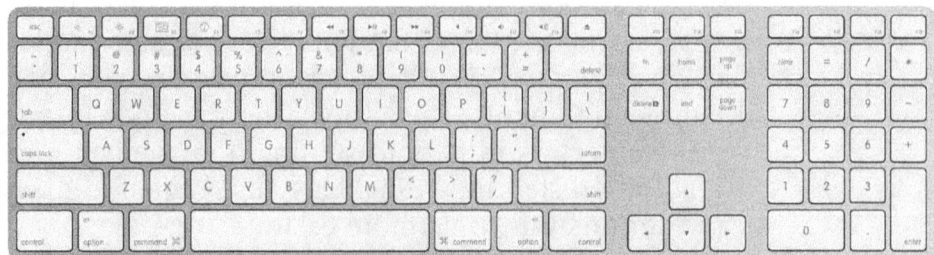

The numerical keypad is essential for style shortcuts and the editing keys are necessary for easy navigation through your book: You'll not like InDesign without the full keyboard. It's needed for custom shortcuts, and many of the standard ones like page navigation.

If you already have a PC: you can use it providing it meets the criteria above. Plus you'll need to be able to calibrate your monitor. You'll need Windows 7 with Service Pack 1, Windows 8, Windows 10, or better.

These are all minimums. You'll actually want 16 GB RAM or more to keep working at speed and to avoid crashes. Each book will add at least a large portion of a Gigabyte into storage. So a 500-1000 GB hard drive is not out of line at all.

You'll also need high-speed internet and a PostScript printer for proofing: You will be uploading and downloading PDFs that are often dozens of megabytes in size. Sometimes this needs to be done many times in a day. It often cannot be done at all with a slow internet connection.

You need the PostScript printer. Other printers cannot show many things. However, your printed proofs can done elsewhere.

Adobe's Creative Cloud

You'll want InDesign CC, at least, at $20 a month. But the full CC package is only $50 a month. Actually, you can get by with CS4 or even CS3 for Illustrator, Photoshop, Acrobat, and the rest, but you need InDesign CC. CC is actually essential & CC 2015 helps a lot. Every version does substantially better ePUBs and that's the core format for ebooks.

Get the non-profit or academic versions: (if you qualify). A good resource for these discounts and information on whether you qualify or not is found at the AcademicSuperstore Website. They just need a valid school ID or a scan of your non-profit paperwork, certificate, or whatever. It is worth taking an accredited class for academic pricing. That will keep the costs down for a year.

Current non-profit/academic pricing: Things have changed a lot for CC. Usually, the full cloud costs around $30 a month. But it's worth checking.

For regular users

- **InDesign CC:** $20 a month [yearly contract]

- **Adobe's Creative Cloud [CC]:** $50 a month [yearly contract] for almost every graphic design app Adobe sells: Photoshop, Illustrator, Acrobat, Bridge, Dreamweaver, Muse, Premier Pro and the Video editing apps, the sound editing apps, the animation apps, and more. (Educational starts at $29 per month)

- **You will need InDesign, Photoshop, and Acrobat Pro:** You may need Dreamweaver. Illustrator is handy. But as I mentioned, older versions of this software will do fine for you—except for InDesign.

In this field you must keep up

Even if you have CS6 for everything else, you'll need to get CC for InDesign, because of all the changes caused by the implementation of HTML5, CSS3, and ePUB3. CC is quite a bit better, plus there are all the yearly changes tied in with the new subscription model Adobe is foisting off on us. Make sure you have a recent computer. I had to buy a new computer to work with CS5. You need to plan on a new computer every 2-4 years. My old computer with its G4 CPU and 1 GB RAM still runs fine. My wife is using it. But I can no longer use it for my work. I was forced to get a new computer last winter with 16 GB RAM primarily because of Mavericks. It's hard to beat the iMac.

You need your own publishing house

On the practical side, you need to think about how you are going to handle your sales. You should do this very early on in the process. For some reason, one of the more difficult areas for an author to get a hold of is the business aspect of writing. If you only have one book of memoirs you are going to give as gifts to your family, then maybe you do not be concerned about these things. If you are a publishing house, you know how careful you need to be getting things set up.

You need to consider the benefits of having a business. Your computer, smartphone, software, writing supplies, research materials, travel expenses for research, and much more can be legitimate business expenses [or a portion thereof]. The time to find out about these things is not after you collect a lot of money and have a huge tax bill. The time to do it is before the tax bill becomes an issue.

You'll need a business account to collect and disperse money. If you are just starting out, I recommend a PayPal business account. It is free (they collect fees from sales) and it will let you collect income, accept credit cards, make payments, and all the other things you need to do as a publisher. Several suppliers prefer PayPal and some require PayPal for royalty payments.

You must start up a business to handle all the legalities. A sole proprietorship is usually free [in all the states I've lived in] and takes almost no time to set up. You may use a dba for your sole proprietorship, set it up as a subsidiary of your corporate identity, or of a 501(3)c if you are a non-profit.

Picking a good name

Regardless of your personal legal necessities dealing with your local governments, you need a name to use. This is not the Big Idea—that great phrase that everyone will remember forever and always associate positively with you, the author. If you can do that—wonderful.

What you need is a name that makes sense to you, which you are proud of, that people recognize as your business. More than that, you need a name which can be trademarked, which does not infringe on any other publisher, person, or company. The best advice is to use your own name, if possible. After all, as an author you are selling yourself, your ideas, and your communication skills. If you have an unusual name, this is an easy and simple way to go.

You need a logo, business card, letterhead, invoice, and all the normal accoutrement of any real business. You do not need to have them printed, but you need InDesign templates of them on your computer to print as necessary—and PDFs to share with clients, suppliers, and so on. Your letterhead will probably be the beginning of your contracts, for example. You'll want your logo on the copyright page of your books. Maybe, like me, publishing is just part of what you do. Regardless, you need some legal method of dealing with the IRS [or whatever tax authority exists in your country], if nothing else.

To be recognized by the industry as a publisher

This is more complex. The best description of this process I have seen is a posting in thebookdesigner.com. Joel has laid it out for us in the post: *How to create your publishing company.*

You will need to buy a minimal block of ISBNs for $295 for ten or $575 for 100 and then go to Bowker (where you bought the ISBNs) and register your company name at BowkerLink. That's all free, once you have bought your block of numbers. But you will need an official name, a real address, a bank account number, and probably a business phone and email accounts. In fact, you'll probably need a good domain name for your business.

 ISBN pricing changes regularly: So go to Bowker and find out what it is this month in the US. They're free in Canada. They were free here until self-publishers triggered a greed reflex .

The basic idea is that they make you pay for the privilege of acknowledgment. For this privilege, you are allowed to print your book through Lightning Source. You need to buy your own ISBNs. You will have to format your book according to their strict specs. You'll need to pay for outrageous proofing charges—every time you make any changes. All of this will allow you to be listed in the Ingram database, and included in the official stats about book sales. You will need to set up wholesale pricing [commonly called discounts], and you will probably have to take returns from any bookstore you can get to stock your book. Because you are wholesaling, your royalty is much smaller. But none of this will sell you a single book.

The book selling will all be done from your marketing. Just because they can order it from a catalog, does not mean they will order any copies—unless they hear the book sells well. That will be up to you. But there's a small problem: brick and mortar bookstores are disappearing fast. The ones which remain can only afford to carry best-sellers.

 My advice: don't go with the Bowker/ Ingram/ Lightning Source option unless you have a book which is already selling well.

At that point, you can market much more effectively to the brick and mortar portion of the industry. Also, by this time, you'll have made enough money to be able to afford it.

For Christian books, if you want to get into CBD, this is your only option

Christian Book Distributors will only list books who are in Ingram and Ingram's Christian list: Spring Arbor Distributors. There really isn't much sense in doing this unless you are writing Romance, Mystery, Thriller, or non-fiction. Plus, you will need to restrict your content to the CBA standards: no sex, no swearing, no violence, ~~no real content~~—oops! *I didn't really write that. I'm sorry. I'm sorry. I'm sorry.*

Other things of which you need to take care

Things you need to do which do not require money [but may require money to do well]. As you will see, these are all tied together.

You definitely need a good email address:
It's hard to convince anyone you are serious with a Gmail or Yahoo account. That goes double for Hotmail or any of the other lesser freebie email addresses. So, you'll probably need online access that provides you with

a way to use your domain name. This is all tied in with the need to pick a good name.

- **You must become involved in your marketing:** This requires consistency. Another reason for a good name, a good domain name, and a good email address. Publishers and advertising services will ask you how many FaceBook friends you have, how many Twitter followers, and so on.

- **You probably need a blog:** A free one will work, but to be serious, you'll need a domain name. I recommend that you choose online access with a company that offers WordPress. org—the commercial version of wordpress.com.

- **The need for a Website may be past:** WordPress enables you to use a blog for your Website and solves many of your Website issues.

How far you go with this is up to you. Just remember the first rule of building your publishing business. Be professional. But there is one final, very important piece of advice [just my opinion, understand].

Do not borrow money to build the business!

There are too many unpredictable variations in selling any book. Be slow and careful. Invest your profits back into the business. Getting in a hurry will not help you at all. Take the long view and don't give up.

CHAPTER FIVE

What is on-demand publishing?

The concept is simple: The printer or distributor stores the book on their hard drives. It is printed or downloaded only after it is ordered and paid for. So, unless there is a demand, it is not printed or downloaded. Much like just-in-time manufacturing, your book is delivered to the reader up**on demand**.

- You upload the digital files: They are stored on the servers of the on-demand printer or ebook distributor.

- They print the document or enable downloads: after they receive payment for an order. There is no warehousing and no storage issues caused by cartons of printed books.

- Your royalty is large: You commonly get 70% to 80% of the money received after printing costs are deducted. For the ebooks, the maximum production costs are 99¢ (commonly nothing). Even with retail books you do much better than you would if you got a contract with a traditional publisher—where a 10% royalty is respectable.

- You receive your royalties quickly: Some pay instantly or weekly. In most cases, you get the money the next month. Some suppliers delay things up to two months, and a few only pay quarterly. All of those options are far superior to the once a year payments of traditional publishers.

- You do not have to deal with wholesale orders and returns: One of the worst parts of traditional publishing comes after your book sales taper off. The retailers return unsold inventory to the publisher for a refund, and you take a loss.

- Sales continue to grow: Unless you are publishing very unique time-limited work, on-demand sales slowly grow and continue to grow. Because there are no warehousing issues, there are no reasons to stop selling your books. In many cases, your sales will continue to build for a decade or more.

  With traditional publishing using brick and mortar stores, there is a huge marketing push and shipments to all the stores, and then all the sales happen very quickly. When that initial rush is over—so is your book. There is no shelf room for books that might sell some day.

It's basically a very simple process

The complexity is added by the fact that the individual on-demand publishers all have different requirements for artwork. The differing formats have unique limitations. The result is that you usually have to convert your book a couple times to get it in the different formats. But, that's a fast and easy process. You can have your book listed at all the distributors very quickly.

You can add new versions as needed: As new distributors appear in the world, it is usually very easy to make up a version for them to sell. As you hear of them, you can try them out. All of these changes were relatively frantic during the early parts of the new millennium. But they have settled down. It has been a while since a new supplier came out who captured any large portion of the market. The iPad was the last, coming out in 2010 and it is a major player.

Android machines are getting very common, but the stats I've seen suggest that there may not be many readers in that group. That's backed up by the horrid sales with Google Play. Amazon is not sitting around. The Fire and its HD variations, for fifty to two hundred bucks, are selling well, as far as we know. As usual, Amazon is not saying. Kobo has picked up a Japanese owner and now supports ePUB3 and vertical Japanese calligraphy. Nook is dying. This industry is rapidly growing & changing: The good news is that it is changing in our direction. The era of author-controlled publishing is here.

I only cover the free options

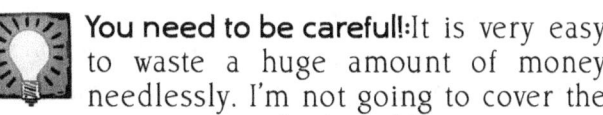

You need to be careful!: It is very easy to waste a huge amount of money needlessly. I'm not going to cover the vanity press options. In this old scenario, you (the author) pay for all the production costs. Several of the subsidy printers do on-demand printing, but the upfront costs are in the thousands of dollars—so in reality they are merely remnants of the old way of doing things.

My focus is on helping non-profits, ministries, educators, and individuals to get their message to the people they serve and the supporters they need.

The new on-demand paradigm is publishing with very few upfront costs. You may choose to pay for marketing and distribution—but they are not required services. Most of you already have good, functional mailing lists of followers—a built-in market for your work. I will talk about some of those options with the services I recommend.

The benefits of the new paradigm

It is very fast!

One of the real changes in the new paradigm is the speed with which you can release books, booklets, posters, and so on. If you have proofed copy that is ready to format, you can get it published and released in a day or so. The limitation is only your formatting speed. With the techniques and workflow explained in this book, you will be able to produce finished formatted documents that are ready to publish and distribute to your readers and supporters in a wide variety of formats: printed and digital.

It is very easy to revise into a new edition

New editions of existing works take a little bit of time because they are usually substantially rewritten. But even a radically revised new edition can be done in a week to a month. This *Book Publishing With InDesign CC* book is a rewrite, expansion, and clarifying of my *Writing In InDesign* books. But even then I've only spent a few months.

Typo fixes are commonly done in a day—unless a particular distributor requires a new proof. Even in that case you can get a new proof printed, shipped to you, and approved in around a week.

You can revise all versions of your book in this time frame *IF* you have your application set up well and *IF* you use the formatting techniques I will share in this book. InDesign CC has added capabilities which make this process even more convenient.

You can publish in multiple formats

Some of the new possibilities really rock your traditionalist world the first time you realize what can be done. As mentioned, at this point I publish in many formats, depending upon the type of book. The different suppliers are listed in Part Six.

CHAPTER SIX

What skills do you need?

The idea is that InDesign can be learned and you can become comfortable enough with the software so that it becomes an extension of your creativity. If you work in it daily, as recommended, it becomes a habitual tool with which you communicate with your readers. If you use it for all your document production, you'll come to love it.

You can do this!

I need to talk a bit about skill sets you will want to have to publish well. Obviously, this new publishing paradigm is radically intruding upon areas held by editors, copyeditors, illustrators, typographers, and graphic designers. It has taken over the skill sets of camera operators, separators, and the rest of the prepress world. That's a pretty daunting list of knowledge and skills.

The key is to realize that like all personal growth it comes line by line, precept by precept. There is help available. Plus, a lot of it is covered naturally by the design and capabilities of InDesign itself. Yet, several of the things you need to know are almost completely unknown outside the industry.

Typography is a good example

This was an assumed baseline skill of any graphic designer in the late 20th century. But that has been eroded by our modern video-centered world. Many modern graphic designers can barely read—if you can imagine that. This is a larger problem than you might think because much of our typographic knowledge comes from all the excellent typography we have been reading since we learned to read.

For us this is no problem

I've never known a writer who didn't love to read. Before 1990, there was nothing printed that was not typeset to a relatively high level. Typewriter output was obviously not typeset, but word processor output had not reached the general public for reading materials like it has now. The Web with its poor font choices and horrible typography was not a factor until the late '90s. The result is that you subconsciously recognize excellence in typographic design (unless you're under 30).

At present, ereaders are contributing to the dulling of the typographic sense of our culture. But excellent typography contributes so much to readability and trustworthiness that adding this capability to ereaders is happening rapidly. InDesign CC moves us in that direction. The iPad and Kindle Fire both support at least portions of ePUB3 and the best of ePUB2. Apple's release of iBooks in OSX and iOS is an excellent step up as the quality of ebooks get better and better.

This is good because your readers expect excellent typography and will consider your output untrustworthy (subconsciously, at least) if you do not provide them with it. All of us who read have been trained by the fact we've seen nothing that is not professionally typeset until the last decade—except for bureaucratic stuff.

The good news is that InDesign has good typography built in—with few modifications needed. I'll cover some of those capabilities in a bit. But before I get into that we need to talk about writing in general.

PART TWO:

Writing
the copy

CHAPTER SEVEN

Where do you start?

My assumption is that this is something you are already doing: You have been writing and you have a body of work you want to publish. If you are not writing, you are not a writer. This book is not for people who say "I really want to write a book about..." some day.

This is for people who have done a lot of writing. You may have a lot of the book written, or a completed book. You want to get it published so you can share what you have written. Or you are a publisher with a finished manuscript. This is for the rabbi who is constantly writing teachings, columns, blogs, and the like. This is for the teacher who is constantly writing handouts, lesson plans, and curriculum. This is for the conference speaker who wants to leave his thoughts with the audience.

The list goes on. For fiction authors and publishers, this is for those producing two to six books a year, or more. The options are endless, and exciting.

So, this is something I do & it's easy

Nope! For me [even with my 45+ years of skills, training, and background] it takes work, perseverance, and a willingness to take risks and simply put my stuff out there for the world to see. I'm certain that you have your own personal issues. We're all different. I'd like to hear your stories. But producing excellent books is a lot of work.

InDesign enables you to get a lot of the busy work under control

Regardless, there is a lot to do. A book is a large to huge project. This is not simple or even easy, but it is fun. You need to find your routine. I write two to six hours a day, six days a week as my normal practice. When I was teaching full-time, I got up earlier and wrote an hour and a half every morning.

You will need to develop your own routine. But as mentioned, I am certain you have done this already. You will need to do some additional reading, studying, and practicing as you turn the corner into professionalism. It is not instant success. In most cases, it takes some maturity. In fiction, there are teenagers with remarkably good stories to tell. For non-fiction, it takes experience to develop the skills required to teach and share your knowledge.

Regardless, this book will not be of much interest to the occasional writer. Authors and book designers have a deep inner need to share stories, convey messages, and teach helpful ideas and techniques. Most of you will write or publish many books. With the development of on-demand self-publishing on a professional level, we start to think in terms of a body of work developed to share lifestyle, culture, and truth.

Now we need to move into the practicalities of writing, book design, production, and publishing. We will start with the words, but you need to understand from the beginning that words, graphics, and layout all work together to help the reader easily understand what you have been given to say.

We are concerned with sharing truth. That is what we are looking for. That is what our readers are looking for. But, these techniques also work for fluff and entertainment. Even escapist stories can help the reader sort out his or her life and lead them toward truth. That is one of the responsibilities of an author. These concerns are the reason why I do what I do.

CHAPTER EIGHT

Writing books fully formatted

This may be causing you confusion or concern. I've already talked about this some. But, I need to explain it better. It will be an unusual writing workflow for many of you—something you have never heard of or imagined.

The focus is on the book as a whole—fiction or non-fiction. You are developing a story, teaching, or guide to help your reader understand the content as easily as possible. The format and layout can not get in the way of comprehension. It needs to aid it.

There are numerous advantages and no real disadvantages to putting a book together as a synergistic whole that is greater than the sum of its parts. The need to learn typography, formatting, layout, graphic design, and all the rest is not a disadvantage but a glorious opening into a new world of reader communication.. It's a true joy if you love beautiful books.

The personalized workflow

We all have different ways of working. Some of us begin with a complete and detailed outline, and many cannot stand that. Often, we begin by posting ideas and concerns on our blogs. Some of these postings are quite lengthy. We have bits and pieces of character development, location research, case studies, personal anecdotes, and a host of other sources of copy. Our books become living entities which almost have a life of their own. They take us on a journey of discovery.

There are many types of lesser software which can be used to produce these bits and pieces. Personally, I write in WordPress quite often. I find it to be an interface which is comfortable. Many writers prefer Blogger or a number of other blogging interfaces.

The problem, of course, is that these bits and pieces are rarely usable *as is* for a book. Blog postings require a lot of reworking. They tend to be choppy, overly dramatic, and pithy to a fault. They have scattered points of view an a varying focus. The same is going to be true of essays, sermons, teachings, presentations, and so on.

The real problem is that blog posts, and blog content in general, is relatively ephemeral. You need to have a place, a system, and a habitual workflow to store your content and work with it easily.

Scrivener is a good choice for some

Scrivener allows you to write, collect pieces, add graphics, develop character bios, build worlds, share culture, describe locations, and organize everything in a surprisingly intuitive interface. This type of work can be essential for fiction—depending on the person. The author must understand and be comfortable with the world through which he or she is leading the reader.

It is equally important for a larger non-fiction book like this as I work toward sharing with you the parts necessary or desired to help you communicate clearly with your readers.

The problem I have with Scrivener is that I never get to see what the book looks like. The formatting options are extremely limited. It cannot handle professional graphic formats. There are no drawing tools. There is no way to deal with multiple columns, asymmetric columns, sidebars, text wrap, or any of the other niceties of book design. Plus, formatting is kludgy, difficult, and very slow.

Beyond that, simply exporting a book as a professional-quality printable PDF is simply not possible. Although the software can handle an immense amount of seemingly unrelated data, and help an author put it into a comprehensive reader experience, it is not enough. It's strength is conceptual development. The actual execution of the book, in all the various formats required, is far beyond its scope.

I use Scrivener to put together my novels. It is of little use for my non-fiction. You may well be different. It may be a wonderfully fluid place for you to write. But, no matter what, the output is seriously flawed.

Word and word processors

Statistically, I can assume that most of you are writing in Word, Pages, or another word processor. I can't hold that against you anymore than I can be surprised by the reality that many of you are masochistic enough to use PCs and Android. >grin<

Both of these situations will make your turn toward excellence a little more difficult. I know, *"no one told you"*. My experience, for the first 10 years, was that I had to work on a Mac and use PageMaker or Quark. Windows did not even support the base technology for book design until Windows NT in 2000 and XP in 2001.

The language I am talking about is PostScript. It is essential for commercial printing. It is still not supported by Scrivener, Office or Word. The result of this focus on business communication, as opposed to typesetting and graphic design, is that the normal practices of book design are either not possible or difficult in any word processor.

I have no problem with you using Word for writing. However, it puts you in a very poor position once you develop the desire to produce excellence in book design. Many things need to be radically changed.

What you need to do, in your mind, is relegate Word content to the category of raw copy. More than that, you will start to see what you do in Word as a hindrance to production speed and efficiency. I will not have to talk you into it. In fact, I will try not to mention it again. InDesign is really that superior.

The good news is that there is a word processor which does what we need built into InDesign. No, it does not have all the fancy bells and whistles found in Word. This is a good thing. Word has a lot of automation built in. The pursuit of excellence will quickly teach you that anything done automatically will—at best—give you average results.

Using the Story Editor

InDesign's built-in word processor is called Story Editor. At any time, while you are working on your book in InDesign, you can open your copy in Story Editor. It is a very streamlined, minimal, word processor. That being said: it is fast and easy to use, very powerful.

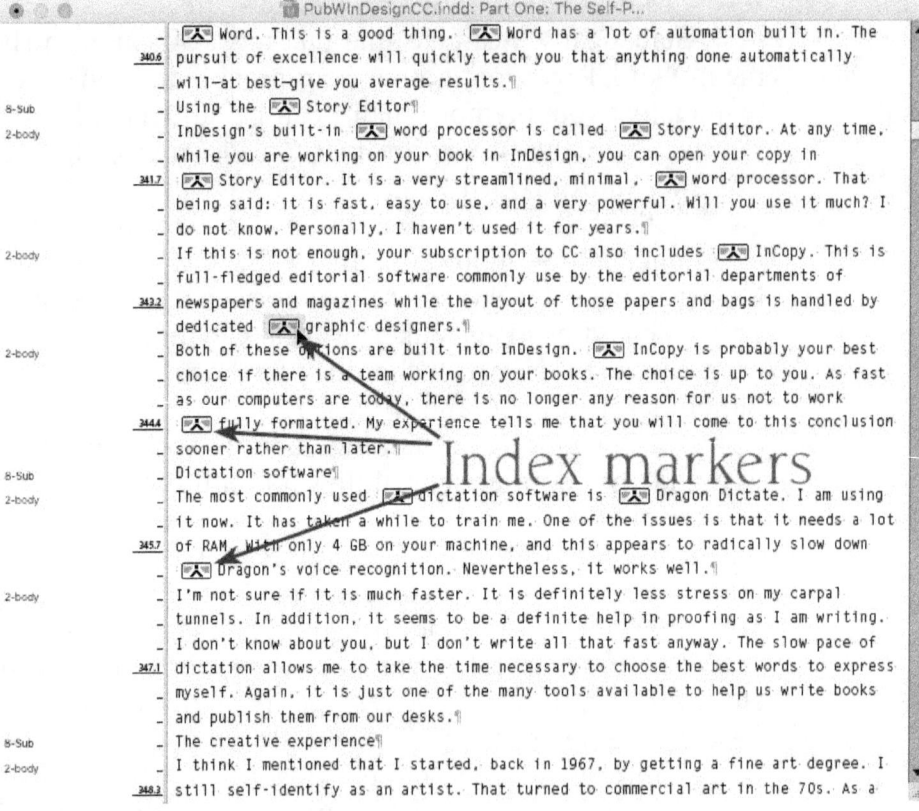

If this is not enough, your subscription to CC also includes InCopy. This is full-fledged editorial software commonly used by the editorial departments of newspapers and magazines while the layout of those papers and mags is handled by dedicated graphic designers.

Both of these options are built into InDesign and CC. InCopy may your best choice if your publishing house has a team working on your books. The choice is up to you. As fast as our computers are today, there is no longer any reason for us not to work fully formatted. My experience tells me that you will come to this conclusion sooner rather than later.

Dictation software

The most commonly used dictation software was Dragon Dictate. I used it until I ran into a greedy update policy. It took a while to train me. One of the issues was that it needed a lot of RAM. I only had 4 GB on my machine, and this radically slowed down Dragon's voice recognition. Nevertheless, it worked well.

The next time I'll use Apple's built-in dictation ability. I'm told that the new Kindle's also do this well (but not into InDesign). I've heard several authors who do this more and more.

I'm not sure if it is much faster. It is definitely less stress on my carpal tunnels. In addition, dictation seems to be a definite help in proofing as I am writing. It uses different areas of my mind which helps proofing a lot. I don't know about you, but I don't write all that fast anyway. The slow pace of dictation allows me to take the time necessary to choose the best words to express myself. Again, it is just one of the many tools available to help us write books and publish them from our desks.

The creative experience

I think I mentioned that I started, back in 1967, by getting a fine art degree. I still self-identify as an artist. I turned to commercial art in the 70s. I learned to take great satisfaction and joy out of serving my clients. In a very real way, I became the artistic skill they needed. I still enjoy that, and I design, produce, and publish quite a few books for various authors.

But I have found that creating a book as a whole is an artistic experience which is a massive step up from painting, drawing, sculpture, or craft. Writing the words is barely the beginning of the process. It's an amazing creative experience and a wonderful joy to have control over such a massive project.

Writing skills

Learn all you can about writing. Work to develop your editing and proofing skills. Train yourself to recognize excellence in book design. Write a lot. Read a lot. Write a lot and read some more. Your skills will build. Your earlier books will become an embarrassment. Take joy in what you do. It's a gift you've been given.

Editing and proofing skills

You need to work at developing your editing and proofing abilities. Even though it is true that you need an editor and a proofer if at all possible. However, for much small niche work, hiring an editor or proofer could eliminate virtually all your profits from the book.

The solutions to this dilemma are many:

- **Study and teach yourself to edit:** Obviously this is a necessity if you are a publisher, but it will help you greatly as an author also.

- **Train your eye to see typos:** Many of these things can only be seen easily in your print layout. It's one of the reasons you need to start with print. It's a typo to have one of your paragraphs flush left when the rest of them are justified, for example. The list goes on.

- **Using a printed version to proof:** this is a different reading experience and you'll see many typos you missed on screen.

- **Proof layouts from a distance:** Looking at your book from several feet, make layout issues become obvious.

- **Use beta readers:** These volunteers are usually your best critics. They truly want to help. They understand your genre and subject matter.

CHAPTER NINE

What skills do you need to self-publish digitally?

The publishing world is abuzz with the impact of the new publisher, the ebook, and selling online. The traditional publisher model may only survive in certain mass market niches. Increasingly they are looking to self-publishing authors as a vetted pool of possible talent. My focus is on helping authors take advantage of the new possibilities.

I want to talk a bit about skill sets you need to have to do this well. As mentioned, this new publishing paradigm is radically intruding upon areas held by editors, illustrators, typographers, and graphic designers. It has taken over the skill sets of camera operators, separators, and the rest of the prepress world. It has brought the author into the marketing arena and this is a mine field. That's a pretty daunting list of knowledge and skills.

Typography is basic

Much of this knowledge has been attacked and eroded by our modern video-centered world. Many modern authors do not read well—if you can imagine that. This is a larger problem than you might think because much of our typographic knowledge, as individuals, comes from all the excellent typography we have been reading since we learned to read.

We need to be aware that our readers may have surprisingly compromised reading ability. The advice for several years now is to write at a fifth grade level or less. I don't worry about that too much for books like this, for obvious reasons. But as an author and publisher, it is a major area of concern as you produce your books.

But all of this misses the basic point of this book. You must understand what typography is before you can produce it. If you have any real hope of communicating clearly and easily with your readers, this basic level of professional typography is essential. Without it your chances of being seen through the clutter will be reduced even more. In this intensely competitive world of publishing you certainly do not want that.

CHAPTER TEN

What is typography?

Here are some dictionary definitions. In truth, they are helpful only to show us what typography is not. You will quickly discover that outside of the publishing industry almost no one really knows what type is. Even graphic designers and advertisers rarely know what the art of setting type is all about.

Dictionaries talk about process not purpose

Here's a few examples.

Webster's: The craft of composing type and printing from it; art and technique of printing with movable type.

Random House: the art or process of printing with type; the work of setting and arranging types and of printing from them; the general character or appearance of printed matter

Cambridge: the style, size and arrangement of the letters in a piece of printing

Wikipedia does the best job of word definition here.

(The) art of arranging letters on a page to be printed, usually for a combination of aesthetic and functional goals

What we are about as typographers is directing reader responses with our craft. My focus here is the craft of typesetting on a professional level—and its relationship to the number one virtue of book design: readability.

What's unusual is that none of the dictionaries really get it.

- **First of all:** they are all tied to printing. Online typography and ebooks are not considered.

- **Secondly:** they describe the physical act, but typography is only secondarily concerned with the physical act of arranging letters on paper for printing, or letters on the screen for reading.

Obviously physical considerations and traditional shapes play a huge role in font design. But typography goes far beyond the actual shapes of the letters, paragraphs, columns, and pages—entering into the cultural and subjective responses of individual readers. Our concern must be presenting the content comfortably to be effortlessly comprehended. It must be reader-centered or it is a fine art exercise.

Not surprisingly, one of the best quotes is from Hermann Zapf, one of the 20th century's outstanding type designers

> ***This is the purpose of typography:*** The arrangement of design elements within a given structure should allow the reader to easily focus on the message, without slowing down the speed of his reading.

My definition is simple:
Typography is the art of communicating clearly and easily with type

Typography is built with fonts. This is like saying cabinetmaking is built with wood. There are well over a hundred thousand fonts available now. Most of them are merely decorative and of little use in book design. What you need to know is relatively simple. But the focus on fonts merely obscures the reality of what we do. We are communicators focusing on specific readers.

People often start with font design

But this brings us to the first major confusion in typography. Many believe that typography is about font choices. If you go to a respected source, like typophile.com, you'll quickly discover that these font choices are the major topic of discussion. They spend a huge amount of time on which fonts to choose and how fonts developed historically. I would call this *majoring on the minors* or pettifogging.

Typography is the art of communicating clearly and easily with type!

This indeed is a good portion of typography, but the excessive pursuit of the perfect font often misses the entire point: The purpose of typography is to use words to communicate. Font choices can help—but this is really a small portion of what we need to be concerned with as typographers and book designers. Communication needs go beyond style.

Know this: Fonts are not typography—fonts are used to create typography.

I am not minimizing the importance of choosing fonts which are easy to read and comfortable for your target audience. But we mustn't confuse the tools and materials with the techniques for using those tools. In addition, we cannot focus on these two areas without maintaining the end product as our primary goal. Here's an example in another field.

Let's consider woodworking for furniture.

- The type and species of wood chosen (as well as the fabric and hardware) &
- The saws, chisels, planes, and power tools used &
- The smoothing, fitting, and joinery employed &
- And the finishing techniques of shaping, adjusting, sanding, polishing, and coating

- Are all subservient: *to the beauty and comfort of the chair being built.*

All the pieces of the process are part of the whole, but they only serve the end goal: comfort and beauty. Plus, of course, how the chair fits the decorating style used. You don't buy a chair because they used a Ryobi saw or mahogany.

In this book, I'm focused on typography for books.

- The fonts chosen (as well as the words & images) &

- The drawing, image manipulation, and layout tools used &

- The paragraphs, columns, pages, graphics, and formatting employed &

- The final adjustments necessary to make the type beautiful and polished

- Are all subservient: *to the beauty, clarity, and comfort experienced while reading and understanding the content of the book.*

A book is all about the author (& illustrator) communicating easily and comfortably with the readers. The readers should not even notice the book, but be drawn into the content unavoidably. If the book design is noticed at all, it needs to be a pleasurable reinforcement of the content. It's rarely an end in itself.

I do not use word processors unless forced to do so. Their documents were a horror when I received them as raw copy when I was working full-time as a graphic designer. In fact, I developed a relatively extensive list of steps to completely strip out word processor formatting to enable good typography to be added within InDesign. I cannot state it too forcefully.

Word processors cannot do *what we need to do as book designers!*

Let's begin with a discussion of fonts to get started.

We begin with the language of type

To begin with, most typographic terminology comes from the dominant printing technology used from 1460 to 1970–now called letterpress. This is changing somewhat, but most of the present terms will remain. Before you can set type, you must be able to speak the language and understand the concepts.

You can tell how severe this issue is as we get underway by learning a new measurement system. Type is not measured in inches or millimeters. It is measured in points. This is not going to change for many reasons.

Today all type is sized in points.

Points were an excellent sizing tool, becoming dominant and standardized in the 19th century. At approximately 72 points per inch, the smaller sizes of body copy could be clearly differentiated. For most people, type that is one point larger or smaller is the smallest increment of size which can be distinguished easily with the naked eye. We can see the differences between 9 and 10 point, 12 and 13 point. Normally, humans cannot see the difference between 11 and 11.5 point type except for certain copyeditor geeks (you know who you are).

Picas (12 points per pica) and points became the standard. Today all type is sized in points. The old distinctions between European and American points have disappeared, but all use points (and will for the foreseeable future).

The computer helped

Apple's Macintosh, in 1984. set the screen resolution at 72 pixels per inch. In the years since that watershed event, the 72-point-per-inch standard has become universal on desktop computers. This is true even though the current high-resolution monitors, Retina displays, and 4K screens make this measurement meaningless.

The nice thing, for us as Americans, is that this is exactly 72 points per inch. At this time the pica [6 picas per inch] is disappearing. In fact, we can safely say it is gone in most cases. But points may never go away. Some software still makes picas their default measurement, but few use it any more except illustrators. One of the first things you do when you install software is fix your preferences. The main preference to change (in those apps still using it, like InDesign and Illustrator) is switching from Picas and Points to whichever measurement system you are really going to use: inches, pixels, or millimeters. As far as I know, the only industry still using picas is newspapers, and they only use it for column widths.

Letterpress terminology

As you would suspect, much of our type terminology comes from letterpress printing. After all, this printing technology was dominant from Gutenberg's Bible in 1460 until a few decades ago. I could give you dozens of letterpress terms that would be of historical interest only. However, it is enough that you recognize the source of many of the terms we use.

A typical example is leading (pronounced like the metal). It would be better (or at least more accurate) to change the term to line spacing. For a number of reasons, that probably won't happen. Leading came from the letterpress practice of increasing the space between lines of metal type by adding strips of lead between the rows. These strips came in standard thicknesses: 1/2-point, 1-point, and so on. In letterpress usage, you could only increase leading and could never have line spacing that was less than the type size. That is no longer true with digital type, but the term remains.

Let's remind ourselves how letterpress type was sized and assembled. Just getting a visual in your mind will straighten out a lot of this. The major fact to remember is that letterpress type was normally cast metal. The letters were cut into dies and cast into blocks of metal. They all had to be the same height, thickness, hardness, and so on. You had to be able to fit them together into blocks that could be locked into place in the chase (the holding frame for the type). If any letter is a lower height, it won't ink up as you roll the brayer covered with ink across the surface of the type. If it stands too tall, it will be smashed by the printing pressures of the steel rollers. Much of our present type usage comes from factors that were determined by the physical nature of letterpress. Below are five lines of type locked together.

A *slug* of type was always .918 inches high and left enough room vertically on the top surface for all the characters in a font of type. Horizontally every letter was a different width. All type had to fit into evenly sized rectangles to line up properly on the composing stick and chase. Often, these terms no longer mean the same things. A slug is now what we call the black bar highlighted when you select type [which indicates the leading].

Face, for example, used to mean the actual printing surface of the letter. Now, in common usage, face often means a type style such as Helvetica or Times—although in that case the word typeface is usually used. As is lamented by grammarians, American English is a living language under constant change.

The same is true of the word *counter*. A counter was the recessed area around the letter above which the face of the character protruded. Now it is usually used (if at all) as a term for the open areas inside a *P, e, g,* or even an *s*. I will give you a diagram in a little bit that covers some of the old terms which remain relevant.

Many of you are probably grumbling to yourselves at this point: You say in your twenty-first-century superiority, "Who cares?" Actually, you care or you will care. Most of you will find that the longer you design documents, especially books, the more you will fall in love with type. Type will become a very important graphic tool for most of you. This importance will increase through-out your career. Often the shape of the letters is the only graphic element in your designs.

The stick controlled a lot

We need to remember how type was set. All the slugs had to be placed in rows on the composing stick – one letter at a time. You can see a stick above. I flipped the type so you could read it in the lower right corner. This is where the rectangles of letterpress were built, and they had to be precise. If anything was out of size, the slugs would move or fall out as they were printed. There are hundreds of specialized terms used for all this equipment. If you are curious, read almost any book written on printing up to the end of the twentieth century.

As a result, many terms in your software are from letterpress and font design. For example, the sizing of type remains the same – from the top of the *ascender* to the bottom of the *descender*, with the capital letters being slightly shorter than the ascenders and all characters fitting within that ascender to descender height. This was determined by the necessities of the composing stick. But there are more words to define.

Type parts: the vertical metrics

The **baseline** is the imaginary line upon which all the letters and numbers sit. The **x-height** is the height of the lowercase *x*. However, I saw this measurement called a *mean line* in a diagram on a typography Web site a few years back [although I have never actually heard anyone use that term]. **Ascenders** are the portions of lowercase letters that rise above the x-height as in *b, d, h, k* and *l.* A *t (and usually an f)* doesn't ascend far enough to be called an ascender. **Descenders** are the portions that sink below the baseline as in *g, j, p, q,* and *y.* The *j* descender is commonly shorter. The **cap height** is the height of the uppercase letters [usually a bit shorter than the ascender by about 4–10%].

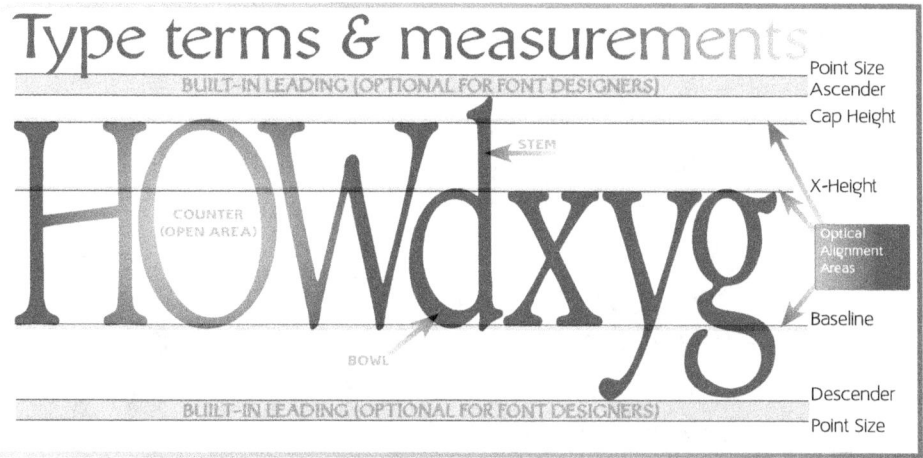

The reason that *x* is specified is that it is normally the only lowercase letter with a flat top and bottom. Curves have to extend over the lines to look the proper height. Yes, it is an optical illusion. These extensions are called **overshoots** in most cases. The same is true of letters such as *A* or *V* that have points. If the point does not protrude past the guidelines, the letter looks obviously too short. Even people who know nothing about type will know that something is wrong. Type design has many of these understandings that have become rules.

You will discover that this **optical alignment** is crucial to excellence in type. You need to even align the sides of the columns optically to make them seem straight, clean, and perfect (though only InDesign offers this ability).

TERMS: Some of you may have noticed that a few paragraphs back we used two additional old letterpress terms. Most of you didn't. Those two terms are uppercase and lowercase. The original terms were majuscules for large letters and minuscules for handwriting using small letters. Majuscules came to be called capital letters. Minuscules remained a mouthful. The terms uppercase and lowercase come from a common hand-setting practice where two wooden cases of letters were used in a standard setup to assemble type (commonly called California job cases.) The upper case contained all the capital letters. The lower case contained all the minuscules laid out by how often each letter is used. In other words, the common phrase caps and lower case (or C&lc) is just one of those things we do in English [though more properly, it is U&lc—upper and lower case].

The upper case
THIS HELD THE CAPITAL LETTERS

The lower case
this held the miniscule letters

Each font and each point size had its own set of cases.

Grandin Building: moveable type cases on 3rd floor [where Book of Morman was published for first time in 1830]

By Mangomal 88 wikimedia commons

The major point to remember is that all letters of a given typeface and a given size fit into rectangles that are the same height. They have to or the lines of letters would

Everything has to fit in the same height!

never align correctly. This is yet another assumption no one ever thinks of—except for typographers.

We've spent a lot of time on this because it is an important concept to understand. Often paragraphs or lines of type look very different in size, but in fact they are the same point size. This is primarily due to variations in x-height and built-in leading in the specific font chosen. Any letter that goes exceptionally high or low changes the size of the entire typeface.

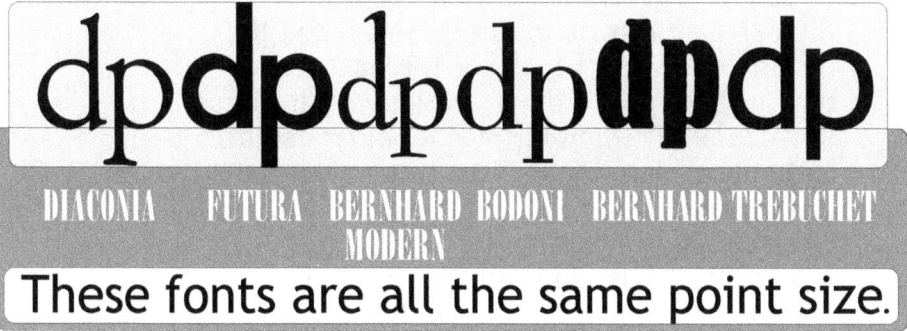

DIACONIA FUTURA BERNHARD BODONI BERNHARD TREBUCHET
MODERN

These fonts are all the same point size.

For example, examine the graphic above very carefully. As you can see, there are huge differences in x-height between Diaconia and Bernhard Modern. Bernhard Modern has a lot of built-in leading also. Bernhard is even more extreme. Even though Diaconia and Futura have similar x-heights, you can see that Futura has no extra leading built into the font, whereas Diaconia has some. The result is that type set in 10-point Futura will look as large as that set in 11-point Diaconia (and maybe 18- or 20-point Bernhard Modern). These things must be taken into account when you pick your fonts for your projects.

Type (or font) measurements

🔹 **Type size:** Type size is measured from top of ascender to bottom of descender in points (plus the built-in leading). Capital letters are usually approximately two-thirds of the point size, but a little shorter than the ascender. The x-height is normally around one-third. The most important factor in visual or comparative size is the x-height. Sans serif faces, covered in a bit, commonly have larger x-heights. Many fonts have some amount of line spacing built in above and below the characters that is included in the point size.

 Leading: Sometimes called line spacing, leading was traditionally measured from baseline to baseline. In other words, leading was the distance advanced to leave room for the next line, measured from the baseline of the original line to the baseline of the following line.

To use typewriter imagery: when you hit the carriage return, the roller advanced the distance necessary to allow the next row of type to be typed without overlap. It was simple to calculate leading in traditional typesetting by using a pica gauge. Now, it is a visual process you watch on your screen in InDesign. You can see the leading by highlighting your copy. Adjusting it up or down is done by watching what happens on the screen.

Type speak: Point size and leading are often written as a fraction. The point size becomes the numerator and the leading the denominator. It is written 10/12. This would be spoken "ten on twelve", meaning ten-point type with twelve points of leading.

As mentioned, many fonts already have built-in leading. You need to be aware of things like this when you pick a font, as mentioned. A font like Futura has almost no built-in spacing and therefore needs to be set with extra leading for readability (AS IF YOU COULD READ FUTURA ANYWAY). A font like Bernhard Modern has so much built-in leading you might be tempted to use negative leading as in 14/13.

A more extreme leading problem comes with type set in all caps (or small caps). If you are using a font that is all capital letters, you may want to set the type as 24/18 or so. Visually, there is far too much space between the lines with the bottom third of the point size blank [because there are no descenders].

THIS HEADLINE IS SET WITH A NEGATIVE LEADING OF 27/25

The leading slug

I mentioned that the meaning of the word slug has changed. While you are getting used to your software, it is helpful to highlight your type and examine the result. The height and vertical location of the black box containing the reversed out type is what software manufacturers now call the slug. This is also the easiest way to see how your font fits the leading which you are currently using. If you have ascenders or descenders sticking out of the slug you are in trouble as far as readability is concerned. It means that your leading is too small and that lines of type will overlap when an ascender and a descender match up between two lines.

 The main thing about leading is that it greatly affects readability: Normally, the longer the line length, the more leading is required. We will talk about producing workable line lengths as we proceed.

Fonts and font design

There are many more things you need to know about typefaces. First, as you will surely notice, this book uses the terms typefaces, typestyles, and fonts interchangeably—as exact synonyms. This is common practice; but it is not entirely accurate. My goal is to give you the common language spoken by your peers—not to be a grammatical Gestapo. But some words you need to know well.

A font, for example, is a very specific thing. This meaning has changed a lot since the second world war. In the days of letterpress, before phototype in the 1950s, a font was all the characters in a given point size. You had Times 12-point, Times 14-point, Garamond 18-point, and so on. In some old fonts, this was hundreds of characters. Gutenberg used over three thousand different characters in his fonts for his bible.

When phototype became available in the 1950s, a font could produce several different sizes. The common machines charged you about the same for a font as was paid in the 1800s (several hundred dollars). But these film strips could be enlarged through various lenses to give you a dozen or more sizes for your money. A common setup, using twelve lenses in a turret, produced 6, 7, 8, 9, 10, 11, 12, 14, 18, 24, 30, and 36 point type. Zoom lenses were the most exciting. For example, one phototypesetting machine went from 6-point to 72-point in half-point increments and 72-point to 144-point in one-point increments.

Today, in the digital arena, a font is simply a complete set of characters for a given style: In InDesign, for example, a font can be set as any size from a tenth of a point to 1296 points. Below I am showing you the font used for this book, named Librum Book (which I designed), showing some of the 484 characters available in it. Notice the three styles of numbers (among other things—like the heifer for the mu).

Librum Book

This is an oldstyle font with a fairly large x-height and small descenders that is very comfortable to read.
ABCDEFGHIJKLMNOPQRSTUVWXYZ 1234567890
abcdefghijklmnopqrstuvwxyz 1234567890
ABCDEFGHIJKLMNOPQRSTUVWXYZ 1234567890
!@#$%^&*()!@#$%^&*()_+{}|:"<>?,./;'[]\=-¡
½¼¹³¾³²¦-×~ÄÅÇÉÑÖÜáàâäãåçéèêë
í""ïñóòôöõúùûüt°¢£□•¶ß®©™¨ÆØ∞
±¥℞ª°æø¿¡☞✐☙⊥«»...ÀÃÕŒœ--""''÷ ÿ Ÿ/ ◊fi ✠ „‚‰
ÂÊÁËÈÍˮÏˮÓÔÒÚÛÙı˜˘˙˚˛˝˗˘

Hundreds of characters

However, hundreds just barely begins to cover the characters needed for type-setting. Typewriters were limited to about 88 characters, although that varied a little. We had the QWERTY keyboard and then those same keys with the shift key held down. The shift key was called that because it physically shifted the entire set of let-ters—lifting them high enough to use the second set available on all the metal keys.

Many of you still think that these are all the letters we need. This is not true—not even close to being correct. In fact, we need access to several hundred characters,

QWERTY keyboard

The story I have always heard was that our current QWERTY key-board was originally designed to be difficult to use because they had to slow down typ-ists. They had to type slow enough so that the keys didn't hit each other and lock up the machine. This was evi-dently a major problem when typewriters were first invented.

as professional typesetters. Even in English we are really limited. But first, we need to mention one of the major differences between PC and Mac.

7-bit ASCII: the PC limitation

When Bill (Gates) and the crew designed DOS, they knew nothing about typesetting. As a result, they were very pleased to offer 7-bit ASCII. ASCII is just an acronym for a regulating group setting a standard numbering order for letter characters, but the key here is 7-bit. Remembering your digital code, 7-bit is 128 choices. So, with 7-bit ASCII, PCs had 128 characters. Good, you say. That is much more than the 88 found on a typewriter. And, in fact, these machines were used only as glorified typewriters. In truth, there wasn't much glory there, but that's another story.

8-bit ASCII: the Mac limitation

When the Mac came out, it supported 8-bit ASCII. We Macophiles have used this for years to lord it over our poor restricted buddies using PCs. However, even the 256 characters of 8-bit ASCII do not even come close to what is needed for typesetting. It does enable us to set type professionally in most European languages—sorta.

Upper ASCII

8-bit ASCII is essential for desktop publishing—both print and ebook. Without all 256 characters, there are many things that are a real pain. There are many special characters that you will need to use all the time.

As a PC user, you will run into that pain very quickly. On a PC, these characters are called upper ASCII characters and are only available by holding down the Alt key and typing four numbers on the numerical keypad. The chart on the next page shows all 128 upper-ASCII characters. Those from 129 and up require the Alt+four-number routine. The number is in the gray bar to the right of the character the character.

The code in the middle column is for the Mac keystroke: O = Option, S = Shift.

This is not to say the Mac is much better. However, all these extra characters are available with the Option key.

Keystrokes for the upper 128 of the ASCII set

Mac & Windows shortcuts for the standard characters in most fonts

Glyph	Mac	Pc: Alt+	Glyph	Mac	Pc: Alt+	Glyph	Mac	Pc: Alt+	Glyph	Mac	Pc: Alt+
		0129	€	SO-2	0164	Ã	On-A	0195	â	Oi-a	0226
,	SO-0	0130	¥	O-y	0165	Ä	Ou-A	0196	ã	On-a	0227
ƒ	O-f	0131	¦		0166	Å	SO-a	0197	ä	Ou-a	0228
„	SO-w	0132	§	O-6	0167	Æ	SO-'	0198	å	Oa	0229
…	O-;	0133	¨	SO-u	0168	Ç	SO-c	0199	æ	O'	0230
†	O-t	0134	©	O-g	0169	È	O`-E	0200	ç	Oc	0231
‡	SO-7	0135	ª		0170	É	Oe-E	0201	è	O`-e	0232
ˆ	SO-i	0136	«	O-\	0171	Ê	Oi-E	0202	é	Oe-e	0233
‰	SO-r	0137	¬	O-l	0172	Ë	Ou-E	0203	ê	Oi-e	0234
Š		0138			0173	Ì	O`-I	0204	ë	Ou-e	0235
‹	SO-3	0139	®	O-r	0174	Í	Oe-I	0205	ì	O`-i	0236
Œ	SO-q	0140	¯	SO-,	0175	Î	Oi-I	0206	í	Oe-i	0237
		0141–0144	°	SO-8	0176	Ï	Ou-I	0207	î	Oi-i	0238
'	O-]	0145	±	SO-=	0177	Ð		0208	ï	Ou-i	0239
'	SO-]	0146	²		0178	Ñ	On-N	0209	ð		0240
"	O-[	0147	³		0179	Ò	O`-O	0210	ñ	On-n	0241
"	SO-[	0148	´	SO-e	0180	Ó	Oe-O	0211	ò	O`-o	0242
•	O-8	0149	µ	O-m	0181	Ô	Oi-O	0212	ó	Oe-o	0243
–	O--	0150	¶	O-7	0182	Õ	On-O	0213	ô	Oi-o	0244
—	OS--	0151	·	SO-9	0183	Ö	Ou-O	0214	õ	On-o	0245
˜	SO-n	0152	¸	SO-z	0184	×		0215	ö	Ou-o	0246
™	O-2	0153	¹		0185	Ø	SO-o	0216	÷	O/	0247
š		0154	º	O-0	0186	Ù	O`-U	0217	ø	Oo	0248
›	SO-4	0155	»	SO-\	0187	Ú	Oe-U	0218	ù	O`-u	0249
œ	O-q	0156	¼		0188	Û	Oi-U	0219	ú	Oe-u	0250
		0157–0158	½		0189	Ü	Ou-U	0220	û	Oi-u	0251
Ÿ	Ou-Sy	0159	¾		0190	Ý		0221	ü	Ou-u	0252
		0160	¿	SO-?	0191	Þ		0222	ý		0253
¡	O-1	0161	À	O`-A	0192	ß	Os	0223	þ		0254
¢	O-4	0162	Á	Oe-A	0193	à	O`-a	0224	ÿ	Ou-y	0255
£	O-3	0163	Â	Oi-A	0194	á	Oe-a	0225			0256

≤ ≥ Ω ◇ = π ∏ ß ∑ √ ∫ ≠ These Option characters are not available on a PC. On a PC, hold down the Alt key and type the ASCII number on the numerical keypad. The blank Mac keys are Control characters not normally available. For a Mac, S = Shift and O = Option. For Mac composite characters like Ô [Option+U then the O], you type the combination to access the accent [which remains invisible] and then type the letter you want the character to appear over — at which point the accented character will be typed.

You do have to memorize the shortcuts. But, Option-8 for a bullet is much easier to remember than Alt+0149. And, Option+-

Shift+8 for the degree symbol makes visual sense, at least. Many Mac keystrokes are easier to memorize.

Plus, once you learn the double-stroke combinations to add accents, they are simple to remember: Option-n, then n gives you ñ [ntilde], for example. Option-e, then any vowel will add the acute éáó [eacute, aacute, oacute]; Option-u adds the umlaut (or diaresis) ü [udiaresis]. In fact, if you have a strange letter that looks like another letter, try it with the Option key. For example, the ø [oslash] is just Option-o.

This chart is available as a PDF at Scribd.com— just search for Bergsland and keystroke table

The cross-platform issues

In early desktop publishing this was a major issue. Not only were PCs 7-bit and Macs 8-bit, but PCs could not read Mac fonts and Macs could not read PC fonts. InDesign solved this problem, but no one else did. As we will see in the next couple of pages, the problem is so huge that a solution had to be found, and it has been. We'll discuss this OpenType solution after we look at some special characters.

Additional characters

Few, if any, of these additional characters are available except in limited fonts which eliminate normal characters like lowercase letters, lining numbers, and so on.

Small caps

One of the typesetting options in most professional software (and many word processors) has been the use of small caps. Most of you are probably familiar with this from tutorials of any of the professional publishing programs. Small caps are capital letters that have been reduced to the x-height and used in place of lower case letters.

The problem is that you may have never seen true small caps. WHAT WE NORMALLY GET IS PROPORTIONALLY REDUCED CAPS. This makes small caps look much thinner and lighter than the capitals they are with. WITH TRUE SMALL CAPS, THE STROKE WEIGHTS OF THE SMALL CAPS ARE THE SAME AS FOR THE

CAPS AND LOWERCASE OF THE NORMAL FONT. There are quite a few specialized fonts that have no lowercase — just caps and small caps. There isn't room to fit true small caps into an ASCII font that already has lowercase letters.

Oldstyle figures

Some of you may have noticed that the numbers used in the body copy of this book seem to flow with the type a little better than usual. That is because the font I am using has oldstyle figures. Most of you probably think that numbers always look like this: 1234567890 These are called lining figures. (Actually, I tend to call them book-keepers' numbers, because I think that is the only place to use them.) But that is another story. For Librum Book, the font used here, the numbers look like this: 1234567890 instead of the lining figures. In fact, because it is one of my OpenType fonts I have the choice of Lining 1234567890, Oldstyle 1234567890, and SMALL CAP 1234567890 figures.

Lining figures are appropriate for use with capital letters, but nothing else. In fact, they look like capitalized characters in the flow of regular C&lc copy. Oldstyle figures are far less intrusive and flow much better when reading. Small cap figures are used with small caps. They flow so much better that it is likely that many of you didn't even notice that I was using them until I just mentioned it. There isn't room to fit oldstyle figures into an ASCII font that already has lining figures [& certainly not small cap figures].

Ligatures

In some cases, letters simply do not fit very well. The typographic solution has been to make special composite characters where two or more letters are made into one character that looks better. In Gutenberg's 42-line Bible, since justification hadn't been invented yet, he used over 3,000 ligatures to help justify his copy. However, in many fonts, through the years, ligatures have been essential to the beauty of the type. Again, the problem has been the 256-character limit. Usually there are only eight ligatures or less in most fonts: fi, fl, ffi, ffl, Æ, œ, Œ, and œ. Librum Book has many more: Æ, NE, NN, UR, Th, Wh, ch, ck, ct, ffy, gg, ry, sp, st, sh, sk, ty, bb, ft, and a few more.

Swashes

With some of the old fonts, especially those that mimicked handwriting, specialized character variants were created to add grace and style to the type. These swashes also were lost when we went to the 256-character limit.

The Lord is my Shepherd; I shall not want.

He makes me to lie down in green pastures;
He leads me beside the still waters.

He restores my soul; He leads me in the paths
of righteousness for His name's sake.

Yea, though I walk through the valley
of the shadow of death,
I will fear no evil; for You are with me;
Your rod and Your staff, they comfort me.

You prepare a table before me
in the presence of my enemies;
You anoint my head with oil; my cup runs over.

Surely goodness and mercy shall follow me
all the days of my life; and I will dwell
in the house of the Lord forever.

In the PDF above [JPEG in ePUB & KFX], you see the twenty-third psalm set in Caflisch Script Pro from Adobe (horribly chewed up by 72 dpi resolution in the ePUB and Kindle versions). This font has many dozens of swashes and ligatures added automatically. Especially notice the k in the word walk in "Yea, though I walk through the valley" in the middle of the psalm when compared to the k in makes (the second line). This swash at the end of the word was added automatically by the font. Also notice the d in goodness compared to the d in days (the 3rd and 2nd lines from the bottom of the psalm).

Fractions, numerators, denominators, superiors, and inferiors

To typesetters, fractions are a real problem. Most PC fonts have ½, ¼, ¾, plus 123. But, what do you do about 61/64 or something like that? In reality, that should look more like this $61/64$. But again that only works when you have an OpenType font with Numerators and Denominators. There isn't room to fit fractions, numerators, denominators, superiors, and inferiors into an ASCII font—or any of the options individually for that matter.

Superscript and subscript

These are conceptually the same as superiors and inferiors except that they apply to all the caps, lower case, and numbers. The most common place you see them is in mathematical and chemical formulas. An algebraic expression might be something like this: $a^3 + b^4$. A chemical formula might look like this: N_2O_3. This type of thing obviously does not work very well with oldstyle figures. It's a little better with lining figures though they still need fixing by moving figures up and down. The problem with this is the same as with true small caps: these characters need to be designed smaller but with the same stroke weight so they look like they fit. Plus, by now you know there simply isn't room to fit all the superscript and subscript characters into an ASCII, 256 character font.

Expert sets

The only solution, before OpenType, was what are called expert set fonts which have all of the oldstyle figures, true small caps, ligatures, swashes, and so on for the normal font. These are a pain to use and they are very rare. If you find one, you are faced with constantly changing fonts. There is certainly no automatic substitution. They do add additional 256 characters to the mix, but even that is not really enough. As you have surely guessed, it would take several expert sets to give us the characters really needed.

The OpenType solution

This relatively new font format solves most of these problems. InDesign was the first professional application to use the format. The Creative Suite is about the only place where they are in constant use. OpenType is completely cross-platform. For the first time you can use the same fonts on a Mac and on a PC. But the new format goes far beyond that.

So, what does the OpenType format do?

First, it completely solves the number of characters limitation. OpenType fonts can have over 65,000 characters. Few do, but they can, if needed. What this means on a practical level is that almost all of the options we have talked about are available (or can be made available) automatically in InDesign as you write: oldstyle figures, true small caps, inferior and superior characters, automatic building of true fractions, ligatures, swashes, plus Greek and Cyrillic alphabets. All of these are optional settings in InDesign—to be used easily.

Kabel Book
Kabel Medium
Kabel Demi
Kabel Bold
Kabel Ultra

Bodoni Book
Bodoni Roman
Bodoni Bold
Bodoni Bold Condensed
Bodoni Poster
Bodoni Poster Compressed

The problem is they are only partially supported in Word and not easy to use.

Font families

Over the years, font design has developed groups of fonts that are obviously variants of the same basic font. They are called font families. These families can have differences in weight and width. Commonly, they have also have italic variants; but that is really a special case, as we will see in a bit.

Font weight

Weight is the thickness of the stroke. Here are several of the common weights arranged in order from thin to thick: Extra Light, Thin, Fine, Light, Book, Regular or Medium or Plain or Roman, Semi Bold or Demi Bold or Halbfett, Bold, Heavy, Extra Bold, Ultra, Fat, Display, Poster, and Ad. Book is usually the most elegant. It is designed for use in books. It is a little lighter than regular (medium) and a little narrower. This makes it possible to get more words on a page.

These radical weight variations are relatively new to font design where most of our standard fonts are four to five hundred years old. The first to appear was Bold, and that did not show up until the eighteenth century.

As advertising became a major force in graphic design, many specialized fonts were developed for the ads. Because these ads were commonly called display ads (as opposed to classified ads), these fonts became known as display fonts. Many of these display fonts showed extreme weight variations, but they were not linked to normal fonts. As far as I have ever been able to tell, extended font families are primarily a late twentieth-century phenomenon.

Font width

Extreme font width changes can look very bad.
For examples, look at the word study below.

20%   100%   220%

Notice on the 20% the horizontals are much thicker than the verticals. On the 220% wide, the unmodulated stroke has become modulated. The t looks very strange that wide.

Notice on the 20% the widths are simply messed up. The serifs have become stubby slabs. On the 220%, it's not too bad—though it is obvious that it would take some work to make this into a true expanded font. The serif width is ridiculous, for example.

There also used to be separate, usually individual, fonts with different apparent widths. There are narrow, extra-condensed, condensed, expanded, wide, extra-wide, and so on. At this point, the demand for fonts with these variations has diminished because any decent publishing software can do what was done to that poor *study* on the other page (to the horror of traditionalists). However, this is certainly one of the descriptive characteristics of a font.

You can see the difference between **Bodoni Bold** and **Bodoni Bold Condensed**. The **Bodoni Poster Compressed** is quite a bit narrower. Whereas **Bodoni Poster** is very wide.

Italics and Obliques

One standard for type is the carved type in Roman columns honoring emperors' great deeds. They are still the classic standard. You should check out fonts like Trajan, Augustinian, and their ilk. To our eyes, they look extremely elegant, and they are. The name has remained in the fact that many people call vertical type roman, to this day.

The problem with these carved letters was that they were all caps. What we now call lowercase letters crept in as people wrote the words. As they wrote faster and faster, monks and scribes developed minuscules. These forms were roughly codified by the scribes and officially adopted by Emperor Charlemagne in the late 900s. Called Carolingian minuscules, he made them the standard for education. They are definitely recognizable as what we now call normal lowercase letter shapes.

The second time this happened was in Italy in the early Renaissance. In Venice, a man named Aldus Manutius developed a font based on the handwriting of his day, which he called *Italic* (from Italia). It became very popular, but because of the narrowness and tight fit of the letters, it was not as legible − and still isn't.

Italics were completely separate fonts and they were not used on the same page as roman fonts until the pomp and ebullience of the Baroque. They really weren't married well until Garamond in the 16th century.

In this day and age, every normal vertical style has a matching italic −Librum Book delights and *Librum Book Italic delights*. As you can clearly see in these six words, italic is a very different font. The *a, e, n, h, g, k r,* and *∂* show the most obvious differences. With some fonts, the matching of these two type styles is done very well and elegantly. In other cases, the two fonts are seemingly just forced into the same bed.

Triage *Triage* Triage
Triage Triage Triage
Italic   Oblique   Regular

One of the aberrations of the digital age is a new phenomenon of fake italics called *oblique*. These are not true italics, but merely slanted roman characters. This is not a true italic. Obliques have been known to drive type purists nuts (but for most of them it's just a short putt anyway)! You can see two example fonts above. You need to pick a font family with good italics.

I tend to think they should get a life and simply not use the fonts they don't like, but then that's just me. In some cases, obliques are a good solution. For the radical geometric sans serif fonts of the 1930s, a true italic would be pure foolishness.

What you definitely do not want are the faux italics produced by software which simply skews the letters. Thankfully, current versions make this optional in most cases. This should be the choice of the type designer. Believe me when I tell you people will notice if you try to get away with it.

Some font terminology

Before we get into specifics of different fonts, I want to define a few descriptive terms to help me explain to you some of the differences between the fonts. The terms are a little esoteric, but I think you will find them helpful to categorize things in your own mind.

- **Stems:** the vertical strokes in letters like h, k, l, r and so on.

- **Bowls:** the rounded parts of letters like *b*, *d*, *g*, *o*, *p*, and even *c* and *s*, according to some.

- **Crossbars:** the horizontal strokes on *A*, *H*, *e*, and so on.

- **Head and foot serifs:** the serifs at the top and bottom of a stem as in *h*, *l*, *k* and *d*.

- **Adnate or bracketed serifs:** when serifs flow smoothly out of the stems.

- **Abrupt serifs:** cross strokes at the end of stems with no bracketing.

- **Terminals:** the endings of the curved portions of letters like a, c, r, C, G, and so on. Lachrymal terminals are tear-drop shaped.

- **Axis:** the angle at which the pen was held to produce the modulated stroke of calligraphers.

- **Humanist axis:** the axis for normal right-handed calligraphic penmanship.

- **Aperture:** the openings of curves on letters like *a*, *c*, *e*, *s*, and so on.

- **Slope:** how far italic and oblique letters slant in degrees.

- **Stroke:** the lines that make up the characters from the old assumption that letters are calligraphic and drawn with separate strokes of a pen or brush.

- **Modulated stroke:** a stroke that varies in width as it proceeds around the letter form.

- **Contrast:** how much the stroke is modulated.

There are more, but this will be enough for our purposes. As you can see, type can get very technical—and I have barely scratched the surface. The differences will seem insignificant to you now, as you start.

But they are really very important. Aperture, for example, tends to control the friendliness and readability. Axis changes from a humanist slant of -12° to mechanical vertical [0°] strongly influence our reaction to the warmness or coolness of a font. But we'll discuss these things as we go, giving you examples so you can see the differences.

Picking fonts

Now that we have briefly discussed what typography is, it is time to look at type styles and the actual design of the fonts you use. In an attempt to get a handle on the different styles, many different classification systems have arisen. Most of these are of mere historical interest—though, in truth, many of you will find these distinctions increasingly important as you grow further as a digital publisher.

One of the things you will discover early on is that traditional typographers really ought to get a life. I can say that because *I are one*. Even from the inside, I find most typographic wranglings to be far beyond nitpicking and well into anal and/or compulsive. Some of the lists and forums I have been on spend months wrangling over insignificant details that will never be noticed by the reader.

My goal in this book is to give you a quick handle on what you have available in our tools of choice: InDesign and a Mac (it's more difficult on a PC or in Office on either platform). Plus, I want you to end up with the beginnings of a procedure to pick fonts on purpose to help with communication. Font choice is one of the prime determinants of your personal publishing style.

In the broad spectrum of available fonts, there are four general classifications:

serif [Bergsland Pro]

sans serif [Frutiger Light]

Handwriting [AuntiePat]

DECORATIVE [ROSEWOOD]

It would probably be a bit better to split handwriting into script and blackletter; but these four have served well over the years. I will only be covering fonts that work well for book design. So, for our purposes in this book, there are two classifications: serif and sans-serif

Serif	Sans Serif
Type	Type

Some sample fonts:

SERIF	SANS SERIF
Librum/Bream	Librum Sans
Bodoni Book	Bergsland Fashion
Baskerville	Gill Sans
Adobe Caslon	Frutiger
ITC Cheltenham	**Arial**
Adobe Jenson	Buddy
Century Schoolbook	ITC Franklin Gothic

Font design books will give you many more classes. For example, they'll break serif into three to nine sub-categories; the same with sans serif. These breakdowns are mainly historical. The functional differences between fonts designed for book design are minimal. We'll leave the more complete categorizing to those who care.

 Historical appropriateness is usually only important to historians: If it makes you happy, do it. However, readers are looking for comfort and ease while reading. Because design is often best when spontaneous rather than structured, this book avoids the legalistic approach as much as possible while still trying to make your choices clear. After all, they are **your** choices.

First, we must define a serif.

Serif Sans Serif
Type Type

A serif is a flare, bump, line, or foot added to the beginning or end of a stroke in a letter. Originally, they were the finishing touches added to the end of strokes produced by pens in the hands of scribes. They have become very stylized over the centuries. There are hundreds of different serif stylings, but do you know their importance?

They seem totally insignificant, but they certainly are not. They strongly influence how we react to type. In fact, on a subconscious level, serifs can be one of the most powerful influences on the reader's reaction to your writing.

Reading has many habitual associations.

The type read during an event or about an occasion takes on the flavor of those events. Many of these typographic reactions are very personal. For example, you may find that your favorite script font happens to be the font on the menu the night you became engaged. Your favorite serif probably comes from that book you read as a teenager which changed your life. Your favorite sans serif could be a result of the marketing brochure about a great, well-loved product you bought.

In our homogeneous, franchised, marketing society, most of us see the same things every day. The result of all of this is that virtually every person in the United States has similar reactions to various type styles. However, there are large differences between the habitual viewers of CBS and Disney when compared to the habitual viewers of Hallmark or the Science Channel. The fonts used are chosen to help identify these differences. The fonts picked to promote Ford pickups are very different from those selected for Lexus and Cadillac touring sedans.

The dominance of serif

Almost every good book you have ever read was set in serif type. Virtually every textbook was also. This one is set in a font I designed called Librum Book. Virtually all body copy before the 1950s was serif. Because of these things, serif typefaces are perceived as warm, friendly, nostalgic, and easy to read. Some of the more modern serif fonts have that edge which was in style in the 1990s, but most are beautiful, quiet, and comfortable. Designers began to use these connections consciously during the 1950s and 1960s. The marketing research boom in the 1970s simply reinforced this trend.

As a result, serif faces are used to promote quality, stability, good value, integrity, and warmth. They are also used to reinforce family values, patriotism, and the emotional content of character traits considered positive by our culture. They are the main choice for the body copy of books—especially fiction. They tend to be seen (at least initially) as trustworthy or at least reliable.

Sans serif is relatively new

Helvetica

ABCDEFGHIJKLMNO
PQRSTUVWXYZ
abcdefghijklmnopqrstu
vwxyz 0123456789

The first widely fashionable sans serif typeface.

Even though sans serif faces (without a serif) have been around since at least the early nineteenth century, they were never popular until the 1950s. Up until the 1950s, sans serif faces were used extensively only by groups like the modernist, Bauhaus movement in Germany during the 1930s, where geometric type was promoted as modern. Futura, Bauhaus, and Kabel are classic examples of this style. They were plain, unadorned—but often they were aggressively modern.

There was quite a bit of large extra-bold sans serif used in the wood typefaces cut for the Victorian explosion of advertising. But those connotations again had little to do with readable copy. Hucksters shouting at us like they did in those broadsides with that huge type usually do not bring pleasant memories except perhaps nostalgia.

In the late 1950s, Helvetica became extremely popular. It was designed by Max Miedinger in 1957, though the name was not chosen until 1960 (it simply means Swiss as Max was Swiss). It was quickly accepted as a new standard type style by many in the business, scientific, and advertising communities. Sans serif faces, in general, became the normal choice for scientific publishing.

Most of the reading associations of sans serif type are anything but warm and friendly. The only exception would be within the youth cultures like extreme jocks who, in cultivating rebellion and adrenaline rushes, have made sans serif their "normal" type classification. But recently, humanist sans serif faces have become quite popular. Books are rarely in sans serif—except some non-fiction.

These usage normals were almost unanimous until very recently when desktop publishing started bringing in designers with no design education. So the reactions are predictable enough to be very useful.

- **Sans serif faces:** are clean and modern.

- **Serif faces:** in general, are more elegant and beautiful.

As mentioned, these distinctions are being greatly muddied by new trends toward very readable sans serif fonts designed for body copy. For my headers and sidebar copy, the sans serif fonts I am using are Librum Sans—a companion sans I designed to go with Librum.

The Times/Helvetica problem

One of the more interesting phenomena of digital publishing is the use of Times and Helvetica. Although these are well-designed typefaces, their excessive usage resulting from their specification as the default fonts in so many nonprofessional applications and operating systems has completely changed their perception in the mind of the typical reader.

Most professional typographers avoid these two fonts like the plague. As a result, the only place people see them is in output by people who are untrained in publishing and simply use the software defaults—think schools, bureaucracies, the IRS, collection agencies, (not very good company) and self-publishers. Because of this uncaring usage, Times, Times New Roman, Helvetica, and Arial have been virtually ruined for serious use by designers. They bring up too many bad associations.

Typically, you should pick a serif for body copy & a sans serif for heads

However, this is simply the norm. You need to pick font combinations which appeal to your readers of your book within the limited niche of that book. As mentioned earlier, these choices are fairly limited. I will give you some options as we go. You will definitely find your own as you develop as a publisher. Time spent at MyFonts.com will be great fun for you and a wonderful help to your font style education!

Our needs are specific

As book designers, we need fonts which are easy and comfortable to read in large quantity, and without strong personality. Our font choices cannot get in the way of the content. If the reader notices the fonts used, that fact takes away from the actual writing. In addition, we need something else—variety for emphasis. What we need, to do what we do, are font families. These are sets of fonts with different styles and weights.

The typical font family

Ah ha! You think you know this one, right? Well, maybe. In the word processor world, especially on PCs, fonts come in regular, italic, bold, and bold italic. But you will discover that this is a modern word processor limitation. It is true that there are many four-font families. However, there are also many 2-font, 3-font, 5-font, 6-font, and 8-font families. There are even some 30+ font families [like Helvetica].

The body copy family I am using for the printed version of this book is Librum (one of my most recent designs). It comes in four fonts, as you can see. But font families can be much larger than this. Adobe Jenson Pro comes with 32 fonts. Helvetica and Helvetica Neue (a recently updated version) have a total of nearly 80 fonts in the two families. The fonts that were installed with the Creative Suite that are designed for reading and books commonly had six fonts. This is true of Caslon, Garamond, and Minion. But Chaparral has eight and Myriad has ten.

What you will find, is that the system fonts which come with your operating system, and fonts which were installed with Office usually only have four.

As typographers and book designers, we need a minimum three-font family—regular, italic, and bold: Italic is necessary for periodical names and emphasis. Bold is used for proper names and headers, As you saw at the start of this paragraph I used a sans serif bold through the colon to emphasize an important point. But regardless of which font family you choose it must satisfy several basic requirements of book design.

What do you need in a font family to make it exceptional for designing books?

That is what we need to cover in this book. Good font families for book design are relatively rare. I'm prejudiced toward my designs (after all I designed them to meet my needs), but you need to be aware of which fonts might work for you and why. These fonts are a careful choice. Let's start with some basic criteria for book design fonts.

- **Readability:** Body copy set with the fonts you choose must be exceptionally easy and comfortable to read. Reading comfort is imperative to help the reader enjoy the book.

- **Extremely smooth type color:** Type set with the font you choose must have excellent letterspacing and produce a smooth even texture when the type is set in paragraphs. That smooth, medium gray type color generated by the body copy is the background that you must have to easily contrast the headers—to make heads & subheads pop off the page, as it were.

- **Legibility:** The fonts chosen need to be quickly absorbed when being used for headlines, subheads, captions, pull quotes, and the like. This is not the place for fancy scripts, or wild decorative typefaces. You need to be sure your readers can quickly comprehend your fonts.

- **Oldstyle figures:** It would probably help if I called them what they are: lowercase numbers. 1234567890 They are essential for good type color—where lining figures [1234567890] are shouting just like ALL CAPS SHOUT in an email.

- **Variety of weights:** You will really need regular & bold weights, but light & black weights will help immensely.

- **True small caps:** As we will discuss ahead, small caps are required in several instances.

- **True, but readable, italics:** Obliques [slanted letters] simply look wrong to an educated reader. But many italics are closer to a script with all of the attendant readability issues.

Studying Studying

Here's a comparison of oblique & italic in Garamond

I could add more to this list, but that should be enough for now. In the 1980s and 1990s, fonts which could supply these things were not common. What I saw in the textbooks perpetrated on my students angered me. Most of the textbooks I was given to use were useful for little other than readily available examples of terrible typography. My students all complained how hard they were to read.

So, I made student reading comfort the primary focus of my textbook designs. I started designing fonts to help me in that quest. I started hearing student comments like: "I started reading my assignment for the first week and read five chapters before I noticed how far I had read." Actually, I've only heard that particular comment once—but it was (and is) really gratifying… It's one of my motivations to write.

Readability

I've talked about this already, but you must remember the importance of this characteristic of book design typography. Your font choices are major factor in readability. In fact, for book design it can be said that comfortable readability is the core of typography. Below is a little graphic to show you some of the things that influence how easily you can read a font.

Readability comparisons

	Helvetica	Gill Sans	Caslon	Jenson	Bodoni	Brinar
Writing Axis	Op	Op	Op	Op	Op	Op
	No axis	No axis	Varied Axes	Humanist	Modern	Humanist
Aperture	ace	ace	ace	ace	ace	ace
	Closed	Mostly Open	Mostly Open	Open	Closed	Mostly Oper
Modulation	RN	RN	RN	RN	RN	RN
	No	No	Yes	Yes	Excessive	Yes
Slanted crossbars	Ae	Ae	Ae	Ae	Ae	Ae
	No	No	No	Yes on e	No	Yes
Double story	ag	ag	ag	ag	ag	ag
	a only	a&g	a&g	a&g	a&g	a&g
Circle/Oval	OG	OG	OG	OG	OG	OG
	Slight Oval	Circle	Barely Oval	Slight Oval	Oval	Slight Oval
Calligraphic	rag	rag	rag	rag	rag	rag
	No	No	No	Yes	No	Vaguely

Everyone has too much to read. *If you give them any excuse, they will quit reading your work and go on to the next piece in their long list of writings they have to read.*

I've seen my wife throw novels away because they were too hard to read. Difficult to read books have become commonplace, One of the attractions of ebooks is the ability to change the type to make it more comfortable to read (although true typographic control in an ereader is minimal).

If you ever took one of my classes, you know how much I harp on readability—especially the importance of aperture and other factors concerning readability. There are many technical font design issues which control this. It's not important that you understand the seven character-istics on the previous page at this point. What matters is that you see that Jenson, Brinar, and Caslon (in that order) are the most readable out those six font choices.

Other good books on typography

- *InDesign Type* **by Nigel French:** This is the best basic book I have seen on setting up type in InDesign

- *The Elements of Typographic Style* **by Robert Bringhurst:** This is the industry classic. It's pretty heavy-duty but an excellent read.

- *Stop Stealing Sheep* **by Erik Speikermann:** The title comes from an old quote by Frederic Goudy who said that anyone who would letterspace lowercase would steal sheep. It's a very entertaining yet highly informative read.

Not surprisingly, because book designers are typog-raphers, there are many books on the subject. The sad thing is that most of them are very dry, ridiculously techni-cal, and full of strong opinions stated as facts (been guilty of that m'self). As you grow in skill as book designer, you'll probably read several of them.

Check out your local library.

What fonts should you use?

You can spend a lot of money on fonts. The good news is that the Creative Cloud comes with many excellent fonts for book design. You get a free subscription to Type-Kit. Included are these five good fonts for body copy, plus many more. If you had older versions of the Creative Suite like CS6 or CS5, then you already own some of these fonts.

- **Adobe Caslon Pro—6 weights:** in TypeKit
- **Adobe Garamond Pro—4 weights:** in TypeKit
- **Chaparral Pro—& variations— dozens of weights:** in TypeKit
- **Minion Pro & variations—dozens of weights:** in TypeKit
- **Adobe Jenson Pro—& variations— dozens of weights:** in TypeKit

The Mac OSX software gives you several more—including those used on the iPad. They are quite pretty.

- **Baskerville—6 weights**
- **Cochin—4 weights**
- **Hoefler Text—4 weights**
- **Optima—5 weights**

Many of you will also have others installed by various hardware and software you have purchased over the years.

What you are looking for is a professional quality serif font. Check Font Book on the Mac. It is a free piece of software that comes with OSX to install and view the fonts you have installed on your computer. You may be surprised at some of the gems. Another you probably have is:

- **Palatino—4 weights**

Any of these font families will work for you as you get into the industry and learn your craft. Eventually you will probably buy something special for your taste and style—but it's certainly not necessary. If you like the fonts I am using in this book, email me and ask. I will sell you the 12 Fonts used in previous books: Contenu Book (4), Contenu (4), and Buddy (4) for $30. List price is $25 each for the twelve fonts and that's below average. The fonts used in this book: Librum (4), Librum E (4), Librum Sans (4), and Bream (2) go for $99—half the normal $199.

A general overview of font classifications

What I want to do next is quickly give you an overview of font design history and some things to look for when deciding on your font use. Font designers will likely give me a rough time for simplifying the choices to this degree, but my goal is practicality. It is actually absurd to define oldstyle fonts as all fonts designed before 1750 or so. Technically oldstyle is a very specific class of type design. But in reality, the readers of your books couldn't care less about those classification niceties. What they want is reading comfort, and their eyes are not trained to see the subtleties of the more extended font classification lists. However, as a typographer, you need a bit more. So I want to give you a simplified, useful list.

A practical list

As mentioned earlier, the four basic classifications of all type are: Serif, Sans Serif, Script, and Decorative. All that really matters for book design are serif and sans serif. We'll start with the majority: serif typefaces. Serif fonts have been the dominant standard for typography for 500 years. Only with the new millennium have we seen a genuine movement away from serifs toward the newer, more readable sans fonts being released. This basic serif classification is broken up into sub classes that are bewildering in their complexity. But the general consensus is as follows.

Minimal Serif Font Classifications

Oldstyle (Adobe Jenson Pro)

Transitional (Baskerville)

Modern (Bodoni)

Slab (Clarendon)

I'll briefly cover other classifications from other systems as we go through our quick overview. You will read and hear many strongly worded opinions about these things as you continue your education in typography. My goal is to get you started and ease some of the confusion.

Old Style fonts: readable and beautiful (1500-1750 or so)

For practical purposes, I include all fonts designed before the mid-eighteenth century in old style. In this book we'll break them out a little, but "normal" people cannot see any of the differences. That's how everyone reads them. The distinctions are only interesting to type designers & type nerds. But then this is a book for us, isn't it? Just don't expect anyone else to care much.

The originals used by Gutenberg were in blackletter, what is commonly referred to as Gothic or Old English by most. This has had its own development and we will include it if I decide to have a discussion of handwriting fonts or scripts after we cover serif and sans serif.

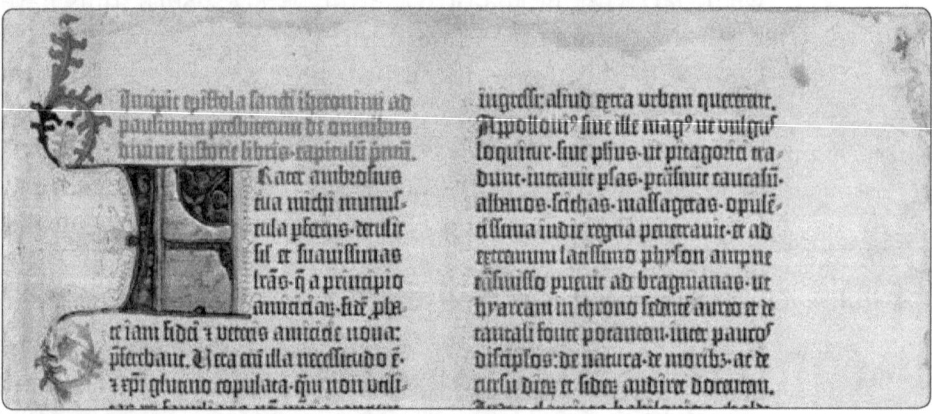

From a scan at the Ransom Center of the University of Texas at Austin [WIKIMEDIA COMMONS]

You can see why we'll skip right over Gutenberg's beginnings. The fonts we are most comfortable reading are those based on character forms from the fifteenth to the eighteenth centuries. I include most of the font designs developed for early printers. These start with the earliest fonts from the Renaissance. Remember printing triggered the Renaissance. It was the beginning of font design also.

These fonts are the standard to which all other fonts are compared. They are full of smooth sensuous curves. They are light, and open—beautiful, comfortable, and elegant. The stems are vertical. The bowls are nearly circular.

The crossbars might rise to the right (but usually only the e). The axis is mostly humanist until the end of the period in the mid-1700s. The aperture is comfortably open. There is enough contrast to help but not enough to dominate.

Humanist axis: All of the basic Oldstyle category uses a slanted axis roughly caused by the angle in which the pen was held for calligraphy. This axis varies in degrees but is always slanted from upper left to lower right—the basic right-handed bigotry that forms many of the assumptions about type design. But then I'm a little subjective on this topic being sinister myself (a lefty). This is opposed to the Rational axis found in Modern fonts.

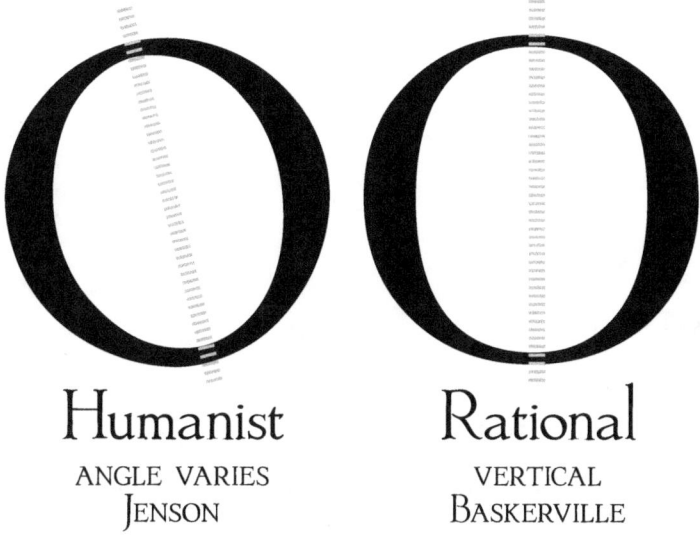

Humanist

ANGLE VARIES
JENSON

Rational

VERTICAL
BASKERVILLE

Baskerville is technically a transitional style, leading into the "Modern" font designs.

Bringhurst's List of font classifications

There are many font classification systems. Robert Bringhurst, in the currently accepted standard reference on typography, *The Elements of Typographic Style*, Hartley and Marks, 1992, uses historical markers. He sets up categories based largely on the historical periods of fine art as you can see below. It is, indeed, a fascinating journey through history. Robert presents his case extremely well. He's an excellent writer and a poet. You will acquire a great deal of useful knowledge by reading his book.

It is a bit over the top, though. Plus, he skips a lot. Bringhurst clearly does not like Victorian letter styles, so he does not mention them. He skips all of the modern variations like Art Nouveau, Art Deco, and the more extreme elements of the early twentieth century. He barely mentions the slab serifs of the late nineteenth century because he thinks they are coarse. In other words, he presents the type he likes in an excellent setting.

- Scribal or Carolingian
- Renaissance
- Mannerist
- Baroque
- Rococo
- Neoclassical
- Romantic
- Realist
- Geometric Modernism
- Expressionist
- Elegiac Post-Modernism
- Geometric Post-Modernism.

My list draws from many sources

One of the more entertaining resources on the Web was Jonathan Hoefler's *Typography 101* writings on typophile.com. It seems to have disappeared recently. Like Bringhurst, his classes made a lot of sense and I'll include them in my practical list as we go through. He starts with two that are fun. They really have no place in a general classification system other than the fact that they show the historical roots of type in European culture. Remember, the study of type is a European thing.

Our carved roots

Lapidary: Jonathan distinguishes Greek Inscriptions from Roman. Basically, the Greeks did not use serifs. He uses Lithos by Carol Twombley from Adobe in 1989 as his standard here. It was the fashion standard of the early '90s. I ALWAYS THOUGHT HERCULANUM WAS CLOSER THAN THE MORE STYLISH LITHOS.

Lithos

ABCDEFGHIJKLMNOPQR STUVWXYZ1234567890

Inscriptional: Here's the Roman variant. Hoefler uses Twombly at Adobe again with her font called Trajan, from the Trajan column in Rome. These are superbly elegant caps. Personally, I find the B, P, R, & S too narrow, and I really dislike the 2—but that's merely an example of what I was telling you about opinionated typographers.

Trajan

ABCDEFGHIJKLMNOPQR STUVWXYZ1234567890

Carol Twombley

It is difficult to overrate the effect Carol has had on typography in the past couple decades.

"American calligrapher and type designer, a graduate from Rhode Island School of Design where her professor was Charles Bigelow. Joined the digital typography program at Stanford University, also under Bigelow. Working from the Bigelow & Holmes studio she designed Mirarae, which won her the 1984 Morisawa gold prize. Since 1988 she has been a staff designer at Adobe. [MyFonts.com]

WIKIPEDIA SAYS: *"She retired from type design in early 1999, to focus on her other design interests, involving textiles and jewelry."*

These two styles are fun, but not too important to an overall classification system, because there are so few of these fonts. The rest of Hoefler's classes we'll cover in the practical list that follows.

Thomas Phinney, now head of FontLab, wrote a nice little historical piece (but that's gone now also). In it, he uses the more common set of categories currently taught in most design schools: Old Style, Transitional, Modern, Slab Serif (or Egyptian), fat faces, wood type, Art Nouveau, Art Deco, synthesis, and grunge. This covers the basics nicely and we will follow that basic lead. However, let's get real.

The important thing is not historical accuracy, it is readability and decorative style.

The importance of classification has to do with appropriateness. Bringhurst is still over the top here when he suggests using French type for French products and so on. What we should be using is historical type in context. You cannot pull off a Western "Wanted" poster with anything but Victorian type from the late 1880s. All of the recent Retro looks have specifically used fonts from a historical period placed in a hip, fashionable setting. Within a few months there were Retro fonts specifically designed to match the style. At this point in graphic design, the fonts appear along with the new fashion.

Venetian: Adobe Jenson Pro

Shortly after Gutenberg got things rolling in Germany a group of printers in Italy became interested in reviving some of the letterforms instituted by Charlemagne at the founding of the Holy Roman Empire in the 8th century. The creative innovation was provided by Nicholas Jenson in Venice who combined the inscriptional caps with the Carolingian miniscules without many of the cursive additions. The gorgeous result is what we now call caps and lowercase, our assumed alphabet.

Adobe Jenson Pro

ABCDEFGHIJKLMNOPQR STUVWXYZ1234567890
abcdefghijklmnopqrstuvwxyz

Robert Slimbach of Adobe used Nicolas Jenson's roman and Ludovico degli Arrighi's italic typeface designs as part of the family of Adobe Originals historical revivals. *Adobe*

In the original, there were many curious shapes. The neat, crisp digital shapes we are accustomed to did not exist in the lead characters cast from hand carved metal molds The scan to the right is from the University of Florida's Rare Book collection.

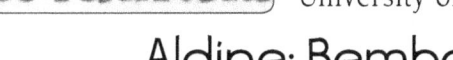

Aldine: Bembo

These fonts are also from Northern Italy. Bembo is a revival of the work of another printer, Aldus Manutius in the 1500s. Manutius was a major influence on type design as we know it. Most of the life and playfulness of the Venetian has been ironed out. The term stately is used of these fonts—cool, formal, and sober..

Bembo

ABCDEFGHIJKLMNOPQR STUVWXYZ1234567890
abcdefghijklmnopqrstuvwxyz

The English used these fonts as a base for what they called Old Face.

Garalde: Garamond 3

These original serif fonts are exemplified by the work of Claude Garamond in Paris in the early to mid-1500s. Garamond was the first major type designer. He was not a printer or calligrapher, he was a freelance punchcutter. Along with Robert Granjon, Geofroy Tory, and others, they were responsible for what is currently called the golden age of typography.

Therefore they say unto God,

This is a capture of P22's Operina Romano taken from Ludovico Arrighi's 1522 instructional lettering book. Like all scans of the very early type examples, it looks really rough to our eyes. Below is Benton/Cleland's italic interpretation:

Garamond 3

ABCDEFGHIJKLMNOPQRSTU
VWXYZ1234567890abcdefghijk
lmnopqrstuvwxyz

This Linotype version of Garamond from 1936 is based on the American Type Founders design by Morris Fuller Benton and Thomas Maitland Cleland, who based their work, in turn, on seventeenth-century copies of Claude Garamond's types by Jean Jannon. *MyFonts*

Garamond 3 Therefore they say
& italic: Therefore they say unto God

One of Claude's major innovations was the conscious decision to design a complementary italic companion font. As font design began, italics were completely separate. The first italic font cut was by Griffo, again commissioned by Aldus Manutius, in 1499. These early italics seem very condensed to us, with elliptical bowls and very calligraphic stroke endings (as opposed to actual serifs). Oddly, many of these fonts have vertical serif capital letters. This was the cursive handwriting of the period. They do not make good companions to modern fonts. They were closer to what we now call script.

As you can see on the previous page, it is quite a stretch to really say these are companion fonts, but this disconnect has become the standard, which we assume is correct. The major thing to remember in all of this is that we are dealing with the popular leader and all of its copy-cat versions. There are hundreds of versions of Garamond.

aaaa

Left to right
Garamond
Garamond 3
Adobe Garamond Pro
ITC Garamond

French Old Style: ITC Galliard

As mentioned, Granjon was another of the new breed of professional punchcutters who developed type foundries in Paris in the early sixteenth century. I find Matthew Carter's interpretation to be the best of the Garalde styles, but Hoefler makes it another classification (probably just to give himself an excuse to show this exquisite design in addition to the required Garamond).

ITC Galliard

ABCDEFGHIJKLMNOPQ
RSTUVWXYZ1234567890
abcdefghijklmnopqrstuvwxyz

ITC Galliard is an adaptation of Matthew Carter's 1978 phototype design for Mergenthaler. Galliard was modeled on the work of Robert Granjon, a sixteenth-century letter cutter, whose typefaces are renowned for their beauty and legibility. *MyFonts*

Matthew calls Garamond's design "stately, calm, & dignified" in contrast to Granjon's "spirited, tense, & vigorous" stylings. Galliard certainly fit well (and had a causal effect) to the styles of the 1980s with the large x-heights and crisp, clean, rounded shapes. His shapes were a revelation to me personally and a major part of my style in the early eighties. Some people even see Granjon's influence in that modern megalith: Times Roman.

Dutch Old Style: Janson

By the 1600s, French oppression had caused the center of typography to shift to Antwerp primarily through Plantin who was based there. This style commercialized the French designs that were so heavily promoted by Plantin. The Dutch influence made the French work more printable, taking out some of the subtleties of Garamond and Granjon.

Their main influence was in England where there was no real typefounding industry until Caslon in the 1700s. These styles were a abandonment of calligraphic roots—mechanically constructed with new elements like the ball terminals of the a, c, g, r and so on. The bdpq characters are no longer based on the o. The diagonal strokes of the v, w, & y are sometimes bowed out to make for better letterspacing.

Janson Text

ABCDEFGHIJKLMNOPQ
RSTUVWXYZ1234567890
abcdefghijklmnopqrstuvwxyz

A faithful recreation of one of the great seventeenth century Dutch typefaces cut by Miklós Tótfalusi Kis. He was a Transylvanian protestant who, sent to Holland in the last quarter of the seventeenth century to learn printing, became one of the leading punchcutters of his time before returning to Transylvania to print bibles. His teacher, in Amsterdam around 1680, was Dirk Voskens. [MYFONTS]

Actually, we would call Kis Hungarian and his name is pronounced Kish—as the s is pronounced in Hungarian with the cs having the s sound.

Lawson sums them up as "not as esthetically pleasing as the French letters, but were more practical for the everyday production of commercial printing." The stylistic Gestapo of the East Coast has downplayed these fonts as somehow lesser creations. Hoefler, on the other hand, says Kis' forms had wonderfully smooth type color with "a typographic rhythm of such evenness" that it was unmatched in oldstyle fonts.

These fonts had huge influence on typography of the 17th and early 18th centuries. They were immensely popular, especially in England. Hoefler says that the English love of the fonts was two-fold: first they were attractive and sturdy—second they were necessary. The English Star Chamber (a secretive court) made newsbooks illegal and so they were all printed in Amsterdam and smuggled into England. Because of these strong restrictions to typefounding, there were no English typefounders throughout the 17th century.

English Old Style: Caslon

Adobe Caslon

ABCDEFGHIJKLMNOPQ
RSTUVWXYZ1234567890
abcdefghijklmnopqrstuvwxyz

For her Caslon revival, designer Carol Twombly studied specimen pages printed by William Caslon between 1734 and 1770. *MyFonts*

MyFonts puts it this way: "William Caslon released his first typefaces in 1722. Caslon's types were based on seventeenth-century Dutch old style designs, which were then used extensively in England. Because of their remarkable practicality, Caslon's designs met with instant success. Caslon's types became popular throughout Europe and the American colonies; printer Benjamin Franklin hardly used any other typeface.

"The first printings of the American Declaration of Independence and the Constitution were set in Caslon. For her Caslon revival, designer Carol Twombly studied specimen pages printed by William Caslon between 1734 and 1770."

Transitional: Baskerville

By the end of this period, fonts had appeared with a rigidly vertical axis (usually called a rational axis). You can see it in Baskerville. This was the time of the Revolution and design was into Retro classical, which was called Neoclassical by the historians. This is the time of Monticello. Franklin was extremely impressed with John Baskerville's designs in England at the time.

Baskerville

ABCDEFGHIJKLMNOPQ
RSTUVWXYZ1234567890
abcdefghijklmnopqrstuvwxyz

John Baskerville had John Handy cut from his own brilliant designs, based on a lifetime of calligraphy and stonecutting. *MyFonts*

Baskerville's influence on typography

Outside of John's very beautiful typeface, his major influence was on the general look of page layout and formatted typography. He liked Caslon's work but wanted to improve on it.

He was an amateur [in the best sense of the word] printer and he made his press a hallmark of excellence. He used a brass plate and a hard impression when the fashion was a soft squeeze. He smoothed his papers by running them through heated copper cylinders, instituting what we now call *calendaring*. Virtually all printing papers are now calendared. He used wide margins and well-leaded copy, beginning the style for quality that we still use today.

As seen in fonts like New Baskerville, John's fonts are still a standard for typographic beauty. Though rational and mechanical, they are clear, easy to read, and elegant.

The entire oldstyle period of font design

Through the 1500s and 1600s, these old style letter forms went through gradual changes. Punchcutters moved continuously away from the calligraphic roots of letter forms. As Europe was caught up in the extravagance and luxury of the Baroque and Rococo, those lavish curves and flourishes made their way into type design as well. But the influence was outside what we now consider the mainstream.

Type design gradually became drawn rather than written. Baroque designers played with letter forms, having stems that varied in slope and bowls that varied in axis in the same font. The entire period was extravagant, but tightly based on classical oldstyle fonts.

The finishing portion of this entire period I am calling oldstyle was populated with rigidly defined, carefully drawn forms. Throughout this period, careful adjustments were tried with axis, aperture, serif style, and so on. However, to our eye in the twenty-first century, all of these fonts are minor variations on a common theme.

Old style fonts are still the normal choice for body copy.

Your personal style will determine which you choose. The variations definitely have their own character and leave their feel in the documents that use them. Beyond that, they are all old, traditional letterforms to us.

The main point is that all of these fonts, to the contemporary eye, look very similar. More to the point, they all provoke nearly identical reader reactions (unless that reader is quite sophisticated graphically—with a trained eye). It is true there are major differences to the typographer's eye, but then there are not many of us. Functionally, these all can be used in the same places, for the same clients. The only differences are ones of taste & personal style.

Revolutionary styles (to locate them by time)

Modern: Bodoni Book

These are type styles of the late 1700s and early 1800s, although their influence remains. To call them Modern, as most of the schools do, is silly. They are 200 years old. To call them Romantic (as Bringhurst does) is equally strange for they are cold fish. They are the natural expression of the radical, revolutionary intellectualism of the period. They are built with hard, tightly structured letterforms which push out the emotional, warm, comfortable type of the Old Style fonts, replacing it with spiky, carved, structured forms.

Bodoni Book

ABCDEFGHIJKLMNOPQ
RSTUVWXYZ1234567890
abcdefghijklmnopqrstuvwxyz

with the rococo, as mentioned. It is hard to reconcile the tightly controlled, rigidly refined shapes of Bodoni with the fashionable stylistic excesses found in the Rococo—though you can see it in the Poster style.

Bodoni Poster

Fat Faces:
Bodoni Poster

In the 19th century, a huge variety of decorative typefaces appeared for advertising use. Many of them we now simply call Display. Hoefler has two categories devoted to them, but they are really minor players. Also, Bodoni Poster really isn't radical enough to be called a Fat Face.

Slab Serif: Cheltenham

Several slab serif fonts were designed when Egyptian discoveries including King Tut were found and the raging fashion in the world at the time. As a result, they are often called Egyptians. As we'll see below, these became more prevalent as a style in the early 20th century.

Cheltenham

ABCDEFGHIJKLMNOPQRSTU VWXYZ1234567890 abcdefghijklmnopqrstuvwxyz

Daniel Berkeley Updike seems to have stimulated the architect Bertram G. Goodhue to design the prototype in 1896 for Ingalls Kimball at the Cheltenham Press. Six years later Morris Fuller Benton at ATF developed it into the design and then the series that we know today."Owing to certain eccentricities of form," writes Updike, "it cannot be read comfortably for any length of time." But he concludes: "It is, however, an exceedingly handsome letter for ephemeral printing." *MyFonts*

These fonts were designed in response to the overwhelming fashion of modern fonts that look great at large sizes, but tend to fall apart in the smaller sizes needed for text. These are sturdy fonts that are surprisingly easy to read, even though they are clunky, heavy, and almost completely lacking in grace.

Geometric Slab Serif

This particular subset of slab serifs is more contemporary. Typical fonts of this type are Memphis, Rockwell, and City. The readability is usually very low. However, the serifs make these fonts a much better choice for readability than geometric sans fonts like Avant Garde, Century Gothic, and even Futura. These fonts are an outgrowth of the modernist movement of the early twentieth century.

Here letter forms are constructed geometrically, most with purely circular bowls, no modulation, slab serifs, closed aperture, and so on. Intellectually, they could almost be considered the scientific extension of the socialist expression found in realism. Currently they are not common but many people like them a lot. They are sort of manly, but I'm not sure that is a complement.

Rockwell

ABCDEFGHIJKLMNOPQ RSTUVWXYZ 123456789 ab cdefghjiklmnopqrstuvwxyz

Realist: Clarendon

Type for the common man—ignored by almost every classification system

Clarendon

ABCDEFGHIJKLMNOPQ RSTUVWXYZ1234567890 abcdefghijklmnopqrstuvwxyz

Slab serif type, when the serif is bracketed, is sometimes referred to as a Clarendon. This font originated in England in 1845 and is named for the Clarendon Press in Oxford. Clarendon was intended to be a heavier complement to ordinary serif designs.

This is a Bringhurst classification. In the mid-1800s, a type design movement began making type for the workers, the common man, the non-educated. Stylistically they are an extension of transitional forms. They were never really popular with designers, but they have had a lot of influence. Many of these fonts were the result of readability studies of the time. As such they were used by newspapers. One of these fonts, Century Schoolbook, is the font many of us used when we learned to read in the first few grades of school. It may be the most elegant of the bunch. In general, heavy, clunky, and old-fashioned are the terms associated with fonts like these.

Century Schoolbook

ABCDEFGHIJKLMNOPQR
STUVWXYZ1234567890
abcdefghijklmnopqrstuvwxyz

Art Nouveau

The swirling curves of Art Nouveau were also used to produce type. It seems like a rebellion against the realists, much as the entire movement was a rejection of contemporary morality and tradition.

Arnold Boecklin

ABCDEFGHIJKLMNOPQRSTU
VWXYZ 1234567890!
abcdefghijklmnopqrstuvwxyz

These are the first fonts with little tie to traditional letterforms. They were never really popular, but certain cultures can take them on for a time. They were the absolute standard for the Spanish culture in New Mexico in the early 1980s, for example.

Fonts like these need to be used very carefully. From a design point of view, they are very interesting. However, they are usually quite hard to read. The larger problem, though, is their ties to a cultural movement known for its depravity. They are used a lot by writers and designers in the occult for these reasons. You need to be aware of these issues.

Current Synthesis

Veljovic

ABCDEFGHIJKLMNOPQR
STUVWXYZ1234567890
abcdefghijklmnopqrstuvwxyz

Nueva

ABCDEFGHIJKLMNOPQR
STUVWXYZ1234567890
abcdefghijklmnopqrstuvwxyz

Many recent serif faces play with attributes of any and all historical styles. Often they experiment with distinctive serif stylings, sharp angular features, fanciful modulations. However, these more playful aspects are often very restrained and elegant. They take pieces from all over and show a wide variety from Times New Roman to Palatino to Veljovic. Often, like in Usherwood, the x-heights are very large—strictly a fashion statement from the 1980s. As a result, many of them had no lasting impact on typography.

Sans serif classifications

There are not nearly as many options in sans serif type. I am only going to give you four general types. I frankly invented these categories to help you make sense of what you run across in your search to build your own font library. Hoefler doesn't even cover them.

Gothic: Franklin Gothic

Sans serif typefaces started in the early 19th century with a single line mention of a monoline font in Caslon's last catalog. The original fonts were all caps. In Europe these are called grotesques. Around the turn of the 20th century, these fonts were very popular.

Franklin Gothic

ABCDEFGHIJKLMNOPQ RSTUVWXYZ1234567890 abcdefghijklmnopqrstuvwxyz

Franklin Gothic was designed by Morris Fuller Benton in 1902 as his version of the heavy sans serifs first made popular by Vincent Figgins in 1830. *MyFonts*

Geometric Sans: Futura

These are largely a product of radical modernism, the Bauhaus in Germany, and the Art Deco movement of the 1920s and 1930s. The letterforms seem to be absolute geometric constructs, but they often have many subtle adjustments beyond that to make them more readable (but just barely). After their introduction the use of Gothics became unsophisticated.

Futura

ABCDEFGHIJKLMNOPQ RSTUVWXYZ1234567890 abcdefghijklmnopqrstuvwxyz

Designed by Paul Renner in 1927, Futura is the classic example of a geometric sans serif type based on the Bauhaus design philosophy. *MyFonts*

These fonts are very stylish and loved by a large portion of graphic designers. They are not really appropriate for typographic use, however. The real problem with geometric fonts is the readability issue. Because all of the bowls are perfectly round and the aperture is usually almost closed, there is little visual difference between an a, c, e, or o. More than that, an ol looks a lot like a d, an rn can look identical to an m, and even a cl can seem to be a d. They can work fairly well in headlines, but using them for body copy is usually a serious mistake. Locally, here in southern Minnesota, several of the local colleges have chosen to use Futura or its more radical cohort Avant Garde as the official font for their school. Their official documents may look "modern" [1980s], but they certainly are difficult to read—which kind of misses the point, don't you think? Typical fonts are: Futura, Kabel, Avant Garde, Century Gothic, and Bauhaus.

The German Bauhaus technological school headed up by the architect Walter Gropius was especially involved in pursuing revolutionary new font designs. One of its instructors, Herbert Bayer, developed a geometric sans with no normal C&lc relationships. He advocated a character redesign to bring it more into line with normal speech patterns—basic intellectual drivel.

afghan president's

Populist commoner: Helvetica

"Normal" fonts—the default sans—neo-grotesques

These are what I call the normal fonts like Helvetica and Univers. (Arial/Geneva are the Microsoft/Apple versions of this classification.) These are part of a large effort in the 1950s to clean up Gothic font families and make them truly usable typographically. Most of them have many subtle curve adjustments, but the stroke is virtually unmodulated. The aperture is closed up tight in most of them. In general, even the best of them "feel clunky", for lack of a better word.

They are difficult to read—though very legible. They tend to cause what I call "bureaucratic" reactions in the reader—simply because so many bureaucracies require their use. Their ubiquitous, default usage has relegated them to background noise of modern typographic style. There is no doubt, however, that Helvetica is the most popular font of the 20th century. Helvetica can be used well, but you have to be very careful.

These fonts were the raging fashion in the 1950s—especially Helvetica. For logo design, Helvetica Black almost took over the decade. They came to symbolize business—cool, objective, clean, and so on. The font has recently been redesigned or modernized and called Helvetica Neue. Helvetica has become one of the most popular fonts of all time, running far up on MyFonts best seller list and on the list of Monotype's best sellers as well.

Helvetica

ABCDEFGHIJKLMNOPQ RSTUVWXYZ1234567890 abcdefghijklmnopqrstuvwxyz

Helvetica was designed by Max Miedinger in 1957 for the Haas foundry of Switzerland (the name is from Helvetia, Latin name for Switzerland). *MyFonts*

Stylized Sans: Gill Sans

The relatively friendly sans serif styles

This is what I am calling those fonts that have a style that seems relatively warm and friendly, even though there is little or no modulation of the stroke. Many type designers include these fonts in what is called the Humanist Sans classification, but they do not have the necessary characteristics. Without modulation there is no axis that could be called humanist.

Gill Sans

ABCDEFGHIJKLMNOPQ RSTUVWXYZ1234567890 abcdefghijklmnopqrstuvwxyz

Designed by Eric Gill and based on the typeface Edward Johnston designed in 1916 for the London Underground signage. *MyFonts*

Many of these fonts make relatively good body copy in short bursts. They all have a distinctively warm feel—relative to other sans serif faces. Common faces in this genre would be Gill Sans, Frutiger, Corinthian, Skia, and

Trebuchet—among many others. Myriad has become the Adobe default sans. They are very popular for good reason. Dell used Gill Sans for quite a while to distance itself from the Helvetica of the typical business PC competitors, and to seem more friendly, warm and accessible.

Humanist Sans: Optima

Optima

ABCDEFGHIJKLMNOPQ RSTUVWXYZ1234567890 abcdefghijklmnopqrstuvwxyz

Hermann Zapf created this one in 1958 for Stempel. This humanist sans combines features of both serif and sans serif design.

Readable, modulated sans serif fonts for text

These fonts are actually neither fish nor fowl. Instead of serifs they tend to have slight flares, They have a modulated stroke and a humanist axis. They are the most elegant of the sans serifs. Most commonly available would be Optima, Poppl Laudatio, and Zapf Humanist.

Humanist sans serifs are radically growing in popularity. They are very readable. They have become the fashion for body copy in the new millennium. It remains to be seen if this is fashion or a radical change in our page layout formatting. Humanist sans serif typefaces are very clean, neat, and unobtrusive. They are increasingly chosen for body copy in contemporary design.

What about the rest of the type styles?

What about all the type that is outside the classifications we just covered? First of all, proportionally there isn't that much of it. Most of it is either serif or sans serif anyway. However, there is huge variety—in every artistic style, for every historical period. Many are so rigidly categorized that they can hardly be used for anything else.

Decorative is the term for this miscellaneous grab bag. Decorative type is defined as typefaces that are so highly stylized that they cannot be read in body copy sizes.

You need to be very careful in the use of these fonts. Legibility is the obvious problem.

> ## Decorative
>
> # HERCULANUM Kino MT
> # PRINCETOWN Rubino Sans
> # ROSEWOOD MESQUITE ECCENTRIC

That being said, this is where you usually look for fonts to be used for logo stylings. There are so many of these fonts in such a wide variety of styles that you can usually find a font the matches the personality of the company you are designing for. Of course, usually, the font design is just the start as you modify the letters that make up the name into a logo worth remembering.

Mimicking handwriting

There are hundreds of fonts, maybe even thousands by now, that mimic hand writing. There are styles for every historical period and every cultural niche. They range from graffiti to impossibly elegant Spencerian scripts. The main thing to remember is that they are a new phenomena with virtually nothing in existence before the 20th century. In fact, they were so hard to produce for hot metal letterpress typography that they really didn't start appearing in large quantities until the advent of photographic production.

Lawson makes a valiant effort at categorizing scripts, but it's really a waste of time. This is a category determined entirely by what you like:

- **Calligraphic:** flat-nibbed pen
- **English Roundhand:** Formal joining scripts
- **Brush Scripts:** Produced with a brush

But these ignore attitude, style, period, history, & all the rest. Basically, you need to make sure you have what you need for your particular design.

Zapfino

ABCDEFGHIJKLMNOPQR
STUVWXYZ1234567890
abcdefghijklmnopqrstuvwxyz

Brush

ABCDEFGHIJKLMNOP2R
STUVWXYZ1234567890
abcdefghijklmnopqrstuvwxyz

Use a companion font for the heads & subheads

This font family needs to be carefully chosen. It needs to have enough contrast to the body copy font to make the heads stand out. But it must have the same, or a very similar, x-height. This way you can use it comfortably for things like run-in heads, where the first few words in a paragraph are used as a contrasting low-level subhead. Your family choice should probably have a similar width. It should emphasize your stylistic decisions which were made to appeal to your readership. These choices are the main determinant for the basic historical and decorative style which is used in the niche with whom you are trying to speak.

There are very few serif/sans combos which work for run-ins

The difficulty is in finding similar x-heights and pleasing weight combinations. You can do very nice things when this is used. In the following paragraphs, notice in the first example using Buddy/Contenu, that a regular sans gives a beautiful, subtle contrast to the text font used for the rest of the paragraph.

Buddy/Contenu

⚜ Readability: Body copy set with the fonts you choose must be exceptionally easy and comfortable to read.

Futura/Garamond

⚜ **Readability:** Body copy set with the fonts you choose must be exceptionally easy and comfortable to read.

Verdana/Cochin

⚜ **Readability:** Body copy set with the fonts you choose must be exceptionally easy and comfortable to read.

Gill Sans/Jenson

⚜ Readability: Body copy set with the fonts you choose must be exceptionally easy and comfortable to read.

The Futura is much too large and heavy for the Garamond. The Verdana/Cochin combo is very bad. The Gill Sans/Jenson combo is pretty good as far as size is concerned though the styles clash badly. Now look at now different it looks with a bold version of the sans.

As seen on the next page with the bold sans fonts, only the Buddy/Contenu pair works at all. In the other three, the sans is much too strong and the x-height differences have become irritating. None of the bottom three pairs could be used for run-ins.

Buddy/Contenu

⚜ **Readability:** Body copy set with the fonts you choose must be exceptionally easy and comfortable to read.

Futura/Garamond

⚜ **Readability:** Body copy set with the fonts you choose must be exceptionally easy and comfortable to read.

Verdana/Cochin

⚜ **Readability:** Body copy set with the fonts you choose must be exceptionally easy and comfortable to read.

Gill Sans/Jenson

⚜ **Readability:** Body copy set with the fonts you choose must be exceptionally easy and comfortable to read.

You really need to think of these things as you begin to design and lay out your books. For novels it doesn't matter as much. But for non-fiction it really makes a difference in readability.

Type color

Finally, we need to discuss one of the most important attributes of copy set with excellent font choices—the smoothness of the color of the type. What is called the *type color* is created by the design of the font character shapes and the spacing of those characters as well as the spacing of the words, the leading between the lines of type, and the paragraph spacing.

This is one of those places where you want an excellent font. In quality fonts, the characters fit very evenly and smoothly. This character fit is called *letterspacing.* Beyond that is a very careful use of spacing throughout your documents, in general. This is your responsibility. This is the core of typography. This is one of the major places where word processors are left in the dust. Even excellent fonts will not help a word processor much.

The professional page layout programs, like InDesign, have very precise letterspacing and word spacing controls. Leading can be controlled to a ten-thousandth of a point. Baseline shifts up or down of individual words and even entire lines of type can be adjusted very precisely.

Paragraph spacing is controlled to a ten-thousandth of a whatever (inch, millimeter, point, kyu, cicero, pica) by the space before and space after fields in the paragraph formatting dialog box or palette. In addition are the margin and column gutter controls, plus the ability to make optical margin adjustments so the edges of the columns appear cleaner. The level of control needed by typographers goes far beyond word processor abilities.

Professional type should have an even color. When your book is seen from far enough away so that the body copy can no longer be read, it must blend into smooth gray shapes. You will come to see that this even type color is imperative. It is what allows the control of the reader's eye which you need for clear and comfortable communication. You will learn to keep your type as smooth as possible, breaking that only to make important points that the reader really needs and wants to know.

Smooth type color needs to become one of your major concerns.

This smoothness is what makes headlines, sub-heads, and our specialized paragraph styles work. The white space surrounding specialized paragraphs stands out from smooth type color. This white space attracts the eye and leads it to that statement. Without smooth type color, you are forced to make your headers much stronger and the reader often feels like you are shouting at him or her. That is definitely not a comfortable reading experience. Smooth type color needs to become one of your major concerns.

Typography determines reader reactions

It goes far beyond your font choices—important as they are. This is the first and most important thing you must understand. You are not only trying to control or at least predict the reaction of your typical reader to your content. You are also working you make your book a comfortable, friendly, and familiar part of the life of a typical reader within your specialty.

Now we are going to talk about basic things that you must add to your writing style or correct in supplied copy: Many of these things run contrary to what you were taught when you learned to type. This is especially true if you ever took a typing course. You will find you have many things to unlearn.

1.   No double spacing

Typing classes teach that one should always double-space after punctuation. This was made necessary by the typewriter characters themselves. All characters on a typewriter are the same width. This is called a monospaced typeface. The result is that punctuation becomes hard to see. The double space emphasizes sentence construction and makes it visible. When you are using monospaced fonts, this type of extra spacing is necessary.

You can see an example of the horrors of mono-spaced type below. You need to examine it carefully.

```
If you look at this paragraph
closely,  you will see that the
spacing looks far different from
the paragraphs above and below.
It is set in Courier,  which is a
monospaced font.  As you can see,
the spacing is horrible.  Much of
this is because of the letter
shapes themselves. But the main
problem is that all characters
have the same width — including
spaces and punctuation. As a
result,  everything lines up
vertically. This is what
monospacing means.
```

In the sample shown, the paragraph in Courier was a real pain to typeset: There are so many automatic controls in InDesign that the monospaced characters would not line up correctly. I had to make a separate text block and turn off all the controls to make this demo. Even yet, the monospacing has been modified a little to make it work like typewriter type.

We use proportional type

Typesetting, in contrast, is done with proportional type. This means that every character has its own width that is designed to fit with the other characters. Typeset words form units characterized by even spacing between every letter. In fact, professional typesetting is judged by this smooth type color, as we just discussed. Double-spacing is not needed because the better-fitting words make punctuation a major break. In addition, there is extra white space built into the typeset punctuation characters themselves. Double-spacing after punctuation puts little white holes in the type color. These speckled paragraphs are not nearly so elegant, beautiful, or clear.

This double-spacing typing rule is taught even though most people using word processors have not used monospaced type for years. The rule is just taught because *"We have always done it that way."*

2. No double returns
No multiple text blocks, if possible

Keeping your type in cohesive text blocks: One of the major difficulties you will have as you begin setting type is keeping your copy in coherent blocks of text. Ideally, all of the copy on a book page (except for the sidebars and possibly the captions) needs to be in a single text block. In some layouts, it may be a single frame per column, but the concept is clear. If you use multiple text blocks, you lose any easy alignment control. This is where you should really use multi-column text frames.

Paragraph spacing
Spacing between the paragraphs is not done with the Return key: It is done with the Space Before and Space After fields in your Paragraph panel or dialog box. The extra space between paragraphs helps the lines of type in the paragraph hold together in a unit. It is especially important to do this in bulleted lists where the paragraphs are short — two or three lines.

The reason for controlling paragraph spacing this way is that spacing in typography uses adjustments that are so small, you cannot control them by eye. Although you can clearly see the relationships, hand-adjusted consistency is impossible on a 72 dpi monitor because most of the adjustments are less than a point—or smaller than a pixel. You can only adjust type relative to itself in increments of small portions of a point.

The first place you will run across this dilemma in our current discussion is with paragraph spacing. Space between paragraphs must be controlled with the space before and space after paragraph options in the indents & spacing page of your paragraph style—not with multiple returns.

**Opinion:** Here we come to a place where there is major disagreement between typographers. You will have

to decide. Your decision on most of these matters will help determine your personal sense of style.

Spacing helps to communicate, it doesn't just make a pretty page.

Some of the more anal typographers demand that you put no space between paragraphs, and that all vertical spacing be a direct multiple of the leading. This is to produce that prime virtue, in their minds, of text blocks that are lined up horizontally top and bottom. Beyond that, they want all lines of type in parallel columns to be lined up. Type should fit a tightly defined grid.

IMHO, that type of rigid structure is deadly to clear communication. I do not want all of the lines of type to line up horizontally. That is one of the ways that readers can easily stray from the column they are trying to read. This type of symmetrical rigidity contributes to the boredom of many layouts. Yes, we must have spacing under control. Yes, we must maintain consistency in our layouts. But rigid grids are as stifling as prison bars.

Double return problems

With these concepts in mind, how should we set up our paragraph spacing? First, be aware that double returns add huge, horizontal white bars that run across your pages—disrupting type color. When cleaning up secretarial copy, you will regularly come across multiple returns—maybe a dozen or more. This is because most secretaries have no clue about the flow of copy. These things are not taught in word processing classes. So they simply type multiple returns to get to the next page.

You want to establish a rhythm to your pages that makes the paragraphs easy to see without being obvious. A couple of points before or after each paragraph is enough. If you do not use a first-line indent, you will probably need to use four to seven points before or after your paragraphs. Try to use as little extra spacing as possible while still making your structure easy to follow while reading. To keep it consistent, this spacing needs to be built into your paragraph styles. Then you can control it globally as your sense of style develops through the writing of your book.

For headlines and subheads, their positioning is controlled to a large degree by the space before and the space after a paragraph. You want more space before a header and less after so the header is tied to the copy that follows.

3. Space, space and a half, or double space?

None of the above! This is why we use leading instead of spacing. Spacing is old typewriter terminology. The three options listed above were the only ones available for typewriters. In almost every case (unless you are trying to mimic a typewriter) a single space is too close, a space and a half is too far, and a double space is ridiculous. Again, the focus has to be on readability.

 Before we go on, another review of type speak is required: Point size and leading is expressed as 10/12 or 21/21.5 plus the alignment. This is pronounced ten on twelve or twenty-one on twenty-one and a half. In these cases, 10 and 21 are the point size and 12 and 21.5 are the leading in points.

So, a common statement would be something like this: body copy is normally 10/12 justified left. This would be a paragraph with 10-point type and 12-point leading set justified with the last line flush left—like this paragraph and all the body copy in this book. When the point size and leading are the same, as in 16/16, it is referred to as being **set solid**. If the leading is less than the point size it is **negative leading**.

Leading is determined by font design, point size, line length, and reading distance. All fonts have differing built-in line spacing. If you recall the graphic we looked at early on in this book, it proved that Futura had none and Bernhard Modern had a lot. Bernhard Modern also had a very small x-height. As a result, if we accept that normal body copy is 10/12 (and it is), then Futura should probably be set at 10/13 and Bernhard Modern at 15/15 or even much larger.

Autoleading: One of the things you need to get under control is autoleading. The factory default is 120%. This means the leading will be 120% of the point size.

This sounds good, and works well for body copy (10/12). However, it is disastrous for headers. I usually have the autoleading set at 105% (or less) for them. This is something you control in styles on the justification page.

 Even worse is when you drop in an inline or anchored graphic as a character in your paragraph: The autoleading adjusts to give room for the graphic. In these paragraphs, you will need to turn autoleading off. This also happens if you make a letter, a word, or words larger in a paragraph.

Some leading norms for normal reading distance:

- **Tiny type:** Type smaller than 7 point is usually set solid. With type set that small, you usually don't want people reading it. It is used for the small type used to produce legalese [which no one reads anyway].

- **Body copy:** This is the normal reading copy in your documents. It is rigidly required to be 10/12 by traditional publishers, as mentioned. However, when you have the control, those figures should be adjusted by x-height and built-in line spacing. Larger x-heights require smaller point sizes. A large amount of built-in spacing between the top of the ascenders and the bottoms of the descenders in the line above takes less leading. Long line lengths require more leading. In general, bold, sans serif, or condensed fonts need more leading.

This is your job: to figure out what reads best.

- **Headers:** Headlines and subheads are commonly set solid. The larger the point size used, the less leading is needed.

- **All caps:** Setting type in all caps often requires negative leading. This means that the leading is less than the point size. If you think about it, the reasoning should be clear. All caps have no descenders. Descenders are about a third of the point size. So headlines in all caps might well be set 36/28 or so.

This header is set with negative leading: 24/20

4.   Tabs and fixed spaces

Spaces cause many other problems for people trained in typewriting. On a typewriter, the spacebar is a known quantity. This is because every character in monospaced type is the same width—even the space. This is definitely not true for type. In fact, in type, the space band is often a different size than it was the last time you hit the key. This is caused by several factors.

Justification

Here are several sample rows of type to demonstrate how justification works in your paragraphs.

Leftover space at the end of a line is divided by the number of spaces and added to each space. Fixed spaces are not adjusted by this.

Here are several sample rows of type to demonstrate how justification works in your paragraphs.

The way this works is as follows. When you are setting a line of justified type, you are dealing with a justification zone. When the last word that fits in a line ends in this justification zone, any remaining space in the column width is evenly divided and added to the word spaces in the line. If the last word does not reach the zone, the length of the zone is divided and added to the spaces in the line (any additional space is divided and added as letterspacing between every letter in the line). But there are some real problems with this.

What this means is that the spaces on every line are a different width in justified copy. Look at the gray boxes on the first and third line on the previous page. Most software gives large variations from line to line. InDesign works hard to minimize this by justifying the entire paragraph as a whole.

Other factors in word space sizing

First, the word space character in various fonts varies in width. There is no standard. This space also changes with point size, of course. This is not a problem with typewriters because they only have one size and one font. Because of typewriter-based training, most people accustomed to word processors do most of their horizontal spacing with multiple spaces. This is one reason why the first thing you usually have to do with secretarial copy is eliminate the double spaces.

More than this, word spacing is one of the defaults that should be set to your standards. Page layout programs give you very precise control over word spacing. Finally, word spacing varies with every line when setting justified copy. But aside from justification issues, word spaces are different from paragraph to paragraph whenever size, font, or defaults change. As a result, you never really know how wide a spacebar character will be.

Fixed spaces

The problem of predictable spaces has been solved by using some more letterpress solutions. When type was composed, it was brought out to a rectangle no matter what the alignment was—right, left, centered, or justified. The characters used to do this were blank slugs, called quads, that were a little lower than type-height so they would not print accidentally. These quads came in three widths: em, en, and el, plus what were called hair spaces. The el space is long gone; it is now usually called a thin space. InDesign has all four types plus several more. A quarter space, third space, and sixth space have been added and more.

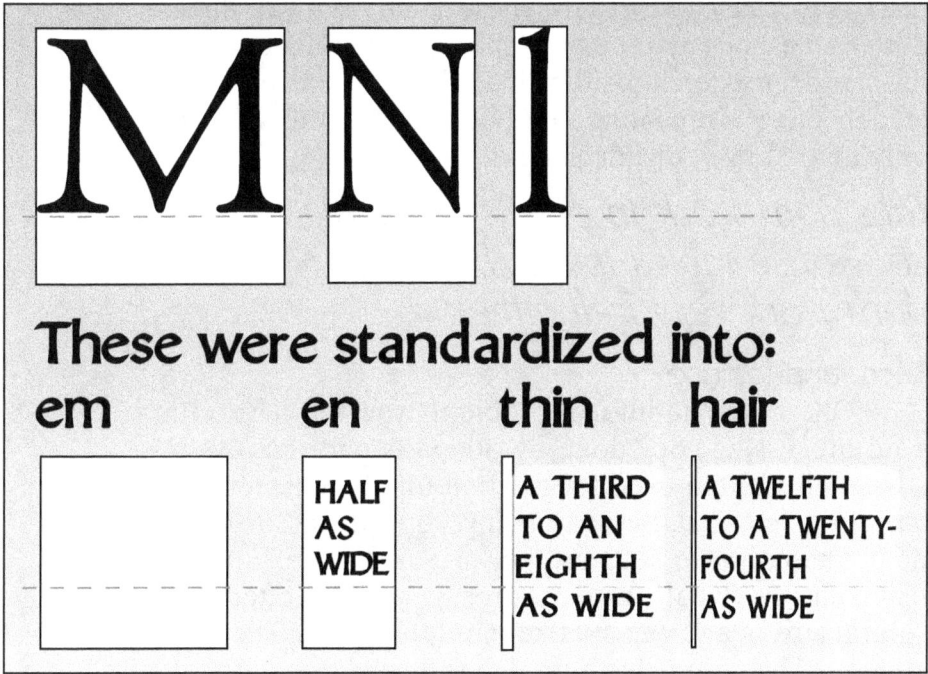

Originally these characters were blanks the width of an *m, n,* and *l,* respectively. Of course, they were standardized. These spaces are now defined as follows: an em space is the square of the point size; an en space is the same height, of course, but half as wide; and a thin space varies. InDesign's thin space is an eighth of an em, and the hair space is one-twenty-fourth of an em.

These fixed spaces are used a lot. For example, they should always be used for custom hand-spacing, because the spacebar can vary proportionally if you change the point size. Fixed spaces remain proportionally consistent. Another fact to bear in mind is that lining numbers are normally an en space wide. This means that an en should be used as a blank when lining up numbers (an em for two numbers) for accountants and bookkeepers.

Tabular construction

Custom spacing should normally be done with tabs. Typesetting tabs are much more powerful than typewriting tabs. They come in four kinds: left, right, centered, and decimal. Actually these decimal tabs can be aligned on any character you choose like the x in 2x4. All tabs can be set up with leaders which fill the space between the final word and the next tab. These leaders can be lines, dotted lines, or any repeating character you need. Again this has been extended radically so that you can now make leaders out of a repeating set of up to 8 characters. You're only limited by your imagination.

Tabs don't work in ePUBs or Kindle, so we use tables there {but they don't work very well either]

Secretarial tab use

One of the additional problems you will have with word processing copy done by others is poor tab use. A single tab is often used for the first-line indent. You will have to delete that. Because many word processor users do not know how to set tabs, they just use the default tabs that come every half inch. As a result, you will often find several tabs in a row—used like multiple spaces. They will all have to be changed to a single tab. In addition, because most do not know how to do bulleted or numbered lists, every line is commonly returned manually using multiple tabs. I'm certainly glad you never do anything like that. You will have to get rid of all of them. You will get very fast with Find & Change.

5. En and em dashes

The next major change we need to discuss is dashes. Typewriters only have one—the hyphen. Type has three—the hyphen, the en dash, and the em dash. All three have very specific usage rules.

Hyphen: This is the character used to hyphenate words at the end of a line and to create compound words. For example, 10-point is the normal point size for book publishers' body copy. In fact, hyphens are used in no other places.

HYPHEN   EN DASH   EM DASH

So, you have a couple keystrokes to learn because en and em dashes are used quite a bit during the creation of normal copy.

En dash: This dash is an en long. It is used with numbers, spans, or ranges. For example, pages 24–39, 6:00–9:00, or May 7–12. It is a typo to use a hyphen in these cases. The keystroke for an en-dash is Option+Hyphen (PC: Ctrl+Num-).

 A special case: In rare cases, hyphens and en dashes need to be mixed for clarity. I used one a few paragraphs back when presenting the width of a hair space for InDesign. It seemed to me to be easier to read and understand one–twenty-fourth of an em with the en dash between the one and twenty-fourth. This is the typographer's decision.

Em dash: This dash is an em long. It is a punctuation mark. The keystroke for an em-dash is Option+Shift+Hyphen (PC: Ctrl+Alt+Num-). Grammatically it is stronger than a comma but weaker than a period. Other than that, there is no standard anymore.

American English is a living language in constant flux. These changes have accelerated in recent years. In many cases, there are no rules anymore. Em dashes are used more every year. In many ways they are very helpful—but traditionalists tend to have knee-jerk reactions to anything outside the grammar books (written decades ago).

Typewriters use a double hyphen for the em dash. This is an embarrassing error to professionals. In fact, it is one of the sure signs of amateurism.

Em dashes automatically: Word converts two hyphens to an em dash if you have auto-formatting turned on. You can set up the same conversion in InDesign by adding an auto-correction item.

Finally, do not think you will not be caught. Hyphens are about a thin space wide. They are higher above the baseline than en or em dashes. However, they are lower in Librum. Also, they are commonly slanted up with little swashes on the ends (you see swashes for all three in Contenu used in the capture on the previous page).

6.   Real quotes and apostrophes

Here is another place where typewriters are limited by the lack of characters. All typewriters have is inch and foot marks. Quotation marks and apostrophes look very different. This is another typographical embarrassment when used incorrectly. There are more keystrokes you need to learn, though you can solve most of the problems by turning on Use Typographer's Quotes in Type page of Preferences. The shortcut is Command+Option+Shift+' by default.

Feet' Inches" Quotes: "double" & 'single'

Again it is important to use the right characters. An apostrophe is a single close quote. You do need to watch typographer's Quotes when using inch and foot measurements or when an apostrophe starts a word. For inch/feet, you'll need to turn off Typographer's Quotes.

Dumb quotes

The typewriter inch/foot marks in almost all fonts are actually wrong. They are the mathematical marks used for prime and double-prime. True inch and foot marks are slanted a couple of degrees. Some typographers italicize them. Typographers often call prime and double-prime marks dumb quotes from their use by typists. Here's the keystrokes on a Mac for the special characters.

Character	Mac	PC
Open single	Option+]	Alt+[
Close single	Option+Shift+]	Alt+]
Apostrophe	Option+Shift+]	Alt+]
Open double	Option+[	Alt+Shift+[
Close double	Option+Shift+[	Alt+Shift+]

Language differences

One of the more disconcerting things to keep track of in this increasingly global society is usage differences in the languages. For example, in America, we are taught to use double quotes for a quote and single quotes for quotes within a quote. British usage is the opposite.

Other languages use completely different characters or changes like open double quotes which look like close double quotes on the baseline—to our American eyes.

Increasingly, we are designing documents set in multiple languages. It is important to keep track of these things. Consider, for instance, the Spanish practice for questions, ¿Que pasa? or expletives, ¡Vámonos!

Guillemots: ‹ › « »

Single and double guillemots are used by several European languages in place of curly quotes. For French and Italian, they point out like «thus». In German they often point in, according to Bringhurst, using »this style«. But then I am not a linguist so I don't know the ins and outs. The point is to be careful.

 Bringhurst's work: *The Elements of Typographic Style,* has a great deal of information on specific typographic usage in other languages for those of you doing a lot of this work. It is important to do it right so the reader is not offended.

7. No underlines

The next difference has to do with the physical nature of typewriters. Because they only have one size of type, there is no way to emphasize words except for all caps and underlining. Underlining is necessary for these antiques. In typesetting, underlining ruins the carefully crafted descenders. In addition, the underlines that come with the type are usually too heavy and poorly placed. They also compromise readability and type color by messing with the white space between lines.

If you decide that an underline is an appropriate solution, please adjust the color and location with your Underline Options dialog to avoid compromising the readability of the type.

The goal of typesetting is to make clean, elegant type that is read without distraction. Underlining is almost as bad as outlines and shadows, as far as professionals are concerned. They ruin the unique characteristics of the font. At times they serve a useful design function, but this kind of modification should be used very discreetly.

How to deal with underlines typographically—change them

When receiving copy typed by others, you will usually find body copy littered with underlines. Our job, as typesetters, is to convert those underlines to the proper usage. **Proper Names** should be set in a bold version of the font. Periodic names like *National Geographic* or *People* magazines must be in italics. Words that are simple *emphasis* should also be set in italic. **For strong emphasis**, you may want to change fonts.

8.   No ALL CAPS

As mentioned in the underline section, setting letters in all caps is the other way to emphasize words on a typewriter. Typesetting has many more options like *italic*, **bold**, ***bold italic***, SMALL CAPS. Plus we can use a larger size, and more.

There is something else, however. Studies have shown that type in all caps is around 4o percent less legible than caps and lowercase, or just lowercase. All caps is also much longer than the same word set C&lc.

Because our major purpose is to get the reader to read our piece and act on the message, you should never use all caps (unless you have a good reason). For example, all caps is often used to make a piece of type less legible and therefore to de-emphasize it.

Some people say that all-cap headlines are fine, but I would disagree unless you are careful.

Readability

Readability is an interesting and complicated phenomenon. Everyone has theories. What most agree on is that people recognize letters by the distinctive outlines on the top of the letter shapes.

This is the major reason why setting type in all caps is so counter-productive. Because uppercase letters tend to be in rectangular boxes the tops of characters tend to look very similar.

As you can see, the straight line formed by the tops of the caps and the bottoms of the lowercase (even descenders do not help) are not distinct enough to recognize easily. Please, remember that difficulty is not a good attribute of reading material. Readers don't notice, they quit reading.

ΛTTD ΛCTIVE WOMΛN

is not nearly as easy to decipher as

cowardly lion

and the bottom halves almost never work, as in

intellectual snob

(intellectual snob)

 By the way, all caps reversed is even less legible: In fact, text set that way (light on a dark background) will not be read unless you force the reader graphically with size, color, or some other such ploy. The worst, for reading, is type that goes back and forth from positive to negative. You will loose a surprisingly large percentage of your readers by doing that.

On the Web and for presentations, it is true that light, glowing letters on a dark background can be easier to read: This is true for any type used as a light source or backlit. However, you need to remember that on the Web the backgrounds often do not print. White type on white paper doesn't read well at all.

These readability issues are primary to typesetting. You really need to keep track. Remember, you can read it because you set it. Your readers do not have that benefit.

9. Letterspacing, kerning, and tracking

Here is another typesetting capability that cannot even be considered by word processors. We mentioned letterspacing earlier. Letterspacing is the built-in spacing between characters in a font. The basic idea is that the white space between letters should be identical for all letter pairs. Obviously, this is not simple or easy. AT,

OOPS, and silly have very different spacing problems—especially the ill. The better the font, the better the letterspacing. In very cheap fonts, individual letters may be far to the left or right. I bought one once where the lowercase *r* was always at least 9 points to the left.

Tracking

Tracking is the official term used to replace letterspacing in digital typesetting now that we can move letters either closer together or farther apart. In reality, either term can be used and understood. The actual procedure for tracking simply inserts or removes an equal amount of space around every letter selected or affected.

Although tracking is used all the time by typographic novices, it is despicable to traditional professionals. Quality typefaces have the letterspacing carefully designed into the font. Changing the tracking for stylistic reasons or fashion changes the color of the type at the very least. A paragraph tracked tighter looks darker. At worst, it can make the type color of the page look splotchy.

Tracking suffers from the vagaries of fashion. In the 1980s, it was very common to see extremely tight tracking in everything. I was guilty of it myself. May it never be among you. Tight tracking severely compromises readability by obscuring lettershapes.

Global tracking changes: There is one place where tracking should be used—carefully. If you are using a display font for your body copy, it will commonly be set too tight. In this case you may want to increase the tracking, globally, for the entire document. The same is true when using a text font for heads. Here you want to move the letters closer. These global changes work fine.

Kerning

Kerning is a different thing altogether. Here the problem is with letter pairs. There are thousands of different letter pairs. I guess the total would be around 20,000 or 40,000 pairs. There is no way to set up the spacing around letters to cover all situations: AR is a very different situation than AV; To than Th; AT than AW.

Literally thousands of different kerned pairs are needed to make a perfectly kerned font. Some kern together and some kern apart. Most of them can only be seen at the larger point sizes. Here again we see the difference between excellent and cheap fonts. Professional fonts have around 1,000 kerning pairs built into the font metrics. Cheap fonts commonly have a couple dozen or none at all.

As mentioned, quality fonts have kerning designed into about a thousand letter pairs. In addition, all professional publishing programs allow you to adjust kerning for individual pairs. InDesign give you keyboard shortcuts (most often Option+Left Arrow and Option+Right Arrow). Adding the Command key multiples the amount moved.

InDesign offers Optical kerning which automatically checks the letterspacing and adjusts it for you. It does a remarkable job. Some years ago, I put a font up on MyFonts.com to sell that was unusable outside of InDesign. I had forgotten that I had purposely made uneven and bad letterspacing in the font used for headers in my first book on InDesign to show how well optical kerning worked. Then I used it in another application. Needless to say, I had to take it off the market until I fixed it.

 **We are always expected to check the kerning on all type larger than about 18-point:** Yes, you really are required to hand kern all headlines if necessary. It's the only way, in most cases. Unkerned type looks cheap and unprofessional. In body copy sizes, a quality font will cover the kerning necessities.

But kerning doesn't work with ePUBs or MOBI, yet.

10.   Be careful with hyphens.

Because typeset line endings are automatic, so is the hyphenation. You can turn it on or off. Hyphenation is done by dictionary. You can set up the hyphens when you add new words to the user dictionary (see help).

Another problem is that automatic hyphenation can create hyphens for many consecutive lines. Here there is sharp debate. Most of us agree that two hyphens in a row should be the maximum (a three-hyphen "stack" looks odd). Page layout software allows you to set that limit. Many set the limit at one.

Yet another problem comes when you run into some-thing like two hyphens in a row; then a normal line; then two more hyphens. The final problem comes when the program hyphenates part of a compound word. In this case, you usually have to set the No Break attribute for the word. It is worth setting up a custom shortcut to do that quickly as you edit. ***Be careful with hyphens!***

Finally, never hyphenate a word in a headline or sub-head. It just isn't done. In fact, almost all headers should be carefully examined if they go to two lines or more. Normally they need to be broken for sense with soft-re-turns [Shift+Return].

In your header paragraph styles, simply turn hyphenation off. I originally turned hyphenation off for this entire book. I later turned it back on for the body copy—simply because the type color was no longer smooth.

II.   Eliminate widows and orphans

As Roger Black states in his pioneering work, *Desktop Design Power* (Random House, 1990, out of print) "Widows are the surest sign of sloppy typesetting." The problems arise as soon as we start trying to simply define the words. See the subsection below on orphans.

I am using the most common definitions (also the ones used by Black). A widow is a short line at the end of a paragraph that is much too short. What is too short? Again, there is sharp debate. The best answer is that the last line must have at least two complete words and those two words must be at least eight characters total. Bringhurst says at least four characters. (But then his typography is filled with short sentence fragments at the end of paragraphs that look horrible, as far as I am concerned.) You need to eliminate all of them like the word "above" which follows: a-bove.

Orphans (paragraph fragments in columns)

The software and current usage will really mess you up here, if you are not careful. Programmers usually have no idea what a widow is. Often they confuse widows with orphans. InDesign uses Bringhurst's definitions. I do not know any traditional typesetter who uses these conven-tions, but then I only know a few hundred or so. I agree with people like Sandee Cohen, Roger Black, Robin Williams, and many others. Actually, everyone agrees what excellent type should look like. There are only semantic differences—word definitions.

An orphan is a short paragraph or paragraph fragment left by itself at the top or bottom of a column. In Bringhurst-speak (and he is marvelously witty), a widow is an orphan at the bottom of a column. An orphan is one left at the top of a column. A classic example is a subhead left at the bottom of one column with the body copy starting at the top of the next column.

InDesign allows you to control both of these problems fairly well with their *keeps controls*. A keeps control, in the option menu of the paragraph dialog or panel, allows you to determine if a paragraph must stay with the following paragraph (in the case of the subhead, for example). It also allows you to set the minimum paragraph fragment allowed at either end of a paragraph. This is normally a two-line minimum, top or bottom, beginning or end. Be careful—all existing software considers a widow to be an orphan at the bottom of a column and an orphan comes only at the top (they are both orphans).

Fixing widows or runts (last lines of paragraphs)

Bad paragraph widows, or *runts*, mess up the type color. They allow a blank white area to appear between paragraphs which stands out like a sore thumb. It's almost as bad as a double-return. There is no way to eliminate them except by hand. The best way is editorially. In other words, rewrite the paragraph!

Occasionally that is not possible. In that case, you must carefully adjust the hyphenation, horizontal scale, point size, or word spacing (in that order).

Here we get into local formatting. However, a difficult runt can often be eliminated no other way.

1. **Hyphenation:** Often you can eliminate a widow by simply adding a hyphenation point to a word with a discretionary hyphen. A discretionary hyphen is a character that places a breaking point in a word that is invisible unless a hyphen is needed. The shortcut varies. The InDesign

default is Command+Shift+Hyphen. Sadly, this character is often not available on the PC.

2. **Horizontal scale:** Here we get into another of those typographic purist fracases. Using horizontal scaling to condense or expand letterforms makes these guys and gals freak. However, plus or minus 4% is invisible. This is the easiest way to pull back a widow. Even most typographers can't see the changes.

3. **Point size:** Make the point size a half-point smaller. As you recall, a point is about the smallest difference the human eye can see. An entire paragraph with type that is a half-point smaller is an invisible change.

4. **Word spacing:** In justified copy, the word space is elastic. You'll need to customize this setting in the Justification dialog box because the defaults are terrible. Let's say your software is set at 80% minimum, 100% normal, and 115% maximum. If you change the normal to 95%, you move the words a little closer and might eliminate a widow.

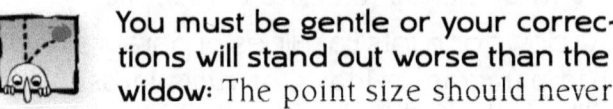 **You must be gentle or your corrections will stand out worse than the widow:** The point size should never be changed more than a half point, for example. Always make your changes to the entire paragraph. Extremely short paragraphs often cannot be fixed, except to "break for sense." This means placing soft returns so that each short line makes sense by itself (as much as possible). Remember, the best method is rewriting the paragraph to add or subtract a word or two or another phrase to get rid of the widow.

The absolute worst orphan is a widow at the top of a new page—especially if it is the hyphenated back half of the last word. Other horrible typos are: widow at the top of a column; subhead at the bottom, as mentioned; a kicker separated from its headline; and a subhead with one line of body copy at the bottom of a column. These errors must be eliminated at the proofing stage. This is what we mean by massaging a document into shape. Corrections like these are among the primary factors that cause people to react to a design. If they are missing, your design will be classed with amateur productions like school and bureaucrat output.

12. Use bulleted lists.

The use of bullets and dingbats is unknown to typists. Bulleted lists are an extremely effective means of attracting the reader's attention. In fact, there has been a lot of study to find out what readers see and respond to. These are the paragraphs you use to attract the reader's eye or to re-attract it if it is wandering in boredom. The readership order goes like this:

❧ **First, picture captions**
- ✛ Everyone looks at the pictures first.
- ✛ Photos are checked out before drawings, unless the illustrations are exceptional.
- ✛ The caption should be the synopsis of the major benefit in the story to the reader.

❧ **Second, headlines:** primarily because of size and placement. The headline should also be the synopsis of the major benefit in the story to the reader. No reader reads everything. You need to tell them why this story is important to them.

❧ **Third, callouts or pull quotes:** these are quotes pulled from the copy or statements about the copy that are enlarged to the point where they become interesting graphics in their own right. They are exceptionally valuable in pages of nothing but body copy to capture the wandering eye. Care must be taken. An improperly pulled quote can change the editorial focus of the article.

❧ **Fourth, bulleted or numbered lists:** like this one. Bulleted lists are read by scanning readers before
- ✛ SUBHEADS
- ✛ DROP CAPS

✦ PULL QUOTES

The assumption is that lists are synopses
of the surrounding copy. Readers
use them to determine if the rest
of the story is worth reading.

Dingbats

There are hundreds of dingbat fonts. Many of them are excellent sources of
fashionable clip art. Here are a few samples from three fonts called MiniPics
-Confetti, MiniPics -LilDinos, & MiniPics -LilFaces.

With typesetting we have even more options than
simple bullets. Dingbats are fonts made up of graphics.
Every keystroke is a different graphic. Zapf Dingbats is a
font that almost everyone has on a Mac. The ones above
are from three of the MiniPics fonts. Almost everyone has
several dingbat fonts, even if they don't know it. In this
book, Librum and Librum Sans fonts have several dingbats built into the fonts in the 256 slots used for ePUBs.
are some of them.

Font creation programs allow you to use a logo in a
font. Top-quality dingbat fonts are a good way to pick up
a collection of clip art that can be used as you type. For
a time, dingbat fonts became one of the best sources of
fashionable art. Using dingbats for bullets increases the
attraction of the list. Just be careful that the reader is led to
read the copy and not simply be amused by your graphic.

**Often dingbats are graphic enough
to make excellent starts or pieces of
logos:** You may want to buy several of
these resources. MyFonts.com has a huge collection. Several type designers specialize in
dingbats. A current search (March 2016): http://
www.myfonts.com/search/dingbats/all/ shows
13,755 digbat fonts are available.

13. Use small caps.

Small caps are a specialized letterform. As mentioned earlier, they are a smaller set of capital letters (often a bit larger than the x-height), used in place of the lowercase letters, which are designed so they have the same color as the rest of the font. Many of the OpenType Pro font families have real small caps.

There are only a few places where small caps are required. However, I strongly agree with Bringhurst here. He has many other places where he recommends small caps. What we are basically saying is that strings of caps within body copy should be small caps. OTHERWISE THESE ACRONYMS AND ABBREVIATIONS APPEAR TO BE SHOUTING.

There are several things attached to this position. First of all, this use of small caps is coupled with the use of old style numbers (or if you use my fonts, small cap figures). Second, small caps are often, but not necessarily, used only in body copy. Your task, should you accept this venture, will be to convince your copy editor that this is correct procedure. Most of them are using old, newspaper-based, manuals of style. Basing typographic style on newspapers is like basing fashionable dress on Wally World.

Nevertheless, there are a few places where you use small caps even if you do not have true small caps. For times and dates, the proper use is not A.M. or AM or a.m. but AM. The same is true of PM, AD, BC, BCE, and CE. In these cases, you always use small caps with no periods.

But what about statements like USA 1776? Here the determining factor is whether or not you have oldstyle or small cap numbers in your font. In general, you should always use oldstyle numbers in body copy, at least. So, all strings of caps like this should be small caps: ASCII, USA, UN, USSR, CIA, NASCAR, and so on.

Small caps in ePUBs and Kindle books: Here we have a problem because most true small caps are OpenType features and most ereaders do not support OpenType features. Here your best shot is to use a character style in a smaller point size set to all caps. If you are embedding a font family which has book, medium, bold, and black, it often helps to go one stage darker with those smaller caps. If your body copy is 12 pt. book make your small caps 9 pt medium. But then distributors like Smashwords will reject your ePUB for too many font size changes. It's an issue with no good solution.

Adding letterspacing for readability

To increase readability, you will need to add letter spacing to the small cap strings (though a good font will have this built in). This should be designed into the font you use. You should also do this if you are using all caps for headlines. Seriously, any time you are using words made up of capital letters you need to add space between the letters until they become readable. The guiding principle is to add as much as you can without causing the letters to separate into individual characters instead of a unified word.

Lining numbers with all caps

Even though we have stated that lining numbers are really only appropriate for bookkeepers, accountants, and CPAS, there are other appropriate uses. One of these is in the midst of all caps.

GOD BLESS AMERICA! REMEMBER 9/11/2001 & 2008.

Yes, there are occasions you will be using all caps. You will have to letterspace to help readability. In this situation oldstyle numbers would look foolish.

14. First-line indents

We have briefly touched on first-line indents for body copy paragraphs. This is the preferred method of telling the reader that a new topic sentence is being developed—a new thought expressed. I also mentioned my occasional practice of adding a point or two after paragraphs to help the reader see that first-line indent on a busy page.

The amount of that first-line indent is up to you. You're the designer. The norm is somewhere between a quarter inch and a half inch. Robert Bringhurst says that the minimum is an en, but that is far below what I would call a minimum. An en just tends to look like a mistake. Some say the indent should equal the lead so when using 10/12 you should indent 12 points. Many specify an em, which in the 10/12 example would be 10 points. That is barely over an eighth of an inch—too small for me.

The first-line indent should equal the left indent of your lists.

Actually, I think the first line indent is more inter-twined than any of those intellectually fine sounding indents of fixed spaces. One of the things to consider as you set up your paragraph styles and page layout is that second consistent interior line which is made by your first-line indents, the left indent of your lists, the left indent of your body heads, and the left indent of your quotes.

As a result, I have personally arrived at a first-line indent of .4 inch. You may want to use less or more, but IMHO anything less than a quarter inch (18 points) just looks like a mistake. It is not really visible; so it merely irritates. Anything more than a half inch makes the eye feel like it has to lunge in to find the beginning.

15. Drop caps

One of the typographic devices used to indicate the beginning of a story or chapter is the drop cap. In this use, the first letter or letters of the first paragraph is (are) made large enough to be three, four, or five lines of type tall and inset into the paragraph.

The first-lines of that paragraph are tabbed around the letter or letters. First of all, this is very easy with page layout software. InDesign's implementation allows you to drop as many letters as you want as far as you want—inter-actively. You can just click the buttons in the Paragraph or Control panel until you like what you see.

If I speak in the tongues of mortals and of angels, but do not have love, I am a noisy gong or a clanging cymbal. And if I have prophetic powers, and understand all mysteries and all knowledge, and if I have all faith, so as to remove mountains, but do not have love, I am nothing."

If I give all I possess to the poor and surrender my body to the flames, but have not love, I gain nothing.

Love is patient; love is kind; love is not envious or boastful or arrogant or rude. It does not insist on its own way; it is not irritable or resentful; it does not rejoice in wrongdoing, but rejoices in the truth.

Love bears all things, believes all things, hopes all things, endures all things."

[I CORINTHIANS 13: 1–7]

Often, the drop cap is in a radically different font. It can be set very dramatically in a flowing script that hangs off in the left margin. It is often in a different color. Commonly used are the illuminated capitals of the medieval scribes.

Mainly, it needs to be dramatic & rare

The largest mistake with drop caps is overuse. They need to be used very sparingly. As you can see in the four sample paragraphs, multiple drop caps are merely confusing. They should never be used more than once on a page. Really, they should only be used once—for the first paragraph of a story, article, or chapter.

16.   Proper accents for languages

When you are using a word or phrase from another language, always accent it properly. Some of these things are commonly missed. Words like résumé, moiré, façade, and the like have entered common usage in English. But if you are using the pine nuts from the Southwest in your cooking, they are piñon nuts. Being from New Mexico, I know the ubiquitous and unique New Mexican hot peppers are chilé. Chili is that weird stuff (to my taste inedible) with beans and/or meat from Texas.

This type of typography is only common courtesy. You need to be aware that in the old Commonwealth it is still cheque and lorry. In those countries, corporations get plural verbs—as in: Shell Oil are drilling five new off-shore wells south of Norway.

In America, you need to be very careful of local usage. I mentioned the chilé example already. In speech, what is sillier (or more annoying) than an outsider calling the fertile valley south of Portland the Will•i-a•mette' Valley instead of the Will•**am'**•et as it is locally pronounced? You will find that all locales have local usage. You need to use it.

17.   Ellipses...

If you really want to start an argument, ask a group of typesetters how to set an ellipsis. The definition in Wikipedia is, "a series of marks that usually indicate an intentional omission of a word, sentence or whole section from the original text being quoted. An ellipsis can also be used to indicate an unfinished thought or, at the end of a sentence, a trailing off into silence, (aposiopesis), example: 'But I thought he was...' When placed at the beginning or end of a sentence, the ellipsis can also inspire a feeling of melancholy or longing. The ellipsis calls for a slight pause in speech or any other form of text, but it is incorrect to use ellipses solely to indicate a pause in speech."

The point is that typographically, an ellipsis is a character or glyph accessed with the Opt+; (PC: Alt+0133) with no space in front of it. Go to the Wikipedia page to get a glimpse of the controversy.

We have just gotten started.

I could go on for many pages with typographic niceties. This is just a first introduction to type. The Chinese showed their wisdom again by considering calligraphy to be the highest form of art.

Once you understand type, you will see its beauty. Well-drawn type is absolutely gorgeous—especially if it is nicely kerned. After a while, you begin to understand why some of the best graphic designs are simply type.

This goes far beyond simple beauty, though. Excellent type is much easier to read. It eases customer fears. It helps make good experiences (think about a dinner menu at a fine restaurant coupled with a marriage proposal). It is what makes your book a joy to read (assuming great content).

Typographers

An underlying thread to this whole discussion is that there are three categories of people producing words on paper—typists, typesetters, and typographers. We have been discussing the first two. Typographers go beyond this to make typesetting an art. You should now have an inkling of how difficult that is. They are some of the finest artists in existence.

Becoming a typographer is a worthy goal. It will take you many years. I'm just beginning to develop the knowledge, control, and attitude necessary after forty-five years. What I want to impress on you is that a surprising number of you will head in that direction.

Book design becomes so involved with type that you fall in love with it. My only request is that you remain kind and recognize that there are many opinions about type. Strange to say, almost all of them are subjectively correct. Keep an open mind and experiment.

They are simply elegant creative solutions to the communication issues of the book.

That is the bottom line: clear communication between author and reader. This is what matters.

PART THREE:

Graphics

CHAPTER ELEVEN

Using InDesign to produce graphics?

Yes, that is what I'm suggesting. More and more I hear designers talking about how InDesign has become the

drawing software we lost when FreeHand was done away with. In the book to the left, you will discover that it is very easy to quickly make a PDF graphic in InDesign while working on your book. Many of these graphics work much better in color. To get them in high resolution color you can buy the full-color book, *Graphics In InDesign*, or you can get the downloadable PDF. The cover of this little booklet on the subject was produced completely in InDesign with the addition of a few paths pasted in from old FreeHand drawings. It's all vectors.

Can you guess which ones are FreeHand?

The word InDesign was traced from a hand-drawn marker script. The butterfly was laid back in perspective in Free-Hand many years ago: Beside those two, everything was drawn in InDesign. The effects [embossing and things like that] were applied in InDesign to the words: InDesign, Typographic Manipulation, and VECTOR ILLUSTRATION. The Screen Mode applied to the arc was done in InDesign. It all went quite fast—a few minutes once I had the pieces assembled.

More than that all the typographic effects are applied to live type. *The type can still be edited like normal type!*

InDesign has many of the important Illustrator and Photoshop tools built in. But we will talk about that as we go. You will still need Photoshop to crop, sharpen, adjust levels, and all the others things which need to be done for photos. I had to use it to convert the color PDF of the cover to a semi-readable greyscale version. You'll especially need Photoshop to rasterize the PDFs used for print into JPEGs used for ePUBs.

But the bottom line is that I have a copy of Illustrator—in fact I have the entire CC package of apps, plus the CS6 Web & Design Premium Suite. I keep several of them installed out of habit, but all I use are Acrobat, Bridge, Photoshop, & InDesign. And I use old versions of everything except InDesign. Even quite old versions of Photoshop can do what we need.

The newer versions have many fancy features for illustrators—especially 3D images. They work very well, but most book designers have little use for them.

CHAPTER TWELVE

Image production in InDesign

One of the real benefits of writing and assembling your book in InDesign is that it is also an excellent graphic production tool. There is nothing better for the production of your cover—especially in print where you need the front cover, back cover and spine all in one image produced to exacting size restrictions. In addition, it is an excellent tool for graphs, charts, maps, and the rest of your needs for graphics in your books. I'll discuss cover designs at the end of this part of the book.

But for now, you need to understand that image production has become much more complex with the addition of the ebook formats. There are radical differences between what is needed for print and what is needed for an ePUB or Kindle book. You have many options for graphics. What I want to do is explain these options and show you how to deal with them.

 **The changing standards:** The ebook standards are in constant flux. The good news is that ePUB and KFX (the latest Kindle format supporting typography) have become close enough so that the graphic

standards are nearly identical. However, the iPad Retina display has doubled the resolution available for ePUBs. But the Fire HDX does also as do other Android tablets. But little of this has changed ePUB production so far because the high resolution images carry way too much file size to be practical for most ebooks. In print, it's 300 dpi CMYK or vector images. EPUB FXL needs 150 dpi. Reflow ebooks use 72 dpi.

The hidden truth: InDesign is the best replacement for FreeHand

To rephrase that thought: when compared to Illustrator for graphic creation, InDesign is quite a bit easier to use. Back a decade or so, there were two professional illustration programs: FreeHand & Illustrator. Adobe bought FreeHand and killed it. It was the best and easiest to use illustration application, especially for typographic illustrations. As Ole Kvern and I commented a while back on an InDesign list, InDesign is the best replacement for Free-Hand. For simple graphics, logos, and typographic illustrations, InDesign is far superior to Illustrator. If you are not a professional illustrator, InDesign is better for you.

InDesign makes superior PDFs for print, and they are very easy to rasterize to size in Photoshop to use in ebooks. In fact, all my illustrations are done in InDesign and Photoshop. They are drawn as needed while I write my books. InDesign makes wonderful maps and floor plans for my novels, as an example. There is nothing better for typographic illustration because everything can be done with live type.

Adding graphics to your book

Here we have another word processor problem. Graphics in Word are not usable professionally. In fact, in many cases Word cannot even add professional graphics to a Word document. Print graphics need to be vector (PDFs, EPSs, or AI files) or bitmap (Photoshop files, photographs, and the like). Bitmap files must be 300 dpi. More than that, photos must be sharp, in focus, with good contrast. They should be CMYK (the color space of print). Even though some on-demand printers now use RGB images, the colors will change when they are converted to CMYK for printing unless you are very experienced with color. Word can handle almost none of this.

But for most of your printing, your graphics will be high resolution grayscale—so you will need to store high resolution color versions for conversion to use in your ebooks. The print version of this graphics part of this book requires greyscale images. This makes many of the demonstrations hard to see. That is why I told you about the full-color printed version of *Graphics In InDesign*, the downloadable PDFs at Scribd and Gumroad or the fixed layout Kindle textbook and ePUB FXL in iBooks. We will talk about this in much greater depth later in the book. But I must mention a few things here.

One of the most obvious areas of amateurism is found in the images many self publishers use to promote and market their books. Even worse are some of the graphics I have seen used inside of these ebooks. Many of them are so blurry they cannot be read. Even if they are not blurry, they are commonly quite ugly and of poor quality.

You must use professional grade images. Traditionally, an excellent professional photo cost around $300 for a single use. The truly superb images still cost that much. But in most cases, those prices are long gone. Many of the stock photo websites will sell you an image for $25 or less. In addition, there are excellent sources of free images. But, you must be careful to get images for which you have a legal license.

Many of these stock photo companies also offer professional quality vector graphics also. This is what you will need for those maps in the front of your novels, for example. I'll show you what a vector graphic is a couple of pages down the road in this chapter.

Using photos (the most common graphics used)

The best solution here is to use photos you have shot with a good digital camera. Images from your smart phone may not do. The problem is that printing quality requires 300 dpi. The latest smart phones come close to that—as long as you don't do much cropping of the images. For example, images in this book are usually five inches wide or more. That means I must have images which are 1500 pixels wide or better—after cropping. I usually get red flags on the print editions of my books when I submit them to the printing company because I use a lot of 72 dpi screen captures. In some cases, I've had to sign a release stating that I'll pay for the printed results regardless of how bad these screen captures print.

You can also use royalty-free images from the Web that give you free rights to publish as you wish. There are many sources for images like these. Wikimedia Commons is good—as are MorgueFile and Pixabay. Sites like Fotolia offer professional quality images at very reasonable prices. Just make sure you read the rights copy carefully. Many images have some restrictions, even if it is only adding a Photo Credit line next to your image. Just make sure they are large enough in pixel dimensions and in color. .

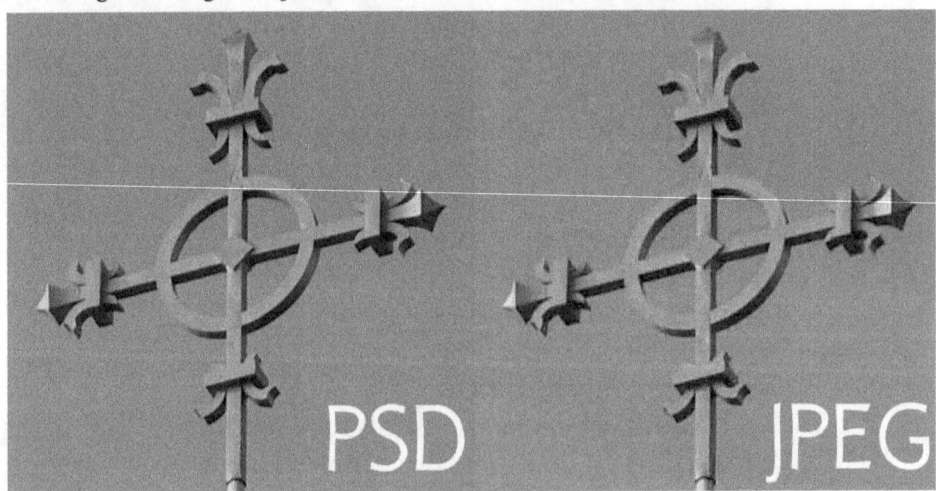

JPEGs: You need to be very careful with JPEGs. The method of compression uses averages where you are not only lossy (image data is deleted), but they also produce bad artifacts around all the contrasty edges of the image. These can actually destroy the image beyond usability. Above you can see an example of extreme JPEG compression:

The images above are three times the resolution. Even here a lot of the damage looks very small. However, at 72 dpi the image below is completely unusable except as a bad example—for print. However, 72 dpi is what is used in ePUBs and Kindle books. In color they work better. Plus a Retina Display can work wonders. Maybe they both look equally bad in an ereader, but in print they're horrible and the JPEG is much worse.

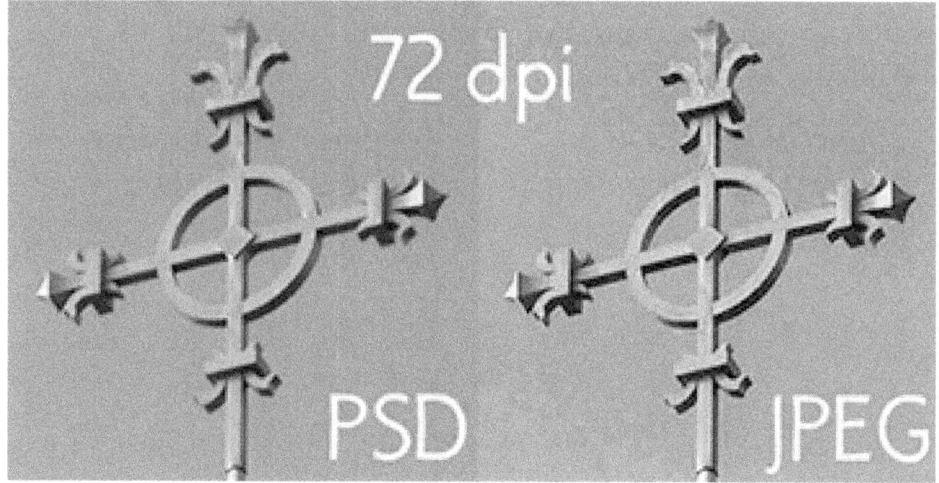

Using drawings & paintings

Paintings are done in Photoshop (or converted in Photoshop), so they have the same resolution problems as we see above. For now, you'll just have to take my word for it about the quality of the 600 pixel wide ebook images. We'll talk about it more in the sections on ebook conversions.

Scanned art: this would include scanned pencil drawings, inkwork, or anything else. As soon as it is scanned the identical resolution and JPEG artifact issues arise.

Vector art [the native output of Illustrator and InDesign]:

Because vector files can be resized with no problems and rasterized at any size or resolution you need, you can have one graphic master file for all your needs in the various formats. It is also much easier to change color spaces with vector images—especially if you are using InDesign for your drawings. The Swatches panel in InDesign makes conversions like this very easy—as long as you have sense enough to have a predefined color palette. Obviously, I highly recommend this approach.

Vector versus bitmap

I do not expect you to forget about the bitmapped extravaganzas commonly developed in Photoshop. However, developing excellent type illustrations in InDesign and then rasterizing them in Photoshop will give you much better typographic control of your graphics. I will talk about this process later in the book.

Scan of an old B&W greyscale ink painting

A vector conversion of the same image

Vector drawing is one of the most misunderstood tools in our arsenal. Digital drawing, sometimes known as PostScript illustration, is one of the indispensable tools of digital publishing. However, it has been lost in the hype of smart phones and digital cameras. Back in the bad ol'days (before computers), when we >gasp< had to do everything by hand, things were clearer. There was camerawork, ink-work, typesetting, and pasteup. These areas have been replaced by image manipulation, digital drawing, word processing, and page layout software. InDesign does all of these except for camerawork and image manipulation. Camerawork and image manipulation are the main pur-pose of Photoshop.

Let's start with an actual graphic

It is obvious that vector drawing is very different from a painting, photograph, or any other scanned object. It's not to say that one is better than the other—they are simply different. The painting is soft, subtle, more "real-istic." The vector drawing is clean, crisp, easily resizable, with a much smaller file size.

With vector graphics, we are now talking about ink-work instead of camerawork—digital drawing instead of image manipulation. What does that mean? It means that we are looking at an entirely different type of artwork. This artwork is not focused on soft transitions and subtle effects. The purpose of this type of art is fun-damentally different. These are images that are crisp, precise, and direct. This is where we leave the natural world and enter an environ-ment with no dirt, no scratches, no broken parts, no garbage.

It is also extremely easy to add pro-fessional-quality, easily resizable type to a vector drawing: Any type added to the original painting must be drawn by hand. Even if you are working with a scan of the art in Photoshop, type is limited to large point sizes and fuzzy edges. Pho-toshop type needs 1200 dpi to 2400 dpi to be sharp enough for printing.

As you can see to the left, the vector landscape from the previous

Hamlauben Valley Fair
September 21–25
NOON TO MIDNIGHT

On the Ramlen Spring Glade
SOUTH OF DUMBARTON ON HIGHWAY 17

Admission: $2.50

page can be easily resized and have type added to it. There is no fuzziness or pixelation. The type is crisp and sharp, even if it were printed out at 500% or 2500% of the original size of the drawing. If this were a Photoshop file, it would be pixelated here. By pixelated, we mean that you could see the jagged edges of the individual picture elements or pixels.

Finally, the Photoshop type would be very crude at 200 to 300 dots per inch, whereas the vector graphic has type at the typographic standard—1,200 dpi to 2,400 dpi (or whatever the resolution of the printer is). Imagine if we printed it out at two foot wide or more. The vector image would still be sharp.

Below on top, we see the vector version enlarged 600%. You can see some of the drawing deficiencies, but the image is still crisp. The same would be true if we enlarged it to hang as a billboard on the side of a sky-scraper at 50 yards wide. There would be no pixelization.

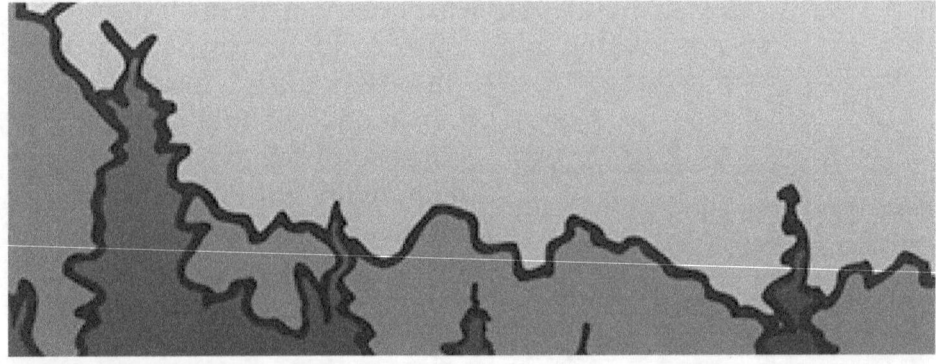

However, that sharpness is not true of scanned, or bitmap, images: The Photoshop (bitmapped) version is ruined at two feet wide, as you can see in the bottom image. When the image was enlarged to two feet wide, the pixels could not change shape. So, we now see what that bitmap really looked like.

The only reason it looked smooth originally was that the pixels were a three hundredth of an inch each and that is far too small to be seen by a naked eye. In the enlargement, the pixels are nearly an eighth of an inch square and easily visible. Also, this enlarged bitmapped image was 235 MB. Full page high resolution full color images like you use on your covers are often 25 MB or more. If you use many of these images in a book like this one, the file size gets huge.

The vector image remains 49 KB no matter what size you use for output. Yes, that is 235 million bytes as compared to 49 thousand bytes of data. Obviously, there are some real advantages to vector illustration.

There are two major advantages to vector art:

- **It is completely resizable:** Vector art is what is commonly referred to as *resolution independent.* There is no resolution to a vector file. All of the shapes, and this includes all the type, are defined by mathematical outlines that can be enlarged or reduced at will. The resolution is produced by the printer, screen, or Photoshop.

- **The file size is normally much smaller:** This is not always the case with very complicated vector images. However, the 49K versus 235MB comparison is very common.

This means that I can make my original artwork for the print version of the book and then easily resize, recolor, and convert it into any file type, size, and resolution needed for the rest of the versions.

I can open it in Photoshop and convert it to 72 dpi (rasterize it) at the size needed for the JPEGs, GIFs, and PNGs needed for Kindle or ePUBs. I can enlarge the image to a poster or book cover and/or reduce the size to a dingbat used for bulleted lists all from the same original. This cannot be done with a bitmapped image.

InDesign produces excellent vector images: We'll cover some techniques later on in this part of the book. Your concern, at this point, is to make sure all of the images you use are of professional quality. You cannot use Web images for print.

The lizard is an old FreeHand drawing. I used the original from 1996 in the print versions. But I gave up on fixing it in Illustrator and colorized it in InDesign for the ebooks. It was simply too difficult to work on it within Illustrator.

The fastest and most common graphic

Speed is one of the reasons to use words as graphics. However, this does not touch on the real reason why words are most commonly used for graphics. To cover that reason, it is helpful to remember that old saying attributed to some ancient Chinese wise man, "A picture is worth a thousand words." Actually it sounds more like Shakespeare, but it makes no real difference. There is truly a major problem with that old proverb. A picture does indeed speak volumes. The problem is found in controlling (or even predicting) what the image talks about. Why are the lizards on this page?

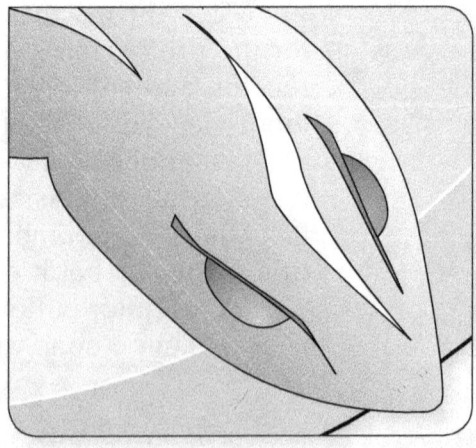

They show that vector images can be resized at will. Now, back to the point. I am not saying that an accurately focused, impeccably crafted illustration is not a wonder – and extremely effective. The problems are the normal ones: time and money. Excellent illustrations are very rare and expensive—if you can even locate one. Now, you may be one of those incredibly talented (and fortunate) designers who wind up working for a superstar publisher as one of their primo talents. Then you don't have to concern yourself about those two little worries just mentioned.

Just listen, then, while the rest of us talk about the real world of illustration and digital graphics. In self publishing, the margins are real tight. Kawasaki in *APE* talks about the need to sell 2500 books to make a profit with base costs of several thousand dollars. That's all very nice, but I don't have anywhere near that kind of budget and my niches are normally too small to support that many sales. I need graphics I can do for free [or close to it]. In addition, they must be professional to avoid the need to lower prices because my quality is so low. The result of all of this is that graphic treatments of words will regularly be the solution of choice.

The frequency of this choice is increased by the simple fact that often there is no real graphic conceivable to describe what you really need to help sell that point about selling product, the need for faith, or that support book for your seminars offering help with depression. Words are clear, concise, and can be graphically strong.

Words are direct and precise

When you really need it, and can say it accurately, what works better than **FREE**? How about a snappy graphic saying whatever you need? The plug-in graphic above would not make a good headline or logo; it's not strong enough. But it certainly adds interest as a subhead on a page where some sort of graphic is visually necessary. It could be used as a subhead or an added illustration—even a drop cap graphic.

In general, you will find many occasions when a quick graphic made of words will solve your graphic dilemma handily. Often you don't even have to write those words – they are offered as part of the story you are writing. So, what we want to do here is give you the tools and structure to effectively use words as graphics. What we need to do now is give you conceptual control of what you have been doing.

There is no such thing as a bad font

Your main task is to pick fonts that are appropriate in style and readable. You have a huge variety to choose from. In fact, a large part of your personal design style will be the font library you build. This is something to start working on now. Do not just pick styles that you like. There are too many instances in which a type style that you find abhorrent is the perfect solution to a design need for a particular book's readership.

But enough talk, let's look at a real project [I redid an old FreeHand graphic in InDesign and it is much better quality in the InDesign version]. I have a little type foundry that sells type online. I needed a small graphic, almost a logo, to identify the foundry. All I had was the name, Nue-voDeco Typography, and a strong sense that the logo-style should use only the  fonts from the foundry. I started with the word portion, DECO. I wanted it to be dominant, so I used one of my fonts called Adept-Heavy (I no longer sell this one).

Because I wanted this word fragment to be

a solid unit, I tracked and kerned it tightly. I deleted some of the excessive Celtic flares. The even/odd overlap of the D and E had to be eliminated, so I subselected the two outlines and used the Add command. Finally, I filled the entire word fragment with a gradient and added a quarter-point stroke to lighten it a little. Now the four letters looked like a unit. You would probably do it much differently. That's fine. I would also do it over, now—20 years later.

Next I added the word *typography*. I must have used five or ten different fonts. They were all too stylized for this location, so I finally settled on Nördström Black. Nördström is conservative—yet friendly and seems to fit the need well.

The word fragment *Nuevo*, in contrast, needed more style, almost a handwritten look. Of course, I had the option to use handwriting. However, I was limiting myself to NuevoDeco fonts. So I chose one of my nostalgic fonts from the fifties, AeroScript.

I had to do what I did with DECO here also. The word is skewed and scaled; converted to outlines; ungrouped and the paths split; all of the outside shapes were made into one path with the Unite command. Then I subtracted the counters of the e and o. And the word was joined together again with a light basic fill and the half-point stroke.

Do I think you know what I am talking about here? NO: But we'll cover all of that in this part. It's really quite easy—though a bit complex. Please, let me finish.

Because I needed a small graphic for my Web page, I decided that I needed a frame to hold the graphic. So, I dropped a round-cornered box with vertical gradient (because it compresses better) behind the words. I added quite a bit of color. However, the color made the word *TYPOGRAPHY* disappear into the background, so I added a one-point white stroke around it.

Finally, I took the DECO art and added some fun effects to it, debossing it into the surface and playing with the color to get enough contrast to make it all readable. (Remember, this is all about my personal taste.)

The whole process took an hour or two. I think it accurately gives a sense of my typographic style in the mid-1990s and shows off three of my fonts which I was selling at the time. I wouldn't do it the same now, of course.

What is an appropriate font?

In general, you have to define that. There is a general sense of what works and what doesn't. The stop sign below would be proof of that. It's doubtful that the logo next to it would sell much $300-per-ounce perfume either [though I've seen something similar for some "manly" cologne]. Sometimes type usage is this obvious. Most of the time it is not. Normally you have to come up with a general sense of the style of type that appeals to the readership of your particular project and accurately conveys the style of the place and culture being talked about in your book.

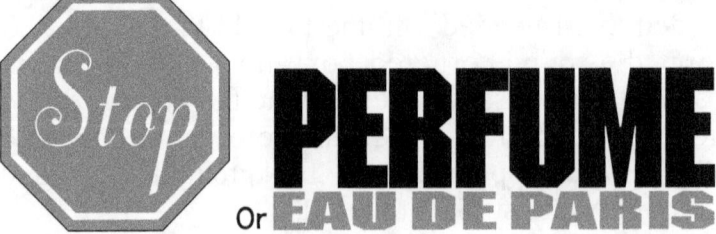

This is something you need to train your eye to recognize. You can get a feel for this by watching television show openers that are targeted at specific demographics. There is a large difference in the style of type used by RFD-TV and A&E or Bravo, for instance. Hawaii 50 has a very distinct typographic style that is very different from Two and a Half Men. It's fascinating to observe the continuous differences between Fox News Network and CNN in all areas.

Another area to watch is fashion retailers. In New Mexico, for example, the extremely expensive, high-fashion boutiques in Santa Fe around the Plaza use very different typestyles from the malls in Albuquerque. The malls are much closer to the national usage found on TV in ads for The Limited, Eddie Bauer, Sears, Penneys, and other national chains. Austin will have a different style from Dallas or Houston. San Francisco is different from LA is different from Seattle. If you want to see a clear regional style that has spread worldwide, look at Starbucks, from Seattle. You will not only have to educate yourself, you will have to continuously feed your eye and your mind with current images for the rest of your career. It's part of being a writer and book designer.

More to the point, genre covers: We have to see what our genre uses. A political/military thriller for example almost certainly needs the White House, Congress, presidential seal, CIA seal, or something similar. A romance? Two or three people large with a scene from the locale of the book in the background is usually standard. *Angie's Decision*, as seen to the left, would probably not do well as a romance cover. The same applies to non-fiction, reference, or any type of book. You need to spend some time browsing in your local bookstore and in the online stores. Interior graphics also have a style for different types of books: fantasy maps, for example.

The bottom line?
A book designer is a graphic designer

That is a simple fact which many new self publishing authors fail to take into account. **Pay attention!** When you decide to self publish you are responsible for the graphic excellence of your books, just as much as you are for the written content. You have two choices: you can do it yourself or you can pay someone else to do it. Regardless, it must be done well.

Some basic guidelines

Now that I have given you one of my examples, we can probably talk a little more clearly about basic typographic choices. When you first begin, choosing an appropriate font runs into two problems: "I really like that one," or, "Oh my gosh, which one is the right choice?" To rephrase, you tend to pick fonts because you like them or you're unable to choose because of all the choices (and you might be wrong).

The first option: your personal taste

When you begin as a designer, this is almost always the wrong choice. Your eye is not educated enough to have good taste. Your personal font favorites are appropriate only when you are a member of the readership. Like everyone else, your taste is a result of your personal experiences: cultural, academic, social, and political. If you are less than sixty years of age, your typographic choices are greatly affected by the television shows you have been watching since youth. They have been trained by ads for the Gap, Millers Outpost, Levi's, Sears, L. L. Bean, or wherever you buy your clothes. They have been trained by the print book covers you have purchased and read.

Unknowingly, you have been herded into a demographic grouping (even if that grouping is *the rebellious ones*). I remember one of my more talented students, whose entire existence was colored by the graphics and lifestyle of snowboarders. He kept talking about the typographic freedom his group used, and how he wanted to design for them. It was a massive comedown when he realized how rigid the graphic style was that had been used to appeal to him and his "buds."

It took almost two terms before he realized that the "freedom" he was so excited about was really a very rigid style. The rule was simple: "Break all the rules!" He eventually became an excellent typographer once he realized that he had an easier time than most understanding normal usage. It was simply the absolute opposite of his group's norms. If he liked sans serif body copy, the norm is serif. He found that he could effectively design for very conservative clients by simply choosing the opposite of his natural inclinations.

The problem with personal taste is personal experience

It took me several years to grasp why my clients, students, and readers always seemed to pick my least favorite choice when I gave them a set of options for a logo or layout. Over the years, I have listened to countless book designers who were virtually spitting on the people commenting on prospective covers, *"They picked the ugliest one. I almost didn't include it. I should have tossed it."* Then one day I realized, while doing a flyer project for a client, that the one I liked best simply reminded me of some of the posters I had designed for my rock group back in Minneapolis in the 1960s. It had nothing to do with good taste. It was all about happy personal experiences.

Since then, I have seen countless examples of designers who made absolute statements of taste and style based on good memories of former times. You are also strongly colored by bad periods of your life. For example, the Retro fad of sixties nostalgia triggered many horrible memories in me and all of my friends. You will never convince me that stuff from the fifties or sixties has any value at all. Mid-century modern? Give me a break! I have spent much of my life fighting that culture and mentality.

Our personal tastes are all based on those types of emotional reactions to fonts, colors, layouts, styles, and so forth. We have to train ourselves to recognize the difference between merely personal taste and genuine excellence in design – between personal taste and truly ugly graphics. More than that, we have to learn what appeals to various cultural subgroups and readerships. For example, I know that the group known as the Spanish (in New Mexico, as distinct from Mexican or Latino or Chicano–though including all three) was strongly attracted by Art Nouveau fonts in the 1980s. This probably has little to do with similar ethnic subgroups with different titles in Southern California or Miami, but it certainly worked around there. This is what you have to learn. I just designed a book for a couple who had spent a decade ministering to the street children of Acapulco. They loved the Art Nouveau type I used. I didn't.

> *We have to train ourselves to recognize the difference between merely personal taste and genuine excellence in design – between personal taste and truly ugly graphics.*

You must learn your local culture. We were strongly, and proudly, multicultural in New Mexico, but it was entirely Anglo, Spanish, and Indian. Now that I'm back in Minnesota, the culture defines multicultural in terms of the Somalis, Hmong, Blacks, and Mexicans who live around the small farming city I live in. There was a strong Japanese influence that I really liked in Oregon, especially around Eugene where I was living.

You must become intimately familiar with the graphic heritage of your area and your genre. It's a language you have to speak fluently. The America culture has become too diverse to pin down. You need to discover the visual language of your readership. Look at books sold to your readership–especially the really popular ones. As mentioned, for genre of military/political thrillers, the cover almost requires a presidential seal, the White House, or the Capital Building to reach the normal readership. Other genre have similar requirements.

The cover on the next page has done much better for me than the original cover with military images and violence depicted. I'll probably redo it again–when I get a better idea to appeal to my readers. This is due to the fact that trouble in the book is the administration, not the Congress. I need to fix that. In the new self-publishing, you can do and redo until you get it working.

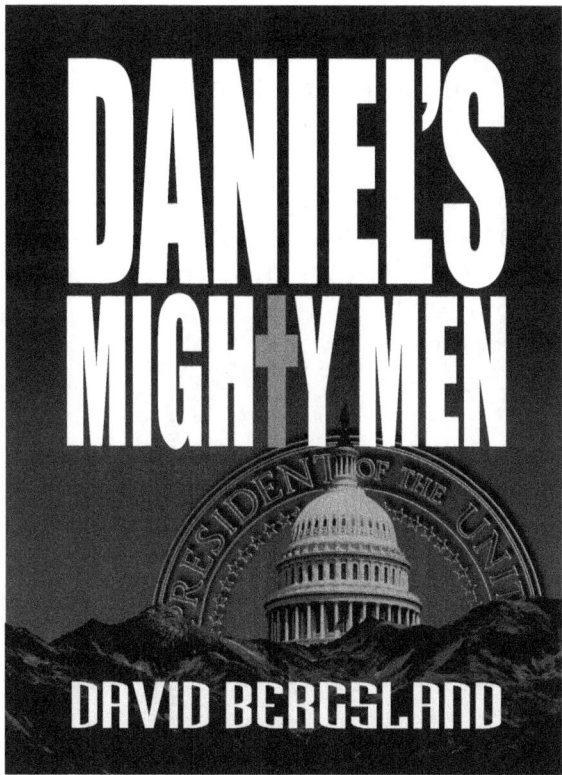

The second problem: overwhelmed by choices

One of the major problems faced by my students was their reaction to the font list I gave them at the beginning of every term. I have about 5,000 fonts, and I printed out a restricted list of the 300 or so that I made available on all the computers in my lab. This list varied yearly, with new fonts added and ones I was bored with removed. However, the reaction was usually the same.

Most new designers (and self publishers) are overwhelmed by the choices. Beyond that, they can hardly see the differences between Baskerville, Garamond, and Caslon. It is always fascinating to watch who chooses which fonts to use in their projects. When I start explaining why Avant Garde or Helvetica is a bad choice for body copy, for instance, they fall into bewilderment. They plaintively ask, "How do I know?" The fact is that it is fairly easy to learn to make good font choices, but it takes a bit of effort. You can learn good taste. All you need to do is look at the examples in the best books within your genre.

The best way I know is to immerse yourself in excellent design to the national market. Communicating graphically to the entire nation requires two things. First of all, you have to avoid all local stylistic distinctions. Secondly, you have to make excellent, classic typographic choices to avoid boredom in your more generic audience. It gives you a solid design background without the local distinctions.

You also see it every day in the traditionally published books you read. If you are reading cheap Kindle books, you may have a problem. You need to look for excellent, well-designed books and magazines. I would suggest going to your local book superstore and perusing the magazines and the best-selling books. This time, avoid those that really appeal to you. I am always sucked in by Taunton Press and Fine Gardening, Fine Woodworking, and the rest of their line, for example. They are excellent and a good source of graphic style. However, for our purpose here, you need to inspect Look, People, Time, and magazines designed to appeal to the mass market of North America. There are similar publications in New Zealand, Australia, Europe, and Southeast Asia. Currently there are massive numbers of specialty magazines—one or more of which are targeted directly at your readership. These magazines, and the people who advertise in them, have made a science out of typography that offends no one yet remains interesting and visually appealing. Look at the two music channel logos to the right. They're obviously going for different niches.

Study the books in your genre or target market. Examine their basic layouts. Which fonts do they use? How are they structured? Look at ads for the major car companies and ask the same questions. Closely analyze advertising from Procter and Gamble, Sears, Wal-Mart, and others that have made such an impact on our national graphic taste. The people who design for them often have research budgets that would make us blush (or turn green). They rarely use type styles by whim or by accident. Take their ads and try to match the fonts used to your font lists. If you have few choices, at least get a good font catalog from Adobe, ITC, Agfa (Monotype), or Bitstream (MyFonts).

Build off these choices. The classics will almost always work and work well. In general, the fancy decorative fonts are used only for the most prominent headlines or logostyles. Most of you will have at least one of the Garamond families or Caslon. Once you learn how to handle one font family well, it is much easier to move on to other fonts. It is a marvelous exercise to design complete documents with only one font in various sizes of caps, small caps, and cap/lowercase. Beyond that, the use of only one font is often an extremely elegant solution to the graphic needs of a book.

It takes a while to build a good font library

Good fonts are not cheap. Invest wisely. After over twenty years in the industry I have several thousand fonts to choose from—not to mention that I have designed over a hundred to fit my personal taste.

If you find a font for less than $25, ask yourself, "why is it so cheap?" I regularly sell mine for $9 each because I am such a small player in the font design world. However, free fonts can cause you real problems. A corrupted font can wipe out a PC's hard drive. On a Mac, it can corrupt your documents so they won't print, or the PDFs are torn up, or many other issues.

In many cases, cheap or free fonts are obvious. Your readers will notice your choices—subconsciously, at least. Pick the fonts you use carefully and wisely. A romance, for example, is usually going to require an old-fashioned serif typeface or maybe a legible script. A science-fiction novel will probably do better with a much more modern-looking font choice—especially for the chapter heads and cover.

CHAPTER THIRTEEN

Drawing in InDesign

Why would you ever draw in InDesign?

Better tools and unique capabilities are the answers: While it is true that InDesign has a very limited set of Illustrator's tools, it uses them in a much better interface. True, InDesign is not a full-featured illustration program. However, most book graphics do not require or even want the full features of blends, gradients meshes, perspective, and the rest of the fancier Illustrator capabilities.

Most book illustrations are relatively simple tables, dingbat chapter heads (the one above is the Lozenge character from Librum), and line art info graphics. While it may be true that Illustrator can do them better, Illustrator greatly adds to your learning burden as a writer in InDesign. If you have Illustrator skills, certainly use them. But do not think they are required.

Why you want to make graphics in InDesign

As mentioned, one of the little secrets in digital publishing in recent years is the fact that increasing numbers of designers are using InDesign for all of their graphic production except for photographs and scans. InDesign's drawing interface is uncluttered and works remarkably well. The primary reasons for using InDesign to draw are the seven we list beginning on the next spread. But the real issue goes much deeper than that. Unless you are a professional illustrator, the drawing capabilities of Adobe's Illustrator are far too complex and take too much time to be used in book production.

Typographic graphics:

The core of my reasoning is simple. The graphics which are not photos are usually (often, at least) type. Even the pieces built around photos are commonly made with a lot of type. You do not want to make these images in Photoshop because the type will end up rasterized at far too low a resolution. As I have said, type for print is normally output at 2400 dpi or at least 1200 dpi for the cheaper technologies. Photoshop images are 300 dpi, at best. The result is that type in Photoshop images is pretty chewed up. The only way type in Photoshop works well is if it is larger than 18 point.

It is true that you can save Photoshop graphics that contain high resolution type—but our on-demand suppliers cannot handle that (at this point). For our purposes, Photoshop is a bitmap application, working in pixels that are precisely defined. Photoshop is a tool you will need to learn (at least in a minimal manner) to handle many things in on-demand publishing—it's one of the very few photo manipulators which can work in CMYK, for example. Even Photoshop Elements cannot work in CMYK. The bad news is that this powerful capability to render very tiny pixels with a great deal of control is also its greatest limitation.

The good news is that InDesign has all you need to produce beautiful graphics.

In fact, it has several attributes that lead me to create most of my graphics within InDesign, because in these areas InDesign is definitely superior to either Illustrator or Photoshop. There is nothing better for assembling graphics from different pieces: drawings, photos, and type. I have mentioned several of these abilities already, but they center around three basic capabilities: type, color, and PDFs. No software handles these three components together better or more quickly.

Typography: Nothing else comes close. It is easier and better, in most cases, to do all your type in InDesign. Even when you are tearing type apart to make logos and graphics, InDesign is easier and faster than Illustrator in many cases. It can do many things with type that are impossible in Photoshop—simply because InDesign creates vector art.

Live stylized type: In InDesign you can do anything to the type short of tearing apart the individual outline or using Pathfinder operations while the type remains editable. This includes gradient strokes or fills, and any of the Photoshop Effects.

Color palette control: No other program has the color palette control of the Swatches panel in InDesign. Nowhere is it more easy to build a predetermined custom color look for a specific project. You can easily control the color of a large project like a book in InDesign (and keep control across all the various formats). This is much more difficult in Illustrator and almost impossible in Photoshop.

Gradient strokes: This seems like a little thing, but it is huge. Many typographic decorations like rules are simply lines. Only InDesign can make gradient lines easily. Plus, these gradient lines remain editable. Any gradient in Photoshop requires rasterized art and type. *[Yes, I know that Illustrator has finally added gradient strokes. But, as usual, the implementation is so complex that it is daunting.]*

Individual corner controls: Built into every frame, InDesign has corner controls that allow you to control the type of corner used all at once as well as each corner separately—by directly manipulating the frame.

Photoshop effects: Many of the basic effects (Photoshop styles) are available in InDesign. The Effects panel is remarkable with individual controls for the entire vector object (or group of objects), or only the stroke, only the fill, only the text, and any combination thereof. Drop shadows, inner shadows, inner glow, outer glow, embossing & debossing, plus transparency feathering are easy to apply. Plus, the type remains editable.

PDF generation: InDesign simply produces the best PDFs. I use InDesign almost exclusively to make PDFs of logos, book covers, product graphics, and all the rest. This is especially true if these graphics must be rasterized into high resolution JPEGs and PNGs for our suppliers.

Createspace covers, for example, demand rasterized artwork. In fact, strange as it may seem, they require a Photoshop PDF– which is very unusual. The InDesign file is much more editable and rasterizing it into Photoshop for Createspace's (Amazon's) purposes is quick & easy. You do not want to be doing your back cover type in Photoshop–even though Createspace requires you to give it to them that way.

Type manipulation

This is even more true with typographic art. Digital drawing goes far beyond simple pen work. Its main power is found in type manipulation. One of InDesign's major assets is its ability to rapidly convert a word or two into a powerful graphic very quickly. Of course, there are some major differences between InDesign and traditional fine art drawing with brush, pen, or pencil.

Formerly, we had to hand-draw the line to the proper width. With vector shapes, I can specify any fill with strokes (outlines) of any color or any width—virtually infinite flexibility, with a precision that was incomprehensible before the late 1980s when the first PostScript drawing programs were released: Fontographer first, followed by Illustrator and then FreeHand. Above [and below in the sidebar] is a simple one: the Radiqx Press logo—which is two words, a couple gradients, and a cross punched out of the modified R [using the Pathfinder panel in InDesign].

 **I drew this in InDesign:** For color the dot over the i is a red radial gradient. For logos there is nothing better. Logos have to be the most flexible graphics imaginable. They will be used very small, very large, and everything in between. There must be black-and-white versions, grey-scale versions, process color versions, and in addition, low-resolution RGB Web versions.

Digital drawing using PostScript paths is almost specifically designed for this purpose. InDesign enables very tiny file sizes that are resolution independent. In other words, they will print at the highest resolution allowed by the printing press, printer, or monitor.

The Create Outlines command (in the type menu) converts your selected words or letters into a collection of editable shapes. With fonts converted to paths, you can use any font and not have to worry about including it. It is still the best way to get fancy decorative fonts on the Web or into an ebook. Rasterizing your converted type into Photoshop is very easy.

Charts & graphs

Many graphics in common usage are charts and graphs. All of the common software, like spreadsheets and presentation software, produce horrible-looking work that is designed for a monitor. To translate, that means they are in the wrong color space for most color printing and far too low in resolution. Basically, every chart or graph you receive will have to be tossed completely or scanned and used as a rough template in the background while you recreate the graphic to professional standards so you can use it wherever you need it in all of your book formats.

As you can see from the sample showing usage of watercolor board to the right, even the best I can do with the received graphic is terrible. I received the image as a 72 dpi, RGB TIFF generated from a PowerPoint slide. Even for this example, I have done a lot of work in Photoshop: cropping tightly; resizing the image to half size, thereby increasing the resolution to 144 dpi; and converting the image to grayscale.

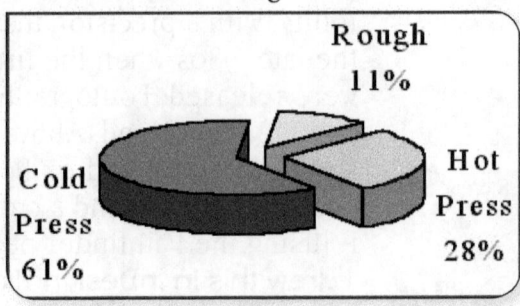

The result is still hardly inspiring. The font choice is clumsy, at best—not to mention that it does not fit my style. The type alignment, leading, tracking, and so on are very amateurish. Worst of all, there is no explanation to help the reader determine if this knowledge is helpful, useful, or even relevant. In all ways, this graphic is useless unless it is used as part of a well-spoken, entertainingly written, enthusiastically presented oral explanation.

We have to remember, as authors and book publishers, that our explanations are found in the professional presentation of our copy. Poor font choices cannot be covered with glib jokes or even pithy commentary. Our readers are going to make choices based on the attractiveness and usefulness of our layouts.

First of all, they will decide whether they are even going to read our work. If it is not clear in concept and easy to comprehend, you have lost them. In your book, you rarely get a second chance. So, with that in mind, let us redesign this awful pie chart.

Before we can start with that, we need to know what it represents:

By talking to the client and asking questions, I discover that it refers to the usage of watercolor board by the art department of an architectural design firm for the past year. They are in the process of making a presentation package that they can use to show their changing focus and capabilities to prospective investors and clients as the firm expands.

As I learn this, I also find another bar chart showing, paradoxically, that **sales resulting from the use of the boards give a very different view:** The rough board is used for hand-painted gouache illustrations, for which this firm is developing a real reputation. The cold press sheets are used as mounting board for client presentations to use as they seek to fill the spaces of the various projects with targeted tenants. These presentations are increasingly digital. The hot press is used for quick visualizations, models, and as a mounting board for general signage.

Rough
Our Best Investment & New Focus
11% Expense
57% Sales

Cold Press
61% Expense
32% Sales

Hot Press
Mostly Non-billable
28% Expense
11% Sales

Cold Press 61%

Rough 57%

Hot Press 28%

32%

11%

Artboard Usage in 2012
Showing the importance of our illustrations
Segment Area: Percent of Expenses • Segment Height: Percent of Sales

It turns out that the expensive d'Arches 300# rough watercolor board is used for illustrations that generate 57%

of all income. The cold press board used for client presentations and to present proofs to the clients for printed materials in support of their buildings represents 32% of the income. The hot press board is second as far as expense is concerned, but it only accounts for 11% of the income.

With that in mind, I quickly traced the ugly Power-Point slide (by hand, using the Pen tool), extending the height of the various slices (adjusting by eye) to provide the additional data from the second chart. I then added more stylish type giving both sets of figures; added a title line; and colored in the shapes. It took about a half hour to fix up the graph. However, there is a much greater likelihood that it will actually be read now. More than that, the data now makes an important point which can clearly and easily be seen. I just needed to double-check with the client to make sure it was making the proper emphasis. It was.

Ebook graphic solutions

It might seem as if the low-resolution (72 dpi) monitor graphics of the Web are a clear place for bitmap graphics. However, even here the creative freedom and flexibility of vector graphics give you a decided speed and efficiency advantage over people who are limited to Photoshop or less when it comes to graphic creation for online use. Bitmaps are very difficult to edit [often impossible] unless everything is in its own layer.

Bitmap painting programs are extremely clumsy for quick, clear graphic production. PDF graphics from InDesign can easily be rasterized as GIFs, PNGs, or JPEGs at any size, resolution, or color space you need. By using color PDFs that can quickly be rasterized to the exact size needed, you obtain a design freedom and image control that are very difficult to accomplish in Photoshop.

The first time you try to make type fit a certain size, transform it, or simply scale type in Photoshop, you will long for the freedom of InDesign. Modified type in an InDesign PDF rasterizes clearly and sharply when compared to transformed type done in Photoshop

The tools available

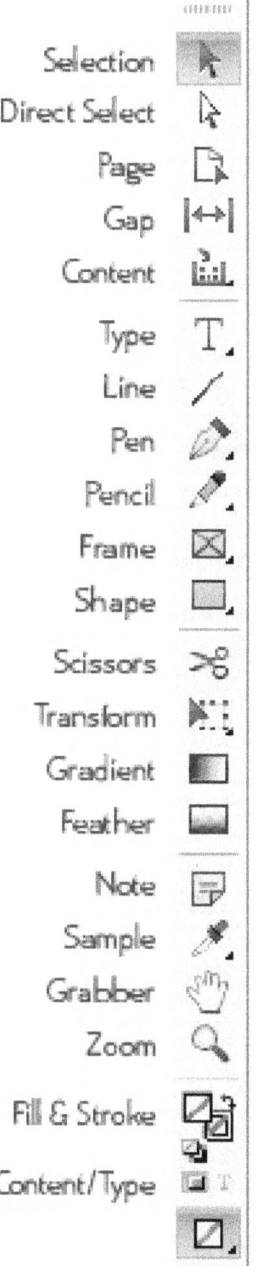

Selection
Direct Select
Page
Gap
Content

Type
Line
Pen
Pencil
Frame
Shape

Scissors
Transform
Gradient
Feather

Note
Sample
Grabber
Zoom

Fill & Stroke
Content/Type

InDesign does have most of the relevant Illustrator tools: but they are laid out in a way that is instantly recognizable as page layout. Strange tools like the graphing tool, gradient mesh, blending tool, and so forth are missing, as they should be. This is a page layout program. This is not primarily a graphics creation program—vector or bitmap. Yet, the basic drawing tools are all here.

The toolbox looks comfortingly familiar. If you are used to Illustrator it seems streamlined and clean. The dizzying cacophony of dozens of tools on pop out menus from the toolbox are largely missing.

What tools are left are the path manipulation tools—and they are really all you need. If you need a fancy 3D drawing with realistic shadows, you belong in Illustrator. If you need realistic textures you need to go to Photoshop. But my guess is that InDesign will be all you need much of the time.

You've been using several of these tools throughout the book already. But once you start drawing with them, their usage changes and I need to be sure you know their capabilities.

The Selection tools

The Selection [V] and Direct Selection [A] tools are very similar to Illustrator's in appearance. The hollow pointed or white arrow does path editing. If you need to move a frame or resize it, you need the Selection tool. If you want to modify the shape in any way, you need the Direct Selection capabilities. You also have to go to one of the selection tools to modify the wrap on the text frames. The Selection tool also includes the Rotation tool.

TIP: One of the disconcerting aspects of this new page layout setup is the simple fact that you can have two separate text wraps on the same object. One for the selected frame, and another for the selected frame content. Don't confuse yourself. Be careful.

The Pen Tool [P]

InDesign's Pen tool is very definitely Illustrator's four part Pen tool: It has all of the same advantages and disadvantages. However, I have found that InDesign's version works the way that I wish Illustrator's or Photoshop's did. It is very smooth and easy to use.

For those of you who are not familiar with Adobe's pen tool, it makes paths by clicking [placing a corner point] and click-dragging [placing a smooth point] in a connect-the-dots fashion (more on that in a bit).

You have to closely watch the tool when producing or editing a path to find out what is happening. If you see a little plus next to the tool (over an existing path), clicking will add a point. If you see a little minus, clicking will subtract one. If you see the little open pointer, clicking will change the point type from smooth to corner or vice versa. The shortcuts are the same as Illustrator's.

The basic advice is to remember that holding down the Command (Control) key changes you back to the last selection tool you used. Holding down the Option (Alt) key switches you to the Convert Point tool. The most disconcerting aspect is that there is no way to drag out handles on a corner point. All you can do is drag out the handles with the Change Point tool creating a curve point. Then move the Change Point tool over the handles that result. This allows you to drag the handles individually converting the curve point to a corner point with visible handles. InDesign's implementation seems very elegant and obvious.

Using The Pen Tool

The Pen tool is the core of PostScript illustration: This tool started with Fontographer 1986. This is the exact same tool

Photoshop and Illustrator use for drawing paths. What I am trying to say is simple: "You must become fluent with the Pen tool!" This is not an option.

How do you add that skill? This is a very strange tool that does not seem intuitive at all: There is nothing like it anywhere else except in PostScript drawing programs. So let's talk a little about how you gain skill. I found this out when I went to the University of Minnesota in the late '60s to learn to be an artist.

When I went to the orientation session of my first drawing class, the final thing the professor said as we left (planning on coming back on Monday morning to have him "teach" us to draw) was,

"Oh, by the way—when you come Monday, bring sixty drawings that you have done over the weekend. I don't care what you draw, but you must bring sixty new drawings done in the next three days."

During that first nine-week course, we all drew nearly 600 drawings in pencil, conté crayon, charcoal, crowquill, and heavy bamboo dip pen. The first ones were horrible and I threw them away.

I wish I had them now. All I'd have to do is look at them to realize I've gotten a little better, at least. The first year was all quantity over quality.

I didn't produce my first "keepers" until my second year, after four drawing courses, two painting courses, three courses on color theory, and so forth. By that time I had produced thousands of drawings, hundreds of stupid exercises, and

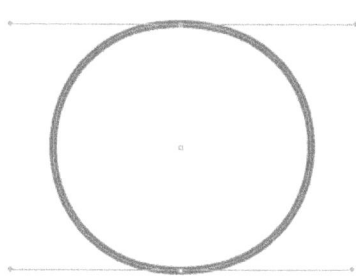

The 2-point circle
A deceptively simple project
Using your Pen Tool: Click-drag sideways, holding down the Shift Key [until the two handles look like what you see at the top of the circle]. Then release, hold-down the shift key again and click-drag below the top point in the other direction dragging the handles until they match the top handles. Then click-drag again on top of the top point, dragging to the left until your smart guides show things are lined up. I have a 3 pt red stroke on my circle.

more than twenty large paintings. They were starting to get fairly good.

Surprise, surprise: You will have to do the same thing with the Pen tool. You just need to draw. Your real assignment, for the next few months, is to draw at least two dozen simple drawings a week, or more, with the Pen tool. In reality, I hope you will do many more than that. By the time you finish, you will be getting pretty good with the Pen tool.

How do you draw with paths?

You use various tools to place points. The points are placed in order around a shape & the path is produced by connecting them. These points are controlled by mathematical formulas to produce a path that can bend and change direction under direct control. These modifications are determined by point location & handles with control points. Each point has two handles. Drawing short lines and connecting them is an exercise in futility. All shapes need to be drawn as one continuous outline or path.

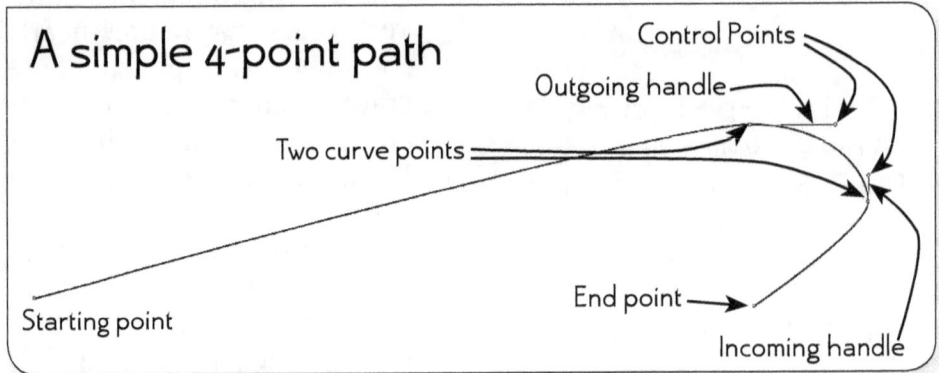

A simple 4-point path

Control Points
Outgoing handle
Two curve points
Starting point
End point
Incoming handle

Corner points, Curve points, & Handles

The following descriptions and definitions are almost certainly not accurate mathematically. Who cares? What is important is that they will help you understand how your paths work so you can control them.

Points: These are the dots you place so that when you connect the dots a path is produced. A path has a direction going from the first point to the second point and so on. Our outside paths are usually drawn counterclockwise.

Path segments: A segment [for our purposes] is a portion of a path between two points. That's the old Fontographer/ FreeHand definition and it works to let you know what is going on with your paths. So, a segment is a straight line from point to point plus any length added by handles at the beginning or the end.

Point Handles: These are tangent lines coming out of the points. A tangent is the straight line touching a curve at only that point without crossing the path.

Every segment has two handles: the outgoing handle from the point at the incoming end and an incoming handle from the point at the outgoing end. If a point appears to have no handles, or only a handle on one side of the point, the other handles simply have zero length. Zero length handles produce the shortest possible segment. If both the outgoing and incoming handles of a segment have zero length, you have the shortest possible segment: a straight line from point to point.

Handle Control Points: At the end of every handle is a small ball, x, square, or knob (depends on the app used) that can be grabbed with the mouse and moved to control the length & direction of the handle coming out of the point.

Corner points: When these are produced by a click of the Pen tool, they have no handles—actually, no handles are visible. In fact, they have handles with no length. What that means is that paths coming into that point or going out from that point will go the shortest way possible—modified by the handle at the other end of the segment. If a corner point has visible handles, each of them can be moved independently.

Smooth or Curve points: When these are produced with a click-drag, they have handles of equal length that are locked onto a common tangent. This means if you move one handle, the other handle moves in an equal but opposite direction. If the curve handles have been modified in length they rotate around the point in a single line in opposite directions while maintaining the length of the handles involved.

So, how does the Pen tool work?

So, with that intro, how does the tool work? When you simply click with the Pen, you produce corner points having no handles. When you click and then immediately drag, while still holding down the button, a curve point is produced. You drag out the outgoing handle which produces an equal incoming handle on the other side of the point on the same tangent as the handle you are dragging out. With these two options you can draw anything your little heart desires—easy, huh? Actually, it is that easy. Once you get accustomed to the tool, you will be amazed with its precision, dazzled by its fluidity, and addicted to its editable flexibility. It makes vector lines and shapes.

Constraining the tool: When clicking to produce corner points, holding down the Shift key will keep the points lined up on horizontal, vertical, or 45° angles. When click-dragging to produce a curve point, holding down the Shift key will cause the handles to be on horizontal, vertical, or 45° angles.

Choose the Direct Selection tool first: before you start drawing with the Pen tool. Holding down the Command key while you are drawing gives you the last selection tool you used. This needs to be the Direct Selection tool because you will be editing the path and need access to the points and handles of that path.

While drawing in InDesign, you will constantly want to go to the Direct Selection tool to modify the point or points you just placed. This is normal. You should learn to resist that tendency, however. It is usually better to draw the entire path around the shape you are working on and close it by clicking on your starting point before you begin editing the path to perfect the shape.

Type P to select the Pen tool

Draw path by clicking or click-dragging to produce the points you want. To repeat, draw a single continuous path around the entire object being drawn. To edit a point while you are drawing hold down the Command key.

When you go to editing the path:

The Pen Icon will show you what is happening.

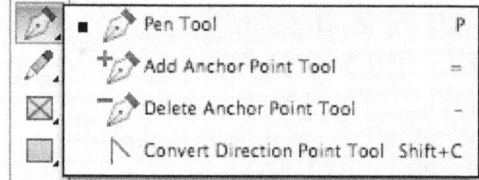

Review: *The Pen tool has four variations that appear automatically, or by holding down a modifier key*

- **If the tool is held over a point with the Option key held down (the Convert Direction Point tool):** clicking will convert that point from a corner to a curve (and you can drag out the handles) or it will convert from a curve to a corner point and the handles will disappear (go to zero length).

- **If the tool is held over a handle control point of a curve point with the Option key held down (accessing the Convert Direction Point tool):** the curve point will be converted to a corner point (without contracting the handles) and the handle can be dragged independently.

- **A plus appears (the Add Anchor Point tool):** When the Pen is held over an empty portion of a segment–clicking will add a point.

- **A minus appears (the Delete Anchor Point tool):** If the tool is held over an existing point–clicking will delete that point.

As you are drawing, if you do not like the way the handles are arranged, or the shape of a segment, simply press down the Command key (PC: Control) to access the last Selection tool used [that should have been the Direct Selection tool]. Click on a point to select it and the handles will appear for that point (the outgoing handle of the preceding point, both handles of the selected point, and the incoming handle of the following point). Adjust the point location and the handles as you decide they need to be set, then release the Command key to go back to the Pen tool, click on the end point to select it and continue drawing the path.

 **Very important tip:** Every shape needs to be drawn in one continuous path. If you need a closed path, you have to draw in one continuous path the entire way around the shape. If you find you have two or more parts to your path, delete all except the first one, click on the end point to select it, and redraw it as one continuous path. This is the most common mistake of beginning Pen users. Yes, parts can be joined together, but it is frustrating, clumsy, and slow to execute. Don't do it! Bad Habit!

Frame generators

The next three tools are a little confusing, because Adobe has made them two separate menus: the frame tools and the shape tools. Frames have no fill or stroke. But with the x running from corner to corner, you can select and move them easily even though they are empty. Shape tools use the currently selected fill and stroke. But, it doesn't make any difference which one you are using. If you have a shape and click in it with the Type tool, it becomes a text frame. If you have a text frame with no type or insertion point in it, into which you place a graphic—it becomes a graphic frame. Graphics placed into a text frame insertion point become inline graphics.

The Frame Tools

The Frame tools have no stroke or fill, yet you can move them around by clicking any- where within the frame [they have a non-printing x though them]. The shape tools (Rect- angle, Ellipse, and Polygon) can only be selected by clicking on the stroke unless you have a fill assigned to the shape.

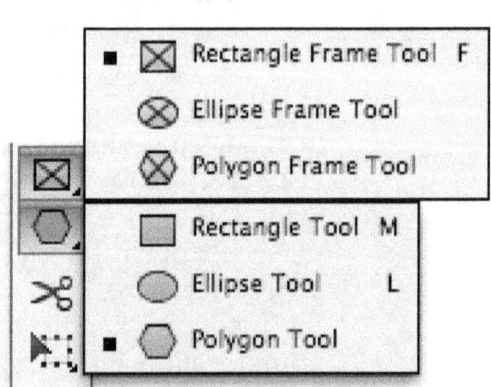

The Rectangle Tool [M] & the Ellipse Tool [L]

These tool are the normal drawing tools. If you hold down the Shift key; the shape is constrained to a square or circle. If you hold down the Option (Alt) key, they draw from the center out. They also draw from handle to handle like any shape tools.

The Polygon Tool

This tool is the normal limited version of the Poly-gon tool available from Adobe products. As you can see from the dialog capture on the next page, the shape of the points of the star must be guessed. There is no pre-view. With an infinite variety of stars possible with every number of points, this makes this tool useless except for drawing frames for regular polygons (hence the name, I guess). Or I guess if you really want a star, you can do and redo until you get something usable.

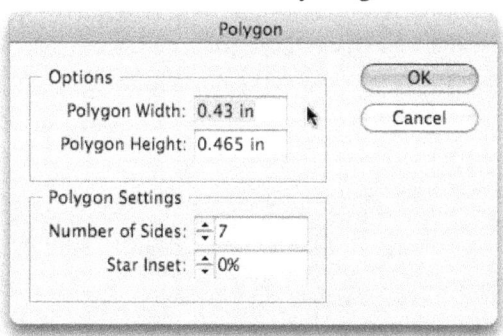

Shape generators produce closed paths

These paths can be edited like any other path with the Direct Selection tool and the Pen Tool. In addition you can modify these shapes with the Corner Options. As you can clearly see on the opposite page, you can quickly get ridiculous with it all. But the controls are easy to use and very quick to execute. Once you have what you want you can leave it selected and make a new Object style which will save all your setting into a style.

The Pencil tool

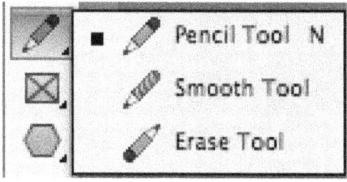

This is a typical Illustrator triple tool: Pencil, Smoother, and Eraser. The Pencil draws freehand paths with no point control. The Smoother progressively smooths out the line (without any real control, although it often does a nice job). You can access the Smoother tool by holding down the Option key while you draw. The Eraser does what you would like it to, most of the time. It must be hand selected.

A really nice capability is that the Smoother and Eraser work on any path you draw, with any tool. The

Smoother, for example, will convert a star into a polygon with concave sides (it changes the entire shape). They even work on type converted to paths, but the effects are rather unpredictable. In general, however, these are a very elegant selection of freehand drawing tools. The main issue is the lack of control over point type or placement. I can't remember the last time I used the Pencil tool.

Converting shapes

This capability is only found at the bottom of the Object menu when you have an object selected. You can convert any shape (with corner modifications or not) into a Rectangle, Rounded Rectangle, Beveled Rectangle, Inverse Rounded Rectangle, Ellipse, Triangle, Polygon, Line, or Orthogonal Line. It works very well.

Corner Options

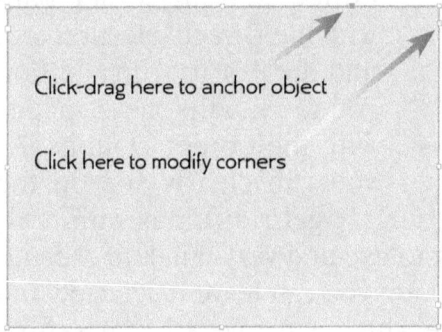

Click-drag here to anchor object

Click here to modify corners

Once clicked the corners look like this. Dragging on the diamond modifies all 4 corners. Option-clicking on the corners will switch them between the six types: None, Rounded, Inverse Rounded, Inverse Corner, Bevel, & Fancy. Shift-clicking will enable you to modify a corner individually. The corner options dialog will help you control and keep track of what you've done.

Then you can color and shape it however you like.

Below is with a Thick-Thin-Thick 7-pt Blue stroke with a light blue Gap, and a radial fill

Good taste is required. This can easily be overdone. Thankfully, you do not do that, right?

Drawing in InDesign is obviously limited

However, even with these limitations in InDesign, the transformation tools are all available as are the Photoshop effects. You'll be surprised how often InDesign's tool set is more than enough. If you are creating a drawing or painting you will either be using fine art media or using Illustrator or Photoshop. Paint and FreeHand work well also, but you'll have a little trouble converting them to a format you can use in InDesign.

The main new skill you'll need is the pen tool: you'll need to practice

This is just a little pen tool drawing, which I use as the logo for my font foundry. It's a typical InDesign drawing. This one only works in color. **Actually:** the leaf blob was done with a large brush in black ink which I then scanned & traced in either Illustrator or FontLab [I can't remember which]. But, the trunk, type, and ground were all added in InDesign.

CHAPTER FOURTEEN

Combining paths

Now that we understand points, segments, handles, and paths, we need to discuss methods of using multiple paths to produce discrete objects. This is often done best with the Layers palette. On a regular basis, graphic production is greatly enhanced by having the separate objects of our illustrations on separate layers that can be turned on and off as needed.

 **TIP: Don't add a layer unless you have a good reason.** A layer should be added to help you organize, not to add unnecessary complexity. Many of my students quickly got lost in a morass of layers that were not only unnecessary, but served only to confuse the designer. If you need a layer, create one. Simply refuse to add a layer unless you have a specific need and a logical reason for that additional layer of information.

However, this section covers those groups of paths that you need to keep in a permanent relationship for various reasons. Sometimes layers will help you sort things out, but that is not what we are talking about here—at all. That type of layer usage is a Photoshop thing. Now we are talking about capabilities that put InDesign and PostScript Illustration far above all other graphic software.

There are basically three ways to combine paths: grouping, making a composite path, and (for now, let's call it) merging. They all have their uses, and it is important to understand their differences in concept. Almost everyone understands and uses grouping. It is probably the most overused capability of digital publishing software. The most common question I was asked by my students was, "Why won't this work?" (Usually with a whining twist.) The first thing I usually had to do was Ungroup several times to get to a place where I could show them how to fix what they were trying to do.

Grouping

DEFINITION: Grouping is the establishment of a permanent relationship between multiple objects, without changing any of those objects in any way. There is no interaction between the objects unless you mess with modes before grouping.

If I group a man's hat with his head, whenever I move his head, his hat moves also. There are a couple of things to remember about grouping. As simple as it is, many think that grouping is the best way to protect yourself from accidental changes. There are some problems with that. They primarily involve changes that make normal workflow more difficult. If you get into the habit of always ungrouping as soon as you are done transforming the group, it will help you in the long run as you work with your graphic.

Please notice that any transformation of the group transforms every piece of the group while maintaining the original relationships. All of the fills remain the same. None of the paths are altered in any way. However, the strokes will vary in thickness as you scale up or down. As a result, there is very little use for grouping other than to gather various paths into a temporary unit to enable transformation as a single piece. Even here you need to be careful.

TIP: Grouping causes any object in an ePUB to be rasterized. In general don't group unless you must. Then ungroup as soon as you can. It's not required—just prudent.

Our other methods of combining paths actually change the paths in some manner.

Composite paths [joining]

An old name for composite paths [joining] is good, for in a real way the paths used are joined into one path. However, it is a very special type of joining. First of all, it has several rules, which we will cover next. Second, it fundamentally changes the appearance of the paths by giving them a single overall fill and stroke.

The rules of joining

- **All paths to be composited must be ungrouped:** When type is converted to Outlines, the entire text block becomes a group.

- **All paths must be closed paths.**

When the two rules are satisfied, all the paths to be joined are selected and then composited. When paths are composited, some very special effects appear. First of all, the new composite path has a single stroke and fill, based on the path farthest back in the layering of the paths. When ungrouped, Paths look the same but they are no longer tied together.

With type converted to outlines: It is converted to a group. If that group is ungrouped, often each line of type remains a group. When each line is ungrouped, you finally have access to the individual paths (except for characters that are composited).

With composited characters, you must use Object>> Path>> Release Composited Path.

Even/Odd Fill

The second, and probably most important, attribute of composite paths is that they should have an even/odd fill. This is where the single fill appears and disappears as it passes through the various sections of the composite path. Here again it is probably easier to show you with type characters, because the most common composite paths are letters.

The only problem is that Adobe doesn't do this very well. You will often find that it is easier to take the interior paths and make sure they are on top. Then go to the Pathfinder panel and use Subtract. This will take the top path and punch a hole in the path behind it.

The most useful part of this even/odd fill is that the unfilled portions are not white − they are transparent, empty, open areas within the composite path. When you think about this, these transparent areas are essential for almost every graphic design. This is why Photoshop is essential, it offers bitmapped transparency. But vector is better.

How would we deal with letters like O, P, R, a, b, d, and so on, if the counters were not transparent? Every time we placed type over a colored background, we would have to manually select the paths of the counters and color them the color of the background. This can be done. But what happens when you want to place type over a photograph or a gradient fill? It is impossible to match portions taken from the middle of a gradient. Type is filled with composite paths to solve this problem.

Of course, this even/odd fill attribute of composite paths can get a bit out of hand. Below, you can see that the word FAST is fairly chewed up. I had to try several fonts for that word before it was legible. As you can see, it is important to look at these joined paths carefully to make sure that readability has not been compromised. [By the way, the illustration on the other page was done in InDesign because I could not do it in Illustrator].

Pathfinder filters

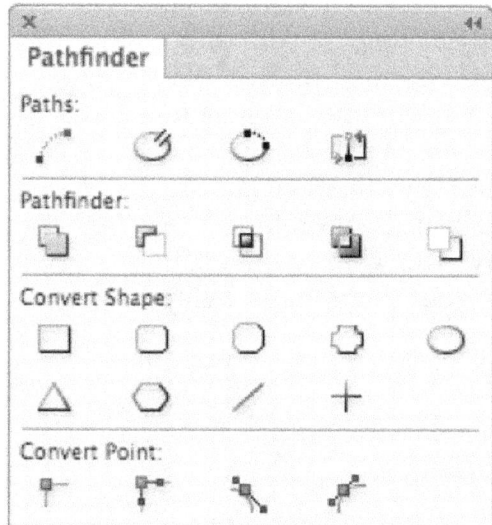

Pathfinder Panel

Paths
Join, Open, Close, Reverse Direction

Pathfinder
Add, Subtract, Intersect, Exclude, Minus

Convert Shape
Rectangle, Rounded, Bevel, Inverted, Ellipse
Triangle, Polygon, Line, Vertical or Horizontal

Convert Point
Plain, Corner, Smooth, Symmetrical

There are several path-combining filters that you will use regularly. These path-combining capabilities, found in the Pathfinder panel, enable you to combine paths in ways that will greatly enhance your drawing production speed.

Pathfinder Panel

This panel hold many commands to modify and convert paths. Simply select the shapes and click the button. As you can see, there are four basic choices: Paths, Path-Finder, Convert Shape, and Convert Point.

Paths

These are very important options that are not really available in Illustrator [though they need to be there].

Join: Connects two endpoints. You can use this for stitching together segments to make a complete path. But it's not fluid and you often add tiny straight line segments between your two end points.

Open: Opens a closed path

Close: Closes an open path

Reverse Path: Changes the direction of the path

Of these four path operations, the last one was critical. This is the one that Illustrator needs but does not have. It is used because, as mentioned, Adobe does not do even /odd fill on its compound paths very well. Compound paths are produced in PostScript by having the path directions reversed. If the inside path is reversed in direction when compared to the outside path, it will punch a hole in the outside path. You see the results of that with the FAST! Graphic on the previous page. However, this is easier to do with Pathfinder by using the Subtract operation. The Pathfinder choices will usually give you what you need. If they simply will not work, one of your paths is probably an open path.

Pathfinder Operations

I started with these three shapes: As I go through these operations, it is important to observe the layering of the shapes and the fills applied to each. Normally the attributes of the top shape will apply. This is a 1-point Black stroke with a 41%-0% gradient fill. Path combination operations in both applications often result in a composite path. Obviously, this is part of the strangeness of working with a collage of shapes – the uniqueness of PostScript illustration.

Start with Add

I've always known this as Unite, which was the old name for it in FreeHand. What it does is obvious. It takes all the selected shapes and makes a new shape which goes around the outside of all the shapes. As you can see it uses the attribute of the top shape.

Next we'll use Subtract

Here we see that the top two shapes were each punched out of the back shape. The attributes of the back shape were retained: 1-point Black stroke with a 12%-77% gradient fill.

Now we'll do Intersect

This gives us the small rectangle where the three shapes all overlap. It has the attributes of the top shape.

Now for Exclude Overlap

This is very interesting. We get a compound path of the three shapes. It uses the attributes of the top shape. Most interesting to me is the fact that this exhibits perfect even/odd fill. That is very rare for Adobe, and far superior to Illustrator.

Finally let's see Minus Back

This one is also interesting. Subtracting the star from the top two shapes eliminated the horizontal rectangle, but left a blunt arrow from the bottom rectangle. But notice the fill. It is the fill of the top shape, but its width is the same as the star so with a gradient we would get the center portion of the gradient showing in the blunt arrow.

As you can see from the preceding examples, these are handy tools. As a practical matter making compound paths, I normally put the shape I want to punch out of the bottom shape on top, select both and use Subtract or Exclude Overlap. I used to use reverse path direction as recently as CS5, but now the path operations work the way I want them to.

Paste Inside

I started with this book cover and the word WARNING! I selected the word and used Type>> Create Outlines to covert it to paths. Then I moved the image on top of the type and Cut it. Then I selected the type and chose Edit>> Paste Into. As you can see the bitmapped image is masked by the shapes of the letters. As you can also see the result is a mess. Neither the word nor the Title on the book cover can be read without a lot of effort.

Here we have one of those commonly used capabilities that is trouble from the start. The idea is to take a shape and fill it with a photo or illustration. One of the reasons Paste Inside is used so often is that it is so easy to understand. It seems to be a simple — and very powerful — cropping tool. In fact, it does not crop at all. It provides a boundary where the images pasted inside are revealed inside the path and not seen outside the path. However (like all clipping paths), the portions of the images that seem to be cropped are merely hidden. All you did was add data telling the printer not to print those areas outside the clipping path. To translate, this means you have added a lot of file size.

The problem with Paste Into is the final result: Aside from the complexity and the possible printing problems, the same question has to be asked, "Does this help communicate clearly with the reader?" In most cases, the answer is a clear, "No!" I am not saying to avoid these options. I am repeating that you really need to keep your priorities straight and work carefully.

To adjust the image inside the paths: With the Selection tool, simply click on the content donut and move the masked image around as needed. If you move it so that it no longer fills the entire interior of the paths, then the original fill color will show [in this case, the bright red fill used for the word WARNING!].

These path combination tools are simply part of your arsenal. You will find most of them invaluable as you run into the deadlines of real-world employment. It's a real shock to many graduates to discover that most graphics are not budgeted — meaning they have to be done very fast. It is not at all unusual to be forced to generate a competent graphic in twenty minutes or less. The power of PostScript illustration, with its ability to freely combine, edit, and manipulate paths, enables this to be a realistic requirement.

Create outlines
[manipulating type]

Previously, I casually mentioned one of InDesign's most powerful tools: converting type to editable paths. There are many reasons why you might want to do this. But first, what does this command do? It converts type characters to editable PostScript paths.

These shapes are no longer editable type

There are many times when this is required. One of the most common is the Paste Into scenario we looked at on the previous page. But it is also used to produce logos and graphics for your books. Book titles on book covers are commonly edited by selecting the title and executing the Create Outlines command in the Type Menu. Then the resulting paths are modified to produce a distinctive title.

I don't think I mentioned it back when I showed you this graphic, but the word FAST had to be converted to paths before I could punch it out of the multi-pointed rectangle.

The word Radiqx in the publishing house logo had to be converted to outlines so I could modify the R and then subtract the cross shape. In fact, those font outlines are already there in the font—used to produce the font, but the Create Outlines command gives us access to them so that they can be edited and manipulated.

Eliminating the need for a font

This is what the word looked like: [for the graphic on the next page] before I converted it to paths so I could make the frame to hold the quote. It is set in Gill Sans Ultra Bold—one of the free fonts which comes with the MacOS. All I did was make the F a bit larger, drag the stem down, add a couple points with the Pen tool, and dragged them sideways to make the rectangle. Of course I had to modify the a so I could unite it with the F, and then move the counter of the a on top and punch it out of the Fa shape. The quote is just set on top of the new rectangle and colored as live type (try that with Photoshop). I forgot! I had to cut and paste back the dot over the i so I could enlarge it, center it, and color it with a radial gradient.

Factoid

Striving for excellence motivates you; Striving for perfection is demoralizing.

HARRIET BRAIKER

I did it all in a new InDesign document, 6"x6", exported it as a PDF and placed it into the copy above. When it comes to do the ebooks, I'll open the PDF into Photoshop, rasterizing it to 600 pixels wide. I'll then save it as a PSD, and Save For Web to get a tiny little JPEG that will work fine in the ePUB and KF8 versions.

Typographic graphics

Making a quick graphic in InDesign is a common occurrence. It is something a word processor cannot do. If you need your images even fancier, you can take your typographic beginnings and finish them off in Photoshop.

Linking graphics

This is one of the most common issues when people begin building their books in InDesign. Many people add graphics by copy/pasting. Worse yet, many want to embed their graphics. Basically, you "never" want to do either of these things.

Embedding bloats file size:

This book, for example, has 69.7 MB of graphics at this point in the design of the print version [229 graphics listed so far]. If I embedded the graphics, InDesign would crash. It does not have enough RAM to keep things going [as if I could afford enough RAM anyway, or find a machine which can hold 80 GB of RAM].

Copy/Paste and/ or embedding make updating almost impossible:

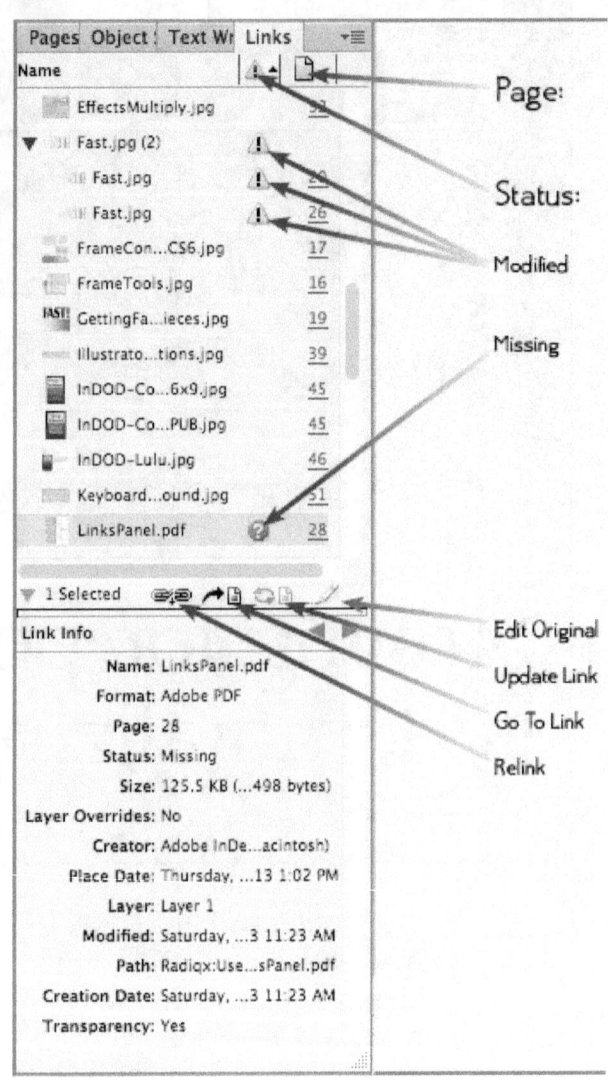

If I make any changes to a graphic outside of InDesign, I have to re-paste or re-embed to add those changes to my document. This goes far beyond tedious.

Linking is one major advantage to InDesign

What we need is a way to add the graphics that keeps them outside the document with a method of updating changed graphics that is simple and easy. This has always been one of the main strengths of professional page layout software. I put all my graphics in a folder called Links inside the folder containing my InDesign document. If I do not move them there first, I move them as I add them.

Links panel

This is actually one of InDesign's strong points. No one does it better. As you can see on the opposite page, not only can you link to graphics with only a placeholder appearing in the actual document, but, you can also easily update any changes. You can relink to a different version [B&W to Color, for example] or a completely different graphic. You can click a button to show the graphic in its actual location. And much more.

Status:

This column has two icons. These both cause major problems if they are not fixed. If either of these icons appear, all that will print is the low-resolution screen image which InDesign has created to show you the graphic within InDesign.

Missing: This red stop sign means that the link to the graphic has been broken. It may be deleted, it may be on a different hard drive, it or a containing folder may have been renamed. Whatever the problem is, it won't print or show up in your ebook. You need to find the graphic and link it again. You use the Relink button below.

Modified: This Yellow triangle means that the placed graphic has been changed or modified in some way. You need to click on Update Link to fix the problem.

Page:

This shows you the location of placed graphic. If you click on a link in this column InDesign will take you to the graphic on that page.

PB: Pasteboard: This means the graphic linked is placed on the pasteboard somewhere [it's not on a page]. You must click on the link to see what the problem is and fix it. Items on the pasteboard will not print, nor will they show up in your ebooks, but they regularly cause serious printing problems and ebooks problems as the printer or ereader goes looking for the non-existent graphic.

Button Bar:

Relink: This enables you to relink to any graphic you have available on your hard drive or server. I'll use this to find and link the graphic which is shown as missing.

Find Link: This will change the page view, centering the graphic on the page where it is used. For example, you can see in the capture that the selected PSD is on the pasteboard somewhere. I need to go there and fix that.

Update link: Sometimes this is updated automatically. Sometimes you actually need to click on this button. You can tell which is needed by the Yellow Triangle found in the second column from the right.

Edit graphic [Edit Original]: This tries to open the original graphic and works well if you have a Photoshop graphic or an AI file. In fact, it not only opens the original graphic, but when you save it, InDesign automatically updates it. However, for PDFs it does not go to the original but tries to open the PDF instead (which is a pain).

Ah well, you can't have everything. Of course, it doesn't help at all if the original is an RGB full resolution graphic stored in originals. All my greyscale images in this book have a full color, full resolution version from which they were saved stored in the Originals folder. Also, it doesn't work when the original is a PSD, from which you Saved for Web a PNG, JPEG, or GIF for your ePUB or KF8 book.

Copy link to folder

If you place a graphic which is not located in the links folder, you can simply right-click on it in the Links panel. This will give you the command seen to the left: Copy Link(s) To... Once you choose your Links folder a copy will be placed there and the link updated.

Must you use a links folder? No: But, You can actually know where all your graphics are located, when it is time for you to make your Color PDF, ePUB, and Kindle KF8 ver-

Relink...

Copy Link(s) To...

XMP File Info...

Go To Link
Embed Link

Hide Link Information Pane
Edit Original
Edit With ▶
Reveal in Finder
Reveal in Bridge
Reveal in Mini Bridge

Copy Info ▶
Captions ▶

sions. If you have all the graphics in a Links folder, and all the full color originals in the Originals folder, file management becomes much easier.

Why have a full color originals folder?

That is simple. When I go to make the color version for the color PDFs, all I have to do is drop the color images into the Links folder. All the greyscale images are replaced by the color originals (they both have identical names). Simply updating does a lot of my preparation work for the downloadable color PDFs I sell through Scribd and Lulu.

When I do my ePUBs

All I have to do is save my color RGB PSDs into JPEGs. They must be resampled to the proper size and then saved into a new Links folder in the new ePUB document folder. Then relinking is relatively easy for that conversion also (though it is not automated because the name has changed). The conversion from vector to bitmap and PSD to JPEG is always tedious.

The Swatches Panel

There is no program which handles color as well as InDesign—not even close.

Even though Illustrator has a Swatches panel, it is very difficult and clumsy to set up a custom palette for your book. InDesign makes it easy. InDesign swatches work very much like styles. They have the same global control as a style does. If you double-click to open the Swatch Options dialog box. You can modify your swatch as much as you like. When you close the dialog every instance of that color [including those used as color stops for gradients will be updated throughout the book. If you import a color, you can delete it and replace it with the colors used in your book palette.

A designed palette of swatches

One of the things that trips up most designers when they start using styles is the fact that styles can only use colors that are already set up as swatches. This may seem like another hassle, but in fact it is a blessing in dis-guise. This situation forces you to set up a designed set of swatches.

Why would you want a special color palette? That is obvious once you think about it. Your color choices are as much a core part of your personal style as the typography & layout choices. We all have a constantly evolving set of colors we use. For most of us (at least at the beginning) these color choices change with fashion. For many of us, these fashion choices remain a key part of our evolving design sense.

What is clear is the factory defaults are ugly

CMY & RGB are building blocks of color. CMYK is printing color. RGB is monitor color. As self publishing using on-demand printing we work in RGB almost exclusively. The six default colors are not to be used alone except in those rare instances where magenta is actually a stylistic statement you want to make. It makes no difference if you like pastels or jewel tones; bold, saturated hues or subtle shades of color. The only universal constant is that no one except the laziest designers uses CMYRGorB. My experience is that we all need the six basic hues (red, orange, yellow, green, blue, & violet), some selected tints of those hues, plus a few gradients. All of these things are necessary for use in developing a gorgeous, truly useful set of styles. Remember, if you do not have them in Swatches, you are going to have to constantly save your style temporarily to go back and make any swatches you need. Then you have to edit the style again to add the colors you just made.

Set up your color palette for all versions before you design the first version

Although it is true that your print version at Cre-atespace and/or Lulu will be printed in greyscale, You will immediately need to change the color palette to RGB for your downloadable PDFs. You will use that color palette for all your ebooks. You will find that really helps to have your palette set up before you start adjusting your styles. It helps immensely to keep the look of the book consistent.

My Current Set of Swatches

On the next page you can see what I am currently using in this book. It probably does not match what you like. But it is probably better than the defaults being currently used by you unless you've customized them. If your panel does not look like this you need to chose Name in the panel menu. We'll cover that menu in a bit.

Controlling the global look with different clients

Because all styles have this color palette embedded, when I begin work on a new book I merely have to modify the existing swatches to completely change the color styling of the piece. To replace a tint of the purple with one of the red, you simply make the new tint and then take the purple tint and delete it. This gives you the dialog that allows you to substitute the new tint for all the instances of the existing tint. Modifying a swatch changes all the tints of that swatch and all the gradients where it is used. **In this way, you can easily modify the custom palette to bring it in line:** with the needs of your differing books and clients (if you are designing for others also). You can also automate the application of these colors with the designed set of styles we've covered.

 **Controlling Gray tints:** After telling you that you can easily delete a color and change all the resultant tints, I need to mention that you might find it helpful to make a NewBlack swatch and make your tints from that. This way you can easily change your grey tints for purple tints by deleting the NewBlack and replacing it with the purple you desire.

Reading the swatches

In order to understand what you are doing in InDesign when applying colors, you need to be able to read the icons Used. They tell you what type of color you are using.

In my earlier books, I had an entire chapter on color usage and Separations. There used to be major problems if you did not keep track of the color spaces you were using. For now, all the free self publishing suppliers use RGB. So, you will do good to do that yourself.

Nevertheless,you need to be careful because not all color prints or views as you might expect. As you can see below, InDesign packs a lot of information into each bar. Aspects like the color space used to display the color, whether it is a spot color, tint, or a process color, and whether you can redefine the color.

First of all, colors in [Brackets] cannot be redefined for output (although [Paper] can be redefined for viewing on the monitor). If you are doing your book on cream

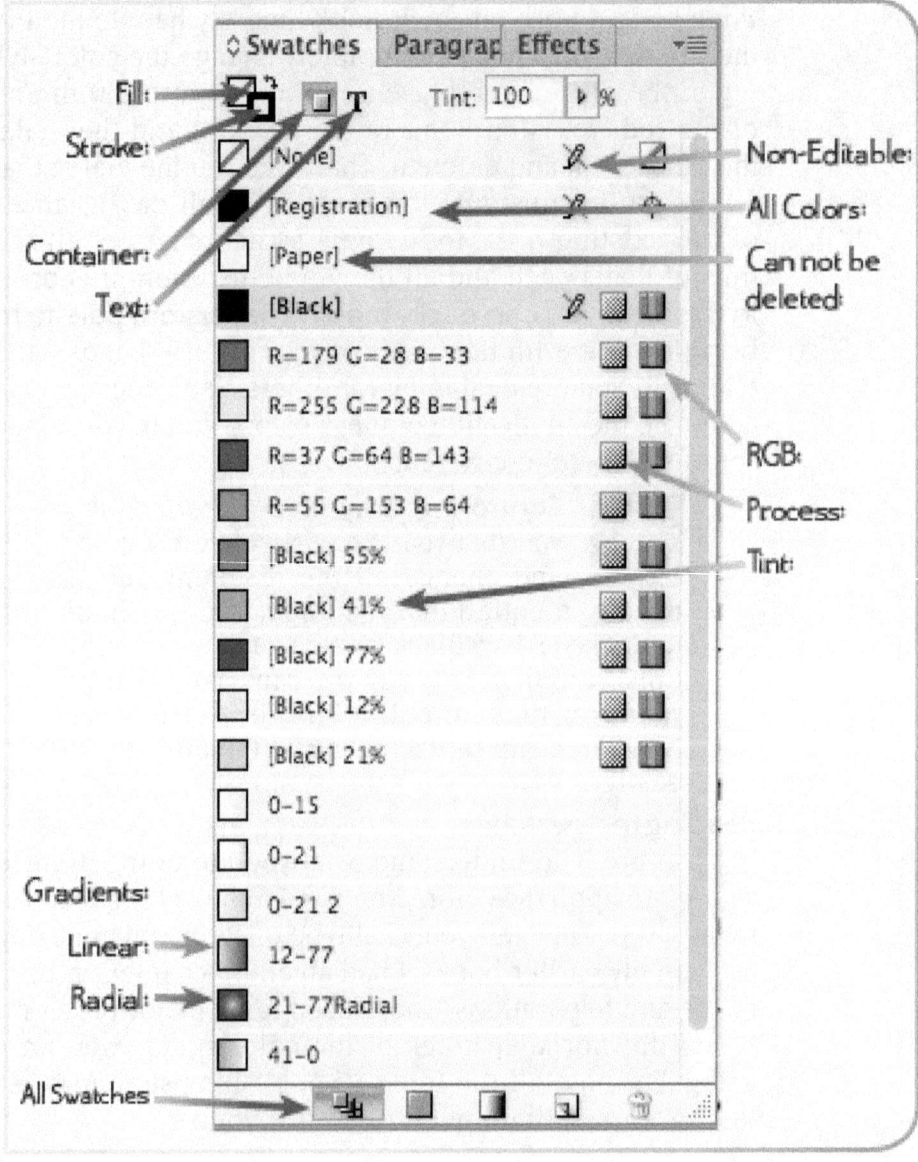

paper, it may help you visualize—but it doesn't change what prints.

Let's start with the top bar.

[None]: As you know, the crossbar in all cases (icon, tool, or swatch) is red. It is to clearly warn you that there is nothing there. It means what it says, None. As you know, we are dealing with PostScript. The PostScript descriptions have no color or dimension until we specify it — in InDesign's case, color is defined by clicking on a swatch including the specification of [None] (not transparent color but none).

Notice: The pencil with the slash through it means that this color cannot be redefined [labeled non-editable].

[Paper]: This is not white, as you know, or is it? Under normal use, Paper is an opaque knockout color with no color that reveals the paper through the knocked out hole. In InDesign you can actually make the Paper color appear to be the color of the paper you will be using. Just double-click the Paper swatch and make the swatch look as close as you can to the color of the paper you will be using. Of course, you can not imitate fiber-added stock, and you have to be aware that it's still just that opaque knockout with which you are familiar once it prints.

[Black]: This, again, is one of those colors never thought about — but it really requires knowledge. First of all, this is process black. Even though it is often treated like a spot color, this is process black (think 70% gray). If you are working in CMYK, you will probably need to create a separate swatch called something like Rich Black. If you are printing it in spot color, remember to specify that the press operator use dense black if it is important. Notice the slashed pencil. This color is yet another that cannot be redefined. By default it always overprints. To the right of the swatch you see the four-sided box that tells you this a CMYK color.

[Registration]: This color prints on all plates and is used for registration marks that must print on all colors. You can change the color that registration colored objects appear on the screen.

[Black] 21%: Here we have a tint of Black. As you can see from the swatch, it is a 21% tint, process color, CMYK. The little gray square that shows us process color shows up for CMYK, RGB, and LAB color. The only way you can tell which model is being used for the color is to look at the second icon just to the right of the process icon.

The final six swatches are gradient swatches. You can tell the top five are linear gradations and the bottom one is a radial gradient. It is a bit frustrating to have to add the gradients to the swatches palette to get any real control over them, but you get used to it after a while.

Swatches Panel Menu

When you are setting up your color palette for your book, you use the three dialogs seen here at the top of the Swatches Panel Menu: New Color Swatch..., New Tint Swatch..., and New Gradient Swatch....

The Mixed Ink Swatches have no use to use in self publishing. They are used for spot color work, mixing tints and shades of two spot colors. They are very complex, and none of the on-demand printing presses can use spot color anyway. This is for extremely top-end commercial printing. You can do amazing things, but not on-demand.

Save & Load Swatches

This gives you the ability to Save your custom swatches into a file which can be imported into any InDesign document where they are needed.

Add unnamed colors

This is not much of a problem for us any more, but colors used which are not named [and therefore showing in the Swatches panel], can cause bad printing problems with

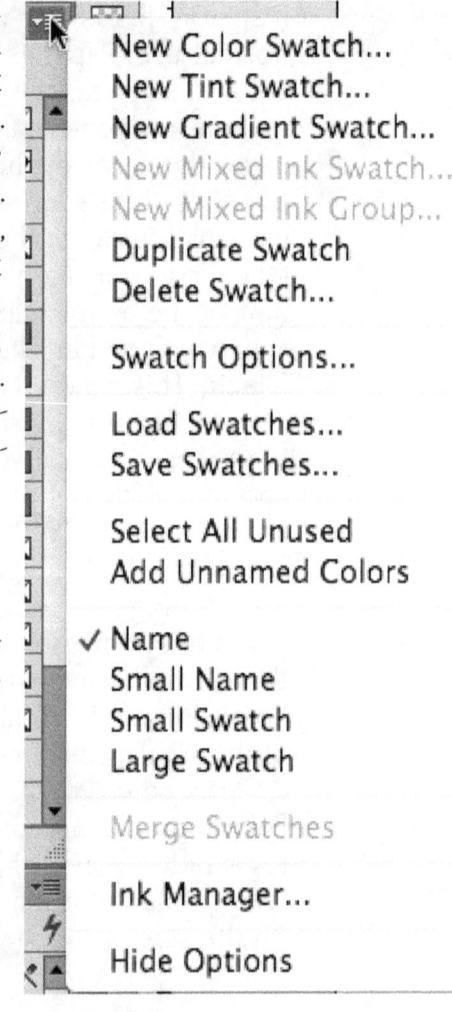

some companies. As long as you make all your swatches with the Add New... dialogs, this is not an issue.

List by name

Always use this one. If you do not, none of the icons we use to determine what type of color we are using are available. You can select a swatch within the panel and drag it up or down to arrange them for easy use. You don't have to do this, but sooner or later it will bite you if you don't.

Creating & Adjusting Swatches

The New Color Swatch dialog is where you start: Actually, you a truly better off if you start [before you've applied any color] by choosing Select All Unused in the panel menu and then delete. This will give you a basic panel with {None}, [Paper], [Registration], and [Black]. These are the four colors which cannot be deleted or changed. You can tell that by the fact that the color names are enclosed in brackets. [Paper] is editable in that you can adjust to be the color of your paper, but it prints white regardless. Plus, we do not really have paper choices as on-demand publishers.

Swatch Name: I still use the color values for the name. You should learn how to recognize color by its color com-

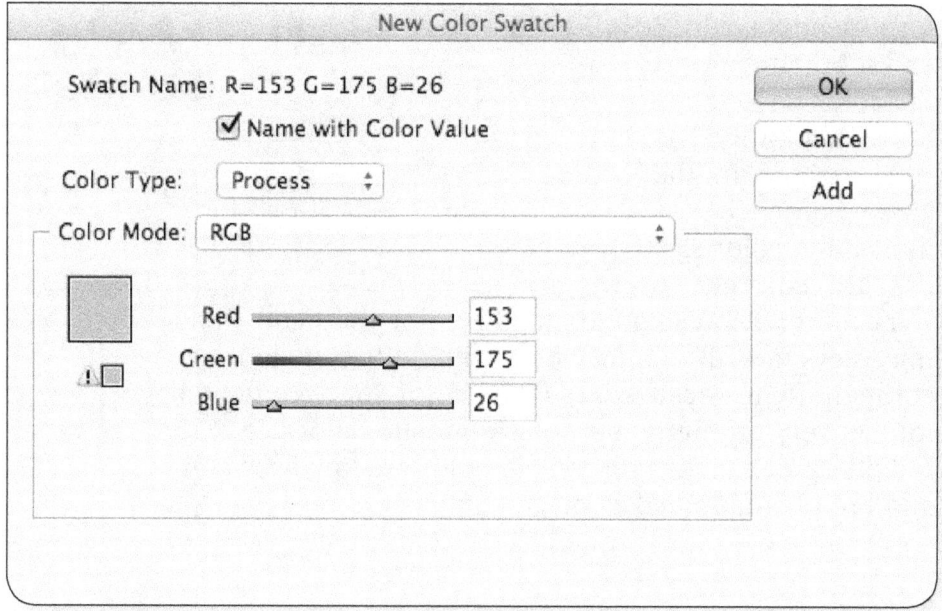

ponents. However, if you uncheck the box, you can name the color whatever you like: such as Dried Mustard or Competition Yellow.

Color Type: Here you have two choices: Process or Spot. Spot color is an important method of saving printing costs when printing traditionally. But on-demand printing always prints in Black & White or CMYK at this point. It cannot print RGB, because RGB is the color space of light not ink.

Color Mode: Our choices are CMYK or RGB. Technically, we should always use CMYK. But there are many problems here because CMYK is the color of ink and computer screens can only show color by blending the three RGB colors.

There can be a fairly radical color shift when converting RGB to CMYK. If you let Amazon or Lulu do it for you, there is no control of those color shifts. However, Createspace and Lulu both do better at matching what you see on your monitor if you send them RGB and let them convert the color for you.

Thankfully, as you can see in the New Color Swatch dialog, the color sliders are colored so

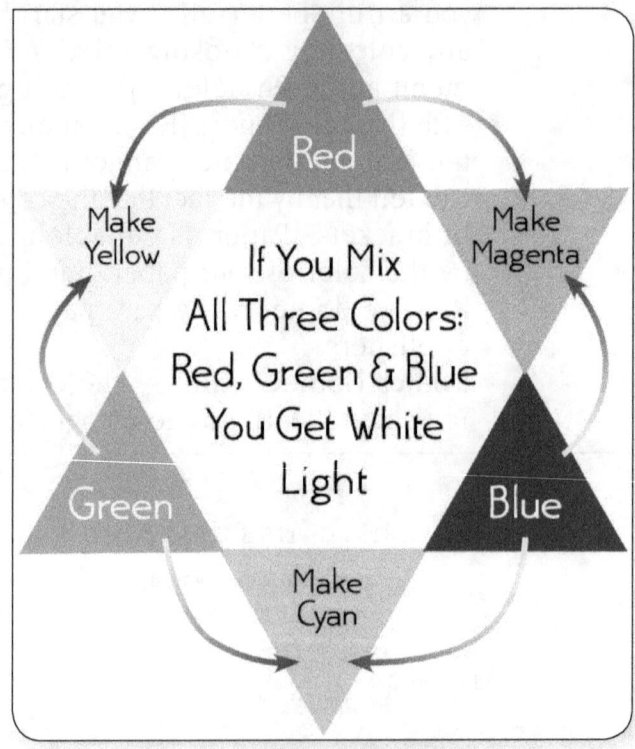

you can which way to go to mix the color you need. Building colors in RGB: You may have some difficulty building colors in RGB. Because this is the color space of light, it follows very different and polar opposite colors. In RGB, red plus green makes yellow; blue plus green makes cyan; and red plus blue makes magenta.

The New Tint Swatch Dialog

This capability is very important: because you can not imagine how complex it is to attempt to make a 35% tint of R=20, G=101, B=38. If you're curious it is R=173; G=201; B=179 (remember more light gives lighter colors). But with the Tint Swatch dialog, it is very easy. Setting up tints of your RGB colors is the best way to set up a color palette before you start your book.

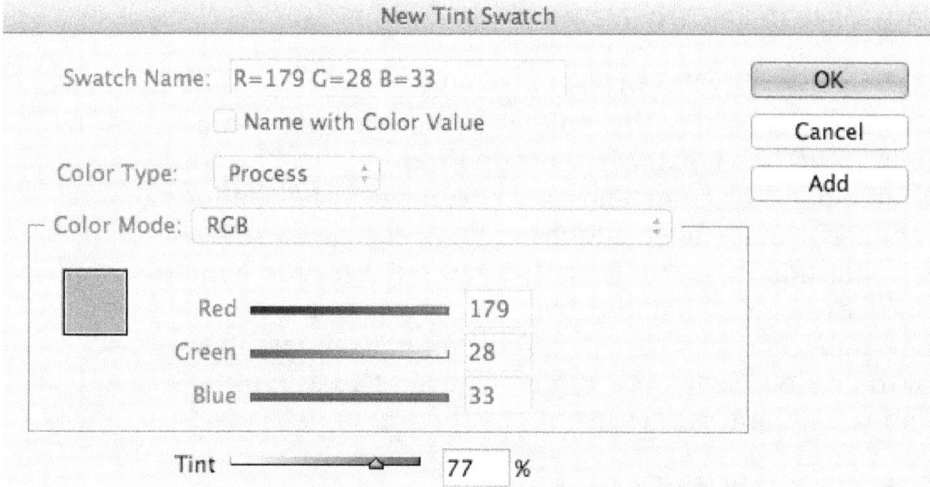

Another issue to remember is that unless the tints are listed as a swatch you cannot use them for building gradients. You will be forced to build all your colors individually, and that is tedious at best.

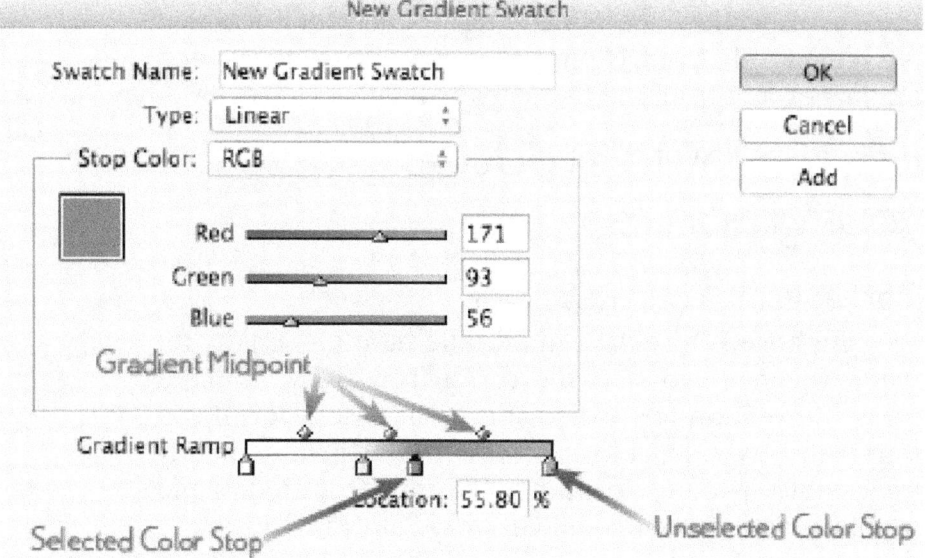

The New Gradient Swatch dialog

Gradients are really nice: I know I overuse them, but they give life to a page. The only real problem at this point is that HTML/CSS gradients are not available to ePUBs or Kindle KF8 books directly exported from InDesign. You can hand-code them for your ePUBs, and I am hoping that gradients will be available soon for ePUB export. You can have as many stops as you can fit on that bar [I think I did forty once in an early book].

The Gradient panel [not shown]

As mentioned, this palette is much tougher to use than the dialog box that comes up when you use the New Gradient Swatch command on the Swatches Panel Options menu. It's confusing to add the colors because there is no specification for them. There is a reverse direction button that has been added. But they are not named, They are not in the Swatches panel, so you cannot use them in any of the various styles you will be using. It's a waste of time and you do not want to use it.

The Color panel [not shown]

This one, also, should be forgotten. The New Color Swatch command is far more powerful and intuitive. This panel changes the color of whichever is active: stroke or fill. It does not add the color to the Swatches palette. Having unspecified colors roaming around your document is asking for disaster. Do not ever use colors in your documents except from the Swatches palette!

How & why to produce your graphics

Start everything in RGB color

Because PDF, ePUB, and Kindle have no penalty for color, you need to start there. You can always make a greyscale version for print, if necessary. However, if you start with greyscale, colorizing the images is often nearly impossible. If you are printing in color, most on-demand suppliers do better with an RGB image anyway. Those who require a CMYK image merely force you to make a color adjustment in Photoshop.

Start your Photoshop files in high resolution

Not only do you want color (where possible), but you also want the highest resolution you will ever need in any of your printed books or marketing pieces. Your modern ebooks (ePUBs and KF8) only support 72 dpi Web graphics at this point. But they need to be 600 pixels wide, at least. For the iPad, something like 1200 pixels wide would be excellent—but I can rarely use the resultant large book file sizes & KF8 has a 127K per image maximum.

Keep images in vector

We've covered what a vector image is. Because of all the different variations you will need for the various formats, you will do better to use vector illustrations as much as possible. These can be AIs (Illustrator files), PDFs (from InDesign or Illustrator), or EPSs (from FreeHand or Illustrator). However, you need to make sure you keep track of the original documents to allow for changes as necessary. None of the final vector images are editable except for .ai files.

Why vector?

It's the most adjustable: Because vector files can be resized with no problems and rasterized at any size or resolution you need, you can have one graphic master file for all your needs in the various formats. It is also much easier to change color spaces with vector images—especially if you are using InDesign for your drawings. The Swatches panel in InDesign makes conversions like this very easy— as long as you have sense enough to have a predefined color palette.

Let me cover some of the possibilities. InDesign works very well with Illustrator, for example. Of course, you can drop in native Illustrator (.ai) files. Because of the Links panel this is the best idea for AI files. What you may not realize is that you can bring in editable paths from AI. All it takes is a little set up to the application preferences.

In Illustrator you need to go to preferences ◇◇◇

In preferences you must set up the Clipboard options. If you have PDF or transparency options set up anything you copy and paste from Illustrator will come in as a non-editable object. However, if you uncheck PDF and check the option which says AICB [no transparency support] and check the button which says preserve paths, you can then copy and paste editable paths into InDesign.

Dictionary & Hyphenation
Plug-ins & Scratch Disks
User Interface
File Handling & Clipboard
Appearance of Black

Clipboard on Quit

Copy As: ☐ PDF
        ☑ AICB (no transparency support)
         ⊙ Preserve Paths
         ○ Preserve Appearance and Overprints

The art on the next page is an ellipse painted by a brushstroke from Illustrator. Let's give you a condensed description of the basic procedure:

- **In Illustrator, first I made a circle:** I chose the Ellipse tool and held down the shift key;

- **Picked a brushstroke and applied it:** These are found in the Brushes panel in AI;

- **Expanded its appearance (under the Object menu):** If I do not expand it, I will have no direct access to the paths and the copy paste will bring in non-editable paths;

- **Ungrouped it:** The brush shapes are attached to the path and bent to follow it;

- **Turned off Preview [Command+Y]:** so I could see the circle the brush artwork was attached to;

- **Deleted the original circle:** this is what would make the brush paths difficult to edit in InDesign;

- **Copied from AI;**

- **Pasted into InDesign;**

- **Selected object with the Direct Selection tool and cleaned up the brush work a bit;**

- Then I made and applied a gradient fill from Swatches.

- I checked Ignore Text Wrap in the Text Frame Options dialog box [Command+B]: and I added the type, breaking for sense and carefully spacing vertically.

InDesign's forte is graphic assembly

This ball of type was quickly created in just a few minutes with a brushstroke from Illustrator and a type-filled circle in InDesign.

The whole procedure I just described took less than a minute—real time. Well, actually, two minutes because I was careful to set the type well. So, I was able to copy/paste a complex drawing into editable paths in InDesign in less than a minute. Obviously, getting editable pieces from Illustrator is quick and easy.

Using the brushstroke as a frame

To make a radical change, I modified the size of the circle to overlap the brushstroke, and and moved it behind the brushstroke. Using the brushstroke as a frame, I pasted a picture of my home into the circle. This took another minute—with the result you see on the next page.

I added the type on top in another 20-30 seconds [the only glitch was that I had to set the new text frame to ignore text wraps as I had put a text wrap on the graphic automatically when I styled it with an object style]. Regardless, the whole thing was done in far less time than it took to write this explanation. It is dramatic if not too inspiring.

If I wanted a graphic I could use anywhere: All I would need to do is copy and paste the new graphic onto a new single page document, save it, and export it as a PDF [which I did]. If you are looking at this in an ebook, you can see it is in g l o r i o u s 600-pixel-wide RGB color—rasterized in Photoshop and exported as a JPEG. For the B&W book, I could have rasterized into Photoshop and saved as a Grayscale PSD at 300 dpi. This is the vector PDF.

A Minnesota winter at home!

You can do graphics like this very quickly In fact, if you have the pieces at hand, any graphic of this nature can be done in less than a minute. Fancy tables with inserted photos and complex typography can be created in a separate document and exported as a PDF to be used wherever needed at whatever size you need.

Graphic needs of the formats: Print, PDF, ePUB, & Kindle 8

The only other thing you need to understand about graphics is what works in which formats. You'll need to hand-adjust to produce the graphics for the various formats. Automation causes many problems. I'm just going to list the four options and their requirements, best formats, and so on.

Greyscale print with color cover

(Lulu & Createspace, plus professional on-demand) You need to be careful. This is digital printing and we are dependent upon the quality of equipment used by the vendors and the quality control exercised in their use. In general, I have had almost no problems with Lulu with print [but they are more expensive].

On the other hand, I have had many quality issues with Createspace. They are the 500 pound gorilla so we cannot ignore them. But, be careful and make sure your artwork is conservative. In all cases, the problem was solved by flattening Photoshop images or re-exporting PDFs limited to Acrobat 4 compatibility [which flattens all transparency]. In one case I had to rasterize a PDF at 300 dpi for a Createspace book. Don't argue. Just give them what they ask for.

* **Bitmap images:** 300 dpi grayscale PSDs, TIFFs, and PDFs. Lulu can handle layered PSDs with transparency. Createspace sometimes has trouble, although I've never had any issues with transparent backgrounds for either of them. Createspace sometimes drops color lighter than 10% (they have a tendency to print a little light).

* **Vector images:** PDFs, AIs, and EPSs. I use Acrobat 5 compatible PDFs for Lulu and Acrobat 4 compatible PDFs for Createspace. Lulu's printing of these images is much sharper. Createspace sometimes drops light tints.

Createspace's books are acceptable or better. Lulu's books are often excellent. This is on-demand digital printing—professional copiers using toner not ink.

Cover art

* **Lulu seems to prefer PDFs:** I use 300 dpi RGB bitmap images with vector lineart and type. Lulu provides a vector PDF of your ISBN artwork. You place it where needed. Their upload cover page gives you the necessary document size and spine widths. I assemble them in InDesign and export them with Acrobat 5 compatibility and have had no problems.

🌐 **Createspace demands Photoshop PDF files:** Their recommended workflow starts with assembling a layered PSD on their template. Their PNG template has a guides layer showing bleed trim areas and maximum area for type. You are required to leave a specific area for the ISBN and they imprint the ISBN into that area.

They leave very little room for type on the spine and enforce their rules strictly. They require 300 dpi RGB. Once you have all the type and images in place and saved as a layered PSD, you then flatten a copy and save it as a Photoshop PDF. They accept nothing else so far [mid-2013].

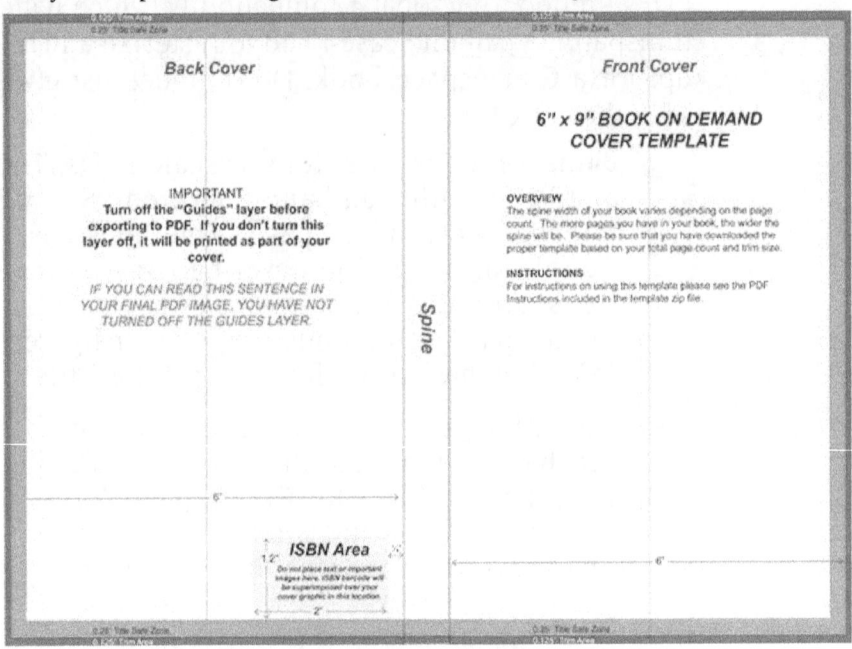

This required rasterization does soften the type (and often fattens it up quite a bit) and they can have problems printing rules thinner than three-quarter point on a colored background (though normally they can print half-point rules with no problem). Make sure your type is large enough and clear enough to handle this.

Color printing throughout (Lulu & Createspace)

I haven't done much full-color printing. When I have, I've used Lulu. Every thing I said about greyscale printing still applies. Lulu works well with CMYK. My best guess is that Createspace likes RGB better (they might require it). *Graphics In InDesign* was my first full-color book with Createspace. As far as I know there were no issues with it. As print sales shrink, full-color print becomes more viable [strange].

Downloadable PDFs (Lulu, Kindle Textbook, Adobe's Publish Online, & Scribd)

Now that Lulu has separated the downloadable PDF from the printed version, there is no reason to avoid full-color. The same is true with the other three options. Lulu can easily handle everything that you can print. Scribd is geared more toward the Word user and has trouble with fancy stuff. For example, Scribd has trouble with paragraph rules, in general, and ruins rules with gradients. Scribd seems to be using a non-Adobe PDF reader, but I have no proof of that.

The bottom line is that you need to be careful proofing Scribd's online PDFs. Also Scribd is more geared to free stuff. But they can give you a lot of eyeballs. I've found they work very well for customized free previews of your books. Adobe's Publish Online option from CC 2015 is a good option, but there's no way to charge for your work.

Lulu has always sold a lot of downloadable PDFs for me. That has slowed a lot now that they've moved PDFs to their own pages (they used to be a downloadable option on the print pages).

Kindle's Textbooks are encapsulated PDFs produced using the Kindle Textbook Creator [free]. They use the print PDF, though you can certainly convert the graphics to color. I've been surprised at how well they have sold.

- **RGB color**

- **Vector if possible**

- **Go for 300 dpi bitmaps:** unless the file size gets too large. Scribd seems to have problems with files sizes much over 5 MB. The other three do not seem to have those issues.

* **Acrobat 5 compatible:** seems to work for all of them.

EPUBs (iBooks, Lulu, Nook, and Kobo)

ePUBs and Kindle books will change radically in the next few years...

Think of this as Web design. It'll help conceptually. All graphics are bitmaps—no vectors allowed. The spec supports SVG, but that has not happened yet in reality. I suspect SVG import from InDesign is coming.

* **Maximum image size:** 600x800 pixels: this has become the interim standard. In specific, image sizes are a bit more complex. The iPad full page image size is 600x860. Nook takes 600x730 pixels. Kobo uses 600x800.The new iPad has a Retina display using 1200x1600 pixels. Some Android tablets are higher res.

* **RGB:** Use color to help

* **JPEGs or GIFs:** Supposedly PNGs work, as far as I know, but use the Save for Web option to help control file sizes.

* **Anchored objects above line for CC:** This preserves the graphics as well as possible.

Right now, iBooks is the one really pushing the envelope: They can handle custom-placed anchored objects, and gradients applied to type via paragraph styles. Single cell tables can be used for sidebars (with care). Embedded fonts work very well here. However, readers of ebooks tend to be unresponsive to better type. But that is because most "fancy type" is produced by the untrained using Word.

Kindle KDP (Kindle Direct Publishing)

If you have an Amazon account, you have a KDP account to publish your books on Kindle. They have the most current requirements listed there. The new format is called Kindle Advanced Typography [KFX], and it was developed for Fire. At present, things are a mess. I was converting my ePUBs with Kindle Previewer to use in KDP with no known problems. Then Previewer did not work with OSX.11 [El Capitan]. Now Kindle Previewer 3.0 seems to work fine. Plus there is a basic problem. Once Amazon gets a hold of them, they can (and do) change things without notice, outside of your control. The conversion from KF8 to KFX happens like that.

 The maximum image size was 127K: Even a byte or two larger and Kindle would resize your image (with very bad results). It was so bad they warned us. Supposedly that is no longer true. But a lot of it is at the whim of Kindle, often after the book is uploaded and released. The better typography of the KFX format is done that way.

You can use embedded fonts with the Kindle Fire: The problem is that the support of tablet reader apps tends to lag behind. They can do much of what is available to iBooks, but only if you own a Kindle Fire HD or Better. Depending on the version, what shows up in my iPad Kindle app varies. Strange because the MOBI files I produce for upload [or the ePUBs I upload] have the fonts and they read fine. So it is something Kindle is doing when converting the file upon upload.

Do all graphics anchored with styles

This comes and goes—as in the little Tip graphic above. In print it's easy—a drop cap graphic. In an ePUB, I can insert an anchored object before the return in the paragraph above. I can make it float left with a text wrap so it looks very close to what you see above, plus the graphic is in color in the ePUB. But page breaks can easily tear this up.

Positioning your graphics in your print version with object styles enables you to simply convert those styles to the Above Line or Custom anchored graphics now possible. CC basically requires all graphics to be anchored. Because of the minimal pixel width available, I still suggest 600 pixels wide images anchored slightly above line if the images contain useful information. I was floating smaller objects left and right with text wraps with unpredictable problems—so I quit it.

The problem is the lesser ereaders

Several of the lesser ereaders strip out all floating objects. So, Draft2Digital will upload a professional version of our ePUB2s with embedded fonts and no problems. But for Kindle KF8 and all the rest, you may need a radically dumbed down version.

Objects Anchored to Text

One of the nice things InDesign added many versions back is the ability to anchor an object to a location in the text. This makes it possible to have a graphic frame or a text frame floating next to a column of type that will move with the type. You can place these graphics very precisely, as you can see below.

The left side of the graphic, in the print version, is on the margin for the sidebars. In addition, I can make these objects behave in a mirrored fashion on opposite sides of the spine—floating right on the left page and floating left on the right page. This allows me to keep a column width next to the objects that remains readable. Of course, it also keeps the illustration side-by-side with the copy which discussed the graphic.

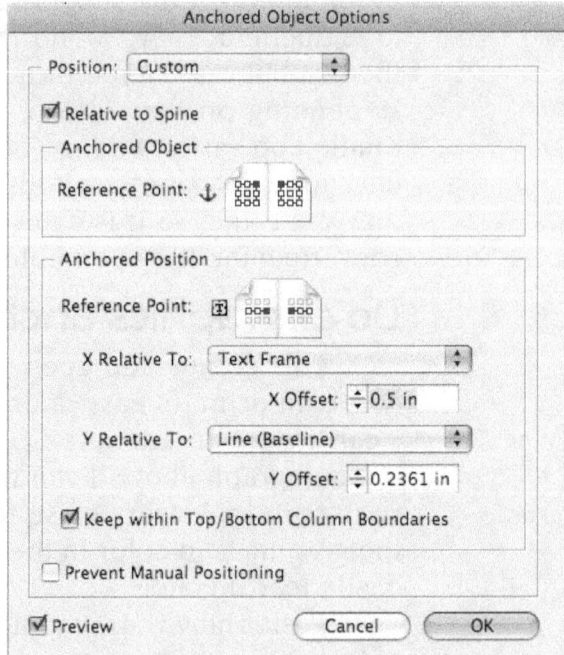

More than that, if you copy or cut the type and paste it in somewhere else the anchored object comes in along with the type in the column. If you cut the object itself, it keeps its anchored attributes. The good news is that you can simply turn on preview and make changes until you have what you want. The even better news is that these options are usually part of an Object style which I will cover next.

Position: Can be "Custom"or "Inline or Above Line". Custom gives you many options: a Relative to Spine checkbox, which proxy handle used to locate the position, and measured from which reference point in the text frame. I use Inline or Above Line for my conversions to ePUB because the controls for exporting anchored objects still need quite a bit of help.

Relative to spine: I am using this almost exclusively in this book and in almost all of my books. This way, if an anchored object is moved from the left page to the right page, the object changes sides. In this book, anchored objects are on the right on the left pages and on the left on the right pages. I wanted to keep the body copy to the outside edges of the book because it makes it easier to read and you do not have to break the spine of the book to do so (hopefully). This automates this choice.

Reference points: The top choice is for the handle of the object being anchored. The bottom choice is for the handle of the frame that contains the Anchored Object Character (AOC) .

X offset relative to: The horizontal offset can be measured from the anchor marker, the text frame, the column edge, the page margin, or the page edge using your chosen reference point.

The Y offset relative to: The vertical measurement can be measured from the line (baseline, cap height, or top of leading), the text frame, the column edge, the page margin, or the page edge.

When beginning, the measurements seem to defy logic: In most cases I find I have to adjust and readjust my anchored object settings to get what I want. That is one reason why I always add my anchored objects with an Object Style (which I will cover next). On practical level, I commonly have to move the objects after they are anchored. But they retain that new location without any issues.

Keep within top/bottom of column boundaries: This moves the anchored frame up or down so it does not extend beyond the top or bottom of a column.

Prevent manual positioning: You can lock it up so the frame is exactly where you want and cannot be moved. However, I always want to massage the location–at least a little.

This does take some practice

There are at least four ways to add an anchored object to your page. The one I recommend as the best (the 4th one in this little list) will be discussed at the end of the Object Styles section that follows this section on Anchored Objects. And I didn't even mention pasting in copy that already has an anchored object attached to it.

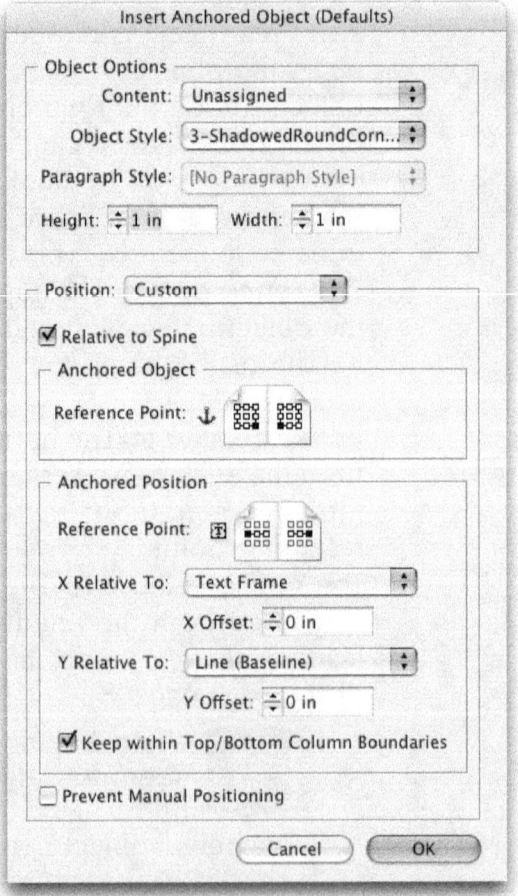

First: Inserting an object into an insertion point

This is the method that Adobe assumes you will be using. n general, this is very inefficient method of using objects. I do not recommend it because you have to set up every anchored object separately and because it demands many locally formatted adjustments to make it work. It does add several extra options at the top of the dialog box. I.

Content: You can choose the frame type: text, graphic, or unassigned. Of course, leaving it unassigned means you can use either option.

Object style: You can pick an object style to automatically be applied to the anchored object. As you will see in the next few pages, this enables us to preset these anchored object options and save it to a style.

Paragraph style: You can pick any paragraph style to be applied.

Size: Height & width of the frame added. You use this to make an anchored object a specific size (you must leave these fields blank if you don't want the original size of the graphic changed when you paste it into the frame).

The process is easy but a little complex. You use an insertion point in the text from which you want the object anchored. Then you choose Object» Anchored Object» Insert... . If you do this a lot you'll want to add a shortcut.

An invisible Anchored Object Character (AOC) is added at that point that looks like a Yen symbol (¥) in the color of your frame .

¥Anchored Object Character

An empty frame will be added that is anchored to that location. You can then add type to the newly generated frame or place a graphic into that frame. The frame will be anchored to the insertion point and move with the type.

Second: Converting an inline graphic

This is probably the easiest to understand. You place or paste a graphic into an insertion point—thereby creating an inline graphic. Then choose Object» Anchored Object» Options and follow the same procedure that I talked about in the first (Adobe-style) method. The options you set up in the Anchored Object dialog are applied to the selected graphic. Again, you have to do this for every object.

The problems with inline graphics: First of all, they add leading to the size of the graphic if you use autoleading. Second, they will be re-rasterized and ruined if you leave them inline for your ePUBs.

Third: Convert a graphic to an anchored object with an object style

Then cut it & paste it into an insertion point. It's almost like magic as the object just pops into position from the insertion point you choose. This is the best method for many reasons.

Text wrap limitations: There is one foible of anchored objects. If you want to put a text wrap around the anchored object, it will only wrap text starting with the line below the anchored object marker. So, you regularly need to make sure you add the AOC marker to the line above where you want the text to wrap around the object. You can copy and paste the object by copying and pasting the AOC, but because it has no width it is tricky to select and move just that character. It is far easier to just select the anchored object itself, cut it, and then place an insertion point where you want to be anchored from—and paste.

Fourth, and best: Here's a variant of three using the new Anchored Object Icon on your text frame

Drag from the Anchored Object Icon on the right side of the top edge of the frame to the insertion point location within the text you need then format and locate the anchored object with an object style: Most people don't use anchored objects much as they begin, but use them increasingly as they discover how well they work for sidebars and the like.

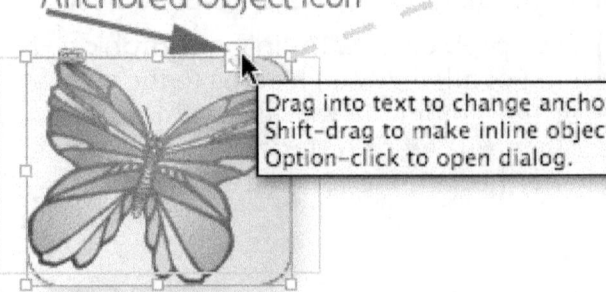

they work for sidebars and the like.

Anchored Object Icon

Drag into text to change anchor position.
Shift-drag to make inline object.
Option-click to open dialog.

CHAPTER FIFTEEN

Object styles

You can have styles for objects as well as text: This will enable you to more easily maintain a consistent look. In these new object styles, you can control everything found in the following panels:

Paragraph Styles	Text Wrap	Swatches
Stroke + Corners	Frame Fitting	Effects
Text Frame Options	Anchored Objects	Story

So: you can set any of the Text Frame Options, turn on Optical Margin Alignment, Adjust the Frame Fitting options, and control the anchored object settings. You can make styles for text frames and for graphic frames.

In addition, you can make any of the saved object styles into your default text frame style or default graphic frame style for automatic text wraps and the like.

This Is One Of Those Options That Is So Complex It Takes A While To Get Used To: As you can see on the next page, the dialog box is a bit complicated. But it will probably become one of your mainstays. Object styles may not seem to be as necessary as paragraph and character styles—but, they certainly help production speed once you have them set up—especially if you have a book like this which uses many graphics.

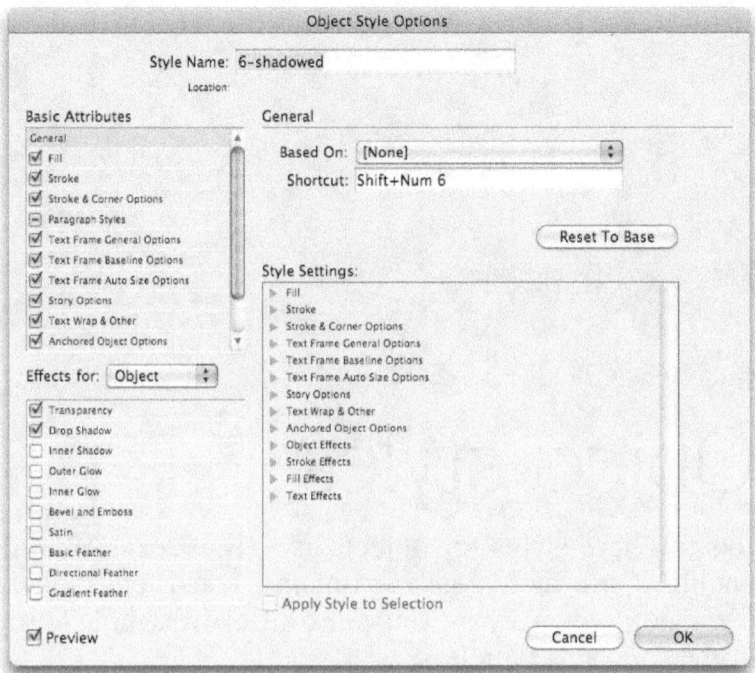

As in the paragraph and character styles, they give you global control of the look of your entire document. They really help with consistency of placed objects. Like with any style, if you edit a style every instance of use is changed. Of course object styles can be based on another style and all of the styles can be applied with shortcuts of your choosing.

Set up Object styles early

Adding anchored objects is a little tedious unless you have some object styles set up. As I discuss in the page layout chapter, designing your columns and sidebar areas before you start your book saves an immense amount of time.

There is no way I can tell how you are going to use object styles and anchored objects. All I can say is that you will use them and that you need to make plans before you begin bringing in your copy and graphics if possible.

As you become used to the idea, you will use it more and more in your layouts.

Then they are relatively easy to convert for use in your ePUBs. The new workflow by InDesign CC for exporting ePUBs basically requires all images to be placed with an object style. All inline graphics will be re-rasterized or worse.

The goal is to develop a set of paragraph, character, object, table, and cell styles that are available by default in all new documents you create.

One of the best uses of InDesign for graphics is in cover design

No other application comes close to the power to layout, produce and export a book cover in all its variations: front cover, front and back plus spine, slipcover for hard cover books, and so on.

Let's talk about that for awhile.

CHAPTER SIXTEEN

Cover design

This area of graphic design has been going through major changes throughout the past decade because of the nature of selling books online: Most of the traditional rules of cover design were geared toward displays at brick & mortar bookstores, magazine and book racks at supermarkets, and the shelf displays of the large discount houses like Wal-Mart, Sam's, Costco, and Target.

Until recently, an additional problem was that an author had no choice in cover designs if he or she was going with a traditional publisher. But, we are talking about self-publishing on-demand in this book. This means that virtually all your books will be sold online. Online sales mean that you need to have a cover design that reads well at very small sizes.

A list of thumbnail sizes in pixels

- **Lulu:** List size: 94 x 140
  Detail page size: 212 x 320
  Approximately 2x3 proportion but their ebooks specify a cover dimension of 612 x 792 pixels which is closer to a 3x4 proportion

- **Amazon:** List size: 60 x 90
  Detail page size: 164 x 242
  Their image specs are: Image dimensions

of at least 500 by 800 pixels; Ideal height/ width ratio of 1.6; Save at 72 dots per inch (dpi) for optimal viewing on the web. They currently ask for 1563x2560 pixels.

Nook: List size: 128 x 192
Detail page size: 300 x 450
A 2x3 proportion but their specs are: "Please make sure that your cover image is a JPG file between 5KB and 2MB. The sides must be between 750 pixels and 2000 pixels in length." Save at 72 dots per inch (dpi) for optimal viewing on the web [like 1300x1950]

Kobo: List size: 84x112
Detail size:150x200
Display size: 220x293
I've just been uploading a 600x800 JPEG

iBooks: List view 105x160
Detail: 220x330
Apple says they want 1440x1873

Scribd: List size: 129 x 167
As you can see, all of these images are very small in size. Worse yet, you do not get much control of them. As you can see you upload them at wildly varying sizes. These uploaded images are then downsampled into very small sizes by the Website. So, what are we supposed to do? I'll admit I do not have a definitive answer yet. But you want to make them exactly to size with the pixels dimensions they ask for. We will talk about a technique for doing this in Photoshop in a little bit.

Your cover design must be clean enough to work with massive reductions in size

What do we know for sure?

Many covers are close to 2x3: Amazon says the ideal is 2x3.2, a 6x9 book is 2x3 in proportion. So let's start with that.

The other standard is 3x4: We need to leave top and bottom margins which allow for adjustments: Lulu's ebook covers, for example, are specified to be 612x792. That divides out to 77% or about 3x4, as I mentioned. In practical terms, this means that I must take my 6" x 9" cover and reduce it to 6" x 8" to get the proper proportions. That's interesting because most people tell us that the maximum image size for an ePUB is 600 x 800 pixels [which is the same proportion].

We need color to the edges: If we leave a white background on the cover, the thumbnails get lost on the page. In fact, several of the companies specifically warn about covers with no background color.

At the small sizes the typography needs to be extremely readable and legible: This is not an problem solved by fancy, swirling type overlaying a complex photo. We really need to work at the legibility of the type. Basically we need to follow the dictum of billboard design: 8 words maximum, sharp contrast between the type and the background, nothing subtle, because all subtlety will be lost as you whiz by the billboard at 60 miles per hour. Remember, that large type at 48 point will be reduced to five point or even less for the thumbnails.

Here are a couple of ideas:

- **One:** We can design the cover to be pure type reversed out of a dark background so we can freely resize it as necessary. The type block should be separate from the back ground so we can avoid type distortions as we resize the background to fit the various proportional needs.

- **Two:** We must carefully redesign the cover to fit each particular circumstance. This is going to be a particular problem if our book simply requires a photo or image on the cover. Obviously, any images used must be sharp enough and with enough contrast so the image is discernible at a half inch or so. Or, they must be so lacking in contrast that we can overlay the type without losing legibility.

The current solution

I now design my book covers as vector PDFs—always. If I have any bitmapped images like photos or other Photoshop artwork I make sure it does not compromise the legibility of the type. I leave large enough borders on all four sides so that I can crop the various covers as needed.

In Photoshop, I have set up custom presets in the Crop tool for Lulu, Kindle, Nook, Kobo, and the iBookstore. Then it is very easy to open my PDF into Photoshop with sufficient resolution to enable me to crop to size. It is never a perfect process, but it has greatly streamlined production of the various cover sizes necessary.

There is no easy solution

First of all we must reduce the copy to a minimum. Online covers are no place for lengthy epistles listing all the content. All there is really room for at these small sizes are the book title and your name. Even a subtitle can be a problem if it is too long. Let me show you a book I did several years ago and the two covers I finally used. It gave the start toward what we are talking about here.

The cover on the left was the original designed for print. I really like it in color on the printed books. But in the online listings, it was always broken up very badly.

As you recall, even the large image on a Lulu detail page is only 212 x 320 pixels. At that size the color still looked very good, but the type was starting break up to the point where readability was bad & I risked poor reader reactions. Yes, the capture from Lulu on the right page looks a bit better than this on the computer screen—but not much. So, when I went to the ePUB version I did the image on the right above. Is that as pretty? No. But it is legible, readable, clear in concept, and probably produces a much better reader reaction when it is seen in a list on the screen.

Looking now I can see I should have made my name larger on all the covers—for I am selling my supposed expertise. In addition, I've been told that it's gauche and a sure sign of amateurism to use the word "By" in front of my name. I fully believe that is a mere fashion of the day, but what do I know? The main thing to recognize is that the author name is commonly more important than the subhead.

I now believe that the real solution is on the side of the ePUB version, but I would want to do a bit more to it and tweak the typography a bit. What is in no doubt is this, the second version has much more impact at small sizes.

InDesign 7.5 On-Demand

By David Bergsland

View this Author's Spotlight

Part of the Wattpad Marketplace

Paperback, 154 pages ☆☆☆☆☆   This item has not been rated yet

Price: $12.95

Ships in 3-5 business days

Help for authors & teachers publishing in the new millennium The focus of this book is very sharp. It is designed for people who are designing books and booklets with very limited capital and few personnel resources. It is a sharing of techniques for the new wave of author/pastor/teacher/designers who need to get their work published digitally & online.

Finally, make sure you look at the covers used by your competition. It's likely they'll show you a design style you should use to look appropriate. But the entire process of cover design is an art, not a science. No one has definitive answers—merely informed opinions.

However, amateur covers are obvious!

The number one mistake is made by adding all kinds of fancy trimmings to your type. Not only does it make the type much harder to read, but all trained designers have been strongly told that NO ONE EVER does that. As a result, there are very few professional covers with type stylized like that. If it is, the type is carefully embossed, maybe beveled, using the minimal amount necessary to get the required effect. If the reader notices the type, the quality reaction to the cover is compromised.

Look at how easy it is to read the top sample. In color, the middle one is almost completely unreadable. But as you can see, even with careful embossing, the bottom example is also much more difficult to read. The extra space between the T and i make even the top title quite bad. Always kern your titles.

The point is simple. If there are any compromises in readability with the full size artwork, by the time you downsample for the tiny online images, that artwork will not be readable at all. In fact, as you can see to the left

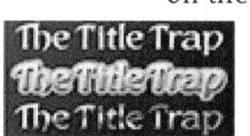

on the next page, even the plain type on the top is difficult to read because all the thin places of the font disappear at this 100-pixel-wide version. You must be sure that you look at your cover designs in a small size to determine the readability of your design. It is absolutely crucial.

Readability is the goal of book typography

In a similar vein, we need to mention that lowercase is more than twice as readable as all caps. Plus, lowercase can be made much larger on a cover because lowercase is much shorter than all caps.

Finally, the readability of the font is very important. In the two examples to the left, both the top version [set in Buddy] and the bottom version [set in Contenu] are far easier to read than the colored samples [set in Cutlass]. In fact, you should be able to see that Contenu is much more readable than Buddy. But you see a simple background color hurts the readability of these also.

The Title Trap

The Title Trap

The Title Trap

The Title Trap

Your name

In the same vein, your name needs to be very easy to read also. Your name is really your franchise. Your most recent book is simply a small addition to the platform.

Because all of our discovery is online, these things are crucial to our overall book design. None of it can be separated out. The cover, description, keywords, title, and so on are all equally important in the presentation of your book to your readers.

Now it is time to take a little break and go through the design of a cover. This was an actual project a year ago, and I am making no value judgment on it either good or bad. The techniques used are typical.

Don't forget the complex background problem

The bad type issues we've just covered are usually severely exacerbated by the complex photos upon which the type is dumped. This is an epidemic with new non-professional self-publishers. It's much worse in novels, but, even in non-fiction, full-bleed photos [covering the entire front cover from left to right and from top to bottom] are the most common background for the title, subtitle, and author name.

Ghosted images

I commonly see lightened or darkened images set in the background of text blocks. The result is absolutely unreadable blurbs on the back covers and severely compromised titles on the front covers.

If the background has a lot of complex high contrast detail, your type does not stand a chance—even if it is a good font set well. White type will not be seen in front of the light or white portions of the photo just as black type will not be seen over the dark areas of a photo. An image which is constantly going back and forth ruins any hope of type readability.

There is no way to fix this problem except to get a better photo. You might place a light or dark rectangle behind the type, but that usually ruins the photo. Just imagine poor Gus [the Corgi] if his picture was reduced to a cover icon 100 pixels wide—and you can simply forget about the type.

A lot of your sales decisions will be based on the professionalism of your cover—like it or not!

CHAPTER SEVENTEEN

A cover tutorial

Something has come to my attention I should have noticed long ago: People do not have any idea how to apply effects to type because they have no experience with being able to add radical styling to live type.

Stylizing live type— only in InDesign

I forget that no one else allows you to even apply a gradient to live type. Illustrator requires you to convert your type to outlines and Photoshop requires you to rasterize it. InDesign lets you simply select it and apply a gradient—of any kind to the stroke and/or fill. In fact, in InDesign you can apply all the Effects available in InDesign—and that is quite a few. But this goes quite a bit further.

So, what I want to do is a small real world example to give you some ideas what can be done. I received a tentative proof of an idea for a book cover. The man who sent it is brand-new to designing in InDesign. He is actually doing very well—given his lack of training.

I critiqued it quite hard. I sent him back an annotated PDF with a dozen or so suggestions for improvement. I told him I thought it looked mid-century modern, and wondered if that would be effective for his audience (I have no idea as I have not looked into that market).

He wrote back that he was going for a similar look to one of his old King James Bibles with a black leather cover. I had no real idea what he was referring to, but I tossed off a quick idea to send back to him.

It turns out that stunned him, He had no concept of what could be done along these lines. I suggested some Photoshop tutorials and he went to look at some of them. His response was that he was amazed at what could be done, and he would let me know what he decided. He also suggested that I add this tutorial—here's what he sent.

One] Make new document with bleed

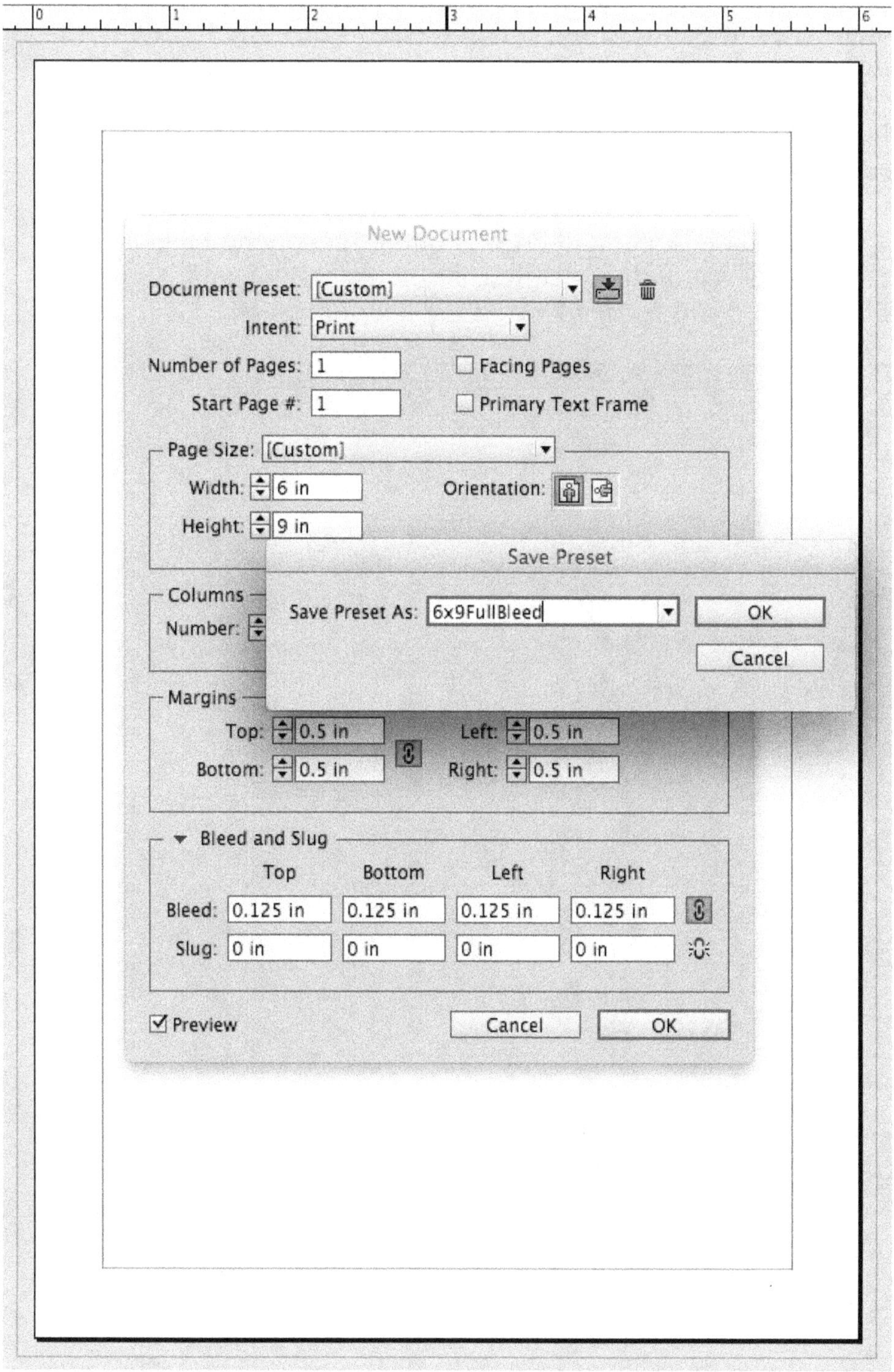

New Document

Document Preset: [Custom]

Intent: Print

Number of Pages: 1   ☐ Facing Pages

Start Page #: 1   ☐ Primary Text Frame

Page Size: [Custom]

Width: 6 in   Orientation: 📱 📱

Height: 9 in

Columns

Number:

Margins

Top: 0.5 in   Left: 0.5 in

Bottom: 0.5 in   Right: 0.5 in

▼ Bleed and Slug

	Top	Bottom	Left	Right
Bleed:	0.125 in	0.125 in	0.125 in	0.125 in
Slug:	0 in	0 in	0 in	0 in

☑ Preview   Cancel   OK

Save Preset

Save Preset As: 6x9FullBleed   OK

Cancel

This is simple, but not often thought of before you do it awhile. I commonly make my graphics documents square and the same width as my column. But for this one I am doing a 6x9 cover and I want the ink to go to the edge of the printed cover. So, I need a bleed. You need to carefully look at the cover requirements at the various suppliers. If you have any questions write them or write me.

In addition, I made a New Document Preset by clicking on the Save Document Preset button. This opened the Save Preset As: dialog. I called the new preset: 6x9Full-Bleed—so I could recognize it in the list of presets.

Two] Add background layer for a template

Next I added a new layer. As you can see I eventually used six layers. Into the new layer I placed the PDF proof I was sent. Then I selected the actual graphic by clicking on the little selection donut in the center of the graphic window. I resized the PDF to fit the new margins of my document. I hit Command+ Option+ C to make the frame fit the resized content. I do not care at all that the original PDF is distorted quite a bit.

With the resized graphic selected, I went to the Effects panel and lightened it significantly by changing the opacity. I do not want the template graphic to confuse me as I draw on top of it. The final step was to lock the new layer. This gives me a guide to draw over—so I can keep the proportions correct. I am going with all new type, so that part of it doesn't matter at all.

Three] Find some leather

One of the things often forgotten when you are doing your own designs for the first time is the simple fact that your background does not have to be blank paper. You can add anything you like as a background color. If you look at the cover of the second editions of *Writing In InDesign* book, for example, you will see that I have put a computer keyboard as a background image. I couldn't find what I liked, so I laid my laptop keyboard in the scanner and scanned it.

For this tutorial, my friend said his concept was an old KJV leather Bible. So I need an image of black leather. There are countless sources for images—and you can easily pay $300 for an excellent one. However, in this instance we are merely looking for texture. We will not get into copyright issues here, but you need to be sure you understand this. Use nothing without rights to it. So, where shall I look?

Sources for free images

- **Wikimedia Commons:** This visual adjunct to the open source online encyclopedia is filled with free images [well over 12,000,000 images at this point]. If you need an attribution, the page will tell you and give you the copy to use.

- **MorgueFile:** This site, MorgueFile, is not ghoulish. A morgue, in designers parlance, is the collection of images you build to use for reference as you draw your illustrations. This site has over 250,000 free images plus images for sale.

- **Pixabay:** A relatively new site with many free images—some of which are very good.

- **My camera:** If you can shoot photos, you have the best images you can use, because there is no question about copyright, at all.

  Just make sure you have any people used in your images sign a model release. You can Google for sample Model Release Forms. This will give you permission to use their images without problems. *Make sure you have permission to modify their images.*

For this tutorial I went to MorgueFile. I searched for leather textures and quickly found a photo of black leather which will work perfectly for what we need.

I downloaded it. Then I opened it in Photoshop [immediately saving it as a PSD], and cleaned it up—saving it at 300 dpi and 6.25" x 9.25" for print use. For a similar bleed on this book, I would use 7.25" x 10.25". The cover must be one-eighth of an inch larger than the trim on all four sides.

Four] Place leather in bottom layer

It will be the foundation for everything we build. At this point, I added a new layer (by clicking the little new layer button at the bottom of the panel) and dragged it just above the leather. I unlocked the original template and move it on top of the whole pile and relocked it. (I also deleted layer 6 which just held the labels for the capture a couple of pages ago. I may want to make it even more transparent so I can work through it and still see what I am doing.

I moved the leather into position, so it covered the entire page including the bleed. I then adjusted the handles of the frame enclosing the leather image to mask it to the exact size of the bleed. If I had needed to move the image around I would have selected the donut in the middle of the frame to select the actual graphic. The color of the handles should change so you can tell what you are working with as you move either the content of the frame or the frame itself.

Five] Draw the top triangle

With the template on top and the leather on the bottom—both locked—it was a simple three click process to trace the triangle on the template with the Pen tool. I worked on a layer between the template and the leather. I choose a strong brilliant yellow-gold to color the triangle. I make it strong and bright because I was going to be making it transparent and additive to the leather texture. This process will radically tone down the color. If I do not make it strong enough, it will disappear completely when I adjust it.

Six] Adjust the transparency

With the new triangle selected and colored: I open the Effects panel and make the triangle 36% transparent—adjusting the look by eye. I also use the Multiply mode which takes the colors of the triangle and adds them to the underlying leather texture. The result is something that looks like a transparent gold covering of the leather. To make it look more real I need to deboss it a little to make it look like it is slightly stamped into the surface of the leather.

Modes in Effects

I've mentioned Modes. Modes were originally a Photoshop thing designed for working with layers.

Modes change how layers interact: A mode will cause the selected object to interrelate with layers and objects below it. Let's look at some quick definitions.

Normal: What do you think? Everything remains normal and the layer does not interact with the layers below it. I think of it in terms of opaque overprinting, but then that is probably just my experience.

Multiply: This basically adds the color of each pixel of the layer to the colors of the pixels under that pixel. In other words, it makes the image darker.

> This is the way to darken and add detail to a very light image. Simply copy the image into a duplicate layer (drag the layer to the New Layer icon) and apply the Multiply mode. For severely light images, you might have to do this several times with varying opacities in the various layers. For some reason, several light transparent layers often work better than trying to do it all in one layer. It is an extremely handy mode. Shadows always multiply.

Screen: This mode is the opposite of Multiply. You can use this to lighten areas. I have seen images which looked totally black on the screen reveal astonishing detail and/or add highlights through the application of Screened duplicate layers.

Overlay, Soft Light, and Hard Light: These three modes apply different combinations of Multiply and Screen using 50% gray as neutral. In other words, they apply effects to the highlights and shadows.

> Overlay, for example, uses the dark tones to darken the dark areas while the light tones lighten the light areas. Hard Light really exaggerates the highlights, often

causing a *"plastic"* look. These modes
can be used very well with filters like
Emboss where the flat area is 50% gray.

Color Dodge or Burn: These two modes increase contrast by intensifying the hues or increasing the saturation (same thing). Color Dodge lightens as it brightens. Color Burn mainly deepens and intensifies the shadows.

Lighten and Darken: These modes work by comparing the pixels in the upper layer with those in the lower one. They do this channel by channel for all the channels. Lighten only makes changes when it finds a pixel in the upper layer that is lighter than the ones in the lower layer. Darken works oppositely by changing only pixels that are darker.

Difference: Here's one of those mathematical wonders. It compares the upper layer and the image below it using black as a neutral. If there is no difference in color between the two, those pixels are changed to black. It usually results in more saturated color, often psychedelic. It's great for professionally ugly stuff. As you can imagine I rarely use the filter.

Exclusion: This is a more subdued version of Difference that creates much less saturated colors (that is, they are grayed out). It is often even more ugly than Difference IMHO.

Hue, Saturation, and Luminosity: Here we have computer geek speak. For those of you with fine art training, these would be hue, saturation, and value. In each case, the mode takes that particular information from the overlying layer and applies it to the image beneath. Hue changes the colors only. Saturation changes the intensity only. Luminosity changes the value (or grayscale info) only.

Color: This mode applies both the hue and saturation – everything except the value.

The key is remembering that all of these
modes can be applied to anything selected,
and they can be applied transparently

One thing where InDesign again demonstrates its superiority is that you can have separate modes and transparency for the fill, stroke, type, and/or the object as a whole. This is immensely helpful and no other application has anything that even comes close to this level of control. It gives you great power in manipulating text frames, as you can imagine.

They remain editable

Effects can always be edited: Just double-click on the *fx* in the Effects panel. They work with live type, text frames, graphic frames, and/or the contents of graphic frames. InDesign effects are immensely powerful and very useful to add graphic touches to your designs. Don't go overboard—only add them if they help your readers.

Remember the adage: If you can't think of a good reason to use an image, color, or effect—don't do it!

Before I could adjust the transparency there were two more things I needed to do.

First, I copied the new triangle and pasted. I clicked the flip vertically and the flip horizontally buttons in the Control bar—and dragged the triangle into position below.

Second, I dragged the layer with the transparent triangles down to the new layer icon and released it there. This made me a duplicate of the layer on top of the first one.

As you will see, when you try this on your screen, this will intensify the color [because it is in multiply mode]. Every time you do it, you basically double the intensity of the Multiply effect in its interaction with the leather texture.

Adjust the intensity by using the opacity slider at the top of the Effects panel.

Then I selected both the triangle layer and its copy (by holding down the shift key and clicking on each layer). Finally I selected Merge Layers from the Option menu of the Layers panel. This saved the look I had developed and made it into one layer. As you can see on the page to the left, this looks surprisingly realistic—even in grayscale.

Finally, I clicked the little *fx* button at the bottom of the Effects panel to add an effect to the selection. Then I chose Bevel and Emboss and made the settings you see below for a subliminal debossing into the leather.

I wanted it very subtle to keep it realistic: The only trick here is that the lower triangle is rotated, so I needed to make the embossing for it up instead of down to keep the shadows on the right edges. It's keeping track of the little details like this which makes the illusion realistic.

Seven] Set the type

I added the type into the two triangles. I carefully kerned it to get the letterspacing looking professional. Then I added a slight deboss (emboss down, remember). It was still not enough to set off the type. So, I added a quarter-point white stroke to the type. This is so thin that it is almost subliminal—but you'll be surprised at how much it makes the type pop out.

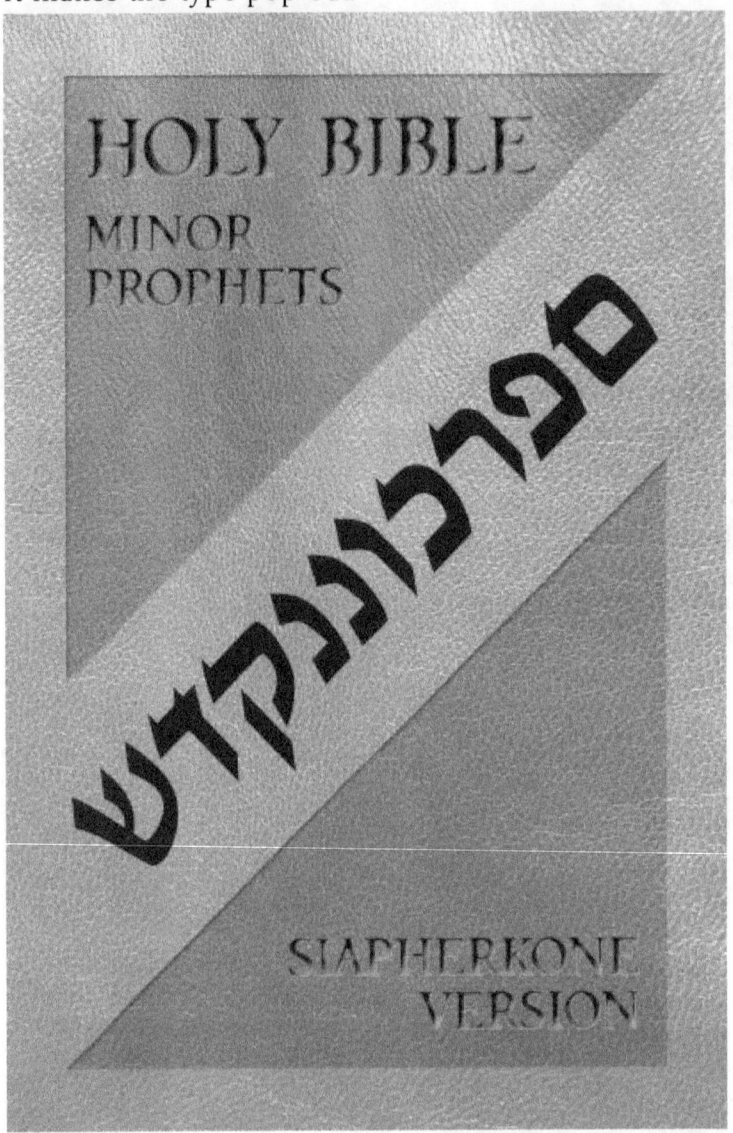

The type still did not have enough contrast to I went to the leather layer and lightened that a bit. I made it 75% opaque (which I later changed to 80%). I think it would work better in color if I made the leather brown also. However, black leather is the choice of the client, in this case. Client choice always trumps a designer's personal taste. As you see above, the type looks like it is carved or stamped into the leather.

Eight] Add the Hebrew

I saved the Hebrew type into a separate file in Illustrator where I could simply copy/paste the type into the InDesign document. If I had the font I could have set it in Hebrew—but all I had was the original PDF. So I dropped it in and it looked like what you see on the opposite page. **The next thing I wanted to do was give the Hebrew an illusion of metal—gold in the color version:** I started this process by making the type a pale yellow. For, as you know, gold is basically a yellow. It needs to be a clean yellow with no blue or greenish hints. I used a new swatch set at 0 cyan, 20 magenta, 90 yellow 0 black. Using this swatch, I colored the type a 35% yellow tint.

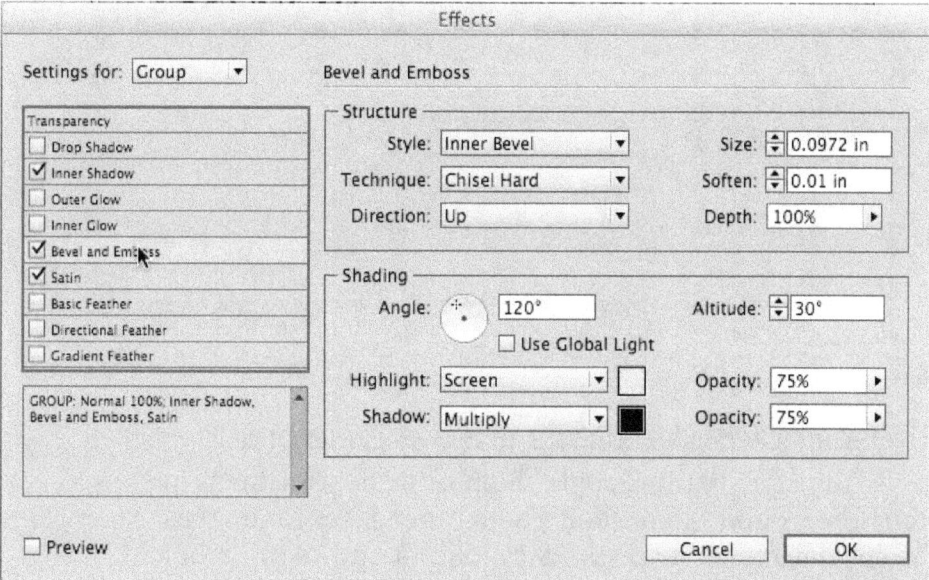

Next I added a set of effects by clicking on the *fx* button at the button of the Effects panel. When it opens, I choose Bevel and Emboss set to 100% depth, up, and the rest of the settings you see in the shading area. In addition, as you can see I added a slight softening with the Satin effect. Finally I added a little bit of inner shadowing. I should mention I added color to the highlights and shadows. If you look closely at the capture above, you'll notice that I changed the highlight and shadows to a gold and brown respectively.

I did the same thing with the inner shadow. When I clicked on the colored box to the right of the mode popup,

I opened the Effect Color dialog. It opens to Swatches, but you can change this to RGB or CMYK and pick the color you like. You can see I picked a warm brown: 15 cyan, 64 magenta, 100 yellow, and 20 black.

The final result looks pretty good, considering it was all done in InDesign. Yes, I can be much more fancy in Photoshop. But it is not necessary. As you can see on the next three pages, this will do fine.

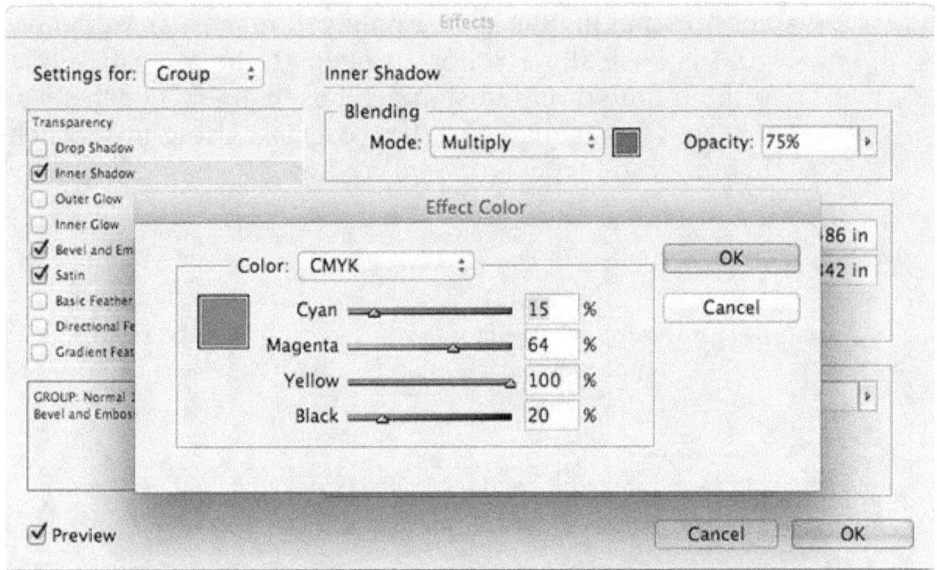

These Photoshop effects are available online

You can simply Google them or search for them in YouTube. You will find step by step procedures for dozens of special effects by Deke McClelland and many other designers. Just make sure you actually need a special effect and work hard to keep any type stylized by these effects readable.

I used Deke's instructions to make the Hebrew on the photoshopped version of the type two pages forward. It does look much fancier, but the readability is compromised quite a bit. The version on the opposite page will probably work best.

Of course, Photoshop does kick it up a notch: as you can see in three pages. But it's not necessary.

The title page image

The final stage in cover design, is to rasterize it as a 300 dpi grayscale image which you can use on your title

page. The only problem you will have with this is that your margins are different proportionally than your page size. There is almost never a reason or an opportunity to use a full-bleed image on a title page. The margins are a much more narrow rectangle. You will have to come up with a solution for that issue. In many cases you will need to build a separate grayscale cover image to use.

A couple of special concerns: If you are printing with Createspace they will require a .75" interior margin for smaller books and a one inch margin for those over 400 pages or so. Actually, this is the distance from the spine edge of the page to the type. But, they will rigidly enforce this rule. This is why many books drop the background entirely and simply use the styled type from the cover.

Another difference with the title page image is that, in most cases, you will be adding the publishing house logo and the locations where it will be published. This is not absolutely essential, but it is commonplace. It is one of the things you can do to make your book look more professional.

If you are using Lulu, Lightning Source, or another printer, they will assume you are professional enough to know what is required. Make sure you leave a three-quarter inch margin for the type on the cover at the spine side, as mentioned.

Other than that all you have to do is rasterize the cover PDF to produce your ebook covers plus the small JPEG's needed for your blog postings, FaceBook and Goggle+ postings, and situations like that.

[Between you and me, this Hebrew, stylized in Photoshop, is not as easily readable. Plus, it does not convincingly lie on the page.]

Deke's Photoshopped version

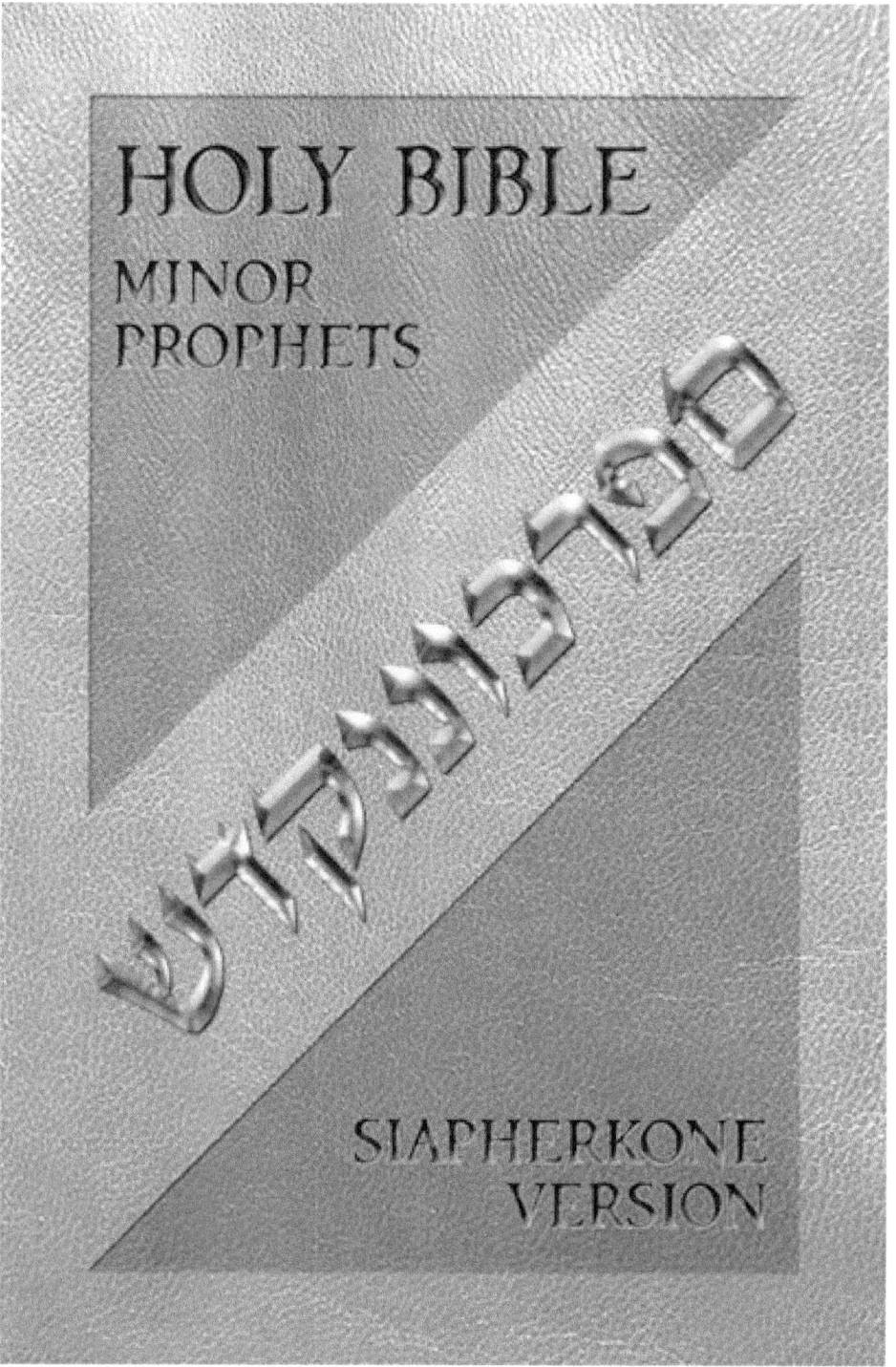

Another quick cover for some more concepts

This is one I did for my book, *The Wife Of Jesus.* I was looking for something dramatic to catch the eye. The response to the cover has been superb. Of course, here in the print version, the greyscale images have much less impact.

First, I went looking for a cover image

I started with Pixabay. After a few searches for wife, love, and whatever else I tried, I came across this one which really struck me.

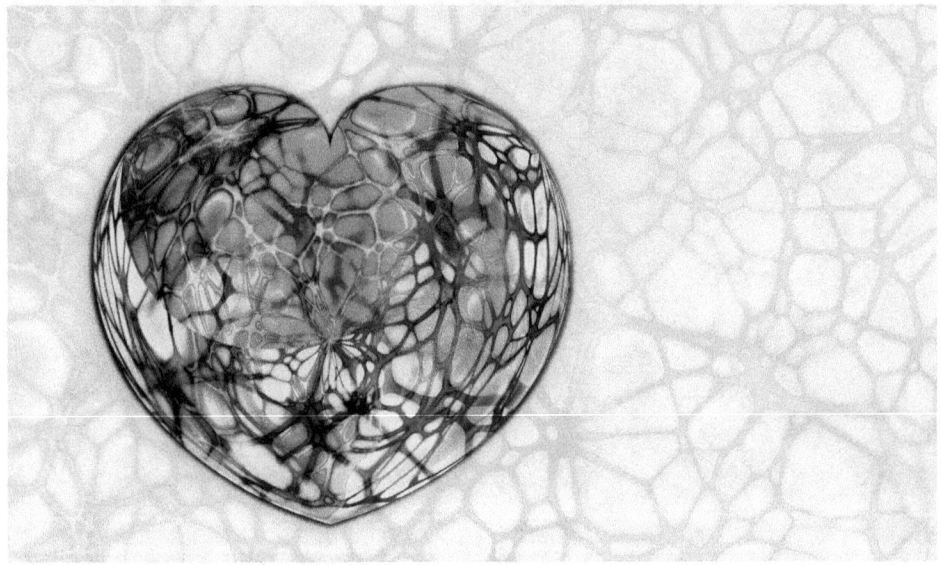

Now, I have no real idea why, but it clicked. It's a huge photo: 5395 px x 3122 px. I need this to make it into a functional cover.

The problem, of course, is there is no room for type on this image. The cover is 7"x10". There's no way I can keep that glorious heart within the margins. Plus the background is too dark and busy.

So, the first thing I did in Photoshop was too draw a path around the heart with the Pen tool. Yes, it is the same Pen tool we have in InDesign. This underscores the need to learn how to use this tool. It is a wonderful selection tool for Photoshop.

Once I had the heart selected. I moved it and shrunk the size as you can see below.

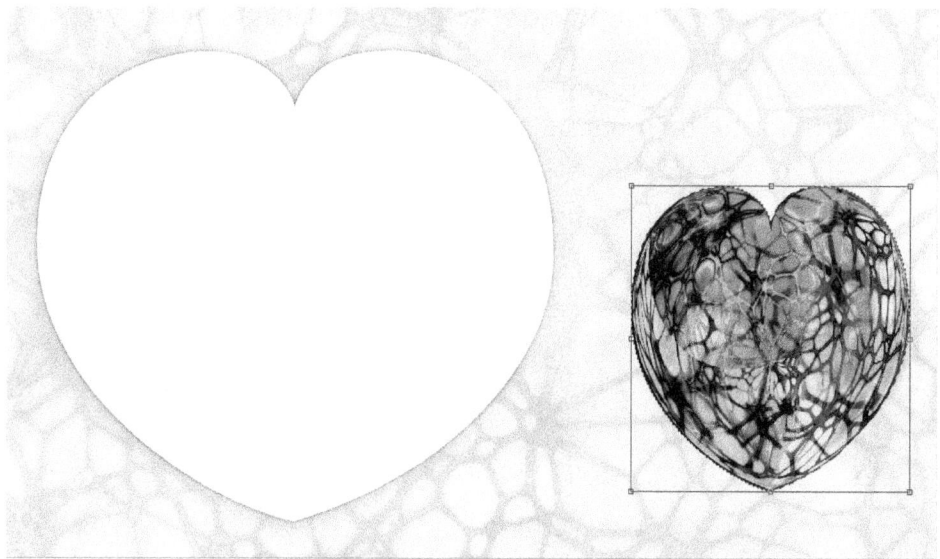

I knew it would take several adjustments, so I cut and pasted the heart into a new layer in Photoshop so I could play with it better. Photoshop is essential to keep the sharpness we need for a professional cover.

Jesus' Wife
No. It's not Mary Magdalene

David Bergsland

The first attempt was pretty poor.

The heart was too round and didn't fit the space well. Plus, I had to do something with the book title. Jesus' Wife simply didn't read right. But I wanted those two words large enough to be easily read in a thumbnail. The sub-title is not important, other than the use of Mary Magdalene as a keyword for SEO purposes.

So, I moved it to the bottom. I reshaped the heart. Once I got it on the page in position, I fixed up the typography of the name. *The* and *of* are not important words. Plus, I believe that even a hint of them will enable all the readers to fill them in with no trouble. So, I made them very small.

In addition, the blank back ground was boring at best. So, I added a border, used it to hold the publisher logo, and used the Multiply mode to dark the background outside the border. Finally I added a small red cross in the center of the heart, set slightly opaque with a thin white stroke. The final result is:

The final result is all vector, except for the heart with its background

The exported PDF will work great for the Print PDF and the downloadable PDF. Photoshop will do an excellent job of rasterizing this cover to whatever size is required by the ebook distributors.

- The original image from Pixabay was 32 MB.

- It was 21.8 MB, as placed into the InDesign document.

- The resulting PDF of the cover is 1.4 MB.

That is why InDesign's PDFs are so important to us as book designers

The typographic control, the high resolution type, the ability to add little things like the cross in vector, the ease with which the border and loge were added, are all important parts of the power available for cover design using InDesign.

I brought in the heart as a PSD file. To make many of the changes, I simply selected the graphic in the Links panel and used edit original to make the adjustments needed. Once I saved the file in Photoshop, it was updated automatically when I went back to InDesign.

The workflow is fast, easy, and comfortable.

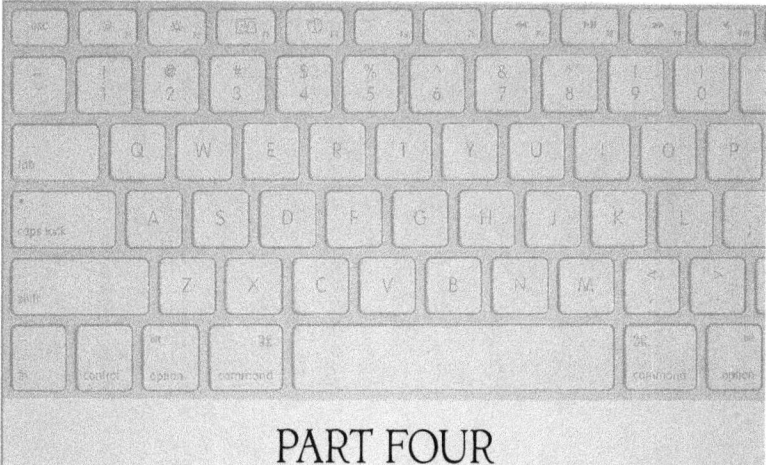

PART FOUR

Layout: Formatting your book

CHAPTER EIGHTEEN

Page layout basics

Setting up your book to be read: One of the more daunting aspects of book design for the inexperienced is page
layout. Most people have Word experience and as I have
said countless times already—Word cannot do professional
page layout. In fact, it is worse than that because Word's
attempts give you bad habits and poor expectations—which
must be corrected.

Many settings have to be covered for every document. Many of these are set up as you go through the
Preferences in InDesign. Every application has important
decisions to be made in Preferences. To repeat, the point
is to set up your applications so they work best for you.
But all I can really do is tell Word users how to get the
manuscript in the best shape so that the conversion to
InDesign is faster and easier.

Starting at the beginning:
Document Setup...

Here we are dealing with the frame or container
of your typography. These decisions radically affect your
choices. First of all, you must accept the fact that you really
need to start by designing a print version of your book.
Print requires high-resolution graphics. You can dumb

them down to ebooks. The reverse is not true. You need to start with high-resolution color. Greyscale images are easy from the color versions.

 **Print PDFs make for proofing ease:** What is largely misunderstood by authors and editors is that layout typos are just as bad as writing error. Print PDFs enable you to proof and edit margins, widows, sidebars, tables, and a host of other things not caught by editing the rough copy in Word. Plus, the editor can note down changes by annotating the PDF directly. You'll probably need to work with your editor, and maybe train him or her to use Acrobat. In addition, most of the beta readers will give comments like, "The main character's name is misspelled in the second paragraph of page 97". There are no page numbers to be relied upon in a Word document.

New document

Though we will be looking at what your different choices are, the first step is to open a new document [Command+N or CTRL+N]. This opens the New Document dialog box. Once you have done this for a little while, you will have Presets set up for your use. As you can see in the capture on the next page, I am using the one I set up for a 7"x10" book. We will go through why I used these settings next.

The Intent

If you click on this pop-up menu, you will find three choices: Print, Web, and Digital Publishing. We can disregard Digital Publishing right off the top, as it is the choice if you are making an app for a magazine. This is a very complex and expensive choice for publishing which none of you will be using, at this point.

Web Intent: This is what we will be using for our ePUBs. We will be converting our print version to another with a Web Intent with dimensions for an ereader page.

Print Intent: This is what we start every book project with. I have already mentioned some of the reasons why we always start with print. Most of these reasons are about editing and formatting needs. However, you should understand that a print version is always desired for a book for beta readers, proofing, and ARCs [Advanced Review Copies]. So here is what I used to start this book. But there are four more choices before we answer: why 7x10?

New Document

Document Preset: 7x10 Book

Save Preset Button

Intent: Print

Number of Pages: 1 ☑ Facing Pages

Start Page #: 1 ☑ Primary Text Frame

Page Size: [Custom]

Width: 7 in Orientation:

Height: 10 in

Columns

Number: 1 Gutter: 0.1667 in

Margins

Top: 0.75 in Inside: 2.25 in

Bottom: 0.75 in Outside: 0.75 in

Bleed and Slug

	Top	Bottom	Inside	Outside
Bleed:	0 in	0 in	0 in	0 in
Slug:	0 in	0 in	0 in	0 in

☐ Preview Cancel OK

We need to choose how many pages, what page number to start with, facing pages, and Primary Text Frame. These are very important.

Intent:	Print ▼	
Number of Pages:	1	☑ Facing Pages
Start Page #:	1	☑ Primary Text Frame

As InDesign works now, we start with a single page, beginning with page #1. We want Facing Pages checked because a printed book has facing pages with a left page and a right page for each spread. Where we are now, for example is page 274 on the left and the next odd page on the right.

The primary Text Frame enables you to add the entire book in one long story from beginning to end. This is required for a book. It is now extremely easy to accomplish with this option checked and all copy pasted into an insertion point in the one story—except for sidebars. But we'll cover that further on.

Document size [page size]

Our first choice [after picking the Print Intent] is the size of the book. In traditional publishing, there were virtually infinite options. This is one reason why traditional publishing costs so much more. All traditional printing is custom work—to meet the needs of the individual designer and specific project.

If you are publishing traditionally you would think that your options would be much larger—but this is only really true for children's books and those designed for the coffee table. Plus, you are always constrained by the paper sizes available to the printer. Books are printed from huge rolls of paper which limit sizes more.

Self-publishers give up even more of that freedom to control costs as we move into on-demand printing. For the on-demand print publisher, many costs are controlled by limiting the options. Plus, the equipment itself has limitations in the type of paper used and paper sizes available. As a result, document size is a given with few options. Here the concern is distribution. The fact that we can publish free is wonderful, but we must live with some restrictions. You need to make wise choices.

There are only certain sizes acceptable to Amazon (and the other retailers offered by our on-demand print suppliers). You must make at least one version of your book in a size that can be distributed through Amazon (even if you have no intention of selling any printed copies—your readers will surprise you and printed versions allow for book signings, book tables at the back of the hall when speaking, and so on). Amazon is the 500[#] gorilla at this point, and by far the best at marketing and selling self-published, on-demand printed books. The other options are all expensive and should be used only if you have a clear, demonstrated audience. The standard trade paperback (as close to normal as you can get) is 6×9.

Amazon accepts 13 standard page sizes

Size	Lulu	Amazon	B&W	Color
5 x 8 inches		√	√	
5.06 x 7.81 inches		√	√	
5.25 x 8 inches		√	√	
5.5 x 8.5 inches		√	√	√
6 x 9 inches (trade)	√	√	√	√
6.14 x 9.21 inches (royal)	√	√	√	√
6.69 x 9.61 inches		√	√	
7 x 10 inches		√	√	√
7.44 x 9.69 inches (Crown)	√	√	√	
7.5 x 9.25 inches		√	√	
8 x 10 inches		√	√	
8.5 x 8.5 inches	√	√		√
8.5 x 11 inches (letter)	√	√	√	√

My norm for books like this one has become 7x10. I find that it gives me more room for graphics and better looking sidebars. For novels, many like 5x8. The problem there is how cramped the space is. We'll talk about these issues more as we go on.

Several more questions enter here

Does the book bleed? I'll cover that process after the size selection is completed. For now all you need to know is that bleed means the ink touches the edges of the paper. I'll assume it does not. It rarely does for book interiors, and it's hard to find a compelling reason to use a bleed. It adds a lot of complexity and expense.

Does it have sidebars? This is a major consideration because of how it affects width choices. You'll see when we discuss column width that a three inch column width is really too small. A sidebar width of much less than two inches is also small. So, you can see the page width needs to be large enough to hold the columns of type and the sidebar plus the margins and the space between the columns and sidebar.

Size and proportion can vary widely. The key is careful control of the column width, font choices, and the words per line. This is the type of decision-making process you need to go through for your book. I tend to gloss over these things because I have made many firm decisions based on years of experience. When I started, I had the bindery department, of the printing company I worked for at the time, make me dummies of the books. You probably do not have that option. So, your process will be based on checking out the book size and feel you really like. Then you can make the decisions necessary to work within the limitations of on-demand printers.

All printers have limitations. You choose the best options available.

You will probably discover the necessity of publishing in various sizes and formats. Once you have your book formatted to your first size, the other sizes are relatively easy. If you do it right, your copy will all be in one piece, everything will be formatted with editable styles, and all graphics will be attached to a location in the copy. This makes it very quick and easy to reflow and reformat your book into any new format you need.

Bleeds

The typical temptations to spend more money than you have! Plus luscious pictures and supposed cash savings.

Logo/address

The dashed line is the actual trimmed size of the document.
BLEED   **TRIM**

A bleed is needed when you produce a design where the ink goes to the edge of the paper. On-demand printers will normally not allow type to come any closer than .375" or .5" from the edge of the trim size. Createspace requires three quarters of an inch (or a full inch for page counts over 400 pages or so.) To produce a bleed, you make everything that reaches to the edge of the page extend one-eighth inch beyond the edge and then trim the piece back to finished size after printing. That's one-eighth inch, nine points, or a little less than four tenths of a millimeter

(.375 mm to be precise). As you saw on the previous page, any place that touches the edge requires a bleed–so the example is a four-sided, or full bleed, even though three of the sides only have ink touching the edge in narrow areas.

The power cutters used in the industry are the reason a bleed is necessary. These huge guillotine cutters slide their knives through stacks of paper several inches thick. They can cut 1,000 to 3,000 sheets at a time. Those huge cuts force the paper to slide around a bit–no matter how tightly they are clamped. The result of these limitations is that cuts are only accurate to plus or minus a sixteenth of an inch or so.

Margins

This seems to be too obvious, but many ruin their job here. The most common amateur mistake is to make margins too small. You can assume that you need to leave .5" margins, minimum–and that is tight in a book.

In addition, margins are often a large part of style. If you are trying for the elegant look of an old book, for example, you will need huge margins. There are many formulas, but here's one you can try: 100% inside, 125% top, 150% outside, and 200% bottom (for example, 1.25" top; 1.5" outside; 2"" bottom; and 1" inside).

"Look at all that empty paper. I can't afford to waste that space!"

It's not wasted space, but room to breathe. You might want to keep some old books to remind yourself. Very high-priced products (or very cultured clients) commonly use designs with one inch to two inch margins or much more. Yes, this is a style issue, and you need to learn about these norms in the industry.

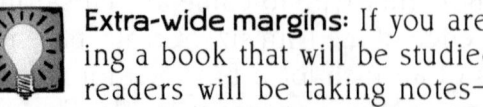 **Extra-wide margins:** If you are producing a book that will be studied–where readers will be taking notes–margins of a couple of inches (at least on the outside) are a real service to the reader. If you remember (and we will cover this in a bit) that the column width rarely goes much above four inches, you'll find plenty of room in an 8" width.

Conversely, if you need to convey the maximization of your money—fundraising materials and the like—you need small margins, gutters, and a lot of rules and boxes. You need to fill every open white space, making the page look like everything is crammed in to save money. Even if it is not strictly true, readers will think it is. You need to understand these common reader preconceptions. Use them to help your designs.

The point to remember is: *the smaller the margins, the cheaper the book looks.*

Minimal professional standards: basically you want the margins to be large enough to engender trust. Most readers have a subconscious reaction to cheapness—making it synonymous with unreliability and many other negatives. You need to be careful to make your work look professional. It really helps your readers relax and open up.

For the new publisher: I would assume a three-quarter inch (.75") margin as my minimum. The gutter margin (toward the spine of the book) should be at least an inch. The on-demand printers tend to cut slightly undersize and even half-inch margins can look very cheap and too tight for your work in the final delivered product.

Columns

Be very careful with your column choices. Your focus must be easy, comfortable readability. Generally, the more asymmetrical (off-center) and the more open you can lay out the piece, the better. Of course, you can go crazy and make things totally illegible. Modern style tends to be chaotic, splashy, and overly complex. But your innate taste and discretion should keep these tendencies in check. The problem, of course, is that taste and discretion have become rare. I know you are working hard to learn good taste and reduce that depressing trend. *Thank you.*

Column width: The first assumption is that you have column widths in good, readable range. Basically you are shooting for seven to eleven words per line. Thirteen words per line is acceptable, but that's the limit. The formula I use for column width is very simple and gives you a good starting point for readability.

Here's a practical rule of thumb that's less complex than most:

40% of the body copy point size in inches or the point size in centimeters ◇◇◇◇◇◇◇◇◇◇

So, 10 point type works well in a column that is four inches or 10 cm wide. 12-Point type may need nearly five inches (40% of twelve is 4.8"). This assumes a normal x-height of about 50% of the cap height or a third of point size. You actually need to count the number of words per line for a half dozen lines or even double or triple that and average them out.

Adjust your margins to leave an appropriate column width: This can be tricky with smaller books. There is a real limit to the smallness of body copy type (about 8 point). This gives us problems with the smaller book sizes.

The normal body copy size is 10 point type with 12 point leading. I'll talk about that elsewhere. But it is a fairly rigid norm. This normally requires a four inch column. For a five inch wide book, this only allows for half-inch margins on the sides. As mentioned that is very tight.

You can probably take the column down to 3.5" with no readability issues, but you dare not go more narrow than that—unless you use a condensed font (just keep the 9 to 10 words per line). On the other hand, an 8"x 10" book leaves you with four inches of margins. This is not a bad thing. One inch margins on all sides leaves you with an extra two inches for the gutter. This makes excellent room for a sidebar and to hold graphics up to six inches wide.

For two-column books: it should be easy to see that you need a page that is at least ten inches wide for any visual comfort. Books this wide become difficult to hold and read comfortably—no matter what you do. It is rarely a good solution (though adding a narrow sidebar can be a real benefit in an 8" wide book).

For a 6x9 book: my normal setup is .75" top/bottom and outside. I set the bottom or the top at an inch to leave a quarter inch to hold my page numbers. I use the resultant 1.25" inside margin to help keep the copy out of the gutter and make reading more comfortable.

For a low price workbook to help your students, a two-column letter-sized book might help: You can set it up with three-quarter inch outside and 1" inside margins, and two 3.375" columns with a quarter-inch gutter between the columns. This will enable you to convert a 200 page 6×9 book to eighty pages or less—enabling a cheap workbook for group studies. Make it spiral-bound to be even more useful.

If you're not sure, make a dummy book & try to read it yourself

Sidebars

In general, sidebars are a wonderful idea. By definition, sidebars contain interesting data that is not essential to the document. They add reader interest. They add graphic interest. They alleviate boredom. They contain graphic and typographic aberrations that are added merely for aesthetic reasons. As you have probably figured out by now, making room for sidebars will usually require a larger book size. There is very little room for them in a 6x9 book, for example. You need to design room for them. **Sidebars in ebooks:** These are now possible with fixed Layout. For reflowable ePUBs, they are much more iffy. You are already running a single column book set up for maximum readability. Adding sidebars to this type of layout is very problematic.

In addition, depending on the type of book you are writing and producing, it may well be read on a smartphone. This is not too large a problem for iPhones with their Retina Display and other phablets. Novels, and the like, have no need for sidebars. A book like this can put them to good use. But they take a wide screen to handle things.

So, my 7"x10" book choices

By now it should fairly clear why I do what I do. I want some breathing room. Plus, I want to leave some paces for notes. I do not want everything crammed onto the page with the resultant bad reactions from the readers. I need a good solid four-inch column, or maybe four and an eighth inch. Plus, I need to leave room for a header or footer with section names and page numbers.

So, here's my solution

New Document

Document Preset: 7x10 Book ▼ 📥 🗑

Save Preset Button

Intent: Print ▼

Number of Pages: 1 ☑ Facing Pages

Start Page #: 1 ☑ Primary Text Frame

Page Size: [Custom] ▼

Width: ⬍ 7 in   Orientation: 🔲 🔲

Height: ⬍ 10 in

Columns

Number: ⬍ 1   Gutter: ⬍ 0.1667 in

Margins

Top: ⬍ 0.75 in   Inside: ⬍ 2.25 in

Bottom: ⬍ 0.75 in   Outside: ⬍ 0.75 in

▼ Bleed and Slug

	Top	Bottom	Inside	Outside
Bleed:	0 in	0 in	0 in	0 in
Slug:	0 in	0 in	0 in	0 in

☐ Preview   Cancel   OK

It solves all the problems and desires just mentioned. I have a nice four and an eighth inch column with room for five-and-a-quarter-inch-wide graphics or even a small three-quarter-inch sidebar for tiny graphics.

CHAPTER NINETEEN

Formatting basics

Before I get started with this, I need remind you about the goal: *a beautiful book which is comfortable to read.*

You need a customized set of styles to enable you to keep your book consistent and give you global control over the entire book as you format. Excellent typography is only possible if you understand how to design paragraphs. Styles make paragraph design possible. We will deal with them conceptually, but you should know this is why InDesign is so good. These options often leave the entire paradigm of a word processor.

Designing your paragraphs

I need to share some basics about setting up your paragraphs. Most of this knowledge is assumed by software manuals and publishing Websites. Somehow they seem to believe that your little psyche will be stifled if any opinion on normalcy is mentioned—or some such idiocy. It's not magic or luck when you produce reading materials that are enjoyable to read. It is the result of setting your copy up (formatting it) in a manner that the reader instantly recognizes and comfortably understands.

You must lead the reader through your writing effortlessly—completely unaware of your guidance. You need to make your writing feel natural, comfortable, and obvious to help the reader receive the content.

 My way is not the only way: As I go through this little presentation, I will be simply sharing what I use. My hope is that you can look at my usage for conceptual understanding. Then convert that for your use. I will attempt to give you the arguments that have convinced me to do things in this manner. But, there is no right or wrong (once you are inside the relatively wide parameters of normalcy).

Our basic problem is that we have too much to read. Subconsciously virtually everyone looks for ways to eliminate content (in order to keep reading requirements within a tolerable range). We might miss a lot of good content this way—but that is the way it is.

In our modern culture, huge numbers of people have difficulty reading. People often know how to read (technically) but they hate to actually do it. I've heard stats as high as 60% of Americans are functionally illiterate. Most people agree it is a huge percentage even if it is as low as a third of adults. They may be able to read [literate in the polls], but: it is difficult for them, in a second language, or they just hate reading [so in practice they rarely or never read]. A Pew poll that came out in early April of 2012 says that nearly a quarter of Americans did not read a single book the previous year. The social media users go far beyond that, of course. I know many young men and women (fifty years old or less) who avoid reading entirely [as much as possible]—even though they are considered fully literate by polls and testing. Many have college degrees.

The need for comfort

The result is that we must go out of our way to make our books accessible to poor readers. Reading is hard to avoid. But many do. We have a large and growing portion of our middle class who get all of their information from social media, TV, movies, and videos.

 **Modern interactive features:** This is an area you need to thoroughly examine. My opinion is that adding video and such to a book changes it into something entirely different. The non-reader may be more attracted to the video content, BUT would they ever buy a "book" in the first place? If you feel the need for video, you should consider whether you actually need a "book" at all.

My best-selling (in the niche) book, *Practical Font Design With FontLab 5*" has developed into a well-liked video course, using the book as the textbook—a reference with further explanations, if needed.

We can argue all we want about these media options and their limited amount of actual content. But, this fact remains: even those who buy our books may well have trouble reading. We must help them as much as we can with our formatting and layout. We must be kind to our readers—gentle and loving. If our readers experience any discomfort or reading difficulty we have probably lost them. They will simply not finish reading our content.

I am a very good and very fast reader. Yet I simply put books aside that are difficult to read—unless the content is required or very compelling. I am not talking about difficult content (though that can be a problem). I am talking about poor layouts, columns that are too wide, fonts that are too stylized, overly busy layouts, and all the rest.

A couple of years ago I was struggling with a book on creationism (my wife gave up and asked me to brief her on it when I finished reading it). The content is exciting. The layout is so poor with photographic backgrounds, glossy paper, excessive line lengths and a host of other problems—I had to force myself to read it. The only difference with me is that I am tuned into this problem so I often notice when I do this with a book. Most people are not conscious of why they put down a book. They simply don't read it.

The poetry filter

Here's another example. I wonder how many of you are like me? I probably shouldn't admit this, but anything in a book which is formatted as poetry I skip (except in scripture). I simply pass over that portion of the copy and continue on. My experience over the years is that the content in poetry is very limited and far too open to interpretation. I am almost always looking for facts—easily accessible facts. In a novel, I am looking for plot and character development. Poetry has never provided this for me. So, I have developed reading habits that keep me from wasting time. I jump to the explanation of the poetry which inevitably follows.

I am sure this horrifies many of you. I am not saying that this poetry filter of mine is good or desirable. I am simply saying that it exists. Again, the only thing strange is that [as a typographer] I am more aware of my reading habits—so I noticed this behavior.

What reading filters do you have?

I suspect you need to examine yourself. It's hard to say what you have been missing all these years. We all have things we just do not read—often for subconscious reasons. As typographers we try to limit those reactions.

CHAPTER TWENTY

Examining the formatting options

Formatting of text is done on two levels: by paragraph and by character. This paragraph, for example, is in my normal body copy style–the one with no first line indent, used after a chapter headline. **However,** I can emphasize certain words a character at a time by simply selecting and applying a character style with the shortcut I define.

Paragraph styles format entire paragraphs. *Character styles format characters within a paragraph.*

First, I just want to talk about the options. The choices you make determine your typographic look. But you do need to know what is possible.

What is a paragraph?

I used to think everyone knew this, but I find that's not true. Every time you type the Return key [Qwerty Enter], you end the current paragraph and start a new one. They can be long or short, body copy heads, & so on.

This one's short!

Paragraph Styles & Character Styles panels

These two styles panels are the enabling concept for typographic fluidity and production speed. Styles panels are a collection of specialized typographic defaults that can be accessed at the click of a mouse or stroke of a key. You can set up styles for headlines, subheads, body copy, hanging indents, bylines, captions, tabular matter, or whatever your heart desires or imagines. You can also set up very complex styles for graphic objects and most parts of a table. Basically, you can globally control the look of your entire document with a little practice.

First let's learn the concepts on paragraphs like you see in front of you. Every paragraph in this book is formatted with these style options—as are all objects.

The best way to find out what's available is in styles

In InDesign, virtually anything that is possible to do to a paragraph is available. So, to talk about the typography of paragraphs we are going to go through the options available in paragraph and character styles. This will show you some or many things you had no idea were even possibilities.

Let's start with Paragraph Styles

These basic comments on paragraph styles also apply to the other different types of styles also, in most cases. This is the only way to get consistent indents and alignments, automatic paragraph rules and leaders for building forms and the like, automatic anchored graphics, automatic drop caps—plus much more. In truth, this consistency is what makes a book look like a professionally designed book.

My intention is to go through all the options on all the pages of the New Paragraph Style dialog box. Most of these options are not understood by new book designers. They give you immense control over your typography **IF** you know what their purpose is and how to set them up.

Going through the pages of the New Paragraph Style dialog box

If you look at the page list in the column on the left side of the dialog box, it might look like nothing changed for the CS5.5, CS6, or CC versions except for the addition of an Export Tagging page—but this is a big deal. However, it has nothing to do with typography.

This is actually a vast improvement to the ePUB export process. I cover what this new capability includes and how to use it effectively in Part 6—which is about designing your ePUBs. Basically, I do it all at once using the Edit All Export Tags dialog box. But it is really a good thing.

You are going to discover there are several basic settings which are very different for heads as opposed to body copy. Some you probably know, like turning off Hyphenation for heads and subheads. Some you don't...

General page

This is where you set up the style name, what that style is based upon, and what you want to happen when you type the paragraph return at the end of your paragraph. Finally, you should set up a custom shortcut for fast access to the style you've created. Yes, you need a numerical keypad.

There is also a field which lists the settings you have chosen for the style. This is an excellent way to keep track of what you are doing.

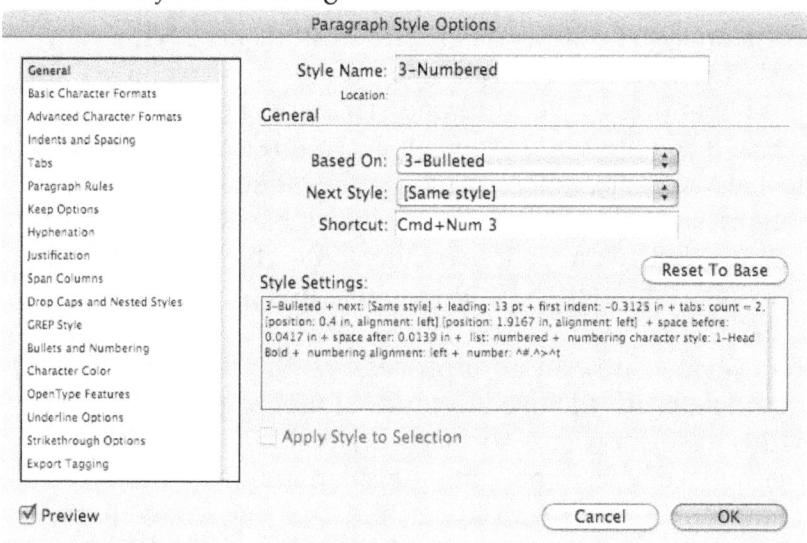

There is nothing on this page we need to cover for typography though it's important to design your style set up.

Basic Character Formats

As you can see, this page contains virtually everything in the Character panel. What isn't on this page is on the Advanced Character Formats page. You can control every aspect of font selection, size, leading, letterspacing (both kerning and tracking), caps, small caps, and scaling. I was assuming you know all of this.

But I can't do that: I've learned though experience that few of you know these things. This is where you make your basic decisions about font usage: family, style, sizing, and spacing.

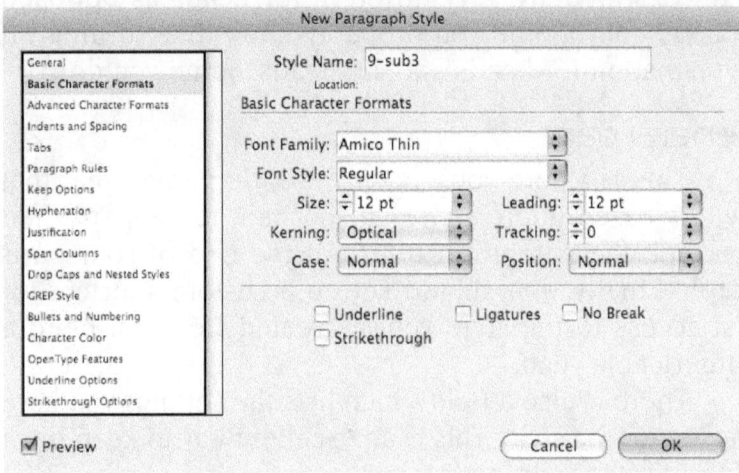

Font family: The up & down arrows work here with your installed font list. You can also hit the up arrow to go to the beginning of the word and start typing the name you need. If you are quick, you can get in three to four letters to narrow your choices. Any font installed on your computer is available. We've already talked briefly about these choices. But you need to have them available and installed on your computer to be able to use them.

Duh!

Font Style: Unlike in word processors, the Bold and Italic commands are not used in professional page layout. This is because there are so many style choices. This is the main place where changing fonts can mess you up. Quite commonly one font will use Bold and the next will use Heavy. You have to watch this. The styles available to the font family you have selected will be available on the drop down list.

Size: You know this one, right? 9-14 point for body copy, quotes, and lists. 24-36 point for headlines. 18-24 point for subhead one. 12-16 point for subhead two. Body copy size for the smallest subheads.

Leading: If you do not like the auto leading setting you are getting, you can change it on the Justification page. Basically, you want the leading to be the same size as the type with the following additions or subtractions.

> ⊕ **Tiny type [5-8 point]:** 0 to +1, as in 6/6 or 6/7

> ⊕ **Body copy [9-14 point]:** +1 to +3 depending on the x-height and built-in leading for the font you choose.

> ⊕ **Small subheads [14-20 point]:** +1 to 0 getting tighter as the subheads get larger.

> ⊕ **Large subheads [18-24 point]:** usually set solid, although they could be slightly negative if set in all caps or small caps.

> ⊕ **Headlines [24-48 point]:** set solid to −10. It depends on the descenders.

Metrics: Optical or Manual. Optical tends to be a little looser than Metrics, but good metrics are only found with good fonts. Cheap fonts often have very bad metric spacing (which Optical really helps).

Tracking: This is the place to compensate for font designer decisions you do not like. Fonts from the 1980s tend to be too tight, for example. Text fonts are often too loose for Display use. Many fonts are too tight for text use and need to be loosened for body copy. The change should be made in the style because then it is global.

Case: The choices are Normal, Small Caps, All Caps, and OpenType All Small Caps. I ask you to bug Adobe with feature requests until we can get the Title case and Sentence case options also. Title case is often required for headlines and sometimes for subheads. Because it is not available here, you are forced to manually change the case as you write or edit the copy.

Position: Superscript, subscript, OpenType Superscript, OpenType Subscript, OpenType Numerator, OpenType Denominator. You can use these options in a character style for fractions and equations.

Advanced Character Formats

Here you see the rest of the Character panel. This is where you need to come for scaling and baseline shifts.

Horizontal and vertical scale: These rarely help.

Baseline shift: This moves the characters affected by the style up or down. Negative numbers move them down. I have used it for Kickers, for example, to move them down into a better fit with the header underneath. But mainly a baseline shift is used a lot for bullets in a character style because many bullets need to be adjusted not only in size and color, but up and down as well.

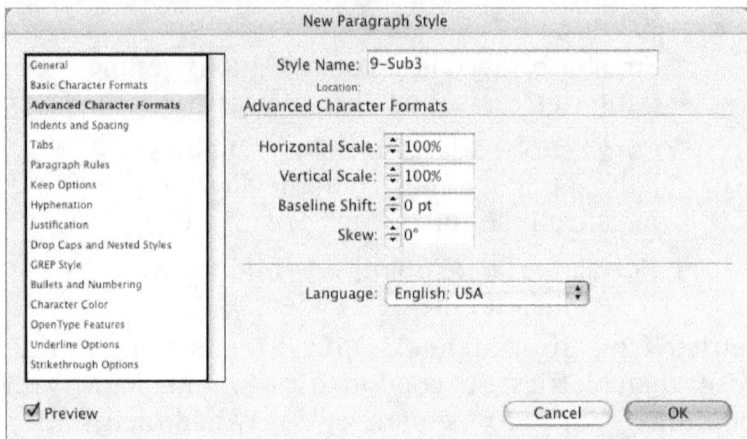

Skew: If you ever use this, I will show up at your door some day to do horrible things to you—mock you, at least.

Language: More importantly, this is where you pick the language used. As we are forced more and more into multi-lingual documents, this will become more important. I can easily see separate sets of styles for English, French, and Spanish (& more than that for EU stuff).

Indents & Spacing

Alignment: Remember, InDesign has seven alignments: Left, Right, Centered, Justified Left, Justified Right, Justified Center, and Full justified. The last option justifies the last line also. It is necessary if you want to justify a single line paragraph. You will regularly be changing lists from Left to Left Justified or the reverse, depending on the length of the paragraphs.

Most recent studies seem to say that justified copy reads better as long as it is justified well. Only InDesign justifies well. For anything else you need to seriously consider flush left alignment to control the word spacing.

New Paragraph Style

General
Basic Character Formats
Advanced Character Formats
Indents and Spacing
Tabs
Paragraph Rules
Keep Options
Hyphenation
Justification
Drop Caps and Nested Styles
GREP Style
Bullets and Numbering
Character Color
OpenType Features
Underline Options
Strikethrough Options

Style Name: 9-Sub3
Location:
Indents and Spacing

Alignment: Left

☑ Balance Ragged Lines
☐ Ignore Optical Margin

Left Indent: ⇕ 0 in   First Line Indent: ⇕ 0 in
Right Indent: ⇕ 0 in   Last Line Indent: ⇕ 0 in
Space Before: ⇕ 0.0833 in   Space After: ⇕ 0 in
Align to Grid: None

☑ Preview   (Cancel)   (OK)

Balance ragged lines: You really need to be careful of this one. This option makes line breaks based solely on line length. It does not break by phrases. The result is often heads or subheads which do not read well.

One of the things you need to become aware of and add to your repertoire is the practice of making sure that line breaks of flush left copy in narrow columns occur between phrases. Let's use the headline below to show you the problem. There is a huge difference in readability between these two choices.

Break for sense to help readability

The above version is much more difficult to read at speed in a book than the following version:

Break for sense to help readability

You are responsible to make sure your headings [those which are large enough to only have a few words per line] have line breaks to help readability. Again, this is called breaking for sense.

Indents: Left, First line, and Right indents. The first line indent can be as large negatively as the left indent is positively. This is what enables the indents necessary to make a list with the bullets or numbers hanging in the space between the left column edge and the left indent of the list.

Secondary alignments

Normally, the left indent is zero. But for quotes, the left and right indent commonly match the first line indent of your body copy paragraphs. You will find that keeping secondary indents the same as your first line indent of your body copy style is a big help.

This interior alignment aids your readers.

- It will go a long way to making your formatting more consistent

- It makes your layout much easier to comprehend

- It requires less effort on the part of the reader.

Please notice in the paragraph below with the dropped inline graphic. The left indent is the same as the first line indent of my body copy. The right indent is also that same size. It's the same set of indents as I use for quotes, but a different font, size, and style, It makes a nice balance. The left indent of my lists is also the same size (as you see in the previous paragraphs).

Again the arrow keys: remember, that the quickest way to adjust things is to tab to the field you want to change, then use the up and down arrows to adjust, then tab out to execute. If you need to readjust, Shift+Tab will take you back to make those changes again.

This does require a larger than normal first line indent to work well. Even the default third of an inch is a little small for me. I have settled on a .4" indent. I've used it for many years now and it works really well.

Align to grid: I don't use grids, so I have no real help for you here. They don't work well in books unless you have a very large book with multiple columns..

Tabs

In this dialog is the complete Tabs panel: Each style can have its own set of tabs. This is where tabs really come into their own. You set tabs once per style and then apply them by style when you need them. Here is the tool you need to set forms by adding leaders throughout your Document. It's much easier and better than drawing rules and trying to line them up by hand.

Decimal Tabs (special character tabs): In InDesign the decimal tab can work with any single character. So, you can align the tab on the x for dimensional lumber, or maybe a colon for a Short Name: short description list.

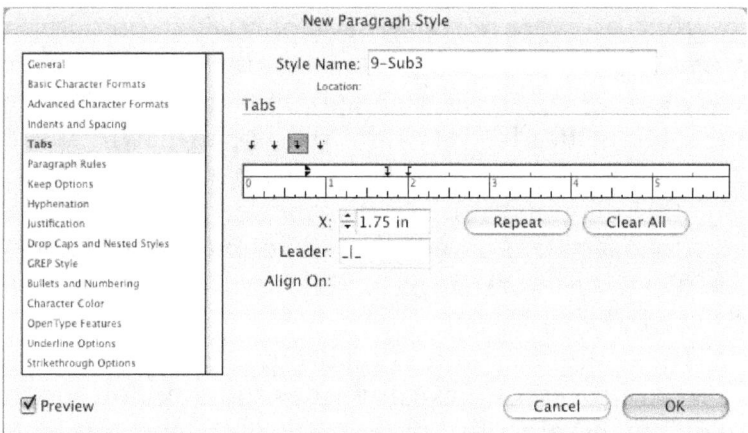

Double stacked right-angle triangles in the ruler: These show you the first line indent on top and the left indent on the bottom. Yes, they can be moved separately, but it's tricky. It's better to type in the numbers in the indent fields.

X: here you can type in the location which really helps for Right tabs at the right edge of a column.

Leader: This fills up the space in a line after the last character over to the next character in the following tab. It can be any characters you can type (up to eight of them).

Align On: This is where you enter the character to use for the decimal tab. You get a period by default.

 You need to keep tables in mind: The only proviso in all of this is that it is often better and easier to use a table than setting up very complicated tabs. Tables have many more options.

The next four pages really only work in styles

They are the complete dialog boxes from the Paragraph Styles panel menu: Paragraph Rules, Hyphenation, Keep Options, and Justification. What you will discover as you learn to add the controls in these options is that this is really where much of the difference between amateur and pro lies. You can do a lot with these controls to make your type look good.

Paragraph Rules

Paragraph rules are normally used only within paragraph styles: They are too tedious to use otherwise. However, once they are set up in a paragraph style the rules are added automatically every time you use that style. If you look at the subhead in the preceding paragraph, look at the fading diamond rule on the right edge with a graduated stroke (a rule is a line which is colored with a stroke). BUT, rules don't work in ePUB Reflows. They work fine in ePUB FXL [Fixed Layout]

These are the professional equivalent of borders in a word processor. Basically rules (plus underlines & strikethroughs) are only limited by your imagination. They can certainly be overdone (I do that myself quite regularly by giving myself the *demo* excuse). But, they are excellent tools for directing the reader's eye–and for controlling emphasis.

Any of these rules can use any of the stroke styles, be any color (including any color for any gaps in the stroke style), any width up to 1000 points, and any location up to 18 inches up or down. Paragraph rules can also be any length up to the width of the pasteboard so a rule in a narrow column can stretch across an entire page if that is what you need.

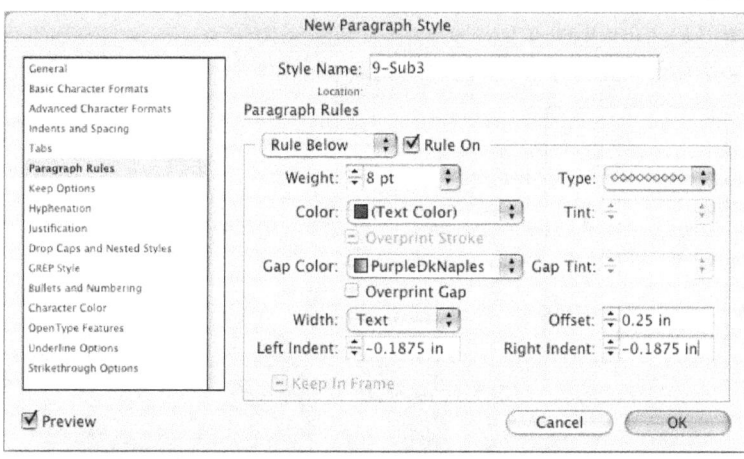

TIP: If you understand how InDesign does rules, you see that each paragraph can have up to four rules attached to it: above paragraph, below paragraph, underline, and strikethrough. (Of course you can use more than this with rules applied by nested character styles.)

There is a great deal of room for experimentation

This means you can use a huge variety of rules to attract attention or divert it. You can make a rule that functions as an automatic tint box in back of your type (like this one). When you need them, they are available.

Just be careful with type in a tint box: Doing this always reduces contrast and makes type harder to read. Be careful to compensate with font choices, point sizes, leading and the rest of the controls in our arsenal.

Keep Options

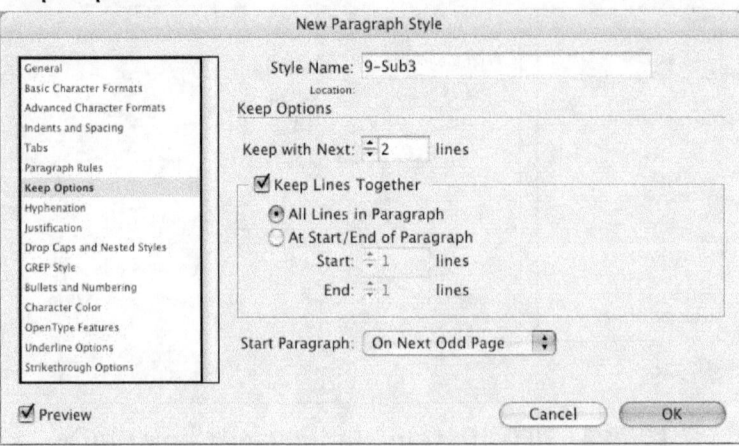

These options are used for almost every headline and subhead. The use depends on the type of paragraph. The Keep With and Together options can almost eliminate orphans (isolated lines and paragraph fragments) They do not help at all with paragraph widows—which always must be edited out by hand.

Keep With Next: with 2 or 3 lines. You certainly do not want a subhead or headline isolated by itself at the bottom of a column—one of the worst orphans.

Keep Lines Together: You normally check All Lines in Paragraph for headers.

At Start/End of Paragraph: I usually use Start: 2 & End: 3 for body copy. End:2 lines often leaves you with a line and a partial line which does not look good. However, if you regularly write four-line paragraphs, you better use Start: 2 and End: 2 to keep the software from a nervous breakdown.

Start Paragraph: This is the place where you can set styles to start new articles or chapters and have them start on the next odd page. (Remember to do that for your headlines or the style you use to start each chapter—it is virtually required that chapters and sections start on the odd [right] page). For ePUBs and Kindle, you just have them start on the next page. This all gives you an immense amount of automatic layout control.

Hyphenation

Again let's use headlines and subheads as an example. They should not hyphenate—ever. Often tightly written, terse lists with short paragraphs are set flush left with hyphenation turned off.

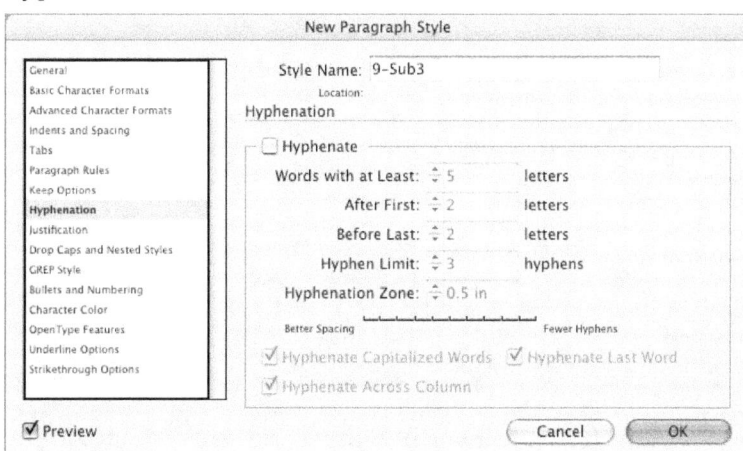

The actual hyphenation setup is something you want to determine before you even start putting together the documents. These settings are determined by grammarians and your usage. For some reason, typographers really get upset about this (even though they rarely agree with each other [which tells me there is no real standard]). Many say you cannot even have two hyphens in a row. Some say a hyphen every other row is terrible. Often you will have to make a case by case judgment as you massage the copy to fit your tidy, well-designed little boxes.

On the other hand, almost everyone agrees that agrees should not be hyphenated after the a in a-grees. Much of this is common sense. The rules are good, but readability trumps everything. For example, would you hyphenate hyphenat-ed? Most wouldn't, but it would be clearly readable. Isn't that right?

Justification

New Paragraph Style

General	Style Name: 9-Sub3
Basic Character Formats	Location:
Advanced Character Formats	Justification
Indents and Spacing	
Tabs	
Paragraph Rules	
Keep Options	
Hyphenation	
Justification	
Drop Caps and Nested Styles	
GREP Style	
Bullets and Numbering	
Character Color	
OpenType Features	
Underline Options	
Strikethrough Options	

	Minimum	Desired	Maximum
Word Spacing:	85%	97%	115%
Letter Spacing:	0%	0%	0%
Glyph Scaling:	97%	100%	103%

Auto Leading: 105%

Single Word Justification: Full Justify

Composer: Adobe Paragraph Composer

☑ Preview   Cancel   OK

Except for Auto Leading, these settings are normally used only when you make the setup for a newspaper or magazine. This is a place where the experts do not agree at all. Everyone has their own opinion. Our choice is to control the word spacing as tightly as possible to make a smooth type color. I go far beyond most recommendations.

In my experience, InDesign justifies body copy with the normal 9-12 words per line exceptionally well. I have changed my default settings to 85% Min, 97% Desired, & 115% Max with superior results. Most say that Desired should always be 100%, but some fonts simply have space characters that are too wide.

Auto Leading adjustments

However, you will want to regularly make Auto leading changes. It is true that auto-leading for body copy is almost always 120% (or 10/12). On the other hand, headers are commonly 105% for C&lc and 80% or less for all caps and small caps (that have no descender). Gradually, you will find that careful adjustments to a style here save you a lot of grief as you actually begin to flow copy into your document.

Auto Leading also changes with the fonts used. Do not simply accept what Adobe dishes out. You are responsible for your typography.

Drop Caps & Nested Styles

Drop caps: You can set a Character Style to use with your drop caps. That is commonly done because drop caps are often in a different font (at least). Drop caps in InDesign are much more powerful than many designers realize.

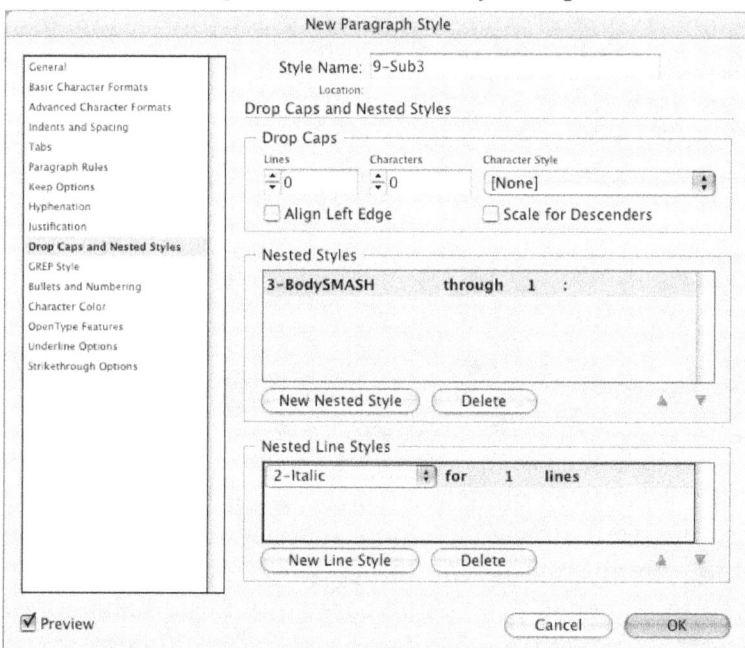

Nested styles: (Yes, these use character styles: I will cover them next.) I always used to call these run-in heads. Adobe's name indicates what they really are—because they are much more powerful than simple run-in heads. Simply put, a nested style allows you to automatically apply a character style to the start of the paragraph until a specified delimiter appears. You can have a bold style run-in until the first colon, for example—a very common addition to this book

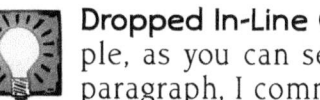 **Dropped In-Line Graphics:** For example, as you can see to the left in this paragraph, I commonly place [import] a graphic at the beginning of a paragraph and then use the drop caps feature to lower the graphic 3 lines with the rest of the paragraph in a run-around. One time for a tall, narrow poster, I dropped the inline graphic 28 lines— down through seven or eight paragraphs below.

Headline font in regular through colon: You've seen this through out the booklet. But I can easily add a second nested style through the first em-dash. You can see something like this at the top of the next page.

Smash through colon: Italic through the em-dash—then back to normal copy. I could even add bold through a second colon—if I Wanted. This is actually quite practical for certain types of lists and bibliographies.

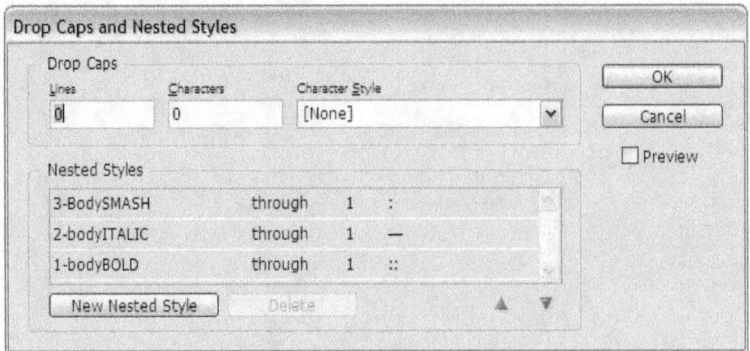

This is the set up I used for the next two paragraphs. Notice I put two colons for the third run-in (it counts the first one used also). Once the style is set up I do not have to do a thing except type the copy or apply the shortcut to apply the style to existing copy. The nested styles just appear like magic.

Publishing With InDesign: by David Bergsland— **Practical training in page layout:** What an embarrassing book that first book was in 2000 (thankfully, it's out of print)!

The Bible: by God's inspiration—**Practical training in living:** now this is truly an excellent book!

Adding new character styles from within the new style dialog: This is one of the major additions CS4 has added. In CS3 or earlier, I was constantly having to close out a partially finished style to add a character style for a drop cap, nested style, and so on [like I still must do with Swatches].

Now there is a New Character style choice in the pop-up menu.

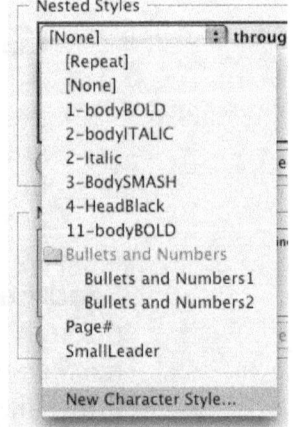

(SEE A SHORT DISCUSSION ABOUT CHARACTER STYLES AFTER I FINISH PARAGRAPH STYLES.)

Nested Line styles: To be honest, I haven't played much with this one. It became available in CS4, but so far in two+ years, I've never found a use. But it would seem to be a nice addition to the repertoire. It allows you to be able to apply a Character Style by line. This has never been a style I liked. One of the more common uses is small caps for the first line. The next paragraph shows another option.

Something like this could be

tried. The 1st line is in 24 point, the 2nd line in 18 point using the header font, the 3rd line in 15 **point using the body copy font, and the 4th line** in 12 point bold. I've also seen the 1st line Black, the 2nd line Bold, the 3rd line Demi, the 4th line Regular, the 5th line Light. You can do the same thing with colors—or with colors in addition to all these things.

To me, it's always seemed pretty desperate—a lack of a better idea. It draws too much attention to the type. Typography should be invisible, simply displaying the content. Too bad that's not true for this book.

Typography should invisibly give you the copy as almost irresistibly readable.

Bulleted & Numbered Lists

InDesign has finally reached the promise of earlier versions with its list options. At least it seems that way to me. Some still complain, but that's always the case. Part of it is being able to add new character styles on the run. But, it now does what I expect when I choose an option. Maybe I've just been trained by the earlier versions.

Bulleted lists

The bullets can be added from any font you have installed on your computer. You can use Unicode to specify a certain character that is available in any font (like a bullet) or a specific character from a specific font (like a dingbat). You can also format the bullets with a character style (a newly added one if that is necessary).

As mentioned earlier, the only real problem seems to be the common necessity of adding baseline shifts for dingbats in unusual fonts set at a larger or smaller size than the rest of the copy in the paragraph that follows the bullet. The bullet needs to look like it is vertically centered in slug of the first line of type—in most cases. But this is very easy to do with a character style.

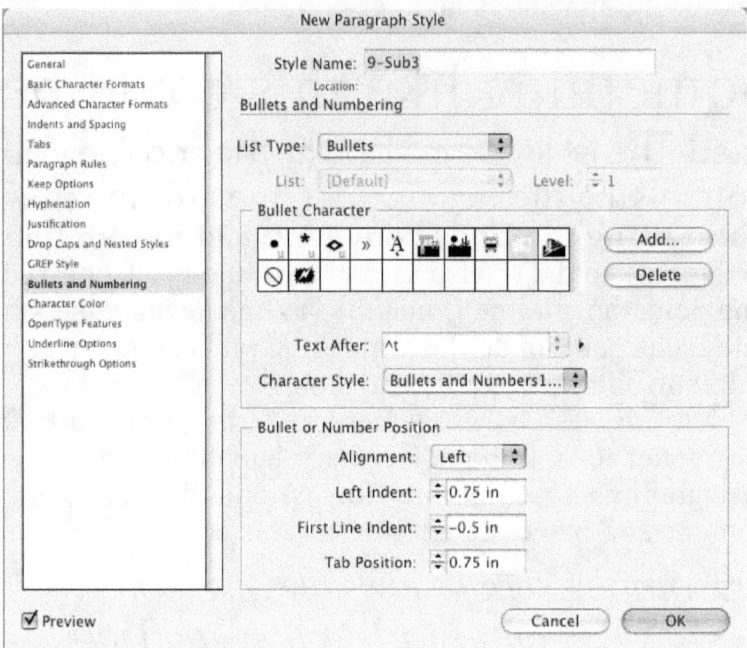

For ePUB Reflow, you can specify a bullet from your embedded font and it will work well—in iBooks, Nook and Kobo. Kindle may well strip it out.

Numbered lists

The numbered list options are more extensive yet. You have any of the numbering formats available to page numbering plus 01, 02 03, etc. You can specify how you want numbers and special characters added at the beginning of a paragraph with very few limitations. [You can't put a tab before the number, for example.] Plus, you can apply a character style to the number to make it a different font, size, color, and so on. And finally under mode you have the choice of continuing from previous number or restarting at a specific number.

Fixing numbering issues in the copy: If you choose Continue From Previous Number, you will regularly want to start over. In the paragraph, a simple right-click enables you to Restart Numbering.

The only two issues I've had are minimal. First, trying to control the numbering when it gets too long. The flush right controls never quite work the way I want them to. Second, restarting the numbers does not work well in ePUBs—they just continue.

New Paragraph Style

General
Basic Character Formats
Advanced Character Formats
Indents and Spacing
Tabs
Paragraph Rules
Keep Options
Hyphenation
Justification
Drop Caps and Nested Styles
GREP Style
Bullets and Numbering
Character Color
OpenType Features
Underline Options
Strikethrough Options

Style Name: 9-Sub3
Location:
Bullets and Numbering

List Type: Numbers

List: Normal Numbering   Level: 1

Numbering Style

Format: 1, 2, 3, 4...

Number: ^#.^t

Character Style: Bullets and Numbers2...

Mode: Continue from Previ... 1

☑ Restart Numbers at This Level After: Any Previous Level

Bullet or Number Position

Alignment: Left

Left Indent: 0.75 in

First Line Indent: -0.5 in

Tab Position: 0.75 in

☑ Preview   Cancel   OK

Automated lists

Be careful of numbered lists. Word, especially, does a lot of things automatically that are very hard to deal with. InDesign is little more polite. But even here, restarting the numbering often breaks in an ePUB or Kindle book. In many, if not most, cases it is better to quit numbering and use bulleted lists.

OpenType Features

Here you can add Discretionary Ligatures, Fractions, Swashes, Titling Caps, Ordinals, and many of the other advanced typographic benefits of an OpenType Pro font. The only problem is educating the readers. Sad to say, many are still freaked out by these typographic treats. I even gave up on using them in this book after getting reviewer complaints.

Mainly this feature is used to pick the type of numbering you want to use. You should use lining figures for copy set in all caps or for accounting copy, oldstyle figures for lowercase copy, and small cap figures for copy set in small caps. (Small cap figures are quite rare, however, so you may be forced to make a bad choice of lining or oldstyle.)

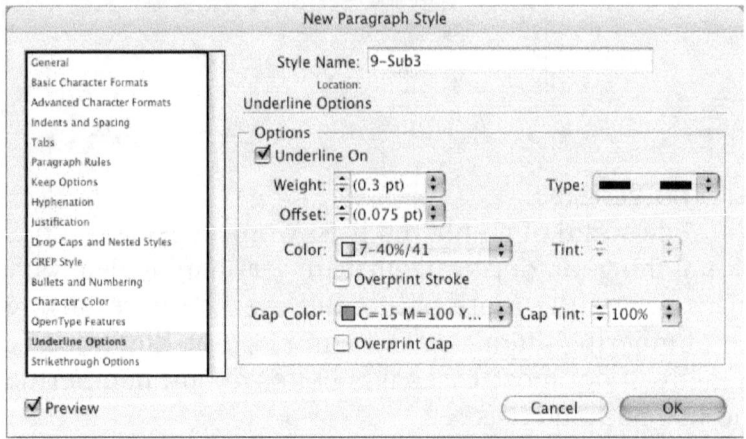

Underlines & Strikethroughs

These options have all the power of paragraph rules but they apply to the specific words. In other words, you can use these options to add rules that appear on every line of a paragraph (unlike paragraph rules that can only appear once per paragraph).

You can see the underline page on the following page. The options are the same for strikethroughs. They aren't used often, but they are an excellent way to add highlighting, for example, if you have a full color book.

Export Tagging

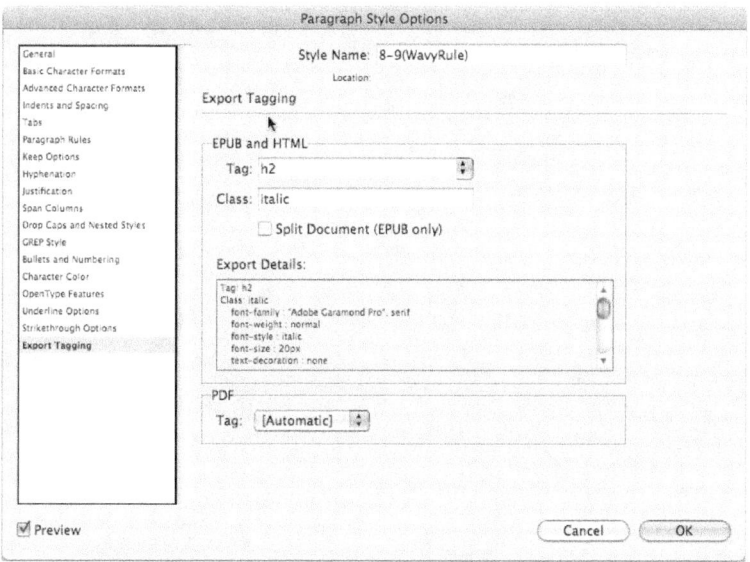

I won't cover this much here. I go over this in depth where I cover ePUB design and production. But this is really a big deal. It enables us to control the CSS produced when exporting an ePUB—which is the best control we can get over ePUB typography (without extensive coding).

As you can see, you can set the HTML tag and class you'll get when exporting to ePUB. It works very well. Normally this is controlled by the Edit All Export Tags... Command from the flyout menu in the Paragraph Styles panel. InDesign has gotten much more stringent about class names with the release of CC, but as far as I can tell it's a good thing. They claim they need to do this to get more functional code. Sounds good to me.

CHAPTER TWENTY-ONE

Dealing with the basic paragraph styles

What I want to do is cover some of the basic concerns for the common types of paragraphs you will be using every day. Remember, my focus in this book is on typography for books and booklets. But if you look at them creatively you'll see how they apply to a poster, letterhead, letter, newsletter, or brochure.

Styling tips for the basic set

Here I want to give you some design tips to use when setting up your set of standard styles. I will go through the basic paragraph needs—explaining the hows and whys as I go. Again, some of my solutions will be different from yours. In most cases, I am just talking about normal usage. You must develop your own setup. This is the core of your layout style. If you do not work on this, you'll pay for that lapse with the extra time spent. Plus, your typography will be haphazard and ineffective. Your readers will not be pleased.

Points: A basic reminder for those just learning. This is the basic measure-ment system for type. A point is now one-seventy-second of an inch. It is the min-imum size that is easily visible to the naked eye. If you ignore points, you'll be measuring in thousandths.

Body copy styles

The first formatting decisions I will be talking about are for the body copy. This is what Word calls Normal. Many of the Word docs you get to setup will be entirely locally formatted Normal. It is the main content of your book, and it must be comfortable to read. This paragraph style is what produces that smooth type color you need for the background against which the contrasting heads and subheads stand out. You really need to focus on making this as comfortably readable as possible. The font choice is critical.

 **Font choices influence these deci-sions:** The x-height and width of your fonts have great influence. Readabil-ity has to do with the number of words per line, the legibility of the font used, the size of the letters, and a lot more. The smoothness of the type color has to do with the letterspacing built into the font.

The font family I am using in this booklet is Librum. It has a normal x-height. But, to maintain the optimal 10-12 words per line I am setting the type in 12-point which is quite large for print.

Body copy or Normal

These are the normal paragraphs of copy. The norm is 10/12 flush left or justified left. All the other alignment options are much more difficult to read. There is a very strong expectation of normal for these paragraphs by your readers. You need to know the normals.

Serif font: This is the standard. Most people still believe that serif fonts are much easier to read. This is being argued. For the new generations, it may be true that a humanist sans font reads very well. But for those born before 1980 or so, all of our reading experience is based on the assumption that serif fonts must be used for body copy.

❧ **Size:** The standard for body copy is 10/12 (10-point type with 12-point leading). **You adjust the point size until there are 9-12 words per line.**

This can vary from 9 to 12 point in size. The leading will be determined by the amount of line spacing built into the font used and the x-height. The larger the x-height, the more leading is needed. The smaller the x-height the larger the point size of the type needs to be. Also condensed fonts can be a little larger and wide fonts often need to be smaller.

❧ **Alignment:** Justified left. Typographers traditionally liked flush left alignment because the word spacing remains constant. However, for books, it will look like an error if you do not use justified body copy. InDesign' superior justification abilities automatically justify copy better than any software program we have had up to this point because it justifies the entire paragraph as a whole.

❧ **Longer line lengths require increased leading:** But the only thing that matters in a book is the 9-12 words per line on average. Many italics also need leading help (or indented paragraphs) because the more narrow italics have more words per line. Formality also needs extra leading—plus a lighter, more elegant typestyle.

❧ **First line indent:** Historically, you used either a first line indent or extra paragraph spacing, not both, Now, however, it is common to see a first line indent with a couple of points of space after paragraph. There is no right or wrong about the size of first line indents. The norm would be somewhere between a quarter to a half inch. (Believe it or not, this topic causes many angry exchanges of dogmatic opinion.)

Body Copy No First

This style is used for the first paragraph after a headline, primarily. Sometimes it is also used under column-wide rectangular graphics. Adjust it to read well with your headers, comfortably clearing any descenders in the heads.

- **Based on (the same as):** Body Copy
- **No first line indent**
- **Extra space before the paragraph**
- **Next style (what happens when you hit return):** It should go to the normal Body Copy.

If you do not use a first line indent for your body copy, you'll need to use some other device for these paragraphs. You can try a drop cap, make the first line small caps, or something like this to help the reader know the content starts here. It also helps set off the headline. It provides additional impact for your major headings.

Body Copy Run-in

This is a common way to format the fourth or fifth level of subhead. It also works well for more informal lists and word definitions. I'm sure you have noticed that I use this device a lot. I commonly use run-ins for lists which do not require the impact of a bulleted or numbered indent. As you can see below, starting with **Based on**, there is far less impact than a bulleted list like you see on the other page.

The only real problem is that a list like this can become very confusing visually. I wouldn't use run-in heads for more than two or three paragraphs in a row. As you can see below, where I use five in a row, it can quickly become visually tiring, boring, or confusing.

Based on (same as): Body Copy

No first line indent: The style becomes too visually confusing if you are not careful (as mentioned). Eliminating the first line indent helps quite a bit.

Extra space before paragraph: Because of the lack of a first line indent and the existence of a subhead, a little extra space before paragraph seems to help in the emphasis needed.

Nested style to format the subhead: I usually set mine up to apply the style until the first colon [as you see above]. This way it happens automatically as I write.

Run-in head uses header font: Depending on the header font used, you may need to use a bold or even black version of the font to give enough contrast for legibility.

As mentioned, I also use run-in heads to help with my lists. My writing style starts a list paragraph with a pithy statement ended with a colon. That is followed by explanatory copy. It probably drives grammarians nuts, but it works well for me (and seems very readable).

Zero and One numbered styles

I have found that for non-fiction books I commonly have more styles based on Body Copy than I have available shortcuts. As a result I have three styles that (if used) are given a shortcut using the Num Zero or Num1 keystroke. This is a relatively new addition to my working style and it differs from the basic starting styles I taught outside of publishing.

Quotes:

Quotes must be obvious. All readers need to be able to easily and intuitively identify quotes.

- **Based on:** Body Copy

- **Indented left and right the same amount as the first line indent of Body Copy:** But, this is certainly not written in stone.

- **Different alignment:** Quotes are also usually set justified when the body copy is flush left and often set flush left or centered when the body copy is justified.

The main thing is to make them different enough to be an obvious solution. Some make quotes in italic, but I find that often makes them too hard to read. If you do it well, quotation marks will not be needed [though you will normally still use them & editors demand them].

In my Bible studies, I no longer use actual quotation marks because it is so obvious where the quotes are. I do this by having my scripture references in a carefully styled paragraph. I use quotation marks for in-line references.

Bio style for articles by various authors

A bio style: You may also want to have a different paragraph style at the end of an article with an indent that allows room for a small picture and a short bio to go with the name and credits. The little bio can add a gentle warm fuzzy to help leave the reader with a good taste in his mind about the article. You can usually use the sidebar styles for this.

Captions

This little item has changed greatly in the years I have set type. Originally captions were commonly set small and italic. Current research suggests that the caption is more important than the headline in attracting readers. So the current norms are:

- **Based on:** Body Copy

- **A little larger than body copy**

- **Flush left**

- **A synopsis of the points the article is making about the picture:** In other words, because the picture is illustrating the article, the synopsis helps the reader decide whether or not to read the articles.

Remember: if it is not truly important content to the reader, he or she will be angry if you trick them into reading copy that has no relevance to their life. None of these formatting tips will help bad, unusable, or poorly written copy.

Sidebar Body Copy

I cover sidebar design in a few pages. This two-item list really doesn't give you any indication in the complexity of the design issues that go into sidebar construction.

- **Based on:** Body Copy

- **Sans serif:** I commonly make it body copy in size with the regular version of the headline font.

Lists need special care

These are extremely important areas in your copy. In terms of reading importance they rank right up there with the headline and the picture captions. Most lists about the importance readers assign to various paragraph styles put captions first, headlines second, and lists third. Some make Headlines first. Many readers look for lists and only read the rest of the copy if the lists are helpful.

- **Flush left alignment:** List paragraphs are usually quite short so justified copy often looks very bad. They will almost always need to be set flush left.

- **Decorative bullets:** As you can see, in this book I am using an ornament. In my Bible studies I use a cross. For marketing work, miniature logos can make wonderful bullets.

Because the reader considers your lists to be so important, you need to work at making them good-looking and obvious. A little care here will go a long way in helping your readers like your book. **Use sparingly:** this section of the book is quite hard to read because I am using several lists per spread [there are three on this page alone].

There are two basic kinds of lists: bulleted and numbered. Numbered lists include lists using Roman numerals, capital letters, or lowercase letters. Technical and bureaucratic writing often have complex and rigid rules about these things.

Bulleted lists

- **Left indent:** the same as the first line indent of Body Copy.

 This second, interior, left indent is a great help in visually organizing your copy: You can see I am using it here in this paragraph [my tip style] as well. It really helps make your formatted copy easy to absorb. It is a sure sign of professionalism. It also shows reader consideration by making the layout easily understood so that the content can be appropriated without the need to figure it what the priorities really are.

- **Bullet location:** The bullet should hang somewhere between the left column margin and halfway to the left indent—as you see to the left here.

- **Custom bullets:** They are certainly not necessary but they really pack a disproportionate amount of visual punch. However, Kindle chews them up.

Numbered lists

1. **Left indent:** the same as the first line indent of Body Copy.

2. **Number location:** The number needs hang somewhere between the left column margin and halfway to the left indent. You need to leave room for the longest number with your indents.

 Watch your lists carefully: Often these paragraphs are so short that you have to break for sense to get rid of the large number of paragraph widows [or runts] generated. Extra care needs to be taken for readability and reader comfort.

If your bulleted and numbered lists are crucial to reader understanding in your book, you may want to make them larger, bolder, and/or in a different font than your body copy. **They are very important.**

Heads and subheads

Ideally, especially for headlines, these need to be written to give the reader the number one benefit of reading the following content. They need to give the reader a reason to read the content—or at least give them the option of making an informed decision. The worst case is to have reader plow forward into a section which is already well-known or completely irrelevant.

Headlines and subheads are your outline. They are also used to produce your Table of Contents—as these are the styles which are collected for the TOC.

- **Short, pithy paragraphs that give a synopsis of the copy that follows:** Readers depend upon them to keep track of where they are in the content.

- **In non-fiction:** subheads are used to demarcate sections of copy, and the next conceptual point within a chapter.

- **Recapture wandering readers:** If you have a section which the reader believes is already known and understood, you often lose the attention of the reader. To recapture them, a well written subhead will pull them back into reading your copy.

- **Headline/subheads need a clear hierarchy:** It must be visually obvious where a subhead lies in this hierarchy. If it is not clear, you often need to make the headlines larger to give you enough size variation to make things work well.

I find that with a good set of styles developed and used, I think in terms of subheads while I am writing. They are simply added automatically as I write. Of course, you can go back and add them, but IMHO this could mean that you weren't considering the reader as you wrote the copy.

Headlines & chapter heads

This needs a lot of contrast with the body copy—in size, color, and/or type style. Typically the heads are sans serif and the body is serif, as you well know. I've been using a large regular sans contrasted with a book weight serif (lighter than regular) for a while now and it seems to work well.

- **Used once:** A headline is used once per article or once per chapter. This is one indicator to the reader that the new content section starts here.

- **Starts on an odd (right-hand) page:** This may not be essential, but the norm here is strong enough so that a headline on a left page looks bad, feels strange, and makes the reader uncomfortable. For ebooks, the headline starts a new page. In print, these headlines are emphasized with a special page style.

- **Size:** The normal size for headlines is 24 to 36 point. Large enough to allow a clear hierarchy with your subheads.

- **Length:** In general, they should be reasonably short and pithy. In other words, they need to give the reader a clear idea of what is coming in the copy following. Though they are different than billboards, the eight word maximum is not a bad guideline.

- **Alignment:** This needs to be closely watched. If the body copy is flush left, the heads need to be flush left. If they are centered over flush left copy they will typically look off center. If the body copy is justified, the heads can be either left or centered. The main concern is ease of reading and logical consistency.

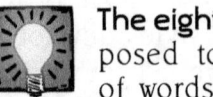 **The eight word maximum:** This is supposed to be the maximum number of words allowed in a billboard. Any more than that and most readers will not have time to read the copy as they fly by at 60 miles per hour.

Chapter beginnings

Books have a unique style which you need to observe. The first page of every chapter needs to have a unique style. Usually the copy starts about two-thirds of the way down the page. There may be an additional heading which simply gives the chapter number. There is often a graphic used to make it obvious that a new chapter is beginning. **Parts:** This is also true for books broken into parts. The first page of a part should have a unique style which cause the reader to know that a major break in the focus of the copy is going to occur beginning from this point in the book.

Often parts have illustrations—commonly antique artwork— to set off the beginning of the part. In an especially dry book, these pages can add a bit of life.

Subhead 1

This needs to be the same basic setup as the headline but about 25 to 33 percent smaller. So for this book, where the headline is 32 point, subhead one is 21 point. Mainly, you need to clearly differentiate & prioritize the headers.

For many years I made the headlines light or book in weight but extra large and then made the subheads bold or black. Sometime I made the headline and subhead-1 the same font and then reversed subhead-2 out of a colored bar. You simply need to design clear priorities to help the Reader. In this way, the reader gets an intuitive sense of the relative importance of the various sections of content. As always, your goal is to help the reader assimilate the copy. You must keep your focus on the reader.

Subhead 2

This is second level of subheads and it is smaller yet and almost always flush left (even if the heads and first level subheads are centered). In this book they are small— only 14 point and regular, not bold. This is why I added the graduated diamond rule to the right of the last line using a paragraph rule with a gradient stroke. For ePUB Reflows, rules are not available. There are many ways to provide this emphasis.

> **Slightly less contrast:** If the 6 and 7 styles are black, 8 subhead 2 is often bold in the same sans serif. These second level

heads do not need nearly as much contrast as the larger, more important heads.

Body heads

This one varies for me. It can have the same left indent as the first line indent of body copy and the same font family, but bold. Or, it can be the body copy sized version of the headers with a flush left alignment.

- **Based on:** Body Copy or Subhead 2, same size as body copy

- **Indent:** same as 1st line indent of copy or flush left

- **Bold or Black:** They often need this additional contrast to make them function as subheads.

These lesser subheads are now largely made irrelevant by the run-in styles already talked about.

None of these paragraph styles are to be used unless they are necessary (in your judgment). The guiding principle is still the same simple concept. *Do they help the reader comfortably and easily access your content?* If they make the layout too busy, pray for a better solution.

Callout & Pull Quotes

Pull quotes or callouts are one of the more important typographic features in long non-fiction articles and books. They are type used as a graphic to recapture the reader's attention (in case it is wandering). Occasionally they get extremely graphic, but the norm would probably be 50 to 100% larger in italicized body copy. They often use paragraph rules above and/or below to set them off.

"(Pull quotes) are type used as a graphic to recapture the reader's attention"

- **If they are actual quotes:** it is a common device to make the quote marks extremely large (400 to 1,000% of the point size of the pull quote). The ones used above are 1000% [10x] larger. By the way, the only difference between the two names (pull quotes and callouts) is that pull quotes actually quote part of the surrounding copy.

- **Not used in busy layouts:** Actually you will see that I use them less and less because most of my non-fiction writing uses layouts which are simply too complex. Pull quotes just become more noise (as they are above). If you are going to use them, you must use almost violent contrast in these cases.

Sidebar styles are important

There are no real rules here, but let's give it a shot. First of all, **sidebars**, by definition, **contain peripheral information**. In other words, they contain data that is interesting and nice to know; but they are often tangential to the main thoughts and concepts of the body copy. It may help you to think of them as a bonus you offer for your good and/or loyal readers—another obscure form of ministry.

 **The key to remember is that the tint in the tint box will mess up your type:** Even at 150 linescreen with 300 dpi tints, the tiny little dots will blur the edges of your characters. So you need to pick typestyles that will not be damaged by those dots. This is why I usually use sans serif for my sidebars. When coupled with the fact that my sidebars are usually very brief, this works well.

De-emphasized a little: You still want the body copy to be primary.

Tinted background: The best way to do this is to put the sidebar in a tinted box. Contrary to common, nonprofessional thought, a tint box tends to make items less important. The tint back ground lowers contrast so the type is harder to read. To make a tint box primary, you will need to place a background image over the entire page—then the light, bright tint boxes will stand out.

Contrasting type: As far as type is concerned, you commonly want a font which contrasts with the body copy. Depending upon how you intend to use the sidebars, you may wish to pick typestyles that contrast with both the main body and its heads.

Multipurpose use: In my books I commonly set up my sidebar styles so I can use them for emphasis within the main copy also. I use the same font as used in my heads, with a plain, light, or medium version of the font for my sidebar body copy.

If you are printing in color: (or for your ebooks) a pastel color background does not chop up the type nearly so much.

If your sidebars are going to be long: maybe even a parallel story alongside your main body copy, maybe you should try something like Century Schoolbook or even a strong contrast like Rockwell or Lucida Bright. Because of the lessened contrast you can use much blacker type than normal. In some cases, an actual Black or Display weight printed at a 70% tint works well.

Tables: I commonly use my sidebar styles in my tables also. The increased legibility helps within the gridwork of a table.

Good formatting is a ministry (a loving service) to your reader

You always need to keep your focus on clear communication with your readers. If your content is important enough to be in a book, it is also worth your time to help your reader easily assimilate the message.

CHAPTER TWENTY-TWO

A Set Of Default Styles

In the past, when I was teaching these materials in a curriculum, I made this information available on the course Website. For this book, I have pulled these instructions off the Website so you are not forced to go there. Here are ten basic paragraph styles to get you started with your formatting. Here is what you are going to end up with in your copy of InDesign.

Setting up the set of default styles

You should have no document open. You want to be setting the Application Defaults so that these styles are available in every document from now on. Any changes made in any of the Dialog boxes, Panels, or commands with no document open will become the new default settings for InDesign as a whole. The result of this little exercise will be ten styles that will be available for every new document you open.

The book template will have a very different set: These basic ten styles are more designed to teach you how to set up your own styles.

A Sample Set of Default Styles

Style	Mac Shortcut	PC Shortcut
0 Kick	Command+Num0	Ctrl+Num0
1 Inline Dropped	Command+Num1	Ctrl+Num1
2 Body	Command+Num2	Ctrl+Num2
2 No First	Command+Opt+Shift+Num2	Ctrl+Alt+Shift+Num2
2 Run-In	Command+Opt+Num2	Ctrl+Alt+Num2
3 Number	Command+Num3	Ctrl+Num3
3 Bullet	Command+Opt+Num3	Ctrl+Alt+Num3
4 Body-Heads	Command+Num4	Ctrl+Num4
5 Quote	Command+Num5	Ctrl+Num5
6 Head	Command+Num6	Ctrl+Num6
7 Sub1	Command+Num7	Ctrl+Num7
8 Sub2	Command+Num8	Ctrl+Num8
9 Callout	Command+Num9	Ctrl+Num9

We begin by setting up the Body Copy Styles

2 Body; 2 No first; 2 Run-In; 3 Number; 3 Bullet; 4 Body heads; 5 Quote; & 9 Callout: All of these styles are based on the basic body copy style 2-body. I number the styles to help you remember the shortcuts.

 **VERY IMPORTANT! Style shortcuts require the use of the numerical keypad:** If you are using a limited keyboard (on a laptop, for example) you will need to get yourself a full size extended keyboard [or buy a special keyboard supplement—as long as is can use the modifier keys]. You need this anyway—as I mentioned much earlier. Setting styles is one of the major reasons why this is so.

Start by opening the Paragraph Styles panel

SELECT ALL THE EXISTING STYLES AND DELETE THEM

You need an empty Styles Panel to start with. All that should remain is [Basic Paragraph] which cannot be deleted.

We begin with the body styles

Start by making a new style: 2 Body

- 💠 **Choose New Paragraph Style... In The Panel Menu, or click on the New Style button at the bottom of the panel**

Then On The GENERAL PAGE:

- 💠 **Style Name:** 2-Body
- 💠 **Based on:** [No Paragraph Style]
- 💠 **Next Style:** [Same Style]
- 💠 **Shortcut:** Command+Num2 (PC: Ctrl+Num2)

BASIC CHARACTER FORMATS PAGE:

- 💠 **Font Family & Style:** Serif your choice, you can change it for individual books
- 💠 **Size & Leading:** Normally 10/12
- 💠 **INDENTS AND SPACING:**
- 💠 **Alignment:** Left Justify
- 💠 **First Line Indent:** 0.4 in [or whatever you decide]

Make new style: 2 No First

- 💠 **Select:** 2 Body & Then Choose New Paragraph Style... In The Panel Menu

GENERAL PAGE:

- 💠 **Style Name:** 2 No first
- 💠 **Based on:** [2 Body]
- 💠 **Next Style:** [2 Body]
- 💠 **Shortcut:** Command+Option+Shift+Num2 (PC: Ctrl+Alt+Shift+Num2)

INDENTS AND SPACING:

- 💠 **Alignment:** Left Justify
- 💠 **First Line Indent:** 0 in

🌀 **Space Before:** p3 [that's 3 points, which will be converted to .0417"]

Next, we need a character style

Start by making a new character style: 1-Body Bold

🌀 **Choose New Character Style... In The Character Styles Panel Menu**

GENERAL PAGE:

🌀 **Style Name:** 1 Body Bold

🌀 **Based on:** [No Character Style]

🌀 **Shortcut:** Option+Shift+Num1 (PC: Ctrl+Alt+Num1)

BASIC CHARACTER FORMATS PAGE:

🌀 **Font Family:** Sans or Decorative your choice

🌀 **Font Style:** Bold

CHARACTER COLOR:

🌀 **It seems to help if you make it a strong color**

Make new style: 2 Run-In

🌀 **Select:** 2 Body & Then Choose New Paragraph Style... In The Panel Menu

GENERAL PAGE:

🌀 **Style Name:** 2 Run-In

🌀 **Based on:** [2 Body]

🌀 **Next Style:** [Same Style]

🌀 **Shortcut:** Command+Option+Num2 (PC: Ctrl+Num2)

INDENTS AND SPACING:

🌀 **Alignment:** Left

🌀 **Check:** Balance Ragged Lines

🌀 **Left Indent:** 0 in

🌀 **First Line Indent:** 0 in

> After creating a character style, make sure you choose {None} again or you might find that character style has become your default automatically applied to all type you set.

- **Space Before:** p2
- **Space After:** 0

DROP CAPS AND NESTED STYLES:

- **Add a nested style; choosing 1-Body Bold through 1 :** (one colon)

Make new style: 3 Number

- **Select:** 2 Body & Then Choose New Paragraph Style... In The Panel Menu

GENERAL PAGE:

- **Style Name:** 3 Number
- **Based on:** [2 Body]
- **Next Style:** [Same Style]
- **Shortcut:** Command+Num3 (PC: Ctrl+Num3)

INDENTS AND SPACING:

- **Alignment:** Left
- **Check:** Balance Ragged Lines
- **Left Indent:** 0.4 in
- **First Line Indent:** -0.25 in
- **Space Before:** p2
- **Space After:** 0

BULLETS AND NUMBERING:

- **Pick Numbered**
- **Set it up like you want**

HYPHENATION PAGE:

- **Turn this off:** It is often a good idea for this style

Make new style: 3 Bullet

- **SELECT:** 3 Number & THEN Right-Click And Duplicate The Style
- **Open The New Style:** 3 NumberCopy

GENERAL PAGE:

- **Style Name:** 3 Bullet
- **Based on:** [2 Body]
- **Next Style:** [Same Style]
- **Shortcut:** Command+Option+Num3 (PC: Ctrl+Alt+Num3)

INDENTS AND SPACING:

- **Alignment:** Left
- **Check:** Balance Ragged Lines
- **Left Indent:** 0.4 in
- **First Line Indent:** -0.25 in
- **Space Before:** p2
- **Space After:** 0

BULLETS AND NUMBERING:

- **Pick Bulleted**
- **Set it up like you want**

HYPHENATION PAGE:

- **Turn this off:** It is often a good idea for this style

Make new style: 4 Body Heads

- **Select:** 2 Body & Then Choose New Paragraph Style... In The Panel Menu

GENERAL PAGE:

- **Style Name:** 4 Body heads
- **Next Style:** [2 Body]
- **Shortcut:** Command+Num4 (PC: Ctrl+Num4)

BASIC CHARACTER FORMATS PAGE:

- **Font Style:** Bold or whatever the options are for the font family you chose
- **Add small caps or whatever you think will make your small heads work**

INDENTS AND SPACING:

- **Alignment:** Left
- **Check:** Balance Ragged Lines
- **Left Indent:** 0.4 in
- **Space Before:** p5
- **Space After:** p2

HYPHENATION PAGE:

- **Turn off**

JUSTIFICATION PAGE:

- **Auto Leading:** 100% or less for caps or small caps

Make new style: 5 Quote

- **Select:** 2 Body & Then Choose New Paragraph Style... In The Panel Menu

GENERAL PAGE:

- **Style Name:** 5 Quote
- **Next Style:** [2 Body]
- **Shortcut:** Command+Num5 (PC: Ctrl+Num5)

BASIC CHARACTER FORMATS PAGE:

- **Font choices:** Make it contrast with the body copy using italic, a regular version of your header font, a larger point size, or whatever solution you come up with. The goal is to make your quotes obvious while keeping them readable

INDENTS AND SPACING:

- **Alignment:** Left Justify
- **Left Indent:** 0.4 in
- **First Line Indent:** 0
- **Right Indent:** 0.4 in
- **Space Before:** p5

- **Space After:** p5

Make new style: 9 Callout

- **Select:** 2 Body & Then Choose New Paragraph Style... In The Panel Menu

GENERAL PAGE:

- **Style Name:** 9 Callout

- **Next Style:** [2 Body]

- **Shortcut:** Command+Num9 (PC: Ctrl+Num9)

BASIC CHARACTER FORMATS PAGE:

- **Type Style:** Italic

- **Size:** 18 point

- **Leading:** 19 point

INDENTS AND SPACING:

- **Alignment:** Left or centered

- **Check:** Balance Ragged Lines

- **Left Indent:** 0

- **First Line Indent:** 0

- **Right Indent:** 0

- **Space Before:** p5

- **Space After:** p5

PARAGRAPH RULES PAGE:

- **Turn on Rule Above &/or Below:**, by checking Rule On

- **The size, color, type, offset, and so on are your choice:** BUT they do really help set off the callout.

- **(You'll probably need to set up more space before and after paragraph to make room for the rules.)**

HYPHENATION PAGE:

- **Turn off**

JUSTIFICATION PAGE:

- **Auto Leading:** 115%

Now we set up the headers

They need to contrast sharply with your body copy—especially in a complex non-fiction book like this one. Most new designers are too timid. Often experienced designers like myself have a tendency to make them too strong.

Start by making a new style: 6 Head

- **Choose New Paragraph Style... In The Panel Menu (With No Style Selected)**

GENERAL PAGE:

- **Style Name:** 6 Head
- **Based on:** [No Paragraph Style]
- **Next Style:** [2 Body]
- **Shortcut:** Command+Num6 (PC: Ctrl+Num6)

BASIC CHARACTER FORMATS PAGE:

- **Font Family & Style:** Sans or Decorative your choice
- **Size:** 30 point

INDENTS AND SPACING:

- **Alignment:** Left
- **Left Indent:** 0 in
- **First Line Indent:** 0 in
- **Space Before:** p7
- **Space After:** p2

HYPHENATION PAGE:

- **Turn off**

JUSTIFICATION PAGE:

- **Auto Leading:** 100%

KEEPS PAGE:

- **Normally, choose start on next odd page:** for most ePUBs & Kindle books, start on next page will work. For the iBookstore, choose anywhere because choosing this style to start your chapters will add a blank page which is disconcerting in an ereader.

Make new style: 7 Subhead 1

- **Select:** 6 Head & Then Choose New Paragraph Style... In The Panel Menu

GENERAL PAGE:

- **Style Name:** 7 Subhead 2
- **Based on:** [6 Head]
- **Next Style:** [2 Body]
- **Shortcut:** Command+Num7 (PC: Ctrl+Num7)

BASIC CHARACTER FORMATS PAGE:

- **Size:** 21 point

INDENTS AND SPACING:

- **Alignment:** Left
- **Left Indent:** 0 in
- **First Line Indent:** 0 in
- **Space Before:** p7
- **Space After:** p2

HYPHENATION PAGE:

- **Turn off**

JUSTIFICATION PAGE:

- **Auto Leading:** 100% or less for caps or small caps

Make new style: 8 Subhead 2

- **Select:** 6 Head & Then Choose New Paragraph Style... In The Panel Menu

GENERAL PAGE:

- **Style Name:** 8 Subhead 2
- **Based on:** [6 Head]
- **Next Style:** [2 Body]
- **Shortcut:** Command+Num8 (PC: Ctrl+Num8)

BASIC CHARACTER FORMATS PAGE:

- **Size:** 13 point

INDENTS AND SPACING:

- **Alignment:** Left
- **Left Indent:** .4 In
- **First Line Indent:** 0 In
- **Space Before:** P5
- **Space After:** 0

HYPHENATION PAGE:

- **Turn off**

JUSTIFICATION PAGE:

- **Auto Leading:** 100% or less for caps or small caps

CHARACTER COLOR

- **Paper:** white or whatever to complement the rule

PARAGRAPH RULES PAGE: Turn On Rule Above

- **Size:** big enough to cover type
- **Color:** Your choice but I suggest a gradient and that means you have to make the gradient BEFORE you can use it here.
- **Width:** Text
- **Offset:** -0.0525 in

- **Left Indent:** -0.4 in (yes this is a negative indent to bring the rule back out to the left column margin)
- **Right Indent:** -0.1 in (negative also)

Make new style: 0 Kicker

- **Select:** 6 Head & Then Choose New Paragraph Style... In The Panel Menu

GENERAL PAGE:

- **Style Name:** 0 Kicker
- **Based On:** [6 Head]
- **Next Style:** [2 Body]
- **Shortcut:** Command+Num0 (PC: Ctrl+Num0)

BASIC CHARACTER FORMATS PAGE:

- **Style:** Bold Or Black
- **Size:** 10 Point
- **Case:** Small Caps

INDENTS AND SPACING:

- **Alignment:** Left
- **Left Indent:** 0 In
- **First Line Indent:** 0 In
- **Space Before:** P5
- **Space After:** 0

HYPHENATION PAGE:

- **Turn Off**

JUSTIFICATION PAGE:

- **Auto Leading:** 100% Or Less For Caps Or Small Caps

PARAGRAPH RULES PAGE: Turn On Rule
Below By Checking Rule On

- **The options are up to your sense of style:** but the underline seems to be essential

Another special style I use a lot

Start by making a new character style: 1-Body Bold

- **Choose New Character Style... In The Character Styles Panel Menu**

GENERAL PAGE:

- **Style Name:** 1 Body Bold

- **Based on:** [No Character Style]

- **Shortcut:** Option+Shift+Num1 (PC: Ctrl+Alt+Num1)

BASIC CHARACTER FORMATS PAGE:

- **Font Family:** Sans or Decorative your choice

- **Font Style:** Bold

Make new style: 1 Inline Dropped

- **Select:** 2 Body & Then Choose New Paragraph Style... In The Panel Menu

> After creating a character style, make sure you choose {None} again or you might find that character style has become your default automatically applied to all type you set.

GENERAL PAGE:

- **Style Name:** 1 Inline Graphic

- **Based on:** [2 Body]

- **Next Style:** [2 Body]

- **Shortcut:** Command+Option+Num1 (PC: Ctrl+Num1)

BASIC CHARACTER FORMATS PAGE:

- **Font Family:** the light version of the header font family

- **Size:** 10 point

INDENTS AND SPACING:

- **Alignment:** Left or left justified

- **Left Indent:** same as body copy first line
- **First Line Indent:** o in
- **Space Before:** p2
- **Space After:** o

DROP CAPS AND NESTED STYLES:

- **Add drop cap of one character and three lines**
- **Add a nested style; choosing 1-Body
  Bold through 1 : (one colon)**

Obviously, the variations are endless.

Let's continue with tables

This is an area of page layout that has only been available for a decade or so. Throughout the '90s, there was no professional application with which to make tables. Many people just did them in Word and ignored the bad type, poor letterspacing, horrible controls, and so on. Now, InDesign has excellent table production tools.

Tables are part of type and edited with the Type tool

A table is a grid of text frames called cells: Each cell acts in many ways like a normal InDesign text frame. You can insert inline graphics, use paragraph styles and character styles. You can save them into Table styles and Cell styles.

You can have headers and footers with multiple rows of each if you like: When the table continues on the next frame, a new set of headers and footers is generated. The point size of headers can usually be quite small as the reader can usually figure out what the headings are with minimal help.

All selections are done with the type tool, as you can see below: The Type tool changes as it moves over different parts of a table. At the edges, it changes to a small bold arrow that at the side lets you select a row; the top, a column; or (in the upper left corner) the entire table.

 Selector arrows: If you move your Type tool over the corner of the table you are working on, this arrow appears. If you click the mouse, you'll select the entire table. Similar directional selector arrows appear vertically at the top of columns or horizontally at the left side of rows.

Tables can flow from frame to frame, column to column, and page to page. They flow like text in general with the small surprise that entire rows jump to the top of the next frame even if there is just barely not enough room. Of course, when you think about it, how could you have a partial row? New headers and footers are added for each new frame.

Tables are separate from the rest of the text

In some ways they function like an inline graphic. In most ways they function like an interconnected group of text frames. There are a few limitations though.

- **You must make a text frame first:** you cannot have a table as a separate object. A table is inserted into an insertion point in the text.

- **Headers & footers can only be selected or edited in the first frame:** In other words, on the first page of a table which extends across two or more frames, columns, &/or pages.

- **Page and column breaks can only happen between rows:** If you think about it, partial cells would be almost impossible to deal with.

- **Shortcuts are often different:** Table has its own context in the Keyboard Shortcuts dialog. You can set shortcuts that only work in tables. In fact, it can be quite disconcerting that many of your normal page navigation controls do not work from within a table.

❧ **Tables can extend outside the enclosing text frame:** In this way they function like an inline graphic.

 However, it can be hard to select type in the cells outside the text frame which contains the table: You'll have to put your insertion point in a cell inside the enclosing text frame and then tab through to get to the cells outside the frame. That's the only way which works reliably. This can cause printing problems also.

Table design

When setting type, there are times when rules, leaders, tabs, and columns are simply not enough. It can be argued (and Bringhurst does in his typography book) that anything more than simple tabs with no rules or leaders goes too far. That may have been true in the last century. But in this one – *He is wrong!*

However, there is certainly a need for restraint. Too many rules, boxes, and borders imprison type and make it feel cheap. Sometimes cheap is what you need, but do it on purpose in that case. Especially in the case of tables you need to keep it light and easy to read.

Table & Cell Styles

Beginning with InDesign CS3 Adobe took the capabilities of Paragraph, Character, and Object styles and used them to create styles for that unique text object, Tables. You can do amazing things with tables once you become comfortable with them.

Assuming that you are familiar with how styles work, Table & Cell styles still take a little preplanning. Cell Styles come first: It will be helpful if you set them up before you make your Table Styles—because—the first choices you make in a table style is which cell styles you are going to apply and where. Of course, it is possible to add new cell styles inline, as you can see in the capture on the next page.

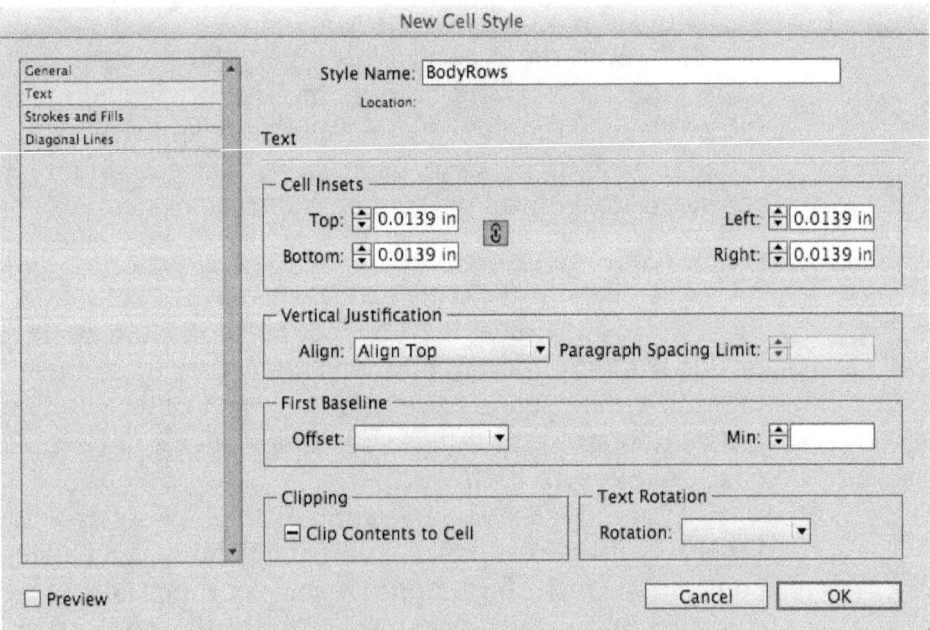

Cell Styles (character styles for tables)

Cell styles format selected cells in a table. You can control the paragraph style used, how the text is located within each cell, the stroke and fill of the cells, and the diagonal lines you might want to use. In the New Table Style dialog are separate choices for header rows, footer rows, the left column, the right column, and body rows. This is much more complex than you will normally use. In fact, I commonly make my table and then format it with my normal paragraph styles by selecting what I want to format with my Selection Arrows.

Text page

This page controls everything in the Text Frame Options dialog: plus the ability to do limited text rotation in 90° increments. You can align the copy Top, Middle, Bottom, Justify Vertically, or (Ignore).

Be very careful of the Justify Vertically option. It sounds very good because the top and bottom of the copy will align with the cells next to it. However, it will wreak havoc with your paragraph spacing. Just like I never use this in normal text frames, I do not use it in tables.

Strokes and Fills

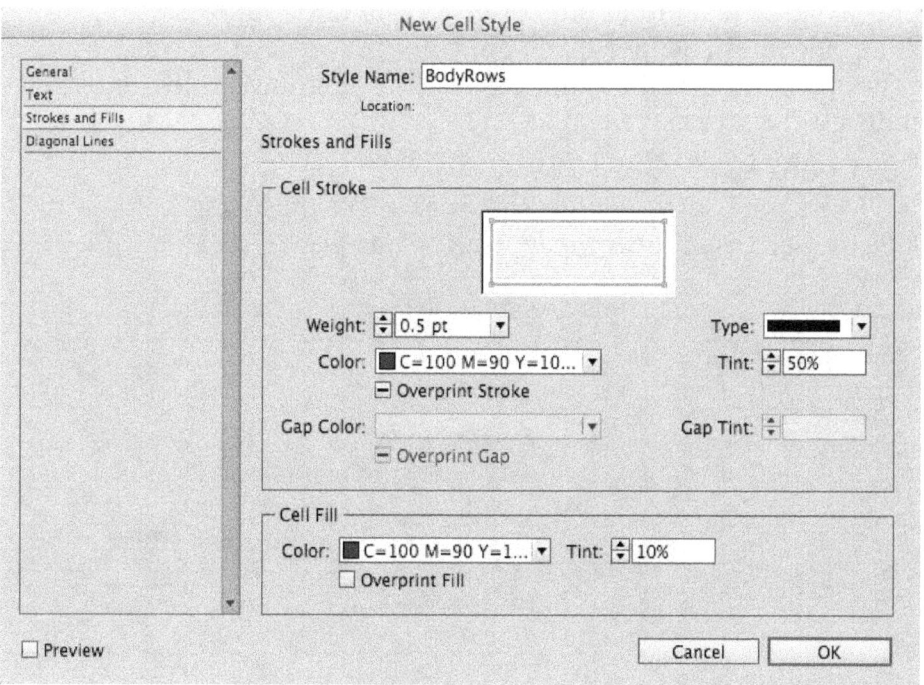

This page allows you to set the stroke for each side of the cell with the normal choices of the Stroke panel. You click on the proxy lines to turn them on or off. Sadly, the colors you choose have to be in the Swatches panel before you start the process, or you'll have to quit and go create the new swatches necessary. Plus, if you use a gradient, you can't tint it.

Coloring the lines around the cell or cells is pretty straight forward. The blue lines in the proxy are selected and will be formatted according to the settings below. In this case you can see all four are selected. The lines will be half point solid rule, colored 50% royal blue, with a 10% Royal Blue fill to the cell.

If I click on any of the four lines, it will turn thinner and black. Those lines are not formatted. These cell strokes are not nearly so important because the table is styled with strokes and fills throughout, but Cell Styles override any settings made there.

For those curious, the Overprint settings are for people printing with spot color. However, with on-demand printing spot color is not an option. So, that control is not used by us at this point. In fact, spot color in general is being lost in the bins of history as CMYK process color becomes cheaper than spot color in our day to day printing. Like varnishes, embossing, foil stamping, et all, they're very expensive.

Diagonal lines

I assume some people somewhere use these? Actually, they are used for companies with long price lists and

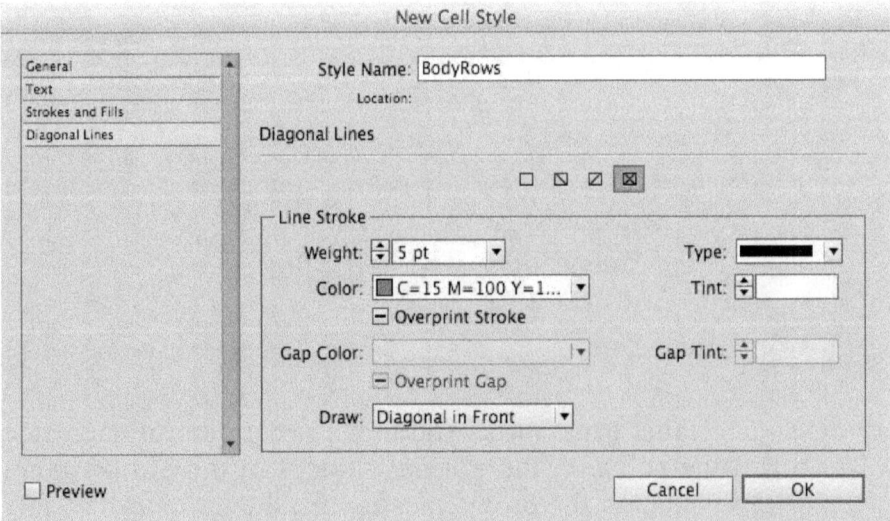

catalogs where you need to block off items which are no longer available or out of stock. There may be other uses, but I've never seen a use in books.

To repeat, you need to set up all your Cell styles before you build your table styles: Actually, you don't but you'll feel better about yourself.

 **InDesign was created to produce artwork for top quality commercial printing:** Many common printing possibilities are simply not available to the equipment used by our free on-demand print suppliers & even less for ebooks.

Table Styles

Table styles use all the controls for tables that you are familiar with plus you can apply cell styles to specific rows like the header rows, footer rows, left column, right column and body rows. This is where you set the overall table border and any alternating strokes or fills you might want. You can also set the space before & after the table here also.

Again the styles are very straight forward and use the same basic concepts and techniques as the text and object styles we have already covered.

Table Style: General [SAME AS TABLE OPTIONS]

Table Style: Setup

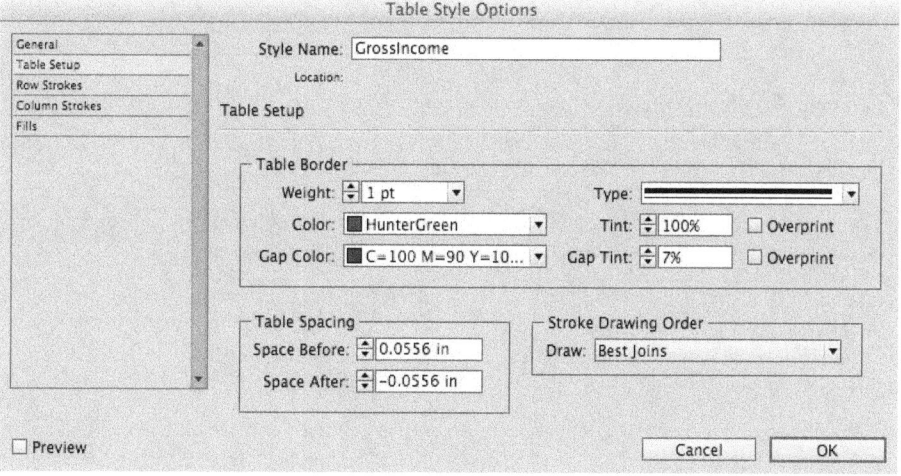

Here you can set the border of the entire table: Cell styles can override portions of this if you wish, because they are applied on top of the table style.

Table spacing: This is the only place you can control the space before and after a table. Even though a table seems to be it's own paragraph, the paragraph spacing controls will not control it. It's a bit of a frustration.

Stroke drawing order: Best Joins is good. The other options are complex and rarely help, usually hurt, the appearance of your table.

Table Style: Row Strokes or Column Strokes

You have many options here: Every Other Row, Every Second Row, Every Third Row, or whatever Custom setup you can imagine with only two choices. Plus, you can skip x# of first rows or last rows.

In most cases, using an Every Other Row fill eliminates the need for any strokes. You can format the rows with fills instead which is much more elegant. So I usually make row strokes 0 points or [None] in color.

Column strokes have the exact same choices vertically. Personally, I have found the making column strokes white [Paper] cleans up tables a lot while still being visible. These column strokes only appear on the filled rows, but that is more than enough for the eye—because the text layout makes columns clear already.

Table Style: Fills

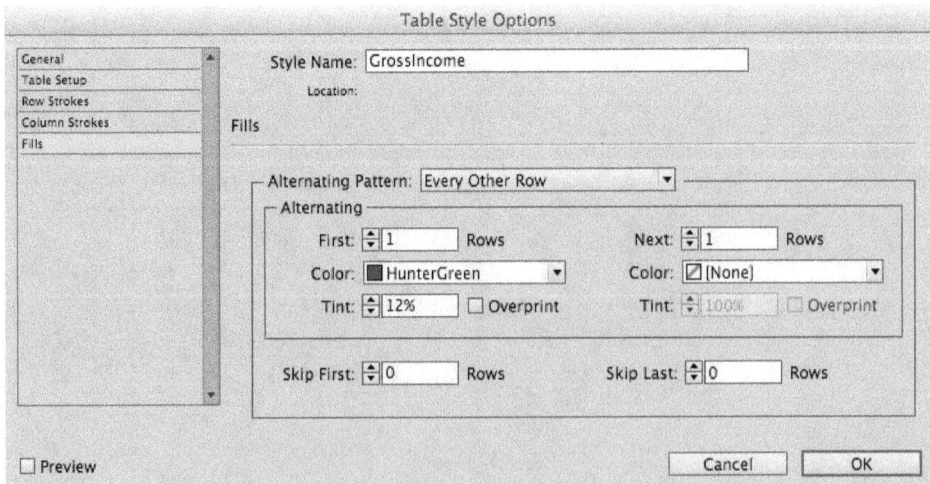

You also have the same alternating choices for fills. The only limitation is that you have to choose whether you will use alternating rows or columns. You cannot do both. You must choose one or the other.

General guidance

The only real limitations are your sense of taste & style. However, remember the goal—presenting written copy in a manner that is easy to read. Each cell is like an individual text frame. So, anything you can do with text, you can do in a table. This includes things like inline graphics, drop caps, lists, and so on.

A Pictorial Guide

Below I show you one of the pages from a little booklet about the cities of New Mexico. This page shows some of the sights around Canyon Road—the gallery strip for fine artists just southeast of the Plaza. I developed a table that flowed from page to page without a hitch. The only production issue was making all the photos the same height—they are placed into the cell as inline text objects. It looks much better in color. There are two header rows and one footer row that appear on every page: The three locations are set off with every other row fills

Cities of New Mexico: Santa Fe

PHOTO	LOCATION	AGE	COMMENTS
	A front door to a compound: close to Canyon Road, the gallery center of the city	Unknown. Relatively recent, maybe 50 years	It is quite common to not be able to see the home from the street
	This door has rough-hewn panels. We think the garden backs up on Canyon Road	Much older, maybe a couple hundred years	There is a lot of parking room outside the door and the compound is very large
	This amazing rock wall must be eight feet tall & run for 50 yards near the state capital	No way to know, but it is very weathered and that takes a while in New Mexico	This type of old, loosely structured detail is the core of what is now called Santa Fe style

ALL PHOTOS © 2001 BY REV. PATRICIA H. BERGSLAND

A course calendar

AD250: Page Layout • Summer 2007 • Submission Schedule & Deadlines

AD250	Tuesday	Lecture	Thursday	Lecture
Week 1	7/17: Welcome!	General Intro: to course and page layout	7/19: 1st Class Email	Getting set up: Chap#1 workspace: Defaults, preferences, workspaces, shortcuts
Week 2	7/24: 2nd Class Email Theory 1: Noon	Reading: Chap #2 Page Layout: project folder, backup, new doc, bleeds, slug,	7/26: 3rd Class Email Tutorial 1 Due: 3 pm	Setting up project: Chap #2 DEMO: booklet, pages, pages panel
Week 3	7/31: Class Email BIO: Noon	Importing text: Chap #3&4: discussion and demo	8/2: Class Email	Text layout tools: Chap#6: Rules and tables
Week 4	8/7 : Class Email Theory 2: Noon	Graphics: Chap #5: Pen tool, shapes, strokes, fills, gradients	8/9: Class Email Tutorial #2: 3 pm	Creating outlines: Chap#5: Pathfinder, editing paths, effects, corner effects

This is one those horrible tables that are necessary. The challenge at a school, of course, is to make them seem non-bureaucratic. The setup above seemed to work reasonably well. It's a two-page table with a header. I tossed a lot of strange color into the mix just to fool them into believing that this might be something relevant to their iPhone, texting, gaming world.

Forms in books don't work very well

The best procedure, if you really want a form to be filled out by your readers is to have a link in your ebooks which they can click and be taken to the site where the form is waiting for them to fill out. It is obviously less powerful to do this in a printed book where all you can do is give them the URL in printed form hoping they will take the initiative to go to a browser and type in the URL.

Single cell forms

One of the resources you may want to remember is the fact that you can make a single-celled table to provide inline text within a bordered box. With some care, it will even transfer well into your ePUBs and Kindle KF8 versions. However, you'll need to save this single-cell table as a PDF, and then rasterize that PDF into a 600-pixel-wide graphic—for now.

CHAPTER TWENTY-FOUR

Book print production

Let's start with a brief review of the process to make sure we are on the same page. Again, this is a very complex process. It is not particularly difficult, but the procedure is certainly not simple. This is subject to fashion, but be careful.

The book production process

Get the vision: You start with your idea. You research the market and try to determine your niche. This is an area fraught with uncertainty, because you really have no idea if it will sell or who will buy it. Even free print books need to be positioned to attract your readers instead of people looking for firestarter.

Pick a size: This again is more complicated than it looks. But in another way it is no real problem. Anything you choose to start with can easily be reformatted to another size once everything is in place and completely controlled by styles. When in doubt start with a 6×9 page.

You need to pray about this or at least seriously think about it. Many times I have been led to a specific size to use for a particular book. Remember who is going to use your book. Know the demographics of your future (and commonly unknown to you as yet) group of readers—your niche. Often it will surprise you once you actually begin selling your book.

 For InDesign, you need to plan things out a bit: You will eventually have many different formats and page sizes. I am just using a Primary Text Frame and doing my additional formats individually. I find I usually need to write new copy or produce new graphics—especially for the ePUBs and Kindle versions where special fonts don't work well and the graphics need to be so radically converted. Start with print and write for all formats.

Using your set of default styles begin writing or adding pieces: All you do is type Command+Num6 (or what ever shortcut you use for your headline style) and start writing. If you are using pieces from essays, blog posts, booklets or whatever else you have written to be a part of this, just paste them in order and format as you go.

You need to keep these styles fluid in your mind: One of the real blessings of using styles is that you can develop your book style over the first few chapters. There will be a real ebb and flow as you adjust your styles—especially your paragraph spacing—as you watch the pages come together.

Front matter & back matter

You need to add your front and back matter as you are putting the book together. You need to be thinking about the entire package throughout the writing and production of the book.

There are several (often many) pages of materials that need to be at the front and back of your book. Many of them are optional. Several are not. Some are required for print but not used for ebooks.

For example, in print, you must have a title page and a copyright page. You almost certainly need a Table of Contents (the actual type should not be in an ebook though the setup must be done). You may or may not need an introduction, a dedication, or any of about a dozen other possibilities. You should have an index for non-fiction (again the search functions of an ebook make this unnecessary and very difficult to implement). The following is deeply indebted to Wikipedia and the volunteer writers and editors who have spent so much time putting information like this together.

Many of these things are not necessary or even desirable for all books. You need to be careful that you don't bore the reader into tears—to the place where they simply put the book down because it is too much trouble to get to the actual content of the book. [Which is why they bought the book in the first place, remember?]

This is especially true for ebooks. Here the rule is as little as possible up front. The minimum seems to be the cover, copyright information and a dedication. But I've even had to be careful with the copyright info. Several times I moved most of it to the back of the ebook.

Front matter choices

- **Advertising blurbs and testimonials:** This would include lists of additional books by the author and quotes from reviewers. I know they are commonplace, but they are certainly gauche.

  Though this is merely my opinion, such self-aggrandizing always seems a bit desperate and is bragging at best (be it on your head).

- **Half Title:** This page just has the title—no subtitle, author name, or anything else. It is the first page inside the cover. You normally use the title font and style from the cover, but smaller.

- **Frontispiece:** This is an illustration on the page facing the title page. As you can see below, this can be a very stylish and elegant way to start your book. If done well, it offers comfort and tradition to your book design.

An old German title page with frontispiece
from 1722 [WIKIMEDIA COMMONS]

Title page: This page is commonly a reduced version of your book cover, unless you use a frontispiece. Ideally the title page shows the title of the work, the person or group responsible for its intellectual content, the place & year of publication, and the name of the publisher.

Copyright page: This is normally on the back of the title page. Some would say that it is absolutely required to be there. It contains copyright owner name and the year, the publishing staff, edition and printing information, ISBN, cataloging details for the Library Of Congress. The lawyers love this page in a big publishing house. Hopefully, we are more merciful than that.

- **Table of contents:** This is built and updated with the Table of Contents… command at the bottom of the Layout menu. It's powerful and I have a tendency to add too much. I am in the process of rethinking my TOC use. I'm moving smaller subhead content to the index.

- **List of figures:** This is more needed for fine art books than anything, but this would be the place it goes, after the Table of Contents. It is also produced with the TOC commands. You'll need special paragraph styles for your captions which can then be collected.

- **List of tables:** If your book is data-driven, this might be a good service for your readers. This is also produced with the TOC commands. You'll need special paragraph styles for your table headers which can then be collected.

- **Dedication:** This where you name the people whose inspiration enabled you to write the book.

- **Acknowledgments:** These are all the people, groups, and Websites who helped you.

- **Foreword:** This is written by a real person, other than yourself.

- **Preface:** This covers the story of how the book came into being, or how the idea for the book was developed. It often includes the acknowledgments.

- **Introduction:** Here you can give the purpose, goals, and organization of your book. This is where you tell the reader the devices you use throughout the book [like little graphics for tips, how you will identify sources, and things like that].

- **Prologue:** Written by the narrator or a character in the book, this gives the setting and background details, some earlier story that ties into this book, or other relevant details. It sets the stage for the real content.

Back matter choices

There are many options here also. These are more reader services and references to help them as they read your book. Where much of the front matter helps fiction, the back matter is almost entirely for non-fiction. Of course, Tolkien loved to add back matter about Middle Earth—which further developed the reality of his fictional world.

It's all up to you. However, if you ignore all of these things, the reader might well feel the book is not complete.

* **Epilogue:** This is a great service to the reader in fiction. For me and my wife anyway, we often talk about books that just dump you off with many of the issues unresolved. We want completion, a sense that we know what happened and that it's all OK.

 To quote from Wikipedia:

 "An epilogue is a final chapter at the end of a story that often serves to reveal the fates of the characters. Some epilogues may feature scenes only tangentially related to the subject of the story. They can be used to hint at a sequel or wrap up all the loose ends. They can occur at a significant period of time after the main plot has ended. In some cases, the epilogue has been used to allow the main character a chance to 'speak freely'. An epilogue can continue in the same narrative style and perspective as the preceding story, although the form of an epilogue can occasionally be drastically different from the overall story."

* **Afterword:** "When the author steps in and speaks directly to the reader, that is more properly considered an afterword."

* **Conclusion:** This is also called a summary or a synopsis.

* **Appendix/Addendum:** This contains additional materials to flesh out a particular portion of the book.

You might consider yet another option as a reader service. As Appendices they can work really well. But, they can also be released as separate booklets for readers of earlier editions and for more advanced readers who might otherwise skip your book.

- **Glossary:** Relevant word definitions

- **Bibliography:** Books used and additional readings

- **Index:** Word and phrase references by page

- **Errata:** No longer needed for on-demand publishing. We simply upload a revised version.

- **Colophon:** "With the development of the private press movement from around 1890, colophons became conventional in private press books, and often included a good deal of additional information on the book, including statements of limitation, data on paper, ink, type and binding, and other technical details. Some such books include a separate 'Note about the type', which will identify the names of the primary typefaces used, provide a brief description of the type's history and a brief statement about its most identifiable physical characteristics." [Wikipedia]

  This is just a fun addition, especially for a book like this that is about book production.

Hopefully, you've been thinking about these things

The appropriate time to add front matter and back matter is during the writing of the book. A passage may suggest an appendix. For example, as I was editing yesterday, I noticed that it was really confusing to refer the reader to my Website to get the instructions to add the basic paragraph styles with which to start your use of them. It seemed good to add the step-by-step for a basic set of styles to this book.

Concern for reader confusion may lead to a prologue to ease them into the main story or content. Mainly you need to be aware that all of these other things exist. Then you will develop them in process while you are writing. It's not good to start dealing with them after everything is written. Often you've forgotten the incidents that will trigger good reader service content like this.

Again! It's all about the reader

Continuously, you must be thinking about serving the reader. You are writing this for them and they deserve all the help you can give them. Often you need to radically shift things.

For example, in my verse by verse Bible studies it finally dawned on me that I was raising an almost impenetrable barrier to reading the book with all my front matter. I had an introduction/prologue that included doctrinal statements, a short (it grew with each book) testimony, and more. The short testimony of my spiritual walk at the front of the book finally grew to over a half dozen pages and was keeping the readers from reaching the real content. So, I changed it to a reference in the introduction and moved it to an afterword in the back matter.

In fact, I have started moving much of this material to the back of all my books in multiple appendices. I leave a brief listing of the appendixes available and then go on with the main part of the book. I did this to give the reader easier access to the real content. Try to watch yourself as you read other books to see what you find irritating.

Excessive front matter

This is especially true of ebooks. This is where I first actually noticed the problem. Front matter is really jarring there. There is really no comfortable way to flip pages and skip to the actual content in an ebook. So you want to get the reader there quickly. I have eliminated or moved all the front matter in all my ebooks except for a very brief copyright statement and the dedication.

But there is no right or wrong here. You need to determine what your reader would like. You might ask them in your blog. For sure, ask your reviewers. Make sure you have people from your target audience doing your reviews. Above all do not use these devices to "bulk up" your book. That's a subtle form of fraud. If the content is not necessary, do not add it to your book. K.I.S.S. (Keep It Simple Stupid) is the principle to follow in all design—especially book design.

The need for these features of the book will become apparent as you are writing. In this book, I am adding much more of the basic information and trying to do it so that as we now arrive at the actual production of the book you have the knowledge you need to get it done.

A basic procedure

Why do we start with print? Simply put: many of the quality extras you can use to help communicate with your readers are not available in reflowable ePUBs and Kindle books. This is especially true of your graphics. Though you can add color in any area you like, the resolution of your graphics will be very poor — 72 dpi in HTML compared to 2400 dpi for vector graphics or 300 dpi for continuous tone [Photoshop] in print. From print you can start the process of dumbing things down to fit within the limitations of HTML, CSS, and ePUB2. If you make a mistake or change your mind about anything, you need the high resolution, typographically excellent master from which you can start again.

- **Make a new document:** Print Intent, at the size you determine, with a single column, and margins designed to provide a good reader experience.

- **Set up your styles:** You will need a set of Paragraph, Character, and Object styles at the very least. This is where you pick your fonts, sizes, spacing, and all the rest. By working in styles, everything is kept fluid so it can be easily modified—globally for the whole book—as you continue to write and assemble it.

- **Add existing copy or start writing:** You can do your writing and editing wherever works best for you. But all the formatting needs to be done in InDesign. No other application has the capabilities you need.

 Plans die with the first shot: As with war, you will discover that, no matter how thorough your plans, they will change radically once you begin assembling the book. You'll discover font choices which do not work, sizing that is wrong in your eyes, graphics which are too small and irrelevant to the book as it evolves, and much more. When you do, simply change the relevant styles [or add new ones to cover the situation]. The styles will maintain the consistency you need for book design.

You are going to be gradually building a set of styles you can use to produce your books. You'll find that you will develop a basic set of styles that you use for all books. In fact, that is your goal.

If you need a graphic, go find it or make it: I've found that the best time to make a graphic is when the idea is fresh in your mind. That way you'll get something that fits the situation exactly. If you postpone it and come back later, you will often make a graphic which changes things—often causing a rewrite.

Place your graphics right next to the portion of copy talking about the graphic: You do not want to try to force your reader to go elsewhere. If that is required, your will probably lose the reader—unless they are only looking to the previous or next page.

There are no color sections: In traditionally published non-fiction, it was and is common to have 4-20 pages of color stuck into the middle of the book. Thankfully, that is not an option with on-demand digital publishing. Books are either black and white, or they are full-color throughout. Keep your illustrations tied to the copy which describes them.

- **If there is a color section:** Design it as a separate brochure. Do not reference pages in the book. Readers will not go to the references and you will confuse them. Make the color section self-sustaining.

The best time to make a graphic is when the idea is fresh in your mind

Some miscellaneous norms

- Chapters always start on a right, odd numbered page.

- Section Title, Part pages, and Chapter heads have no page numbers.

- **Page numbers:** should go on the outside ends of the headers or footers at the top or bottom of the pages.

- **Headers:** have the book name in the left header and the chapter name in the right header.

- Some books have the section name: in the left header.

- Blank pages have no header, footer, or page number

- Half Title, Frontispiece, Title, copyright, dedication, and table of contents have no page numbers.

- The gutter of a book [spine area] is always wider than the outside margins.

You can just copy/paste to add pieces, place word. docs or .rtf files, or write out additional stuff [as I am doing here]. This book is being put together from pieces old and new, plus a lot of material like this which has never been written out before. It's a seamless process that flows smoothly as the book is built.

One of my better new tools has been the addition of dictated materials. The process works remarkably well after you train yourself and the software. I find that it is much faster and much more accurate than my limited typing capabilities.

CHAPTER TWENTY-FIVE

Dealing with large & complex books

One of the important panels for assembling your book is the Pages panel: Adobe, in its wisdom, has made this slightly more difficult for us in CS6 & better. Strangely, the basic issue is that the design of this panel still caters to people coming from Quark, though you are not.

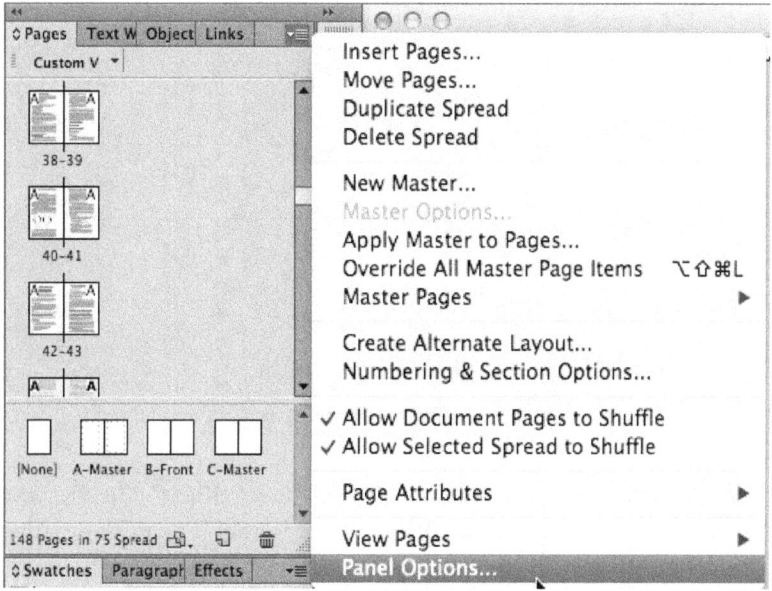

What I am talking about is that the default view of the Pages panel is very clumsy to use in a practical way. As you can see on the previous page, in the default layout, you can only see 3.5 spreads and four masters, and there is an incredible amount of wasted space in the panel. By simply opening the Pages Panel Options dialog, you can make this panel much more useful. You can rearrange things so you can see 8-20 page spreads at the same time—depending on the width of the panel. This became more difficult because CS6 chooses to hide the main horizontal/vertical control for the pages.

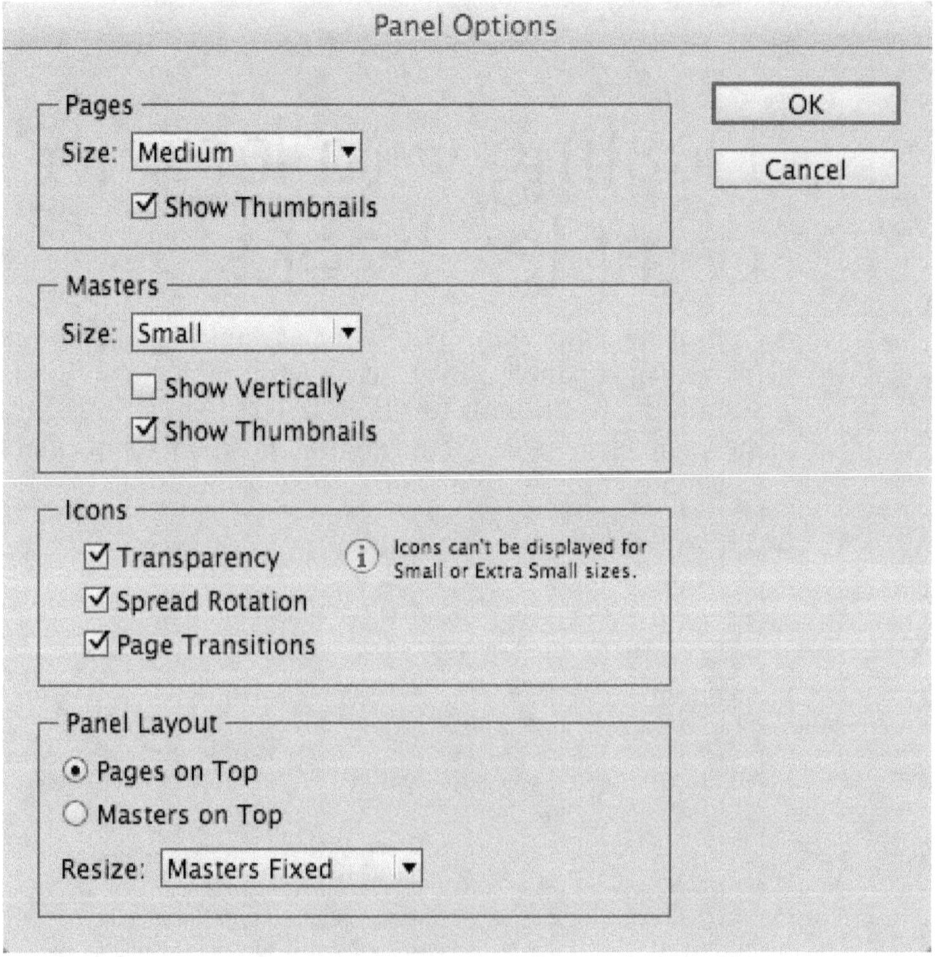

Panel Options

Pages
Size: Medium ▼
☑ Show Thumbnails

Masters
Size: Small ▼
☐ Show Vertically
☑ Show Thumbnails

Icons
☑ Transparency
☑ Spread Rotation
☑ Page Transitions

ⓘ Icons can't be displayed for Small or Extra Small sizes.

Panel Layout
◉ Pages on Top
◯ Masters on Top
Resize: Masters Fixed ▼

OK
Cancel

As you can see above, there is a simple check box for Show Vertically remaining in the Masters section of the dialog. This needs to be unchecked so you can see what was in the capture on the previous page. There has been one of these in the pages portion also—in every version since InDesign One first came out in 1999.

Now to change Pages, you need to right-click on the pages section of the actual dialog box (once you have finished setting the options) or choose the View Pages command at the bottom of the panel menu (as you can see on the previous page. This View Pages command is vertically by default. Change it to Horizontally. This is so important that you really need to change your application defaults by fixing the Pages Panel with no pages open.

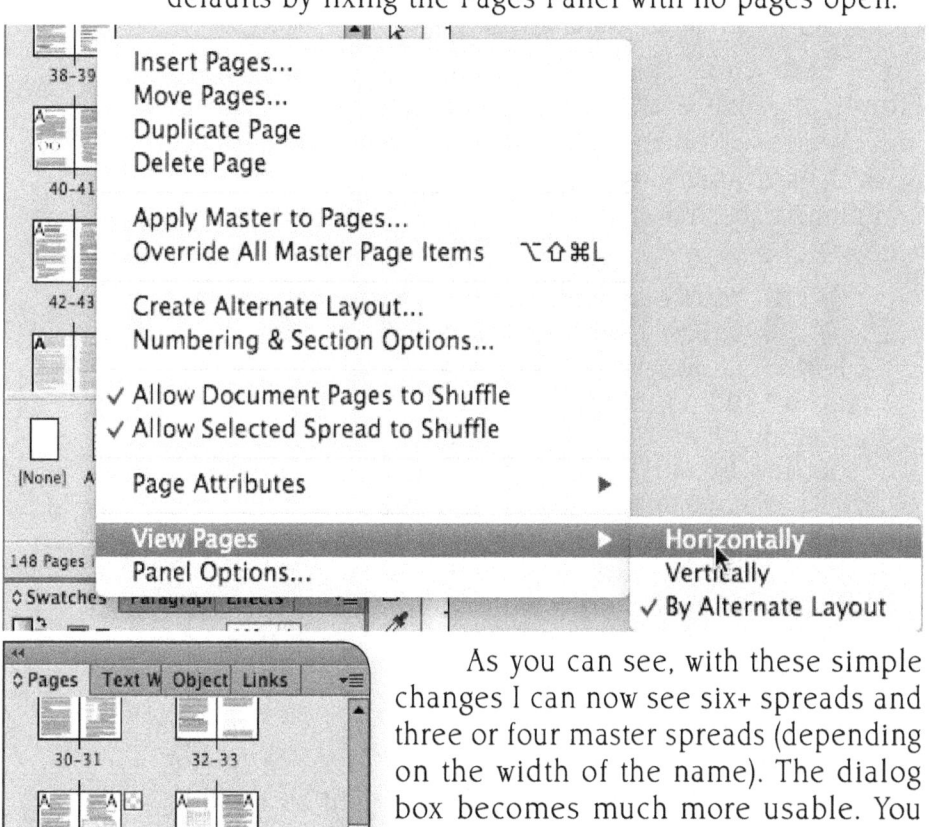

As you can see, with these simple changes I can now see six+ spreads and three or four master spreads (depending on the width of the name). The dialog box becomes much more usable. You can also see how the Show Thumbnails checkbox helps you tell where you are in the book.

Using the Pages Panel

You can drag'n'drop pages within the panel into a new location. You can add pages or master pages by simply right-clicking on a specific page in the pages or master pages portion of the panel. You can apply masters by drag'n'drop (frustrating to control, though), or by right-clicking on the appropriate page or pages in the panel. The easiest is to multiple select [click plus shift-click to select the range of pages] and then right click to apply the master where needed. You can add sections, create an alternate layout if you are working on a DPS digital magazine project, and quite bit more with the commands in the panel menu out of the upper right corner of the panel.

Numbering the front matter pages

There is one special convention you need to follow. Front matter has a different type of page numbers. They use lowercase Roman numerals whereas the body of the work uses Arabic numerals. To set this up you need to add blank pages before your content and make them into a new section.

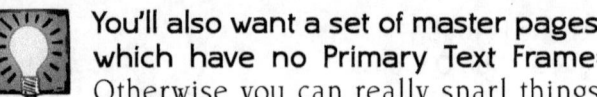 **You'll also want a set of master pages which have no Primary Text Frame:** Otherwise you can really snarl things up by adding things like a table of contents—making it part of the main story going throughout the book. That makes updating the table of contents impossible. You delete the PTFs on a pair master pages by click on the frame then delete it on the right page first and then the left page. Otherwise the left page will continue to add pages which are threaded to the main story.

Separate stories

InDesign defines a story as a single thread of connected frames. The same is true of copyright data and so on. You do not want the front matter part of the Primary Text Frame story at all. Each sub-section, like the Table of Contents, the Introduction, the Prologue, and so on, should be its own story.

Sections

Your book can have as many sections as you need. You can tell existing sections in the Pages panel by the little black triangle over the top of the page in the panel.

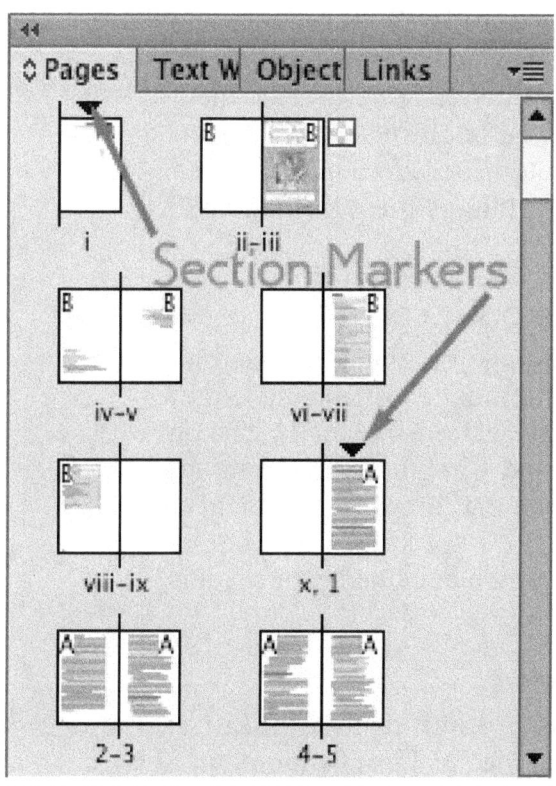

Numbering & Section Options

☑ Start Section

○ Automatic Page Numbering

⦿ Start Page Numbering at: [1]

Page Numbering

Section Prefix: [   ]

Style: [1, 2, 3, 4...   ▼]

Section Marker: [   ]

☐ Include Prefix when Numbering Pages

Document Chapter Numbering

Style: [1, 2, 3, 4...   ▼]

⦿ Automatic Chapter Numbering

○ Start Chapter Numbering at: [1]

○ Same as Previous Document in the Book

Book Name: N/A

As you can see in the capture to the left, this edition is currently running ten pages for the front Matter. That will change and be adjusted as I go through the writing and production of this book. I usually only use these two sections, but I could use sections for the appendixes [if I decide to have any]. But there are always at least two: front matter and the book itself. To make a new section, you select a page in the Pages panel and then either right-click or use the panel menu in the upper right corner of the panel. Choose "Numbering & Section Options...".

For this book, the Numbering & Section Options dialog box looks like what you see To the left for the first page of the actual copy. The front matter section also starts with page one, but uses the i, ii, iii, iv... (lowercase Roman numerals) style. Always check the page numbers in the Pages Panel afterward to make sure they are correct.

Section Prefixes and Chapter numbering are used in technical and scientific writing—stuff for governments and lawyers and the like. Those of you who know me are probably laughing at the idea that I would even know what these are—and it is true I have never used them.

In the Book panel (talked about next) every document after the first one has Automatic Numbering checked. That way the numbers are continuous through the book.

The back matter usually continues the same numbering as the body content

By the way, all of these page numbers are used for the Table of Contents and the Index. So make sure they work well for those uses. Also, Sections normally start on the odd pages (as do Parts and Chapters). These things are not major items, but not doing things in this manner proves to the readers that you do not know what you are doing. It is these little things which convince your readers about book quality.

Dealing with blank pages

Blank pages could use a different master. But as you'll see below I no longer do that. As I briefly mentioned, applying masters to a page is most easily done by selecting the page or pages in the Pages panel. Then you can simply right-click to access the Apply Master to Pages... command. The problem with blank pages is that there is a very strong convention in the book design business to not have anything on the blank page.

The simplest way to do this is to scroll through the Pages panel and look for empty pages. This is where the Show Thumbnails option in the Panel Options... dialog comes into its own. You'll be able to see the blank pages (though it can be slightly confusing if you use a header or footer on your master page).

I formerly used the default [None] master page to clear off the blanks. But that caused reflow problems with the Primary Text Frame. So now I hand delete the master page items on the blank pages by clicking on them while holding down the Command and Shift keys. This removes them from the control of the master page so I can simply delete them. **If you edit:** you may have to add back some of the headers/footers by reapplying the master page.

Full page illustrations

Many people believe that you should also clear off the pages covered with an illustration (or a full page ad). I must admit I find this convention irritating. How many times have you searched through a magazine trying to figure out where you were, because all the page numbers were gone? I have done it thousands of times, and every time it made me mad. My suggestion is to put page numbers on the full page illustrations. You may want to do a different master page with numbers in a different location.

The Book panel

If your books are like mine (very graphically intensive), you may find that certain operations like adding words to the User Dictionary and spell checking in general can cause InDesign to lock up after the book reaches a certain size. That happened to me with this book until I got 4 GB RAM. Now with Mavericks and CC, I had to get a new computer with 16 GB.

I don't like to use this option unless I have to. But if needed, it solves many problems while raising new issues.

Start by opening a new book

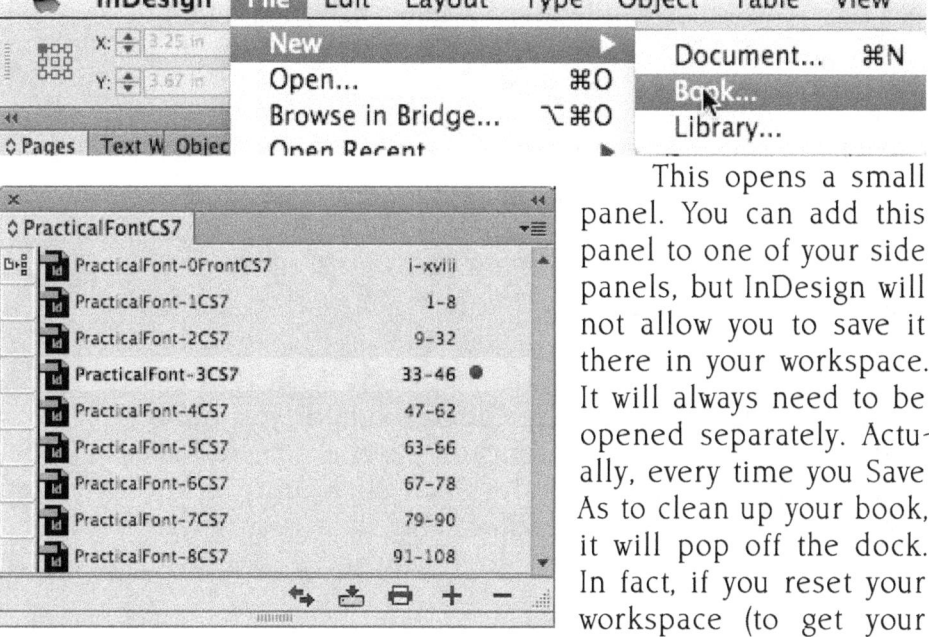

This opens a small panel. You can add this panel to one of your side panels, but InDesign will not allow you to save it there in your workspace. It will always need to be opened separately. Actually, every time you Save As to clean up your book, it will pop off the dock. In fact, if you reset your workspace (to get your panels back to where you want them) the book panel will be removed and placed behind your documents. You'll be able to find it at the bottom of your Window menu. It's a bit of a pain to work with, as you can tell.

You add chapter/sections by clicking the little plus at the bottom of the panel. Add them in order, as there is no way of reordering them once you add them. Once you have them added, you need to open each one (double-click on the listing in the Book panel), and open the Pages panel. Right-click on the little section symbol above the first page of the added document. This will enable you to check Automatic Page Numbering in the Numbering and Sections dialog box.

Once you have checked this the book documents will automatically continue the numbering through out the book (as you can see below). These numbers will change automatically as you add pages while you are writing into your Primary Text Frame.

There are two icon indicators you must be aware of in the dialog. First is the strange multi-shape icon in front of the first document in the capture to the left. The second ones are the open book icon [bullet] you see after the fourth from the top in the list of documents. The first one indicates the Style Source. This is the document that has the styles which will be used when synchronizing the book. The open book bullets tell you which documents are currently open in InDesign.

Synchronizing your book

This works like a champ. You simply select the command on the Options menu (or click on the little double arrow icon at the bottom of the Book panel), and all selected documents will be synchronized to the Style Source.

Of course, it is not quite that easy. What it does is add all styles to the other documents. If you have added styles to later documents they will not be added to the Source document—unless you click on front of the document where you added the style and make that your source. Then you can synchronize to add it throughout the book.

Another minor irritant is that when you synchronize, the alphabetical listing of the styles will be all snarled up. You can choose Sort By Name at the bottom of the Option menu of the panel to reorder the styles. As you can imagine that is a bit tedious if it happens very often. It's one of the reasons I avoid the Book panel, if possible.

As you can see in the Book panel Option menu below, you can Preflight the book, package the entire book (if you have none selected in the panel) or the selected documents {selected contiguously or not], export the entire book or selected docs to a PDF for uploading to print it, export the entire book to ePUB, synchronize, update all the numbering (if necessary), set the page numbering options and so forth. It's all very handy.

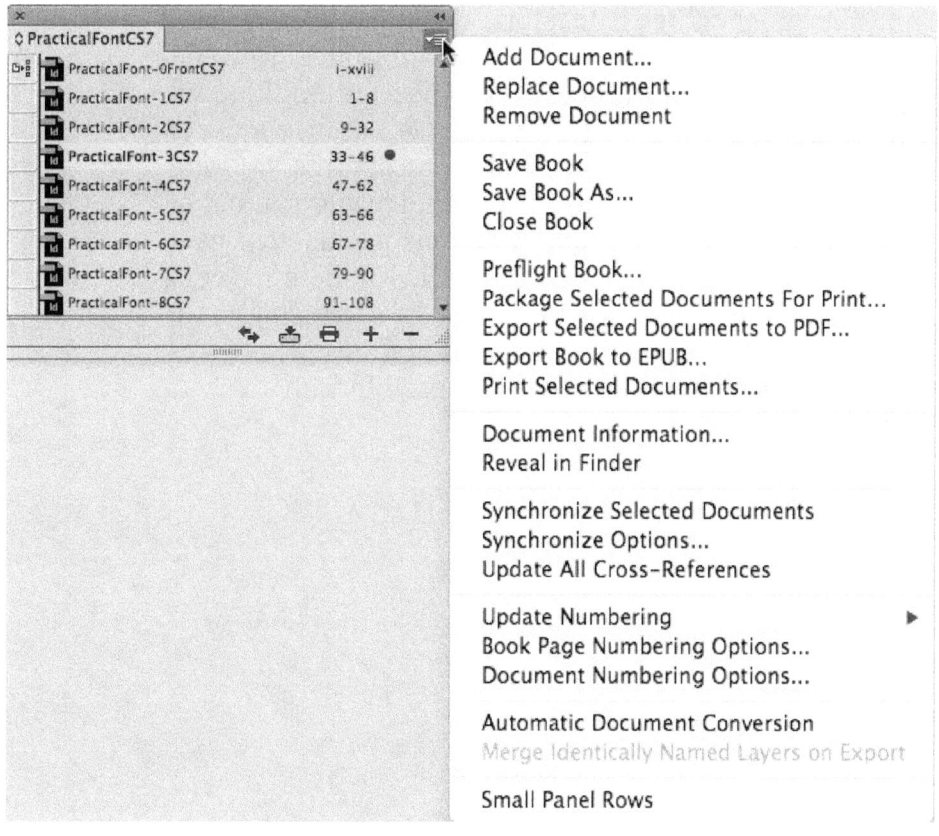

It does take some watching. If you decide to redefine a style, you should do it in the Style Source document, and when you synchronize, you need to go through the all the documents to make sure that changes in paragraphs, anchored objects, and graphics in general have not messed up your layouts. But other than those rather obvious issues it works flawlessly.

Actually using the book panel

In actual practice, the book panel is a necessity or it is not used. Though everything works fine, the actual workflow is greatly complicated by using multiple documents for a single book. Now I know that some publishers require authors to submit each separate chapter as a separate document. In that case, you may be stuck. But this is definitely one of those "you did a wonderful job of implementing a solution for a problem I pray I never have to use". It really does complicate things.

The strange thing is that for a book like this one with hundreds of pages and hundreds of graphics, it would seem that I would certainly need to use the book panel. In practice I do not. But I suspect that is because most of my graphic are PDFs or low resolution captures. If I were using large full color photos, I suspect I would run out of RAM very quickly. So far, any problems in this area have been solved by getting more RAM. Many of the designers, in groups of which I am a member, say they are using 32 GB RAM. Mac Pros can use 64 GB RAM. I know my iMac maxes out at 16 GB. I have no idea what is possible with a PC.

PART FIVE:

The various ebook formats

CHAPTER TWENTY-SIX

All of InDesign's output is an ebook

As you know, almost all of InDesign's output is in ebook form. Even for the print book, we produce a PDF. This PDF reads wonderfully well in iBooks or any ereader which can handle PDFs. However, even that PDF should really be modified for excellent use as a downloadable PDF. The graphics can all be in color, for example.

Now that ePUBs and Kindle books have reached the tipping point [become more than 50% of sales for most of us], we truly need to be sure we make a excellent ebook for sale. At this point, my best sales are again through Createspace [Amazon's print service]. But this is changing fairly quickly. Both the iBookstore and Kobo are growing even faster than Kindle. Nook is shooting itself in the foot.

I've almost completely quit using the KDP Select option which allows me to offer the book for free by giving Amazon exclusivity for three months or more. The free option doesn't seem to work well for anyone other than writers of romances or more distasteful genre like erotica, horror, and so on.

Basically we need to learn to be fluid on these things. There are new startups [almost weekly] trying to break the monopoly Amazon now stakes out on a pure ease of shopping and book discovery level. As soon as one of them gains traction [Tomely, Draft2Digital, BookShout, and at least a dozen more today], book selling will go to the next level. Draft2Digital has, and I use it instead of Smash-words, at this point. We desperately need an excellent shopping service for ebooks for Christians, for example. CBD [Christian Book Distributors] is the best on prices, but the shopping experience is not good. They use a pro-prietary ereader that is very restrictive. Overall, outside of Amazon, the ebook shopping experiences are still at a very rudimentary level.

InDesign is getting much better

There is still a long ways to go, but there is a good deal of hope that future versions of InDesign CC will give us what we need to produce excellent ebooks without any need to do hand-coding. InDesign CS6 was a good step better than InDesign CS5.5. InDesign CC 2014 is really getting pretty close now. Almost all of our problems now are with the distributors and ereaders.

Now that Windows is the second-largest OS and will soon be the third largest—after Android and iOS—there may well be further changes. At this point, it does not appear likely that a tablet [iOS or Android] could handle an app like InDesign. But as the desktop computer fades into niche work, as MacOS blends into iOS, we do not know what the future will bring.

This book is current to the release of CC 2014. But this is a rapidly changing industry. As usual, new information will be posted on *The Skilled Workman* and in other books until there is enough to do the next edition of this book.

ePUB & Kindle design in InDesign

I need to mention two basic assumptions before you can make an ePUB or Kindle book.

- **First of all, you need the book completely written, edited, and proof read:** It's very painful to format a book that is not completed, unless you are actually writing in InDesign [which I recommend, as you know]. Plus, you certainly do not want a situation where you make changes in the ePUB which need to be added to the print version and on and on.

- **Secondly, you need to have the book completely formatted for print in InDesign:** This means that all copy is formatted with styles: paragraph, character, table, cell, and object styles. No local formatting is acceptable. If it is not completely formatted, you will have no way to control your ePUB globally and you will waste many hours and probably many days, weeks, or months.

Everything in HTML is formatted.

You have your book finished & formatted for print

Now, you are ready to start. Why do we start with print? Simply put: many of the quality extras you can use to help communicate with your readers are not available in Reflowable ePUBs and Kindle books [HTML/CSS]. This is especially true of your graphics. Though you can add color in any area you like, the resolution of your graphics will be very poor – 72 dpi in HTML compared to 2400 dpi for vector graphics, 300 dpi for continuous tone in print [Photoshop], or 150 dpi for ePUB FXL. From print you can start the process of dumbing things down to fit within the limitations of HTML, CSS, and ePUB2 or ePUB3. If you make a mistake or change your mind about anything, you need the high resolution, typographically excellent master from which you can start again.

Once you have that baseline, the modifications necessary for your ebooks become relatively easy–though never simple. At this point, for example, you need four versions for the font variations alone.

- **ePUB Fixed Layout [FXL]:** is a real good option for the iBookstore and Kobo.

- **Kindle Print replica:** This is their fixed layout kindle book built from the PDF of the book.

For reflowable ebooks,

- **EPUB Reflow:** Everyone now takes ePUB2 with embedded fonts, any font you have a license to use [through Draft2Digital], except for Kindle

- **KF8 [Kindle Fire] MOBI:** you can try to embed fonts, but their formatting limitations with tables and lists suggest that a simple version with 4-font serif and sans serif font families is best. But all tables and lists need to be very simple, or converted to a graphic.

The problem is that with reflowable ebooks ugly, horrible typography has become the accepted standard. I find this vaguely nauseating, but I can no longer recommend going beyond the accepted–no embedded fonts.

Designing & formatting your ePUB & Kindle book without coding

With my assumption [that you have a finished, formatted and uploaded book for print] comes another equally important expectation. Writers and designers don't normally do well with code. It's not that we cannot understand it or use it. It's more like it is so boring and stifling to creativity that we simply avoid it whenever possible. My experience is that people like us can handle a little simple Web coding like XHTML and CSS (actually, most of us have been forced into it for our Websites). However, most people who do what we do really dislike coding. It is a specialized skill not found often in creative people. Even HTML and CSS code writing is a painful process.

The question is how do we take these givens and produce an ePUB and a Kindle version of acceptable quality? It is not difficult, but you are certainly going to need to rethink your definition of book and of typographic excellence.

Do fancy ePUBs still require fancy coding?

At this point in the development of ebooks, ePUB design is commonly produced by coding specialists. That's no longer necessary. InDesign can export good validated ePUBs: fixed layout and reflowable. Some things are still missing, but they're not just missing from InDesign but from all WYSIWYG applications. This was because of one simple issue. In order to do simple things like text wraps (CSS: alignments), sidebars (CSS: divs), and all the rest, before CC you had to crack the compressed ePUB file and mess with its innards (many files and folders)

CC has made major strides toward solving the text wrap and sidebar issues, plus they've solved many more problems. However, it is still not clean and simple. Plus, there are many design issues which suggest that text wraps and sidebars do not work well in ebooks, regardless. The largest issue is how to handle a div or text wrap which crosses the border of a page break. If the reader changes the font or the size of the type, all the page breaks change also. **The ereaders have no real way to handle a graphic or a sidebar which crosses a page break.**

InDesign has become that simple program which allows you to do this visually—sort of. Anything more must be done on the code level and most of us are simply not ready to do that. It is possible to do the editing in Dreamweaver, but it is not pleasant and it is certainly not a good design experience. You are going to make some tough decisions about your ebooks. This is true no matter what you are using to format.

Bottom line: many things which are easily done in print and PDFs are impossible or difficult in ePUBs or Kindle

Here are InDesign's abilities for the various versions

We will cover the details later in this book. However, I wanted to mention these here because so many people are trying to limp along with older versions. You really need the CC version.

InDesign CS5 and Earlier: have no real way to make ePUBs directly. Copy/paste into your HTML/CSS editor is your only real option.

InDesign CS5.5 can produce validated ePUBs: but your book layouts take a lot of work.

InDesign CS6 did quite a bit to write better code: but it still takes a lot of setup on your part. The ePUBs validate, but lists are compromised and embedded fonts do not work with the iBookstore. The Amazon plug-in for CS6 does better Kindle books than InDesign does ePUBs. But the plug-in cannot handle nested styles, for example.

InDesign CC helps a lot

It validates and writes ePUBs with embedded fonts which upload fine through iTunes Producer. If you convert your lists to text upon export, lists work well. You can now add an index with active links. You can add a TOC anywhere with links to the anchors of the style in the TOC. This makes Lists for Graphics possible, for example.

Anchored object control now works—except for inline objects. They must be anchored as Above Line or Custom. They can now float left or right and it works with a text wrap. Plus the text wrap will let you inset your floating objects from the edge of the column. You can also apply gradients to the type with a Paragraph style. All of this works with iBooks, most supposedly work with Kindle KF8 [but only if you own a Fire HD or better], Draft2Digital accepts ePUB2 with fonts, and if you sell DRM-free versions from your Website or through Gumroad or Ganxy. Increasing portions work in more and more ereaders. InDesign's ePUBs convert well with Amazon's free Kindle Previewer into KF8 books keeping everything until Amazon converts them again upon upload. A direct ePUB upload sometimes even keeps the embedded fonts in my Kindle apps for OSX and iOS. But Kindle remains very frustrating. Lately they have been reformatting the books you upload into the new KFX format.

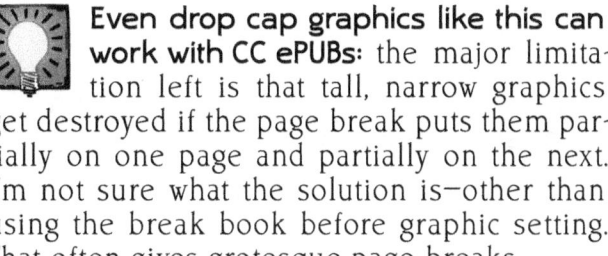 **Even drop cap graphics like this can work with CC ePUBs:** the major limitation left is that tall, narrow graphics get destroyed if the page break puts them partially on one page and partially on the next. I'm not sure what the solution is—other than using the break book before graphic setting. That often gives grotesque page breaks.

InDesign CC is finally a professional ePUB production tool: The largest advancement is the ability to produce Fixed Layout ePUBs. But, major advances have been made with reflowable ePUBs also. Tables now work fairly well with controls for stroke and fill—but no gradients yet. It is still very hard to get the width right also. A graphic will resize. Anchored graphics are now fairly predictable. The graphics now come in with the stroke and fill of the frame containing the graphic [probably without any gradients].

The ePUB limitations

Many of the excellent design possibilities of print are simply not available in ePUBs. What I intend to do is give you a list of changes you must make to get a validated ePUB. The good news is that several things that I would have had to mention for CS5.5 or CS6 are no longer necessary for CC.

Digital books are a very different world. You must rethink your concept of a book in order to design one which will work well for ePUBs and Kindle books. Let's talk about some of these necessary changes. But first:

Why are ebooks so different?

First let's talk about the fixed layout versions. These are very useful—especially if you are producing a book which will be used in a classroom setting. The fixed layout versions keep the page numbers, which are a real help in a group setting. There are three we use:

- **Downloadable PDF:** This is a conversion from the print PDF using a color cover, color high resolution graphics and color in the text. I often do one in readers' spreads and one in single pages.

- **Kindle's Textbook:** This uses the downloadable PDF [single page]—converting it with the free Kindle Textbook Creator. I've been surprised at the good sales of these.

- **The ePUB FXL:** This has some compromises: flush left copy and 150 dpi web graphics, but paragraph rules, fancy tables and all the rest convert beautifully.

Yes, they may seem to only apply to non-fiction. But what about the study groups using your novel? A fixed layout version will keep them all on the same page [literally]. This can be important.

The Reflowable option

The most important factor is adjustable type: The reader controls font sizes globally and can override your font choices. At this point, even as a designer you get limited control over font choice, font style, font size, font spacing, or typography in general. But, the good news is that CC will export most of the CSS you request. The bad news is that the reader can still override a lot of it [and normally will]. **Plus, there are other issues:** OpenType features are not available. CSS2 can handle this, but no ereader I know of is capable. We are back to the very limited 256 character choices. As a reader, in most cases, you get maybe two fonts with up to four styles, a dozen sizes (maybe), and that's it. Often you only get one font family—especially with e-Ink ereaders like the early Kindles, Nook, and Kobo.

As a designer, unless you embed fonts, you get the number of fonts available (just serif and sans serif at best, unless you're on an iPad), four typestyles (regular, italic, bold, & bold italic), largely unlimited sizes & line spacing, alignments, indents & paragraph spacing, nested styles (or hand-applied character styles), a couple of list styles, all set up with p and the six headline styles [h1-h6] plus unlimited classes, and all of this directly out of InDesign.

In most cases (except for e-ink Kindles, Nooks, and Kobos plus their apps on desktops, iPads, iPhones, and Android machines) you are able to control the serif and sans serif choices.

The second major factor is the single column layout: Liquid Layout with its automatic column additions and graphic resizing and mask changes for various ereaders and smart phones has no real bearing on ePUBs. It's developed for use in InDesign's Digital Publishing System [DPS]. That is, app design for magazines with tablets—where multi-column pages are the norm. And that is virtually dead from reader neglect.

We are not there with ePUB Reflowables: There is just not enough width to display two columns or more except for landscape tablets. Even with fixed layout ePUBs, multiple columns are rendered so small that they are virtually unreadable. However, non-facing-page landscape designs should work fine for FXL with a great deal of care.

As usual, this is changing as you read this: Currently, it is recommended that you embed fonts for KF8 [Kindle Fire], the iBookstore, ePUB2 uploads to Draft2Digital, and DRM-free versions sold directly to readers using a resource like Gumroad. InDesign CC embeds fonts well. If I email a copy with fonts to my iPad and open it in most of the ereaders, it works well. The embedded fonts remain and the anchored objects render correctly. But, Kindle has issues.

Even with Kindle, things change rapidly

As I write this, March of 2016, one major problem has been solved. With the release of El Capitan [OSX 10.11.3], Kindle Previewer quit working which made real trouble for Kindle conversion. Now, [yesterday, February 29] there is a new version of Kindle Previewer 3.0 [beta] which seems to work well.

Never forget, Kindle is in its own world with its own rules and proprietary procedures. Many of them remain outside our control. The conversion to better typography [the new KFX format] is done outside our control, without notice, and we cannot proof the results without buying our own version of the book. A 500# gorilla has few constraints. We just have to live with it [or get stomped].

The main problem is bad reader expectations

Any styling you put into your fonts, most of the uneducated readers will consider *wonky*, at best, and horribly ugly for the most part. But you cannot design for them. They will pick another font.

However, if you have embedded fonts, the serif/sans serif distinctions will remain. Any they are the most important font information.

CHAPTER TWENTY-EIGHT

Ebook Design

Reflowable ebooks are like a different species. Of course, the basic difference is that you are reading on a screen instead of on paper. But it goes much further than that. There are many things which can be explained easily using typography in a printed book or even a fixed layout ebook. These can be quite difficult to accomplish in a reflowable e-book. Conversely, except for the e-Ink ereaders like the cheap Kindles, Nooks, and Kobos, all ebooks are available in full color—whether you decide to use their color or not.

So, we change how much? **Everything.**

It is obvious that we must rethink our book designs: The real question is how much do we want to change in the conversion from print to ebook? The unavoidable answer is that we need a complete redo. This goes quite a bit beyond simple repurposing. If you are going to use fixed layout ePUBs you may need two different redesigns: FXL and Reflowable.

Designing for quicker repurposing: This can certainly be done. What it requires is a clear idea of what is going to be needed for the conversion. In order to make your ePUB look as good as possible we need to think reasonably about how to set up our documents so they can be converted quickly. So, your decisions are very important when you set up your layout and formatting in your print books.

Everything must be controlled with styles ◇◇◇◇◇

The major thing to understand is that HTML freaks out with paragraphs which use local formatting, done ad hoc in the document. All type must be controlled by paragraph styles, plus character styles as necessary. All graphics must be anchored and controlled with an object style. I haven't used the new table capabilities enough to have a definitive answer yet; but it is more than likely that table and cell styles are now necessary also.

The first e-book was the downloadable PDF in color

Scribd is a good example of a supplier which provides downloadable PDFs to their readers. But there are many more: Lulu, Gumroad, Ganxy, and hundreds of others [even though most specialize in free downloads and do not sell books]. Scribd, Gumroad, Ganxy, and Lulu are the main ones we are concerned with because they will sell your PDFs.

The production of your color PDF should be very easy if you have followed my suggestions about graphics. If so, you have a Originals folder which has all of the graphics used in your book in full color with the same name. If not, it can take quite a while to find the originals.

Remember, PDFs can use printing quality graphics & vectors

So, all you have to do is package your completed book. This places a copy of your document into a new folder at the location of your choice. All of the linked graphics are copied to a new Links folder inside your new package. You should be able to drag a copy of your Originals folder to that same location. Then you can simply drag/drop the colored images into your Links folder. The grayscale images will be replaced by the color versions.

There are a few other things you should do for your downloadable PDFs. If your print book is normal, you will have a half title followed by a blank page before your title page. You should delete both of those and replace your title page image with a full bleed, full-color cover. Your Table of Contents will now have live links and a complete set of bookmarks in the left column. Other front matter should demonstrate a true benefit to the reader in the front or be moved to the back of the book. Your index will have live links also.

InDesign CC exports fixed layout: ePUB FXL!

I put the exclam on that because everyone is so excited about this ability. It is a big deal. It is essential for illustrated books like children's books. It's still not nearly as good as a PDF. **However:** the iBookstore will sell an ePUB FXL, and that's really good. Kobo Writing Life also accepts one. Neither will sell a PDF. Kindle KDP has their own version (as usual) which is a converted PDF.

The pages look very much like they do in a PDF. You can do headers and footers, page numbers, paragraph rules, and excellent tables. It even handles gradient paragraph rules and gradient strokes and fills on the tables.

However, they are still ePUBs with no OpenType feature support, no true small caps, and so on. They also require Web graphics [150 dpi] like all HTML documents. Some are pleasant surprises like the gradient strokes and fills within text blocks for rules & tables. However, justified copy does not work. I'll cover the rules for FXL as I go through the changes necessary for ePUB export.

Ebook front matter

One of the first changes you should make for your readers is the elimination of as much front matter as possible. It is much harder to skip through such things in an ereader. This is also true with PDFs—even though they look very close to your printed version of the book—without spreads.

The good news is that you can put a hyperlink to where you want the reader to begin on all the front matter pages. Ebooks handle hyperlinks well.

Adding hyperlinks

One of the major differences with ebooks is the ability to use hyperlinks for your footnotes and references. The only problems will be companies like Apple which do not allow links to competitors. Lulu does not allow links in ePUBs. Smashwords watches them closely. The rest of them only object if you have a link which goes to a competitor. Kobo doesn't like it if you have a book link to the Kindle store, for example. .

Adding hyperlinks is very easy. You use the Hyperlinks panel. As you can see below, you simply select what you want linked, open the New Hyperlink dialog, and paste in the URL. Or, in the case of the capture, type in the email address and add a subject line. You can easily add

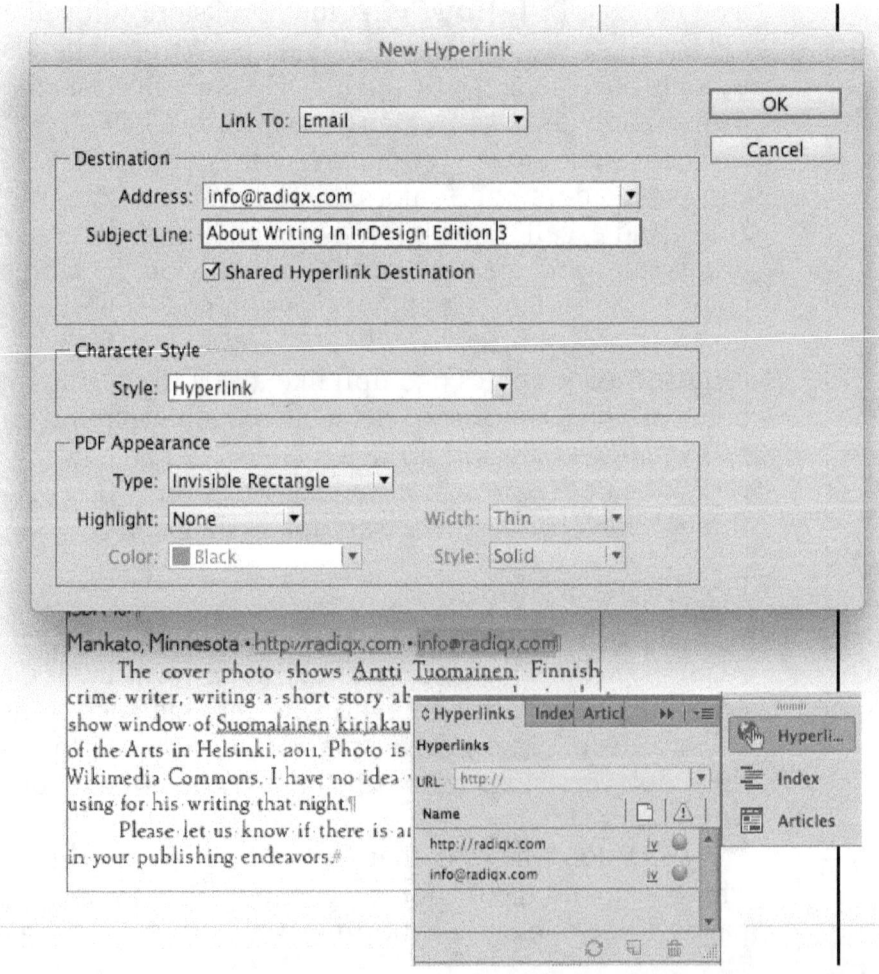

a character style for your linked text. If you do not, the default is usually a blue underline. I've tried special fonts and sizes, but that usually looks very contrived and artificial. The shortcut for a new Hyperlink, with the selected text or object, is Command+Shift+8 in CC.

Contact info

It is very easy and necessary to add links to your email, FaceBook page, Pinterest, Twitter account, and so on. You want your readers to be able to get in touch with you. This is one of the strongest advantages we have over traditional publishers.

Many authors and publishing houses delegate this to staff. That is not a good thing. The readers are looking for contact with the author or publisher. If you do end up with someone screening your email, make sure that personal requests are bounced directly to the author or person being sought out. This interaction with the readers is one of the great benefits of the new self-publishing paradigm.

 Apple will bounce your book for any links to Amazon, Nook, Kobo, and so on: They seem to handle links to your Website with no problems.

ePUB Design

With ePUBs we enter a whole new world. Normally this type of ebook is very fluid. Fonts and font size can easily be changed. Margins can be adjusted. Background colors can be stylized. The brightness can be adjusted to adapt to ambient conditions. You need to drop your preconceptions now!

At this point I am assuming that you have a finished and formatted book for print and probably a downloadable PDF. The question is how do we take this and convert it to an ePUB ebook and a Kindle version? This question has become more complex now that we have the fixed layout option to export ePUB FXL books.

This field of design is changing so rapidly that anything a month old is at least a bit out of date. The good news is that the methods I will cover here will still work. The bad news is that some of them may no longer be necessary. After writing much of this material in the Spring of 2012, many changes happened during the rest of the year. In July 2012, the CS6 Kindle Export Plug-In was released. It was a huge improvement to the plug-in for CS5.5. In the same month, Kobo began offering Kobo Writing Life so we could upload ePUBs directly into Kobo.

By the Fall of 2012, several other things had changed. Image sizing specs became available. A demand for ePUBs and Kindle Fire books with embedded fonts had begun to appear. Now with CC, the instruction for lists has changed. The rules for CSS style tags called Export Tags by InDesign have changed. April 10, 2013, Barnes & Noble dropped PubIt! In favor of a new site called Nook Press. It's had no affect on the tide rising against B&N, but no one knows. The iBookstore no longer requires ISBNs. InDesign CC now exports ePUB2s with embedded fonts which are acceptable to iTunes Producer, Draft2Digital, Smashwords, and which are converted well in the Kindle Previewer 3.0. CC 2014 began exporting ePUB FXL. CC 2015 added Publish Online and Paragraph Shading. These changes will continue.

I remember that it took from the late 1980s until the very late 1990s before desktop publishing for print even started to settle down—and then InDesign changed everything. Now I can say with confidence that print production has not advanced much at all since CS2 or CS3. You can easily use old versions of software for print production. This is not true for ePUBs and Kindle ebooks.

You need InDesign CC. The main problem is now ereader capabilities. This means you need to produce different versions: one with embedded fonts, one without, plus special versions for Kindle, possibly a fixed layout version, and so on.

Document size

At present for ePUBs I am using a document with a Web intent: iPad vertical (768x1024 pixels), with 84 pixel margins right and left; and 112 pixel margins top and bottom. This gives me a Primary text frame of 600x800 which is nearly the maximum image size for an image in an ePUB on an iPad2. The Retina resolution (double the iPad2) has no standardized techniques yet. Nook and Kobo use the same width but shorter images [Nook 760 tall and Kobo 600 square?]. I'll cover Kindle later—but the Fire also likes 600x800 pages though 600 x 500 images are preferred and a 127K file size is rigidly enforced.

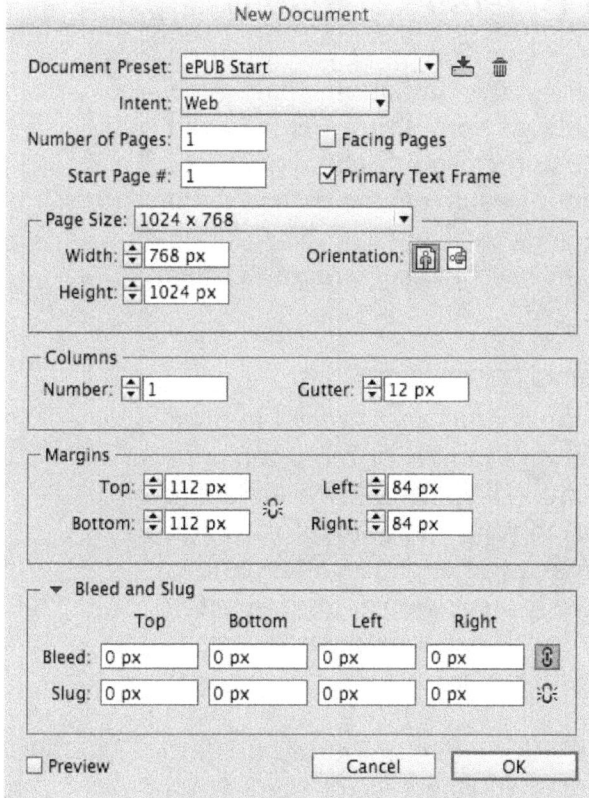

You just have a single master page because you cannot use page numbers, headers, or footers anyway [except in FXL]: Everything must be in a single story from the front page to the last word at the end. This is the old HTML page with infinite scrolling.

It ain't purdy, but it's what we have to deal with. And you can do a lot. Now that we have anchored objects which can reliably float left or right with a text wrap, things have gotten a lot better. The only real issue is floating graphics which cross page breaks. You need to watch this very carefully. In actual practice, floating graphics much taller than 100 pixels will cause problems sooner or later. The problem is that floating graphics which cross page breaks are simply eliminated and the readers do not see them at all.

Page sizing for fixed layout ePUBs

This is still in its infancy. The conceptual change is that you need to be working in an InDesign document where the page is easily readable on screen. You need to make sure your body copy is in the 9-12 words per line standard. I recommend using half-letter up to 7" x 10". For landscape pages, I would shoot for the emerging HD standard: 960 pixels wide by 540 pixels tall. When I get a book which can use it well, I'll be using 9.6" x 5.4" as a starting point. That should easily handle two columns.

Just remember, limitations are the birthing place for creative solutions.

This is always the case. The first thing you do when designing a book is determine the limitations: page size, fonts used, and so on. It's always something. Fixed layout ePUBs exported from InDesign can not display justified copy. This is due to what the InDesign engineers had to do to convert the page to a fixed layout. However, the solution they came up with now means you can use paragraph rules and gradients in an ePUB.

Graphic format, size, and resolution

This one is rough for those of us accustomed to print quality. Ereader graphics always look horrible when compared to print [except for the PDFs]. Even PDFs are stuck with screen resolution {though you can zoom into a vector graphic remarkably well]. What you need to understand is that you will be using relatively large Web graphics—but 72 dpi in most cases, not 300 dpi. This is obviously a serious conflict with the way we have been working for the past two and a half decades.

Basically you need JPEGs— a maximum of 600×800 pixel, RGB. For flat areas of color and sharp contrast, a GIF may look better. PNGs work also, but they are usually larger in file size. You just need to make your choices in Photoshop's Save For Web dialog box. The iBookstore, Nook, and Fire have different image size requirements as we'll see in a bit.

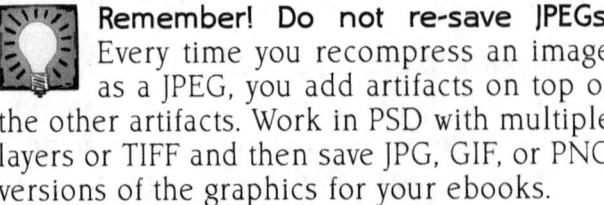

Remember! Do not re-save JPEGs: Every time you recompress an image as a JPEG, you add artifacts on top of the other artifacts. Work in PSD with multiple layers or TIFF and then save JPG, GIF, or PNG versions of the graphics for your ebooks.

This obviously takes some planning ahead as you will be using grayscale images (vector PDFs if possible) in your print documents—in most cases. You'll have CMYK images if you print in color. These bitmapped images will be PSDs preferably, and TIFFs upon occasion. So from the beginning, as you write and create, you need to save RGB versions of your color images. You probably also want color versions of your PDF graphics for easy conversions. Then using Save For Web as a Max quality JPEG [even High] will not noticeably ruin the image.

Reflowable graphics MUST be to size and not cropped: Graphics must be placed at 100% and fit the frame proportionally without cropping. If not, your exported ePUBs will ignore the graphic. There can also be no corner effects, dropped shadows or anything like that. All these things work fine in fixed layout but not at all in Reflowable.

At this point, even though the ePUB3 spec accepts SVG, which is a vector form of graphic, none of the ereaders do—with the possible exception of Kindle Fire and books produced with Apple's iBooks Author. InDesign cannot handle SVG images now, regardless. From what I have heard recently, SVG will work for what we need. . Regardless, we need vector images for ebooks, and they aren't available. But there is hope.

Everything in one story for reflowable

For reflowable ePUBs, you must remember the image of an eternally scrolling Web page. That is truly what we are dealing with. Of course, we want things like sidebars, inset text wraps, and so on. They work well in HTML. With certain limitations, InDesign CC can now export them.

The problem isn't with the ePUB standard

The problem is with the ereader hardware and apps available to read what we publish. I am always saddened when I read my ePUBs in iBooks on my iPad. They look so much better than is possible in the old Kindles, Kobo, or Nook. I know that purchasers of my ePUBs and Kindle books will be stuck with much less. An ePUB is a new capability [way less than a decade]. All I have to do is remember how limited PageMaker 4.2 and Quark 3 were when I began in digital publishing in 1991. Right now KF8/KFX on the Kindle Fire, Readium in Chrome for Android devices, and iBooks on the new iPad are best for type and graphics. Overall, iBooks is probably the best ereader available. But, I realize that many are still deeply tied to their e-Ink Kindles, Kobos, & Nooks. In fact, for many seniors, e-ink Kindle sales are growing fairly rapidly.

Eliminate all separate stories [reflowable]

Remember that everything in an ePUB must be in one story or in a div attached to it floating above line, right, or left. This is a radical conversion in many cases. And you will need to do much of it by hand. The Articles Panel is a help, but in my experience it takes longer to order things in this way and it is certainly not a flawless conversion. On the other hand, it's necessary if you add a linked index.

So, I drag'n'drop any separate stories into an inline location that makes sense—rewriting as necessary to keep the copy flowing well. Again, simply repurposing is not a good idea. ePUBs are a very different reading experience and we must adapt to it.

What I find is concepts which can be easily shown with typography in a PDF are completely lost in an ePUB—even a fixed layout ePUB. I commonly need to rewrite copy to deal with this fact. Type in an anchored sidebar usually needs to be rewritten and placed into a different location to make sense as a part of the one story. Often, all text sidebars must be simply eliminated. Plus, OpenType features don't work.

Live type in an anchored frame now works: BUT, you need to be very careful. The rewraps from point size changes often overfill the frames. The apparent type size is often larger. And in general, they simply do not look good. You can get borders and flat color backgrounds, but gradients haven't made it yet [except in FXL]. You can use a gradient in live type, sometimes. But, conversions to graphics work best.

Easily converted anchored graphics:

For very graphic books like mine with the wrapped graphics, I simply redo the object style for the graphics so that it drops them in Above Line or Custom locations. Moving graphics around to make the most sense becomes easy with the new drag'n'drop anchoring controls built into the frame edge—upper side, right corner. Simply drag them into position and convert them to the object style of your choice with a shortcut. I make many of my graphic conversions 600 pixels wide, because I want them as large as they can be to help you actually read them.

Wrapped graphics are definitely doable. They can float left or right and the indent can be controlled by the outside text wrap, which becomes the margin. The biggest missing capability is in setting sizing with percentages. Now, all you can do is set the pixel width. But the Tip icon in the next paragraph here is very problematic. I usually eliminate it or make a new 600 px wide one.

 Dealing with captions: Supposedly, they are grouped with the graphic and then set off with an Object style. I've had trouble getting the live text to work because it changes size with the rest of the text, and the graphic would need to be a grouped Object. That now works, but I don't trust it.

The Object Style controls

The new Export Options: in the Object Style dialog are pretty self-explanatory. You have three choices: Alignment & Spacing, Float Left, and Float Right. As you can see, you can control left, right, center alignment plus spacing before and after. The only strange thing is that Inline will not work for your Anchored Object Settings. It must be Above Line or Custom. If you leave it inline, no matter what it is, it will be re-rasterized and the result will be a mess.

Setting the text wrap will translate to the margins of the div inserted. So, I may need to adjust the text wrap a few times to get everything to line up as needed by my design. In a PDF, I commonly locally format these problems, but that does not work in ePUBs. You will need to make case by case adjustments.

Be patient with all of this. Adding ebooks to the publishing repertoire is a very complex operation for Adobe. InDesign CC 2014 was a major step upward toward a more stable, more usable, more easily exportable ePUB. InDesign CC 2015 version added some more. We have been assured by Adobe that ePUB3 is very high on their priority list. In fact, I heard they joined Readium to add ePUB3 capabilities to ereaders.

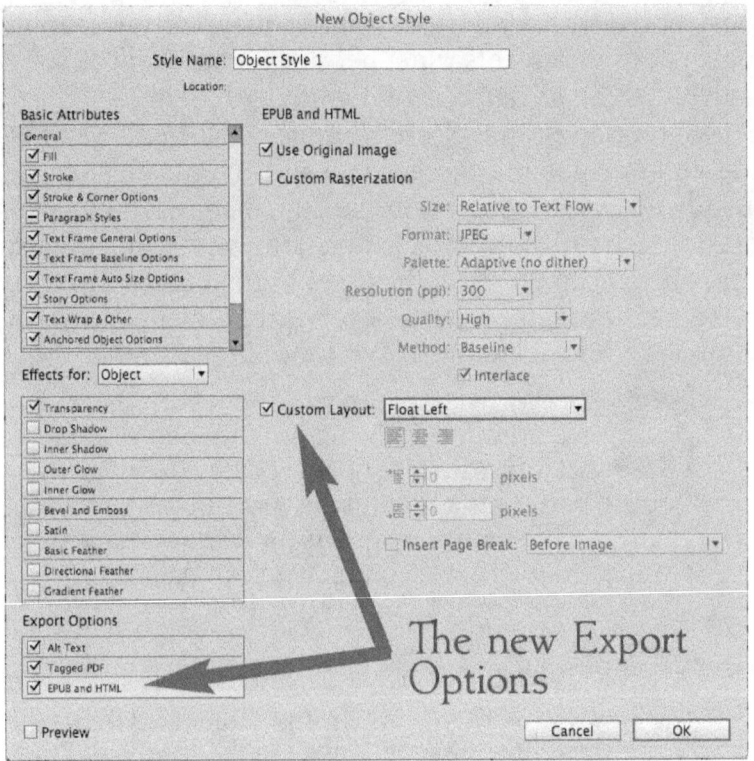

The new Export Options

Adobe has a good reputation of bringing these things online—and for doing it better than we expected. I know I certainly did not expect Liquid Layout, yet we got that for CS6. It may only apply to magazines at this point, but ePUB3 will probably use it more—both in InDesign and in ereaders. The iPad, Fire, and Kobo read simple ePUB3 docs now. Kobo promised full ePUB3 support by spring 2013. FXL works with their Kobo Writing Life. Now, as I mentioned, everything works quite well with ePUB2 Reflow, fonts embedded, and so on.

For CC 2014, I did not expect fixed layout ePUBs. As you know, what I am looking for is full CSS2 support. That's what we need typographically and it's basically available now. The fashionistas are demanding video and audio. The readers do not seem to care about that at all. They've got YouTube for that.

Fixing the styles

Eventually we are going to edit the exported tags. But for now I want to talk about how the styles need to change. The easiest way is to simply start editing the copy and changing the styles as we get to them. We must bear in mind that sidebars or anchored graphics require an object style with anchored object settings.

Again, often I find I need to rewrite copy in my books to deal with the reality of the ePUB reading experience. Do not hesitate to do that. However, my books are on formatting, so that's not surprising. Yours will not be, in most cases. So, little rewriting will be required. The main thing is to help the reader as much as possible.

Font changes

The big news, for me, with InDesign CC is that they can now embed fonts: These ePUBs are accepted by everyone except for e-ink ereaders. You have to encrypt the fonts to embed them. But the finished ePUBs upload fine through iTunes Connect, Kobo Writing Life, and Draft2Digital. Eventually, this will be commonplace and InDesign is leading the way.

Even though the ePUB spec says we can embed fonts, this is still spotty—not because it is difficult, but the ereader and reader support is usually missing. Most readers have gotten so used to the ugliness of standard fonts and limited typography that they change your books to fit their expectations. That will radically mess up your typography. My current recommendation is still to embed fonts for iBooks, Nook, Kobo, Scribd, and so on. For the Fire and Fire HD, we can embed Fonts. But you must make sure that you are using fonts with the proper licensing. You can also read embedded font ePUBs in BlueFire on the iPad and Readium in Chrome on Android.

Font producers like me can use their own, but you'll have a hard time finding a supplier who sells ePUB rights.

I offer those rights with all my fonts. But you have to buy through me. TypeKit , which comes with your CC subscription, offers several hundred fonts with an ePUB license.

Corinthian Light

ABCDEFGHIJKLMNOPQ
RSTUVWXYZ1234567890
abcdefghijklmnopqrstuvwxyz

Created by Letraset Type Director Colin Brignall, this clean-cut, monolineal sans serif typeface was inspired by Edward Johnston's Railway Type and Eric Gill's Gill Sans typefaces. *Myfonts*

Corinthian Light

ABCDEFGHIJKLMNOPQ
RSTUVWXYZ1234567890
abcdefghijklmnopqrstuvwxyz

Created by Letraset Type Director Colin Brignall, this clean-cut, monolineal sans serif typeface was inspired by Edward Johnston's Railway Type and Eric Gill's Gill Sans typefaces. *Myfonts*

Defining typography

- **Webster's:** The craft of composing type and printing from it; art and technique of printing with movable type.
- **Random House:** the art or process of printing with type; the work of setting and arranging types and of printing from them; the general character or appearance of printed matter
- **Cambridge:** the style, size and arrangement of the letters in a piece of printing
- **Wikipedia:** art of arranging letters on a page to be printed, usually for a combination of aesthetic and functional goals

What's unusual is [Embedded fonts aries] really get it. They [Readium or] but typography really has [iBooks] l act of arranging letters on

Obviously physica[l] [   ] [   ]onal shapes play a huge role in type design. But typography goes far beyond the actual shapes into cultural and

Defining typography

Webster's: The craft of composing type and printing from it; art and technique of printing with movable type.

Random House: the art or process of printing with type; the work of setting and arranging types and of printing from them; the general character or appearance of printed matter

Cambridge: the style, size and arrangement of the letters in a piece of printing

Wikipedia: art of arranging letters on a page to be printed, usually for a combination of aesthetic and functional goals

What's unusual is that none of the dictionaries really get it. They describe the physical act, but typography really has little to do with the physical act of arranging letters on paper for [No fonts embedded] [Kindle Mac App]

Obviously physical consideratio[ns] [   ]ole in type design. But typography g[   ] cultural and subjective responses of individual readers. Wikipedia does the

TypeKit gives CC owners plenty of good fonts to embed!

The main thing for us, in this book, is to have a little discussion about what will work and what will not for your ePUBs. Font choices are always a highly personal thing. I'm going to suggest my personal tastes and give you reasons. You make up your own mind. You can use the fonts I use in this book. I'll sell them to you cheap. Go to *The Skilled Workman* and look at the Fonts page to find some publishing font packages I am selling at very good pricing.

Verboten fonts [Courier]

First, I'm just going to mention the ugly ones you should never use: Courier or New Courier. These eight fonts should never be used unless you are trying to evoke a period, make a historical statement, or something strange. But almost everyone believes they are hideous fonts (not to mention they are very difficult to read).

Fonts with bad reader reactions [TIMES & ARIAL]

These fonts are not bad designs, but they have issues—some of them fatal. I don't use them.

> **Arial:** This font family with dozens of styles is the ugly cousin of Helvetica used to avoid the royalties. As far as I know, Microsoft had it designed precisely for that reason. These fonts plus Times make up the core of some of the most overused fonts in existence. Plus they are the default for many bureaucracies.

> **Times New Roman & Times:** These families normally have regular, italic, bold and bold italic. Though the bold pairs tend to be too narrow and ugly with plugged counters, the real problem is the bureaucratic associations. Times always brings up strong negative emotions for most people [except authors]. At best, it looks like a book designed in Word. This is why this tends to be the font family of choice for many authors. Just think "non-professional" to help with your cure.

Bureaucratic fonts: These are the fonts that have been the defaults in Office, Publisher, and similar non-professional page layout tools for decades—Arial, Times, and Times Roman. They are not very pretty fonts. The true situation is that non-professionals who use nothing but software defaults are the only people who use these fonts. In fact, most bureaucracies have standardized them and require their use. The only books to use them are those using Word conversions done by Kindle, D2D, and Smashwords.

They trigger our bureaucratic drivel filter

For example, if you watch yourself when you open your mail or when you receive handouts, you will see that bureaucratic output is quickly consigned to the trash—usually without being read. Most people are fully aware that there is no usable content in these things. Bureaucratic output is produced purely to prove to administrators that something was done—even though we all know that nothing was done except some committee meetings. Our experience tells us these are a waste of time to read. Most of us throw them away unread (unless, of course, we are a member of the dratted committee).

So also, almost everyone simply tosses mail with obvious Word output without reading it—consigning it to the junk mail category in their mind automatically. Beyond that, default Word or Publisher output is barely readable. The default typography settings are very bad and obvious. There are simply too many really bad associations with these fonts to use them.

Versatile fonts for typography

The basic point is simple: You want to choose fonts that read well, have matching x-heights [if you use run-ins], and which will make the distinction between serif and sans serif in the CSS exported with the ePUB.

I also want to mention some of the standards included in TypeKit. These come with an ebook license, as far as I know [it seems to change]. These are font families that are relatively easy to read and comfortable for the reader. There are several fine serif choices, and many sans serif families. There are enough choices for you to be able to make your ePUBs unique, stylish and very readable.

For body copy you need at least regular, bold, and italic styles for your typographic needs. A bold italic is nice—but not often needed. You'll need these fonts installed on your machine to use them in InDesign. Type-Kit allows you to embed the ones which come with CC into your ePUBs.

I used to follow this paragraph with the complete listing of iOS fonts. But that no longer seems useful. The iBooks conundrum is one that I haven't quite figured out yet. It definitely does the best job of presenting your ePUBs with support for embedded fonts, floating divs, and anything that InDesign can export.

However, the iBookstore does not sell books I upload directly very well. Books uploaded through Smashwords and Draft2Digital sell much better through the iBookstore than the versions I upload directly through iTunes Connect and iTunes Producer. It is quite frustrating. I would like to get beyond my dependence upon Amazon, but no one else offers the capabilities of Amazon either for shopping or for ebook display. The only lack is Amazon's poor quality book formatting.

So, what I want to do is simply suggest some font combinations that should work well for you. If you remember our earlier section on using a companion sans for your serif font, you'll recall that I said there that finding a good pair which works well together is difficult. I finally gave up and designed my own—the Contenu/Buddy pair until this year where I designed the Librum/LibrumSans combo I am using in this book. Both of these collections are for sale on my Website, *The Skilled Workman,* http:// www.bergsland.org/hackberry-font-foundry/fonts/

Ebook standards are different

People who read ebooks are a new breed. Many of them are, like myself, shall we say mature. A decent percentage of the new readers using ereaders are in their 50s or higher. We tend to like traditional typesetting, because that is what we are used to. However, even here there are some new trends we need to be aware of as designers.

In ebooks, I have seen several postings suggesting that non-fiction should be done with sans serif body copy. I would be very careful about that, but there is certainly no reason why you cannot choose a truly humanist sans like Optima or even Gill Sans for your body copy. Be sure that you pick one that is very readable. Then you can use elegant serif faces for your heads and get a beautiful book. I suspect that my next font design will be a readable sans to match with an elegant display serif.

Plus, the reader can change fonts at will: Reflow is the goal. That trumps typography in an ebook. Also remember, that an ePUB on an iPad, or converted to KFX for the Fire, is the typographic wonder of the ebook world. All the other ereaders support ePUB. Plus there are many Android tablets with the Readium extension in Chrome. But without embedded fonts the font options remain abysmal.

The various ereaders like iBooks, Kobo, Nook, and Readium all support embedded fonts. The Kindle Fire is certainly headed in that direction by supporting embedded fonts, but the Kindle apps often do not. So things are indeed getting better, but not entirely yet.

The Kindle, Nook, Kobo, and Sony choices may be easily readable on their e-ink devices. But they certainly do not provide good typographic choices for a designer. Your only real font choices might be serif or sans, plus you can add italic and bold. The bad news is that many of the ereaders simply ignore font instructions—but they'll retain the serif/sans serif distinctions.

However, we must remember the ebooks using the currently limited choices are selling like crazy. Kindle still has a majority of the overall market, but the iBookstore is growing rapidly as the iPad becomes the dominant tablet for ereading. If you want to sell to that market, you need to make a book that fits their paradigm. In my case, non-fiction about InDesign and font design sell about twice as much on Kindle as they do on iBooks (but print is still better than a third of sales). Nook and Kobo are still negligible (for me).

These percentages will continue to change regularly as the market matures. Since the Spring of 2013 I have seen radical changes in my sales. In the Spring of 2014, Createspace as still the biggest at 32%. Kindle is only 24% in the US but 32% globally. Gumroad has 12%, Lulu and Draft2Digital are both about 9%. Smashwords is a little less than 4% [it's mostly iBooks and Kobo]. The rest are negligible. In 2015, Createspace had about 30%, Kindle around 27%, and the rest were scattered all over.

In other words, Amazon is under 60% of my sales. They seem to be slowly slipping. The domination of Amazon has run its course for me. I have heard others saying that Amazon's sales are going down. I suspect that will increase. Kobo is really making a push—as is the iBookstore. With iBooks is available in OSX, it should grow a lot. But everything is still controlled by the ebook distributors. One of these days that problem will be solved. At this point, I sell a lot through Gumroad links from my Website/blogs.

The problem is that most excellent text fonts for body copy have fairly small x-heights and there are not many sans serifs with x-heights that small. So, you will look long and hard for true companion fonts. The only font sets you are likely to have [in TypeKit] are Lapture/

Calluna Sans, Sirba/Effra, or other large x-height combinations. Now you can see why I created Buddy and Librum Sans. Otherwise we're the victims of fashion.

Some Sample font pairs

❧ Contenu, Athelas, Garamond/Buddy

❧ Lapture/Calluna Sans

❧ Sirba/Effra

But enough on fonts. Let's get back to ePUB design possibilities. These options get better all the time.

Size & Leading changes

We have quite a bit of control here. In an ePUB the font sizing and spacing must be specified in ems or pixels. InDesign is doing it in ems. Basically, 12 point type is converted to one em. Leading is converted to a multiple of that em. On the iPad's high resolution screen, one em is actually 16 pixels high (I guess that's 32 pixels for the Retina). [But the reader can change it all by whim—though the size proportions you set will remain proportional.] **For fixed layout:** you may well need to increase your point size to get an appropriate number of words per line.

Alignment

This was never a problem until CC 2014. But now **fixed layout ePUB FXLs cannot handle justified copy**. So, you must be sure to convert any style which justifies the copy. It's a small hassle, but it's a result of the coding process used. You just have to carefully proof your ePUBs and make adjustments.

Small Caps & ALL CAPS

Of course, because OpenType features do not work, true small caps are very rare. So, any typographically excellent true small caps would have to be in fonts that have them like Copperplate & Bodoni 72 Small Caps. The OpenType variants will not be picked up. In the subhead before this paragraph, I am using small caps in the print and PDF versions. But I will set MALL and APS in a smaller point size [using a character style, but you will see they are much lighter] for my ePUBs and KF8 variants. Otherwise they would still not work in most ereaders. Even this workaround is commonly stripped out in the e-ink ereaders. **Note:** I've started making ebook versions of my fonts [Contenu eBook & Librum E]. LIBRUM E HAS A SPECIAL FONT FOR THE SMALL CAPS.

No special fonts: CONVERT TO GRAPHIC

If you need a special font, you need to make it into a graphic [unless you can embed it]. For fixed layout, embedded fonts are the norm so this is not an issue. It would seem that selecting the words and choosing Create Outlines would do it. But the resulting rasterized graphic will be a bad size and very pixelated.

Normally, it is necessary to make a separate PDF graphic with that type so you can rasterize it into Photoshop. Then save as a PSD, then use Save For Web to make a Web graphic copy, and place that into your ePUB document. You will be doing this a lot—at least until the ereaders & distributors accept SVG or other vector files.

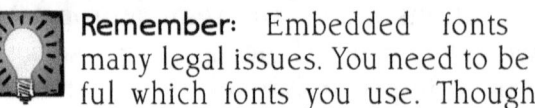 **Remember:** Embedded fonts have many legal issues. You need to be careful which fonts you use. Though you can embed any font you have on your computer in OTF or TTF formats—there are two major problems. In many cases, you will need to pay extra for an ePUB license. So, if there is any doubt (and believe me there is), do not embed fonts unless you are sure you own the rights and that it will look good. You can go to the bergsland.org site and click on the page Hackberry Font Foundry for the fonts I am currently selling for ebook production.

But it is still very rare to buy a font which offers ePUB rights included.

Lists

Lists do not translate well. HTML makes bad lists. For HTML lists, all you can do is delete all special indents you set up. Make it a numbered or bulleted list (with no special bullet) and let InDesign do the translation. It is not good. Remove all indents, left and right from lists unless you have InDesign CC. However, the numbering of HTML lists will not continue to separated paragraphs.

This problem is pretty much solved. It does quite well by using the "Convert To Text" option in the ePUB export dialog. For fixed layout, anything goes except for OpenType feature glyphs. Just remember, Kindle destroys lists using anything other than simple bullets.

Be very careful with fancy bullets: FROM LISTS

Prior to CC [specifically InDesign CC 9.2] this was a real problem. You had to crack the ePUB and change the CSS to use special bullets—from the limited CSS choices. BUT NOW, you can use any character in the basic ASCII set like the delta, lozenge, and so on. The problem is that in the basic fonts, those characters are not very good choices. I have made bullets additions to my book fonts.

In CC, if you use convert list to text, this option embeds bullets with special fonts [including dingbats] when converting to text, but only out of the ASCII characters. The extra OpenType glyphs are not available. You can also make a Character Style with color and size changes to bulk up the bullets a wee bit.

Add chapter breaks with a H1 style

You must set up a H1 style (usually your headline) and specify it as the chapter break. Have it go to next page [not next odd page]. However, for iBooks, you can't do that either because it will add an extra blank page. The good news is that even with H1 setup without the Next Page Keeps control, CC ePUBs still maintain the page controls and move H1 paragraph to the top of the next page.

Eliminate all soft returns.

A soft return is a forced line break in a paragraph without adding a new paragraph [Alt+Enter on PC or

Shift+Return on a Mac]. You will get rid of all of them when exporting a reflowable ePUB. But understand, soft returns are a real problem when the reader can change fonts and font sizes at will while he or she is reading. If you must do a line break, you may well be stuck with special paragraph styles with no space between paragraphs to make it work. Soft returns seem to work fine with fixed layout ePUBs. Just make sure you proof your ePUBs carefully.

Paragraph shading seems to work flawlessly

This new capability is quite nice. No, we do not have border control yet, but we can hope. I don't know yet whether the gradient will work in ePUB Reflow.

Eliminate all OpenType feature use

Nothing can be done about this. Current ebook readers do not support OpenType features—yet. However, they probably will. It is part of the CSS2 scenario and therefore usable in the ePUB standard. This is a major change when moving from print and PDF to ePUB and Kindle books.

Eliminate tabular layouts

HTML/CSS does not support tabs so you'll need to do tables. The good news is that tables now work fairly well—but not in Kindle books.

Use tables [FXL: good; reflowable: eh OK]

For reflowable ePUBs, you will often want to set up a separate InDesign doc for the table, export a print PDF, and rasterize that in Photoshop as wide as is possible [normally 600 pixels]. However in CC 2014, regional cell styles are supported as seen in the capture below. These choices are on the General page to the Table Style Dialog. CC 2014 also supports strokes, fills, and padding. Rules are limited to solid, dotted, and dashed. **A quirk:** A border color of [None} maps to [Black]. I am still regularly disap-

Cell Styles			
Header Rows:	Headers	Left Column:	PartNumber
Footer Rows:	Footers	Right Column:	RowTotal
Body Rows:	PrintStrokes		

pointed at how bad tables look in Kindle. In FXL, they work very well. In ePUB Reflow they are still a bit iffy.

Tables in Fixed Layout ePUBs

Here the problem is solved. So far, everything I've tried has worked flawlessly in my fixed layout ePUBs: gradient borders and fills, any rule style [wavy line, triple line, or anything], and basically anything you can do for a PDF you can do for a fixed layout ePUB.

Eliminate paragraph rules for reflowable

GRAPHICS IN INDESIGN CC FIXED LAYOUT

InDesign's forte is graphic assembly

The whole procedure I just described took less than a minute—real time. Well actually, two minutes because I was careful to set the type well. So, I was able to copy/paste a complex drawing into editable paths in InDesign in less than a minute. Obviously, getting editable pieces from Illustrator is quick and easy.

Paragraph Rule

Using the brushstroke as a frame

To make a radical change, I modified the size of the circle to overlap the brushstroke and pasted a picture of my home into the circle. This took another minute—with the result seen above. I added the type on top in another 20-30 seconds [the only glitch was that I had to set the new text frame to ignore text wraps as I had put a text wrap on the graphic automatically when I styled it with an object style]. Regardless, the whole thing was done in far less time than it took to write this explanation. It is dramatic if not too inspiring.

If I wanted a graphic I could use anywhere: All I would need to do is copy and paste the new graphic onto a new single page document, save it and export it as a PDF [which I did]. If you are looking at this in an ebook, you can see it in glorious 600-pixel-wide RGB color, rasterized in Photoshop and exported as a JPEG. For the B&W book, I could have rasterized into Photoshop and saved as a Grayscale PSD at 300 dpi.

You can do graphics like this very quickly. If you have the pieces at hand, any graphic of this nature can be done in less than a minute. Fancy tables with inserted photos and complex typography can be created in a separate document and exported as a PDF to be used wherever needed at whatever size you need.

A Minnesota winter at home

Fixed Layout ePUBs do paragraph rules well: You can do white or colored type over a gradient rule. You can even extend your rules outside the text frame. The only quibble I found was that these rules are cut off at the text frame border unless there is also a graphic out in that sidebar area as you see to the left.

For the reflowable ePUBs, the only rules you have available are Underline and Strikethrough: without any customizing allowed. If you need the rules, you can create graphics that you can place before and/or after your paragraphs. The only problem with that is the difficulty with spacing control. Plus there is no way to do an overlap so you cannot have a rule as a bar from which the type reverses out to white. On the other hand, we are able to use simple tables with solid top and bottom borders. You just need to test and see what works.

Eliminate borders

You can use borders as a stroke on an object: But it depends on your version. For CC 2014, strokes almost work as expected, but only solid, dotted, and dashed. However, proof carefully. This one is still under development. There was nothing new for 2015, but one of these days we'll get complete border controls—as soon as they figure out how.

 Again, tables will probably be the final solution: In CC, you are able to use single cell tables and their rules.

Type color

You can make your type any color even gradients.

CC now works with nested styles

You can use nested styles in your ePUBs. In the exported ePUB they are converted to spans which you can control with the Export Tags dialog. The only fly in the ointment was that the Kindle Export Plug-In did not support nested styles.

 The Kindle plug-in did not handle nested styles for CS6 & earlier: Because I formerly did my Kindle books first, I was still converting all the nested styles into hand-formatted character styles.

However, for CC I am going back to nested styles. I recently dropped the use of the Amazon Kindle Export Plug-In in favor of making a special ePUB for Kindle [more on that in a bit] and then opening the ePUB in Kindle Previewer which will compile the ePUB into a Kindle KF8 archive. That worked fine, but lately I have just been uploading the ePUBs directly in KDP. If you convert your KF8 books from an ePUB with Kindle Previewer most of this information survives, Kindle books are really frustrating. Sometimes you'll be sure you have it figured out and then the next day it won't work again.

Pages & master pages

Reflowable ePUBs: these are irrelevant as there are no pages in a reflowable ePUB.

Fixed layout ePUBs: Because they do pages, master pages with automatic page numbers work well. I haven't tested yet, but the master page items shown above should work fine. Actually, the gradient paragraph rule worked, but had to take the gradient out of the text itself.

Making these changes & proofing

What needs to be done now is to go through all the styles used in your print document and convert them to work within ePUB limitations. Then export your ePUB and open it in Readium [in Chrome] and in iBooks. For Nook & Kobo, I email the ePUB to my iPad and open it in the readers. ADE4 is making the other ereaders work better. BUT you need to proof on the ereader, it will show your fonts in the desktop computer which has the fonts installed. That will not happen in the ereaders. You can set the export options to automatically open your ePUB in your best ereading app after it is exported.

If you own an iPad, Nook, and/or Kobo: open the ePUB in it to see how it will look there. They all have procedures to sideload ePUBs. Email it to yourself and open it from the email into the reader(s) of your choice with the iPad. It is especially important to check out the graphics and see how they fit. Adjust spacing as well as you possibly can. Be very careful to look for issues which work well in print and PDFs, but do not translate well to HTML—like soft returns, paragraph spacing, OpenType feature use, and so on. Kindle proofing is always very iffy unless you own one.

If you are typographically trained and visually sensitive, this first attempt at an ePUB will be a horrible shock

The typographic ugliness of HTML after you have so carefully crafted your typography in your printed book is a major hit to the senses. Your ebook readers will not be shocked. But, there is no kerning or tracking, and spacing is very crude. All of your OpenType features will be gone. All the controls are very crude—even with the new print quality screens. But most of the new phablets and tablets have 300+ dpi resolution for checking graphics.

Take a deep breath! Now get on with it

You've learned to deal with this level of quality with Websites. [If you haven't–shame on you!] This is the reality of ePUB. Now your goal is to make it as easy to read as possible. It is likely that your first attempts will require you to fix several of your styles. Thankfully, they control the entire document globally because everything is formatted with no local formatting. This is why the use of styles is so critical.

Deal with reality

Do not hang on to impossible requirements. The more simple you make your typography, the better it will work in this greatly restricted environment. There is nothing wrong with ePUB and the ePUB standard. It is simply different and requires a new sense of design. As InDesign has improved we have more control. The largest hurdle at this point, and for the near future, is reader preconceptions.

ePUB does give us much more

If we quit looking at ePUBs from the background of the printed book and start looking from the background of ebooks, then we can see how much we have available in an ePUB. Just focus on readability. If your readers have to work at reading your book, they'll try changing the size–but more likely they'll just quit reading.

Setting chapter breaks

This is a very important part of setting up your styles. Reflowable ePUBs do not support page breaks–with one exception. If you have a style set up as a headline, with the keeps set up to start on the next page, the ePUB will start a new chapter when you use that paragraph style. But you must choose it when you export the ePUB. You find this choice in the ePUB Export Options dialog box: Break Document at Paragraph Style with a popup menu to pick the style.

New for iBooks: The set up just mentioned above no longer works for books set up to upload to the iBookstore. For them you need to leave Keeps set to Anywhere, and then check the style to Break in the Export All Tags Dialog. This will give you the page break without an extra blank page.

Setting the TOC (THIS IS REQUIRED)

You do need to set up a TOC (Layout>> Table of Contents). You will chose this Table of Contents style in the ePUB Export dialog. The styles you choose for your TOC will be added to the bookmarks in the column to the left of your ePUB. You do not use leaders or page numbers like you see in the print settings below as leaders do not work and page numbers do not exist in ebooks [more accurately the page numbers would change all time with

Table of Contents

TOC Style: Print

Title: Contents   Style: 7-Sub 1

OK
Cancel
Save Style...
Fewer Options

Styles in Table of Contents

Include Paragraph Styles:

7-Sub 1
6-Head

Other Styles:

[No Paragraph Style]
Index Level 1
Index Level 2
Index Section Head
[Basic Paragraph]
0-Alphabet

<< Add
Remove >>

Style: 6-Head

Entry Style: TOC Heads

Page Number: After Entry   Style: Page#

Between Entry and Number: ^t   Style: SmallLeader

☐ Sort Entries in Alphabetical Order   Level: 1

Options

☑ Create PDF Bookmarks   ☐ Run-in
☑ Replace Existing Table of Contents   ☐ Include Text on Hidden Layers
☑ Include Book Documents
☐ Make text anchor in source paragraph

Numbered Paragraphs: Include Full Paragraph

reader changes to fonts and/or type size]. **_Practicality rules in these things_**. You can spend a lot of time and money trying to figure out why these things are so or you can publish books.

I publish.

Keep working on ideas. As you add a new technique that works, implement it. InDesign CC will continue to get better. But the basic concept is that you can only do what the software enables. A double-minded person will get nothing done.

Writing the metadata (THIS IS REQUIRED)

You need to write the metadata before you export the ePUB. However, you can enter the metadata within the export ePUB dialog box. As you can see on the next page, this is old File Info dialog box. The important things here are the title, description, keywords, and copyright. You worked all this out when you released your book for print. Right?

You find this dialog in the File menu under the File Info command. It is required to fill out this description page. It contains the information primarily used by the search engine spiders. So, obviously it will greatly help as your readers try to find a book like yours.

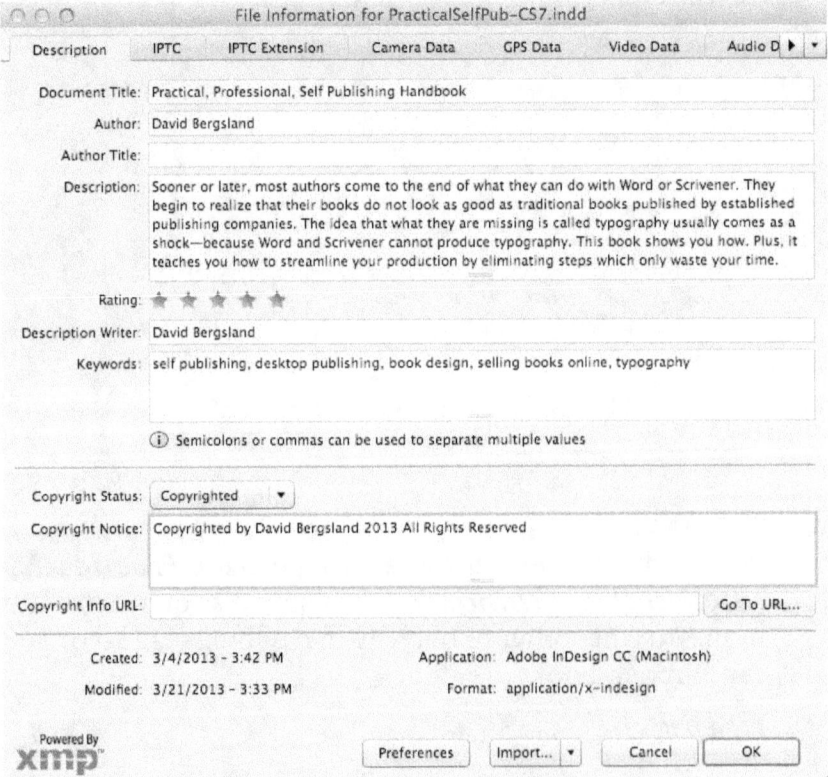

There are some strict rules for metadata

Some of these rules are Apple's rules. However, many of them seem to be Lulu and Smashwords paranoia. It doesn't matter. **Do what they ask.** You do want to sell your ePUBs, right? They include things like the metadata title must be identical to the copy found on the cover. It must be in title case except for a half dozen or so tiny words. There are several others things like this. For example, I had the title of an earlier edition as: Writing In InDesign Second Edition. Lulu made me change Second Edition to a subtitle. I was very irritated, but you can't fight city hall. Here are just a few from Lulu's page (these materials are six years old now. Get the latest versions on the Lulu Website). **Their list of rules is much longer:** In fact, if they didn't sell so many books they would not be worth the effort.

- **Title must match everywhere:** metadata, cover, and book's title page

- **No mention of included materials that don't exist in the digital product:** (Example: CD, poster, etc.).

- **Cannot up-sell to a version of the product that is more complete.**

- **No advertisements or links.**

- **Do not use characters which require entity references in the description:** (Example: &, -, or -, curly quotes, etc.).

- **Cannot mislead buyers or misrepresent the ebook:** (Example: An illustrated guide containing no illustrations or pictures).

- **Do not use font sizes in the description**

- **Subtitles are particularly important for differentiating multiple books:** in a series that share the same title.

- **Improperly formatted HTML tags in the description:** can cause a garbled description in retail channels.

- **Titles and Subtitles incorrectly capitalized. The first letter of all words in the title and** subtitle should be capitalized, except for the following words: a, an, and, for, from, of, or, the, to. The first and last word of the title and subtitle should always be capitalized.

- **Use of HTML lists in description is forbidden**

- **Titles beginning with articles should display properly. EX:** A Tale of Two Cities, not Tale of Two Cities, A

- **Must have a valid description:** Do not use the title.

- **Multiple blank pages:** Especially at the beginning of the book. Please remember to remove blank pages before converting to ePUB

If you do not follow all of them precisely, they will not publish your book. I just signed up with Apple Connect so I can upload my ePUBs directly. I think you can see why—I simply do not need the hassle. However, books sold through Lulu, Smashwords, and Draft2Digital continue to sell much better than the versions uploaded directly. Draft2Digital does not require much of this nonsense.

 There's been a big change, starting in 2015: I started using ePUB2 Reflows uploaded to Draft2Digital for iBook, Nook, Kobo, Scribd, and several others. Most of the metadata rules seem to be relaxed [a little bit]. Plus, we now fill out the metadata in the ePUB export dialog.

Setting the Export Tags

As mentioned, this ability to open a single dialog box and set all the HTML tags and add the CSS classes for each style is huge: It is a real disappointment that we cannot edit these class rules directly, but it makes it much easier to edit the CSS—if you're into that type of thing. CC works well, but it has added a couple of wrinkles. Nothing major.

You can easily force InDesign to write good CSS

Well, that's a bit of an overstatement. The Web developer purists will be shrieking. But, you can easily make

InDesign write CSS that controls all of your type in the ePUB in most cases.

Lists

The only exception is lists. HTML lists are ugly and hard to control regardless—even if you coding directly into a Website, but CC has a solution for this problem also. With CC, it turns out that setting the ePUBs conversion for lists to [Automatic} works well. However, the standard HTML lists will never work typographically. In the Export to ePUB dialog, Convert To Text works best. I change from [Automatic] to p:bullet or p:number for the tag and class. This comes closer to retaining the indents and the special bullets. CC 2014 does retain custom bullets from dingbat fonts. But this does require embedded fonts.

The good news is that cracking the ePUB and editing the CSS is no longer necessary: You can easily force InDesign to write CSS rules that will control all of your type without the need to edit the CSS afterward. What you need to do is make sure that you specify a class for all your styles as well as a tag. The first thing I do is choose the Select All Unused command and delete all usused styles that were selected [except for styles which will be used for the TOC].

Let's take a look at what I just exported for an ePUB with a recent book. I opened the Edit All Export Tags… dialog and set up the tags and Classes. You can see them on the next page.

Notice I added tags for all the styles. I do not leave any set to except for the Object Styles. The CC difference is this: if you do not use unique classes for every style InDesign will scream bloody murder with alerts. I tended to do it like I do with my websites, using the same class for all items in a div. But for an ePUB, this does not work. So instead of: p.norm; and h1.norm I have to use something like p.norm, and h1.normh1. It's a minor irritant and it does solve the problems. The CSS exports flawlessly [at least for everything other than Kindle].

I must decide whether the paragraph style is a subset of p, h1-h6. For character styles, I need to decide if the style is a subset of em, strong, or span. This will work, and it will look remarkably close to what I see in InDesign. I'm no longer editing the CSS in Dreamweaver. In fact, I was so sick of it I quit a little early with CS6. CC improved things. Now with CC2014 things are better. CC2015 was even better. CC2016 will do the same.

Why add the classes?

That's simple. InDesign would not define p, my basic paragraph tag. But it will define p.norm. It will not define h2, but it will define h2.normh2. Is the result wonderfully sleek and elegant XHTML code? No. But it works and all of your typography is controlled. If you do not do this, you are forced to crack the ePUB, open template.css, and add the basic tags. So, the choice is yours.

Edit All Export Tag:

Show: ⦿ EPUB and HTML ○ PDF

Style	Tag	Class	Split EPUB	Emit CSS
¶ [Basic Paragraph]	[Automatic]		☐	☑
¶ 2–body	p	norm	☐	☑
¶ 2–No first	p	nofirst	☐	☑
¶ 2–run–in	p	runin	☐	☑
¶ 3–Bulleted	p	bullet	☐	☑
¶ 3–Description	p	nnobullet	☐	☑
¶ 4–Body heads	h3	small	☐	☑
¶ 5–Tips	p	tip	☐	☑
¶ 6–Head	h1	normh1	☑	☑
¶ 7–Sub	h2	normh2	☐	☑
¶ 8–9(WavyRule)	h2	italic	☐	☑
¶ 8–Sub	h3	normh3	☐	☑
¶ TOC Heads	h1	indexhead	☐	☑
¶ TOC Sub1	h4	indexsub	☐	☑
A 1–bodyBOLD	strong	body		☑
A 1–List Bold	strong	sans		☑
A 2–Italic	em	bodyitalic		☑
A 3–BoldItalic	span	smash		☑
A 3–ListRegular	span	sansreg		☑
A 4–Version	span	smallsans		☑
A Bullet	span	red		☑
A 14 point	span	fourteen		☑
[Basic Graphics Frame]	[Automatic]			☑
[Basic Text Frame]	[Automatic]			☑
3–Inline	[Automatic]	three		☑
4–Anchored	[Automatic]	four		☑
5–SimpleAnchor	[Automatic]	five		☑
6–Left	[Automatic]	six		☑

OK
Cancel

You can now design your ePUB edition of your book in InDesign and directly upload the resultant ePUB with no modifications. The results will look very good. Purists might tear their hair, but I think it's silly to add coding which does not help much—especially with ereaders being so bad.

The reports are that for ePUB FXL the code is better than most hand-written code.

The goal is an easily readable book—not the production of a coded tour de force. You need to closely examine the output for readability. That's your priority.

It is never quite that easy: bad fonts

The problem is that during the massive conversion from your print version to your ePUB version it is likely that you have many styles or locally formatted type that use fonts you cannot use in an ePUB. A couple of years ago, I was looking at the CSS for the first proof of the ePUBs and at the bottom I found many spans asking for fonts I was certain I was not using. They had been added along with old copy.

Find Font

Fonts in Graphics: 72
Missing Fonts: 0

130 Fonts in Document

Font Information	Sync	
Adobe Caslon Pro Regular	☐	Done
Adobe Garamond Pro Regular	☐	Find First
Adobe Jenson Pro Display	☐	Change
Amico Regular	☐	Change All
Amitale Book Bold	☐	Change All
Amitale Book Book	☐	Change/Find
Arturo Book Regular	☐	More Info

Reveal in Finder   Sync Fonts

Replace With:

Font Family: Minion Pro
Font Style: Regular
☑ Redefine Style When Changing All

ⓣ Font Sync is powered by Typekit.com Learn More

We See, above, the Find Font dialog box (Type>> Find Font...) for one of these books. As you can see, the top listings are many fonts I don't want to use in my ePUB, because every ereader would substitute them out into its defaults unless they were embedded [and for some I do not have an ePUB license]. I am using 130 fonts so far. Obviously this is real problem with an ereader like the Nook which only has three fonts available. More importantly, you must be sure it is legal for you to use them. None of these 130 fonts are available on any ereader unless I embed the fonts.

I will use this dialog extensively to check the ePUB version of this book. I must eliminate any font for which I have no license. Plus, I do it simply to control the file size of the ePUB which is already huge, I must convert all of these fonts to graphics. I will carefully decide what to do with each one of those instances where a font is used—deciding how to convert it to a graphic you can read easily.

This may add many graphics to your ebooks: If you have books like mine which are written about book design, you have some unique problems. I had to make many new graphics to show simple things I could easily demonstrate in print like ligatures, small caps, oldstyle figures, small cap figures, ordinals, ornaments, and so on.

If I click the More Info button you can see in the Find Font dialog, it will show me the page location of the font use. Once I locate the font flagged in the actual copy of the book, I find I have one of three issues to deal with:

- **It may be in a paragraph or character style that was never redefined:** In that case I can redefine the style and globally eliminate the font usage very easily.

- **It may be in a graphic:** In this case I must make a rasterized version of the graphic. Live type in a graphic will normally cause too many problems in the display of the type to be used. Sidebars with live type are always going to be a very tricky thing in an ePUB.

🌀 **It may be part of the copy:** This will probably not happen to you unless you are like me and write about typography and fonts. In this case, you can select the type and Create Outlines—leaving the outlines type inline in the copy. That will work, but InDesign will convert that outlined type into a coarse bitmap that looks pretty chewed up. Your best choice (for quality) is to rasterize that type in Photoshop and save it as a high quality JPEG at 72 dpi, 600 pixels wide. You can then place that high resolution bitmap graphic as an anchored object in your copy and it will look as good as possible.

Once you have your fonts cleaned up and your export tags set, you should always recheck your TOC settings and your File Info. Then you can export your ePUB. Type Command+E and select ePUB for your format.

EPUB Export dialogs: fixed layout, reflowable, 2 & 3

With InDesign CC, the ePUB export dialog gives us a lot of tools and options as we fought to control our output. There are six pages and many things you need to set for ePUB 2.0.1, and ePUB 3.0. Now we have two separate export dialogs for FXL and Reflow.

At this point, ePUB2 with embedded fonts works well for Draft2Digital: iBooks, Nook, Kobo, Scribd, and a few others. ITunes Connect and Kobo Writing Life accept FXL ePUBs. The ePUB3 support for reflowable is minimal. This entire area is changing, seemingly by the week, so any updates will be mentioned in my blogs.

The Fixed Layout ePUB export box

This is all ePUB3. In many ways, this option simplifies things a great deal. Fonts are always embedded, for example. The CSS is always written. This entire export process is fairly controlled.

The general page

Export Range: This gives us the normal choices.

Cover: The choices are None, Rasterize First Page and Choose Image. IMHO: you always want Choose Image. Just pick one that matches the page size. Once you choose an image that changes to From Location, as you see above. I design a specific front cover to be used and link it here. It should be the page size and 150 dpi. Just remember to use a JPEG optimized with Photoshop's Save For Web dialog for the cover, at this point.

Navigation: TOC Style: You need to choose the one you have set up for your ePUBs. As you can see I call mine ePUB.

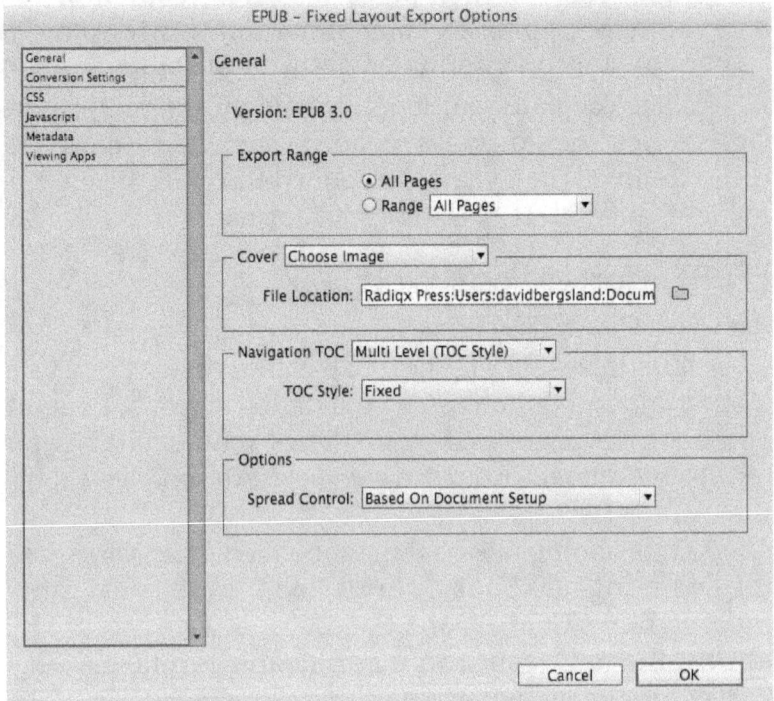

Options: Spread Control. This is very different from anything we've had before. The choices are:

- **Based on Document Setup:**

- **Convert Spread to Landscape page:** Portrait books with facing pages and converted to landscape spreads

- **Enable Synthetic spreads:** Portrait books non-facing can allow synthetic spreads if the ereader supports it.

- **Disable Spreads:** Obvious

Conversion settings

Format: This has four choices: Automatic, JPEG, GIF, and PNG.

Resolution: This also has four choices: 72, 96, 150, or 300 dpi. I've been using 150 dpi as I have tested this out. It seems to work well. The lower resolutions, not so much.

JPEG Options: I've been using Progressive, and High as you can see. In my current workflow, I only use JPEGs. But I for transparency, I go to PNGs.

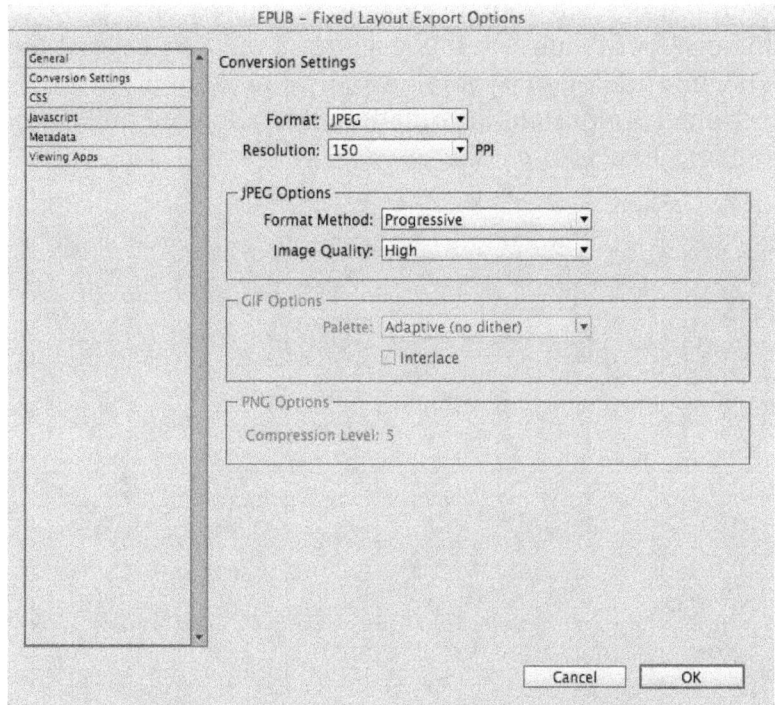

GIF Options: I don't usually use these, but adaptive (no dither) is probably the best.

The real problem

I do not want InDesign to be messing up my graphics. Reconversions always blur the image, at least slightly. So, I'm doing everything I can to avoid that issue. It's not easy and often it just doesn't work. As I get clearer info from Adobe, I'll edit this and post about it in *The Skilled Workman.*

CSS & Javascript

I'm skipping over these. They simply have an attachment button to add your own CSS files or javascripts.

Metadata

This is a major change for CC 2014. From now on we will be filling out our metadata in the Export ePUB dialog box. If you already have the File Info metadata dialog filled out—and that is certainly possible if you are making a conversion from your print PDF to a fixed layout ePUB—InDesign will populate this page from the first page of the File Info dialog. As you all should know by now, this is extremely important information. It is often the major way readers find your ePUBs.

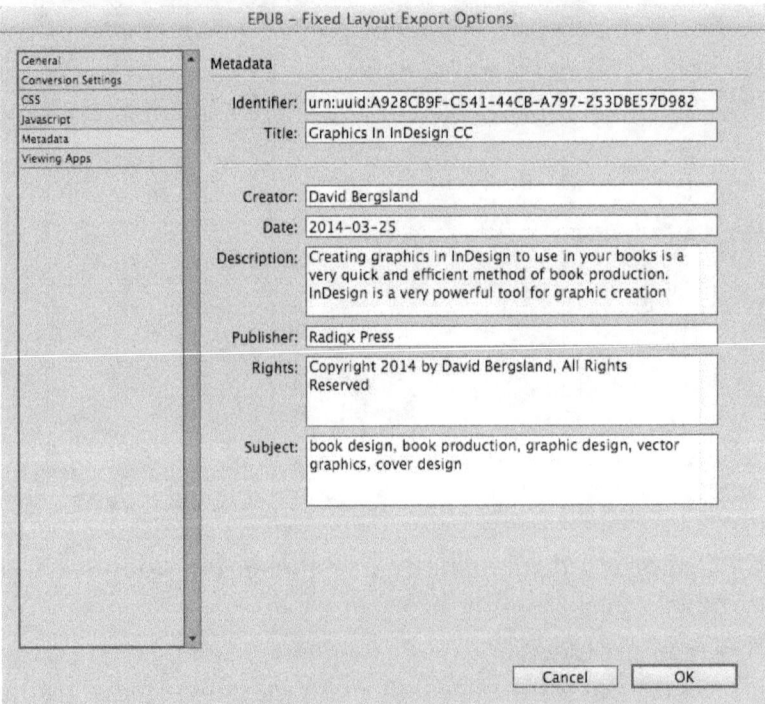

The keywords and description need to be chosen carefully and written well. Both of these areas are as crucial as your cover and title. Spend a lot of thought and prayer over all four of these items. If your books are not selling well, see what your competition is doing here.

Viewing Apps

This is the expansion of the old View ePUB after export checkbox. Now you can list the ereaders you have on your computer and view your new ePUB in all of them for proofing.

One of the things you'll need to do is keep on top of the new ereaders as they come out. Do not be surprised if you export and check out your ePUB, that you need to edit and reexport—often several times. I still have to do this, and I've been doing it a long time.

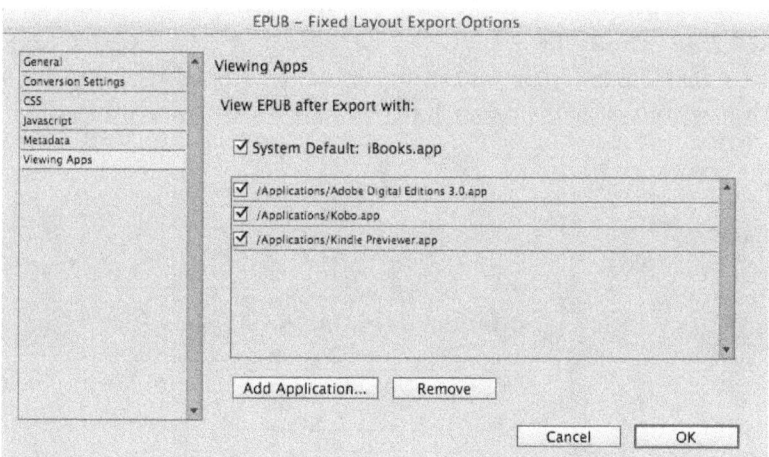

Reflowable ePUB dialog box

This covers 2.0.1 as well as 3.0. As mentioned ePUB2 is still needed for the distributors who will not accept ePUB3 like: Lulu, Smashwords, Tomely, NookPress, and the rest. These suppliers will not accept embedded fonts either. Why do we bother with them? They sell a lot of books. Draft2Digital uses ePUB2 to add a lot of helpful marketing to your books, like adding New Releases at the back of all your books, adding a list of your other books and so on. They cannot do this with ePUB3.

General

Version: the choices are 2.0.1 or 3.0. You will probably need two versions of this: a 2.0.1 with fonts and without fonts.
Cover: The choices are None, Rasterize First Page and Choose Image. IMHO: you always want Choose Image. Just pick one that is 600 x 800 pixels x 72 dpi. Use Photoshop's

Save For Web dialog. That's what they all want. I design a specific front cover to be used and link it here.

Navigation: TOC Style: You need to choose the one you have set up for your ePUBs. As you can see I call mine ePUB.

Content: Based on Page Layout, Same As XML Structure, and Same As Articles Panel. I find the articles panel useless for dealing with sidebars and the like. The only thing it works for is the TOC and Index, but those are added correctly by the page layout.

Split document: You can check the first option and pick the one paragraph style you use for starting new chapters. Or you can check Based On Paragraph Style Export Tags. In most cases, you want the second one as iBooks uses that whether or not you have the first button checked.

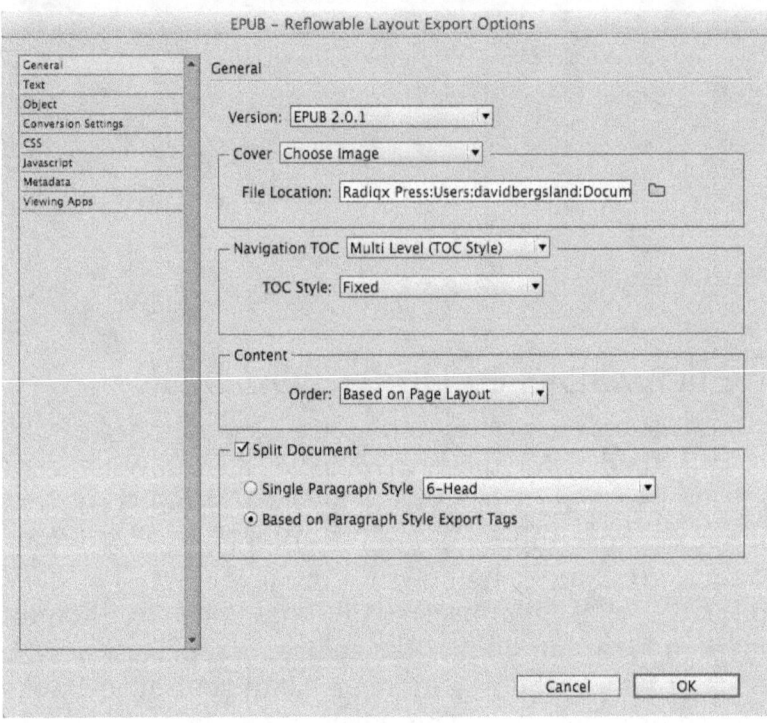

Text

Options

Remove Forced Line Breaks: That's what they are calling soft returns. You must remove them because the type re-wraps horribly when the readers change the size and font (and they will). When InDesign removes these soft returns it replaces them with a space. That is almost always what you want. But check and make sure.

Footnote placement: At the end of the paragraph seems to be the best method for readability of footnotes in an ereader—at least until the pop-up footnotes are accepted by everyone. IBooks takes you to the footnote with a link back to where you were. Most footnotes these days are hyperlinks—where you might actually hope that readers stopped the reading to go and read the source. The pop-up footnotes may well be the best. My clumsy fingers make the pop-up variety untenable.

Lists

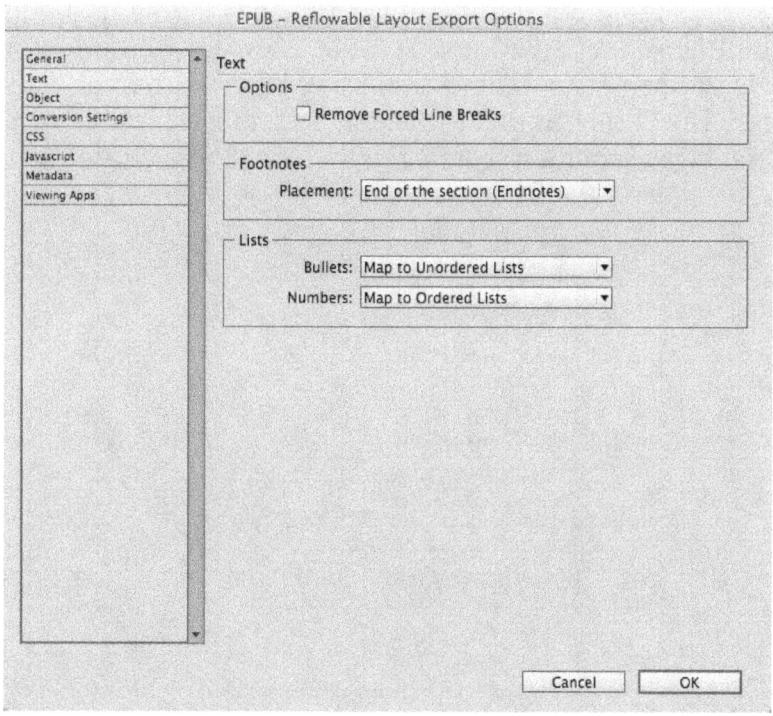

Bullets & Numbers: As mentioned, HTML lists are very ugly. With CC, the best option is Convert To Text. It's not perfect, but the bullets are maintained and any applied character style, plus this comes the closest to the indents you set up in InDesign. But remember, bullets which are dependent upon a font will need that font embedded—I'll talk later about Kindle's distortion of lists.

Object

This is all puzzling. But for most cases, what you see below works best. Fixed CSS Size only seems to work with iBooks. The basic concept is simple: now that it is possible to specify your original image—the one you carefully prepare in Photoshop—you are a fool to do anything else. You check Use Existing Image for Graphic Objects. You really do not want any software automatically doing anything to your images when they are so severely limited by the format. Web images, 72 dpi, are extremely crude. Virtually all detail is lost. For CC2015, images in ePUB3 are broken. It's another reason to stick with ePUB2 for now.

Finding out information on images is like trying to pull hens' teeth (and no, city folk, they don't have teeth). No one seems to want to admit how bad the images really are. The best I can find is that the iPad, most smart phones, and high-resolution tablets require 600x800 pixels or less.

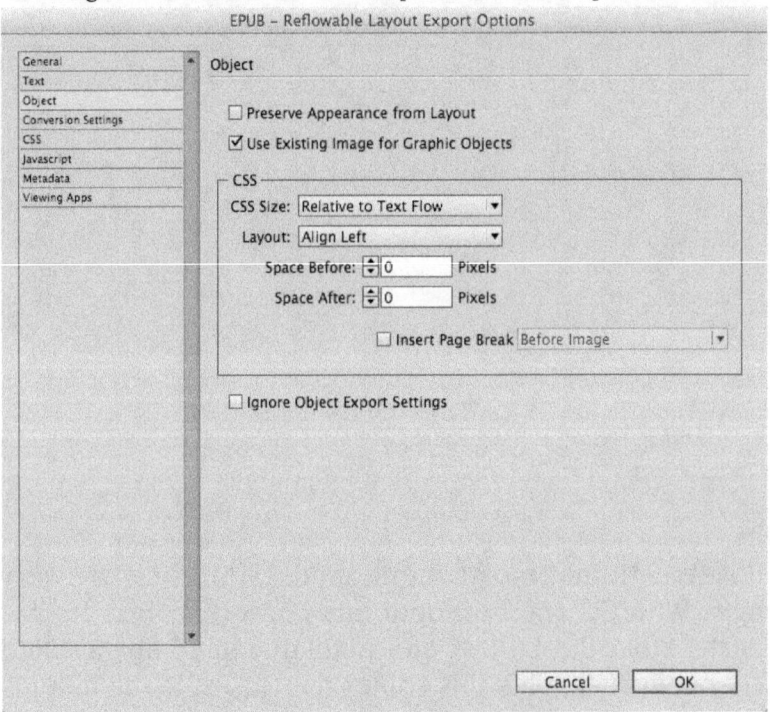

🌼 The iPad maximum is 600x860 pixels.

🌼 Nook's maximum size is 600x730 pixels.

🌼 For Kobo and Fire it is 600x800.

At this point, I make my images to size, and JPEG [in almost all cases]. I make them wide enough to fit the column of type and place them as Anchored Objects. With CC's new capabilities, I can use smaller images more easily. But tall narrow images will always be a problem. I try to do something to make the images wider so I can use the Above Line style if the image is tall. I do this to get as much help as I can with image sharpness. You can make them smaller and have them work OK. But, if you need detail make them as large as possible, and that is 600 wide portrait, and 800 wide landscape.

Remember, ebook graphics are ghastly: I continue to fight the good fight, but you really need to question why you are even including graphics. The iPad does a good job, but the ePUB format itself does not support graphic excellence. Of course there was the hope that the high resolution of the tablets would really help. But the file size is usually too large to use.

Use Existing Image for Graphic Objects: The InDesign automated conversion processes re-rasterize the graphics. So, I am very pleased with the Use Existing Image for Graphic Objects button. My procedure is to open all the graphics from the print version in Photoshop and make them exactly the pixel dimension I need. Then I use Save For Web… to save them as JPEGs. This gives the best results.

For print, I use PSDs (Photoshop's native format) at 300 dpi. I keep the original PSDs in case I want to go back to the way the image was before the JPEG compression. Then I save JPEG versions at 600 pixels wide [or whatever I need] to use in the ePUB. I should be able double the size for iPads with Retina Displays (and the higher resolution Android tablets), but it adds so much to the file size I haven't bothered yet.

Preserve Appearance from Layout: This is now unchecked when I check Use Original Image. The appearance is controlled by the Objects styles.

CSS size: The choices are Fixed and Relative to Page. I use Relative to Page, but again this is controlled by the controls in the object style. I want them as large as possible to be readable because they are basically low-res bitmap images. Fixed works well with iBooks but not elsewhere.

Image Alignment and Spacing: Because my images are all anchored objects, the alignment is controlled by the object style used. But I set this Flush left.

Insert page break: Before Image, After Image, or Both Before and After Image. I rarely use it, but its utility is clear. Remember that page breaks destroy images.

Ignore Object Export Settings: I leave it unchecked because I do not set custom settings for any image. The problem was that Object Export Settings were needed to control anchored objects as sidebars. In CS6 and earlier, these settings really didn't work. Now they are not necessary.

Conversion

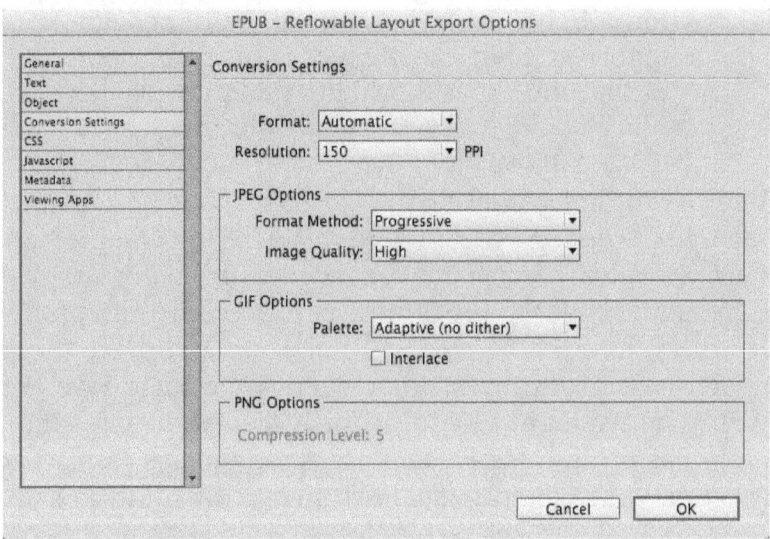

Format: You have four options: Automatic, JPEG, GIF, and PNG. I use JPEGs almost exclusively. With Automatic on, InDesign converts anything it can't use [like a PDF] to a PNG.

Resolution (ppi): I make my large images 600 pixels wide and 72 dpi JPEGs. I've been using 150 dpi for books with fewer graphics. For a book like this one with over 260 graphics, I go with 72 dpi to better handle the size of the resulting ePUB.

JPEG Options: I set the JPEG options to Progressive, High. The image quality in ePUBs is bad enough without any

JPEG artifacts produced by compressing the JPEGs too far. However, for my font design book (with nearly 300 graphics) this made my ePUB nearly 20 MB. But then the ePUB for the professional InDesign book is 22.3 MB. The one for this book will be about 20 MB. So, I am sometimes forced to change the quality to medium. Because the images are almost all screen captures, the new ePUB looks very good on the iPad. I may have to do that for this book also. You must do what you need to do to get the best images possible.

GIF Options: I use Adaptive (no dither). But then, if I make my GIFs with Photoshop's Save for Web, I'll use 100% dither and a bit of lossy compression.

PNG Options: I take what I get.

CSS

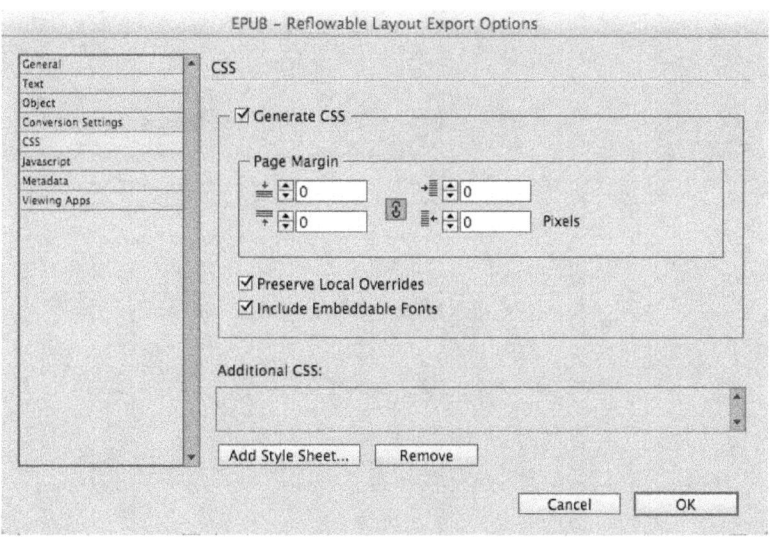

Generate CSS: Unlike fixed layout, where CSS is not optional, it is in reflowable. I can't really think of a reason why you would not want to generate CSS—except for the obvious one: your own CSS is better and you want to use it.

Page Margins: Try it, but most ereaders ignore these.

Preserve Local Overrides: I uncheck this. You usually do not want any local overrides. Clean them up while proofing. They are covered with your character styles.

Include embeddable Fonts: This works for everyone except Smashwords and Nook.

Javascript

I'm skipping over this. It simply has an attachment button to add your own javascripts.

Metadata

This was a major change for CC 2014. From now on we will be filling out our metadata in the Export ePUB dialog box. If you already have the File Info metadata dialog filled out–and that is certainly possible if you are making a conversion from your print PDF to a fixed layout ePUB–InDesign will populate this page from the first page of the File Info dialog. As you all should know by now, this is extremely important information. It is often the major way readers find your ePUBs.

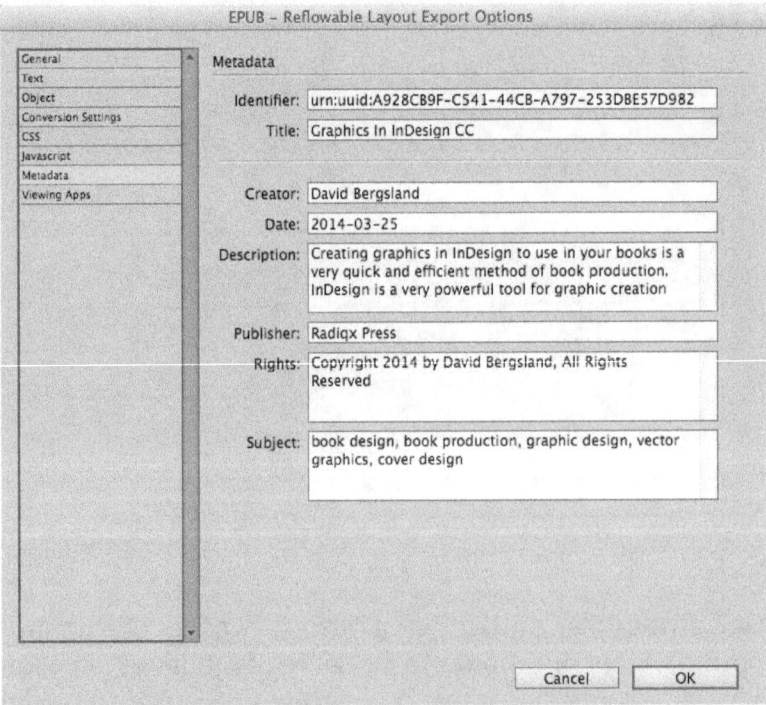

Viewing Apps

View after Exporting: Always check this. This has changed for me lately now that the fourth version of Adobe Digital Editions is out. But ADE4 is still inferior. Readium [requires Chrome] is fairly good. Now that iBooks is in OSX Mavericks, that is the best option. Always look over the exported ePUB in ADE4 before you validate and upload. You also need to check in iBooks. Increasingly, I check it out in BlueFire on my iPad. I am still regularly surprised by something that needs to be fixed.

Always test with crappy ereaders: I have a tendency to only test in the ereaders which show everything. Quite regularly I am surprised and disgusted with what is actually displayed in Nook, Kobo, or the e-ink ereaders in general. Basically, that means you need to test using the apps on your iPad. You don't have an iPad? Then you don't really have to worry because you have crappy already well-defined by everything except Readium and Fire.

This is not a smooth process yet. It is really good that InDesign can now export ePUBs that can be validated. But it probably will not be uneventful until InDesign 2017 or so. InDesign CC is getting pretty good, but there is still a long ways to go.

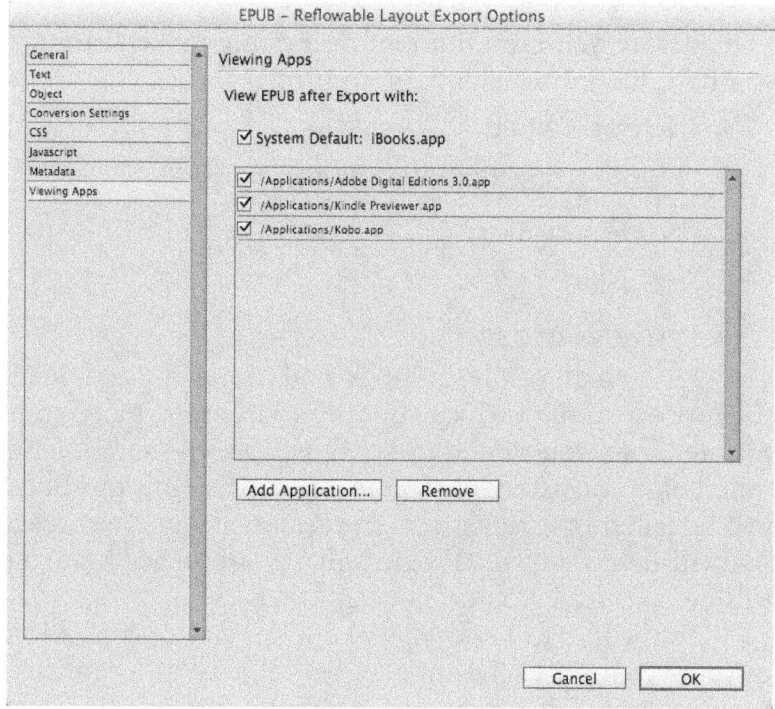

Click OK and you've got an ePUB

It will open in your reader of choice. Proof it carefully in a variety of ereading apps or hardware. Redo as necessary. You will quickly develop a good idea of what is translating well and what does not work for you. I need to reiterate: proof carefully and often. You need to go through every ePUB you export page by page. Adobe Digital Editions 4 is a problem. It will show fonts from your hard drive on your computer which will not show in your ereader. On the other hand, do not be seduced by iBooks. It's in another league. Most ereaders will not do nearly as well as you see in iBooks.

Validate it

Redo the proof as often as necessary. I used to suggest that you go to: http://validator.idpf.org/ for validation. But, I haven't had an ePUB which wouldn't validate for a long time with InDesign CC. I no longer worry about it.

Uploading to the various places

Before you even think of doing this make sure that you have the following under control.

- The book's title
- The book's subtitle (Optional)
- The description
- The price
- The keywords

Without all of these things well in hand, the uploading process to the various suppliers will much more complicated than you want it to be. Plus, you will have a hard time being consistent. If you are not consistent, your book will be listed in various ways in various places. Your readers will be confused. Google will be confused. Amazon will be confused. You do not want that.

You will also need to make a special rasterization of your cover for each vendor. They all have different size requirements. This is one of the main reasons I suggest you have your front cover separate in PDF form. That way each rasterization will be sharp and crisp. The only problem now is that the various covers have different proportions, which for which it can be a bear to adjust.

Never forget these are Web documents

Actually, as you know, they are not exactly that. There are many Web page possibilities which cannot be used in an ePUB. But, the basic capabilities are the same. You are using HTML and CSS with 72 dpi images a maximum of 600 pixels wide in almost all cases.

The major fly in the ointment

Converting to Kindle

Until the summer of 2012, I gave some very explicit instructions for the construction of the HTML and CSS needed to step back in time to Amazon's MOBI format. It was extremely limited in what was allowed. It was all done by writing HTML by hand. Things have gotten a lot better. In fact, in many ways, Kindle's KF8 Export Plug-in for CS6 and earlier worked very well. You could export a Kindle book easily, though it was missing many capabilities.

Now with CC things have changed again. There was a short time period where Amazon's plug-in was doing better than converting an ePUB. This was also the same time frame where Amazon was bouncing all MOBIs made with non-Amazonian software. But now you can just upload your ePUB or convert it in Kindle Previewer.

Kindle Previewer 3.0

One of the less heralded features of Amazon's free Kindle Previewer is that is will do a good job of converting an ePUB using Kindle Gen. This is my current production workflow.

- **First I export an ePUB with embedded fonts:** this is my upload for all my distributors.

- **Next I package the document used to create the ePUB into a new folder:** in the Amazon folder for the Kindle version.

* **In the newly packaged Links folder, I go through all the linked graphics:** [They are all JPEGs at 100% quality to avoid artifacts].

* **Any graphic which is over 125 KB:** Needs to be resized. I to open the original into Photoshop and make a JPEG which is less than 120 KB. Amazon will re-rasterize anything not done this way, badly blur, and otherwise mess up your graphic..

* **I use Save For Web to get the file size of the graphics adjusted to less than 120 KB:** A couple of times I have saved them at exactly 127 KB and Amazon still resized them—thereby ruining them.

* **If I do that, I Save As a PSD:** and save the original JPEG as a PSD in a new Originals folder.

* **Change all the object styles to your Above Line option, flush left or centered:** The fancy anchored objects options are stripped out by Kindle— not uncommonly stripping out the entire graphic.

* **When all the graphics are fixed, I export a new ePUB:** I open it in Kindle Previewer to convert it to a KF8 package for KDP uploads. I use that to Proof.

* **Kindle Previewer 3.0 [Beta] is what we use to see what the Kindle book looks like after we export the ePUB:** It uses KindleGen to convert the new CC ePUBs to KF8 books and then views them. However, if you use Fixed for the CSS Size the preview graphic sizes will be very small. I am told that this is not an issue once the book is viewed in your Kindle. But I don't have one.

So far, the results have been good. I am sticking with this new procedure at least until Amazon's new plug-in comes out [if it does]. Who knows what they will do to ramp up their offering? If I change back I'll blog about it.

Images

Basically, nothing is changed here. For CS6 and earlier, I still recommend that you place all images inline. For CC ePUBs, all images are changed into anchored objects. Kindle Previewer seems to strip out a lot of that information. Quality issues with the Kindle books still remain very frustrating. I imagine it is much easier to deal with if you have a Fire.

The Kindle supports GIF, BMP, JPEG, PNG images in your content. Vector graphics are not supported and must be converted to raster graphics. **The size limit for images is 127KB [120KB actual].** Below this limit, all images will be exported unaltered. While above this limit, images will be automatically optimized [re-rasterized] to be under the size limit during conversion. You should understand this to mean that images larger than 125KB will be ruined. That is straight forward enough.

Here's another warning from Amazon
about images with text:

I'll just quote them on this:

For images containing a lot of text, using the GIF format is recommended so that the sharpness and legibility of the text is retained. Since an image is always displayed completely on the screen, image resolution should be constrained to a maximum of 500x600 [ed: 600w x 500h] so that the image is not scaled, making it hard to read. Minimum font size should be such that a lower-case "a" is at least 6 pixels tall. You can reduce the number of colors used in an image to optimize its size or split the image horizontally to keep it under the size limit. It is highly recommended that automatic optimization by KindleGen be avoided in case of images containing text.

My recommendation is that you do what you need to do to entirely avoid any "optimization" by making your images smaller than 125K and 600 pixels wide or narrower. Notice they specify that images larger than 600x500 pixels will be scaled. This means that you need to keep the height less than 500 pixels also.

Cover image

It's required and it needs to be exactly 600x800. In the past JPEGs were virtually required. I found that unless they were produced by Photoshop's Save for Web command I had troubles. I set up my images exactly to spec before placing them into my InDesign document.

The KDP upload process will have you upload the cover image again in addition to the one embedded in your book, for their use. Their exact recommendation is 1563 pixels by 2500 pixels. It's all pretty straight forward. The KDP Publishing guidelines are linked off the plug-in page. My basic design recommendations remain the same as we discussed for ePUBs, modified only by what you see above.

Bottomline on the Kindle Export Plug-In & Previewer

Since the summer of 2012, everything I've exported with the new plug-in worked as expected and has been accepted by KDP. Then I used Kindle Previewer—which also worked well. I uploaded the CC ePUBs directly in KDP last year. Now I am back to using Kindle Previewer 3.0. Book quality in Kindle is still a problem and will remain so until the give us tools which cover their "better typography". Supposedly you can now use much larger images. I'm not willing to risk that. If I come up with a new and better procedure, I'll keep you up to date on *The Skilled Workman*. The big thing to remember is that the fancy features only work in the Fire, several only in Fire HD and HDX.

Dealing with the old e-ink Kindles, Nooks, & Kobos

These remain popular and for graphic designers, this is horrible news. All anchored object stying is stripped out and the images are placed on their own line flush left. All font information is stripped out—including the serif and sans serif distinctions. I would be concerned about much more. I imagine tables are dumped. The only borders kept are those rasterized within the Photoshop images. These e-ink ereaders are very much like reading your book in NotePad or TextEdit. The thought makes me nauseous.

However, the users of these devices usually read nothing but novels. Novels are very simple books. So, these issues are not nearly as bad as they seem.

PART SIX:

The various suppliers

CHAPTER TWENTY-NINE

Publish

Several days, weeks, months, or years have transpired now. The front matter, body, and back matter is now complete. You have the cover designed and you've written the description. You've researched keywords to help searchers find your book. You've exported test ePUBs and proofed them carefully. As far as you know, you're ready to go.

Dealing with the supplier/ distributors

So, you need to get the book proofed and published. My assumption is that you are an author with very limited capital and few personnel resources. Once I accept this focus, there are relatively few suppliers. [If you hear of another one, please let me know and I'll add it to the book.]

In early-2016, I am going to share techniques that work for Lulu, Createspace, Scribd, Amazon, Kindle, Nook, Kobo, Smashwords, Draft2Digital, Gumroad, and Zazzle. Draft2Digital has become my preferred distributor, even though they take an additional cut from the royalties. But their service and marketing are excellent.

Yes, there are more showing up all the time. But, most of the new ones have up front fees—and often those fees are substantial. The best one I have heard of is Book-

Buddy which required an upfront payment of $19.00 for the ISBN to upload a new book. However, that didn't last too long. Blurb is excellent for coffee table books. But these techniques will almost certainly work for the new startups we will see in the next decade.

ISBN Numbers

To be a traditional publisher, this is required. In this case, you will be using Lightning Source and/or any one of the innumerable on-demand printing companies like Snowfall Press. Usually, these companies are not nearly as user-friendly. They expect you to understand the printing process and often require you to purchase expensive proofs.

One of the major hassles in getting books published in the old paradigm was the ISBN number required to sell your book on Amazon, Barnes & Noble, and all the rest. Both Lulu and Createspace offer free ISBN numbers. None of the ebooks distributors require them anymore. You can use ones you have purchased yourself. But unless you are using Lightning Source it's not necessary or good stewardship. These are essential for print distribution. If you use the free ISBN they supply, they will be listed as the publisher of record—though you put your own name (publishing house) on the copyright page.

Who's really the publisher? You are: Even though you might decide to use the free ISBNs supplied by Lulu and Createspace, you are still the publisher. Although they are listed as publisher of record (because they own the ISBN), they are actually your printing supplier. Createspace, for example, will flag your book if you say they are the publisher and make you correct the copy. Don't worry about it.

If you want to supply your own ISBN: you need to register as a publisher and buy a block of them. ISBN costs are complex and ridiculous. They were free until recently. You can buy them in blocks of 1, 10, 100, or 1000 for $125, $250, $575, or $1000 from Bowker in the US. At the time I wrote this, you also needed to translate them into EAN-13 barcodes at $20-$25 per code depending on the quantity (but there are quite a few free barcode converters online). It seems obvious that Lulu and Createspace have purchased them at a large enough quantity to make their costs virtually negligible for them. The free ISBN option is a wonderful thing for us. **If you want to purchase your own single ISBN:** so that you are listed as the publisher, Lulu and Createspace charge a hair under $100 for that service (a little cheaper than Bowker). That is better than the $125 single number price mentioned above (cut from $275 at the end of 2010). Yes, that's steep, but it is still much cheaper than the smallest publishing package from a vanity press. They tend to start somewhere between $1000 and $2000 and go up from there (plus you are left with boxes of books in your garage to dispose of eventually).

 The only reason you need your own ISBN is to get access to specific retailers (brick and mortar or online): Of course, it may just be a vanity thing for you. If so, go for it. It will make your workflow more complex and add a lot of paperwork, proofing and marketing issues to your life. I don't recommend it at this point.

Consider the size of your niche

For example, my niche [people who produce books and/or self-publish in InDesign] is very small. The total size may be only a few thousand people [but growing]. For me to pay $125 for an ISBN from Bowker would eat up much of my profits. However, if you have a larger niche, buying your own ISBN is a very good investment because you can use it for a number of different printers and it keeps your options open. Plus, many distributors will not distribute your books unless you are a listed publisher with your own ISBNs at Bowker.

You can always upgrade later: Because of the way this works, you can always buy a block or purchase a single ISBN later if one of your books starts selling well and you want wider distribution. All you need to do is publish a new edition with few, if any, content changes. You are really in control in the new publishing paradigm. *Don't spend money that's not required.*

I do want to briefly cover the companies I use and share their basic capabilities.

I will do it in the order I use to release a book. It is certainly not the definitive method. You should do it in the order that makes sense to you. The main thing which you need to understand is that all of these suppliers have different requirements. I always start with print. This is mainly because it takes a little longer to get things proofed for print. For our purposes, print means Createspace and Lulu.

Quality issues

As I have said over and over, the best quality is probably a full-color printed book. However, with a Retina Display, a PDF comes very close to matching that—and color is always free in a PDF. The next capability level is fixed layout ePUB followed by the ePUB with embedded fonts. This enables some typographic niceties not commonly available in ebooks. The next is a plain ePUB, but it is really not necessary any more.

A Kindle book is close to an ePUB with embedded fonts if you are using the Fire or Fire HD. However, the graphic file size limitations are a real problem. For the e-ink Kindles the abilities are quite a bit less than word processor quality.

I am saying this, not because I want to denigrate Kindle books, but to show you the reality. I am talking about simple facts about resolutions and typography. I know that there will be sharp protests from Word users about this. If your market is readers of novels on the Kindle, these arguments have some validity. However, your marketing efforts will also be severely compromised without the printing quality afforded by InDesign. These considerations really do matter.

Because the vast majority of my print sales are going to occur through Createspace, I usually start with them. This is not always the case. For *Graphics In InDesign*, I released it only in KDP Select and offered the five free days to build exposure for this book. I eventually radically upgraded it and re-released it in full-color print and as an ePUB.

Createspace (by Amazon)

To quote them from their original press release,

"Createspace books sold on amazon.com are printed on demand, display "in stock" availability on amazon.com and can be shipped within 24 hours from when they are ordered. The books are automatically eligible for Search Inside!™, Amazon Prime™, Super Saver Shipping™ and other amazon.com programs as well."

Because Amazon is currently the 500# gorilla this is the best source for self published authors to sell printed books. Your only required cost was the cost of a proof. Lately Amazon has been making many in the industry angry because of their strong-arm tactics. But the fact remains, they sell more printed books for self publishers than anyone else, by far.

It really depends on the book. A book like this one will sell mostly print and PDF. Only a third or less will be ePUB or Kindle. A novel is commonly 90% Kindle with the rest at Nook, Kobo, and the iBookstore. However, getting your novel listed in places like GoodReads is much easier if you have a printed version with an ISBN. Some reviewers require a printed version. Book signings obviously require a printed copy.

The printing quality of Createspace is not quite as good as Lulu on the occasions when I printed virtually identical versions on the two sites. It seems like the RIP is limited. For example, they require a rasterized cover at 300 dpi which really compromises the quality of the typography on the cover. Their quality control sometimes slacks off. But you cannot deny they sell books.

 Digital proofing for established authors: Createspace has been allowing the option of no proof or a digital proof. If you are new to proofing, you need to get a printed copy.

 Amazon pushes Createspace books harder: They offer more marketing options and better listings (which they obviously consider in-house offerings). As mentioned, at various times they have cut off many of the books offered through Lulu and Lightning Source (the on-demand publishing standard for "real" publishers with their own ISBNs and distribution).

For printed books, Createspace books have been outselling Lulu's offerings by a huge margin.

Paperbacks

Createspace sells only paperbacks in a slightly reduced variety of sizes (compared to Lulu) and only perfect-bound. They offer black & white (with a color cover) or full color books. With the B&W books you can make a custom trim size (but with limited distribution).

Size	Lulu	Amazon	B&W	Color
5 x 8 inches		√	√	√
5.06 x 7.81 inches		√	√	
5.25 x 8 inches		√	√	
5.5 x 8.5 inches		√	√	√
6 x 9 inches (trade)	√	√	√	√
6.14 x 9.21 inches (royal)	√	√	√	√
6.69 x 9.61 inches		√	√	
7 x 10 inches		√	√	√
7.44 x 9.69 inches (Crown)	√	√	√	
7.5 x 9.25 inches		√	√	
8 x 10 inches		√	√	
8.5 x 8.5 inches	√	√		√
8.5 x 11 inches (letter)	√	√	√	√

Standard sizes: for the best distribution you need to pick from the traditional, industry standard sizes. Let's review the options in Lulu and Createspace. The following list was accurate in 2013. They do change occasionally, but not often.

The trade paperback [6"x9"] is the expected standard. I have found that for the type of nonfiction I do, 7 x 10 works a little better for me. This is your decision.

Large print editions: in most cases this is a good idea. Amazon expects you to use 16-point for your body copy. Using our normal column width formula [40% of the point size in inches], this would give us a 6.4 inch column width. A column of this wide will barely fit an 8 x 10 book.

ISBNs

They provide four ISBN options: a free Createspace-assigned ISBN, a $10 Custom ISBN where you can name your imprint, a $99 Custom Universal ISBN where you name your imprint and supply distribution, or you can use your own ISBN. Both custom ISBN options are offered through an agreement with Bowker. Always check because these options change.

The Expanded Distribution Channels

Createspace has a great deal for expanded distribution. It's now free to get larger distribution. It includes Createspace Direct which provides wholesale books to independent bookstores and book resellers. It also makes the book available to libraries, schools, and academic institutions.

Finally, "you can make your book available to thousands of major online and offline bookstores and retailers, and expand the size of the potential audience for your books". They move quite a few distributed books at about half the royalty. It's an excellent idea—especially now that it's free. Just make sure that you charge enough to cover the larger costs associated with retail distribution. Retailers consider this price to be wholesale and take 50% or 60% as their markup.

Payments

They do direct deposit to your banking account every thirty days (with a 45-60 day delay)—with a minimum of $10 in accrued royalties.

Createspace artwork

This is reasonably straight forward. Be sure to put the ISBNs on the copyright page. List your publishing company as the publisher.

- **They do insist on a .75" interior [gutter] margin:** One inch if the book gets very large.

- **Even if you choose a bleed layout:** you will still be required to keep your copy within standard margins.

- **There is a tendency to have trouble with light tints:** Keep your lightest tints over 10%.

- **Be sure, that the PDF you upload to them is flattened:** Their RIP [the raster image processor in their printing software] has trouble with transparency. Make sure your exported PDFs use a compatibility with Acrobat 4 [PDF1.3]. also be sure that all fonts are embedded and that your transparency flattening is set to high-resolution. I make a PDF preset with these settings and name it Createspace.

Createspace covers

You need to be very careful with your covers. Createspace has very specific requirements. The best method is to let them provide you with a template. They give you a little form where you type in the page size, type of paper, and number of pages.

You are provided with a download which includes PNG file to use as the base to build your cover. Yes, this is a very clumsy way to work. However, they require a flattened 300 dpi Photoshop PDF (it's the only place I've ever used one). The PNG shows you where you are not allowed to place copy. This is especially important for the spine. For some reason, Createspace makes the printable area on the spine quite small. Recently they seem to have relaxed this requirement a bit. But if they flag it, fix it. You do it the way they want you to do it.

They also provide a very specific area which must be left clear [think white] for them to imprint the barcode. It is simply a waste of time to try and fight them on this.

Proofing

When they upload your PDF they will quickly preflight it immediately using a digital reviewer. If you have a lot of experience with printing, like I do, the things they flag might irritate you a lot. It is an absolute waste of time to argue with them about errors and problems – about any of it. All you will do is delay approval. You will have to change it to what they like eventually.

When you have your interior PDF and your cover PDF uploaded, you submit them for review. This takes about 24 hours. If your files are not approved, they will show you the problems in their digital proofer. Fix all of them immediately, and resubmit your files.

Once they come back with no problems, you have two choices. Once you have a lot of experience, you can simply approve the digital proof. However, without this experience you definitely need to get a printed proof. Even if you approve the digital proof, I would suggest that you buy a few copies for yourself. Their prices are very reasonable.

Finishing the uploading and releasing process

After you set your pricing, add your description, and your keywords, you will get the option to automatically set up your Kindle version. You should take that option with the provision that you will upload your own Kindle book. Trying to convert your PDF to a Kindle book is simply disaster.

However, if you let them automatically begin the setup of your Kindle book, the title and description will be transferred. But most importantly, Amazon will sell your Kindle version and your print version on the same page automatically. Otherwise, you will probably have to email them and tell them to combine the two pages.

Lulu

It is sad that Amazon has beat up Lulu so badly. On a practical level, these are the people who started this whole thing in 2002. In many ways they do it better than Amazon. Their concept was to offer on-demand publishing services for free. Their profit comes from a very reasonable royalty of 20% per sale (plus they almost certainly make a little with their production charges).

In other words—you, as the creator, get 80% of the money received after the production costs are subtracted [unless you are offering the book at retail. Retail distribution requires a full 100% markup. So you get about 40% royalty there, but you still get the 80% if the book is sold through Lulu's Website]. For their ebooks you get the full 80% minus $.99.

They just began offering GlobalReach free

They have a large number of options in many sizes and many bindery options—plus, they offer the best printing quality and several unique binding options like case-bound hard cover, spiral-bound, and so on. Amazon has pretty much refused to stock Lulu's more unique options.

One of the things they offer (& very profitably for me) are high quality, printable PDF downloads. But they moved the downloadable PDFs to their own page a year ago which cut those sales significantly. For my niche, many readers are aware of the typographic messes which are currently called ebooks [whether ePUB or Kindle]. My PDF sales were still nearly 25% of my Lulu sales in January of 2012—though they were over 50% for the previous two years. I haven't sold as many since then—but the PDF sales continue.

In overall sales, Lulu is still good. Even Apple bullies them a little. Lulu used to be an official aggregator for the iBookstore. They are no longer on that list. However, their ePUBs is still sell well through iBooks—if you can get them approved by Lulu. The CC ePUBs have been a problem. The old CS6 ePUBs work for Nook. They are extremely strict about their requirements for ePUBs. I haven't come up with a normal working procedure here. Again, I'll post in *The Skilled Workman* when I find something that works.

Paperbacks

They offer paperbacks that can be perfect bound [square spine], saddle-stitched [stapled spine], or **coil bound [plastic spiral wire spine]**. The contents can be black & white or full color. The covers are always in color. They can handle projects from one to 800 pages. The minimum and maximum number of pages depends on the size picked and the distribution plan chosen.

Their spiral-bound workbooks are beautiful. The printing quality is high, and the binding is done well. For a book like this one, I would recommend that you buy the spiral-bound version. They recently severely cut the size offerings for spiral-bound: only offering 6x9 and 8.5x11.

Hard cover

They offer both casewrap and dust cover versions from 24 to 800 pages, depending on the options selected. Plus, they offer two large premium hard cover options: 12" x 12" and 12.75" x 10.75" landscape with premium smooth finish paper in full color for coffee table books. It is too bad that Createspace does not offer hardcovers.

Ebooks

Any of the books can be made available as a downloadable PDF. They also offer ePUB distribution to iBookstore with a free ISBN—as long as you charge for the book. But at this point, I wouldn't worry about their distribution. They will sell ePUBs for you. I don't like their iBooks option because you haven't been able to embed fonts.

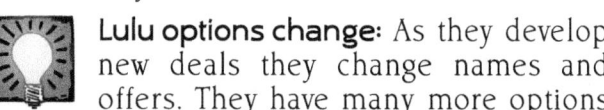 **Lulu options change:** As they develop new deals they change names and offers. They have many more options now than they did in 2003 when I started. However, sometimes these have negative effects like the separation of the printed books from the downloadable PDF.

Downloadable PDFs

I highly recommend that you provide this option through Lulu. They sell a lot of PDFs. There is no reason why you cannot add color to your PDFs, but do not go through the layout revisions recommended for Scribd. Lulu adds a cover in their own unique way. They have no option to view the PDFs online like Scribd does. You'll need to provide a special preview PDF for them. However, you can offer that preview PDF for free as a promo tool on Scribd and elsewhere.

ISBNs & Distribution

If you get a free ISBN number from Lulu (currently called ExtendedReach™), it used to include a listing on Amazon. If you provide an ISBN or purchase a single ISBN, you have to use the GlobalReach™ distribution package (but you can still use the free one Lulu provides if you wish). This gets you wider distribution and is now free. You do have to buy a proof copy and approve it.

With no ISBN

Nothing is required. They used to offer what they named MarketReach™ for $25 to get you listed with Lulu's Amazon Marketplace and eBay.com with a possibility of more to come. At this point, Amazon has cut off that option. This is necessary with coil-bound books, for example, or the more unusual sizes [including the premium coffee table books]. You do have to buy a proof here.

Payments

Lulu pays directly to your PayPal account, monthly—around the fifteenth for the previous month. You do need a PayPal business account, but it is free and can be set up in a couple days. You will need a PayPal business account for your publishing house, regardless.

Artwork considerations

There really aren't many. Lulu does very well with high-quality PDFs for print. They can handle Acrobat 5 level PDFs which do include transparency. Drop shadows and the like use transparency. The same is true for their covers. You need to choose the Advanced One-Piece Cover Designer. This will open a page which will give you all the dimensions you need to set up a single page InDesign document upon which to build your cover.

If you are using one of Lulu's ISBN numbers, they will give you a link to download your barcode. You are responsible to place this vector barcode on your cover. Lulu is much easier to please with text on the spine and cover art. They work well with vector art, and have no trouble with Transparency. So, you can export your PDFs with Acrobat 5 [PDF 1.4] compatibility. The color accuracy is much better with Lulu. I know results vary, but Lulu is better consistently though not cheap.

Scribd

Downloadable PDF distribution doesn't get much better than this. It was founded in 2007 and is designed for free booklets, but it does give you the option to sell your works. Now they even offer a Premium Reader subscription service. These readers read online and Scribd pays you according to the amount of the book read. The site shows off your works well. It's a social networking site. I've sold little here, but it is increasing. My free offerings have been downloaded hundreds of times and I'm over 21,000 unique views—a lot of eyeballs.

Now that Scribd is tied in with Smashwords and Draft2Digital, all of your ePUB books through either of them will be offered by subscription on Scribd.

I look at it as a marketing opportunity that may grow into something. It is built easily from my printing PDF, so it's a no pain, possible gain type of thing. Because it is viewed on the screen, you can do it in full RGB color and have some fun with the design. I believe I mentioned, I get rid of the half title and as much front matter as possible. I start the PDFs with a full bleed full-color cover.

I use the Scribd PDF for Gumroad & Ganxy

My books like this, about InDesign, Fontographer, and FontLab, have had thousands of people read the previews. It may be generating the sales of the printed versions at Lulu and Amazon. For some reason I am convinced that this will be an increasingly good resource in the future. In addition, you can get some idea of interest. This is also the version I send to reviewers and people who have helped me with the book.

Payments

Scribd pays directly to your PayPal account with a $25 minimum. You do need a PayPal business account, but they are free and can be set up in a couple days.

Artwork considerations

This PDF should be full-color throughout. As mentioned I always start with a full color, full bleed cover. I start by packaging my Createspace document into a new folder inside my Scribd folder. This brings over a new Links folder with all the placed graphics. I replace them with my color originals.

You need to remember to take the Amazon ISBN off the copyright page. This version does not need an ISBN. I do use my Createspace PDF settings to produce the new PDF. This is because Script does not seem to handle transparency any better than Createspace does.

ePUBs (the ebook standard)

You will need several versions of your ePUB. I always start out by making one with embedded fonts. As mentioned, only the iBookstore will accept an ePUB with embedded fonts directly and the new FXL ones as well. I have heard that Nook and Kobo will, but so far they have bounced my uploads. However, I sell archives of my ebooks with embedded fonts using Gumroad and Ganxy.

I used to set up a second version of my EPUB using the iPad fonts from iOS6 with no embedding. Lately, I haven't bothered unless I decide to try Smashwords again.

Lulu

They still sell ePUBs for me, but the submission requirements became so odious that I have dropped them. When I go back, and I will, I'll share my experiences in the blog and update this paragraph in the book.

They started the new self-publishing in 2002. They have always been a superior company to work with. I would not count them out. Just their easy support of hard covers and spiral-bound books makes them a badly needed supplier. Self-published print is by no means dead.

Nook Press (Barnes & Noble)

As I mentioned earlier, my best sales through Nook are with D2D and Smashwords. At this point, I do not care much as Nook doesn't sell well for me at all. However, some of my author friends claim a lot of sales through Nook. Sales are not as good as the iBookstore or Kobo, for me. Barnes & Noble is in real trouble. It looks like they may be able to save it, but that remains to be seen.

Kobo Writing Life

This relatively new option seems to work well. They will accept the same ePUB FXL that I used for iBooks. But otherwise it's ePUB2 with fonts. But I sell many more Kobo books through Draft2Digital and Smashwords. This is why I upload to so many services.

Smashwords

Super news! I just uploaded an ePUB2 with embedded fonts and Smashwords is selling it!

Mark Coker brought out Smashwords in 2008. He is a man driven to succeed. In a short time he has developed very high visibility. Sales through his service are growing quickly. He is considered an industry leader by the publishing world. I mention Smashwords because it is turning out to be a good resource—especially now that it accepts ePUBs directly. In some countries, Smashwords is the only access to the iBookstore and Nook. They now take an ePUB2 with embedded fonts. Just do what they ask you to do in order to get it into their Premium distribution. The final file cannot be over 7.5 MB. That means this book will not be going there as I anticipate that the final ePUB will be well over 10 MB and probably closer to 20 MB.

Smashwords' distribution matches or surpasses Draft2Digital going to the iBookstore, Kobo, Nook, Scribd, and the Smashwords site. Mark is pushing the envelope in on-demand publishing.

I have been using Smashwords more lately even though they are releasing to many of the same places. I do not know why but their sales seem to differ from the same books uploaded to Nook, Kobo, or the iBookstore. There does not seem to be any penalty in doing so—so why not? They are an excellent resource for novels.

Coupons

One of Smashwords best abilities are discount coupons for their books. It is a way to offer your books deeply discounted or free without raising flags at Amazon.

Payments

Smashwords pays directly to your PayPal account, quarterly. You do need a PayPal business account.

Artwork considerations

This is yet another place where you make the changes they ask for. Originally they would only take Word documents — specifically Word documents with no styling. They are still very restrictive — obviously geared toward helping new authors writing in Word. Just do what they ask. They will now take ePUB2s directly, with embedded fonts. It's a recent development. Arguing with them will not help you and it will merely delay the release of your book.

Draft2Digital

This is a good option. Their uploads are very simple— using a well-designed ePUB2 with fonts. They take ePUB3, but their marketing work only comes with ePUB2s. They offer uploads to the iBookstore, Nook, Scribd, and Kobo— plus several other smaller outlets. They're still growing. The sales have been good and getting better. They are a very good resource. They are approaching #2 some months.

All reports are that they are very good at helping new authors with their Word conversions. I wouldn't know about that. But they have been very helpful and supportive to my efforts.

BookBaby

I've never used them. They had a limited free option with the only charge being $19 for the ISBN—but I think they dropped it. They remain a relatively cheap vanity press. However, I've never heard anything bad about them.

Blurb

I've never heard anything bad about this company either. They cater to the coffee table book users. They are not cheap, but by all reports the quality is superb. But they are just beginning their offerings of ePUBs. They use InDesign and offer InDesign plug-ins. There is some capital outlay, but minimal as far as I can tell.

New suppliers

There are new suppliers coming online all the time. You need to be very careful. A couple of years ago, one appeared in England which took your worldwide rights and continued to sell your books even if you canceled your account with them. The ones I have mentioned here have proven to be trustworthy. If I discover more, I will write about them in *The Skilled Workman*. You do need to keep abreast of things. The wild ride of change is not over yet.

Bottom line: *If you have to pay anything, you need to seriously question your use of the company as a supplier or publisher*

You are allowing these various suppliers, distributors, and publishers the opportunity to offer your books. Traditional publishers will give you an advance and a small royalty of under 15%, and normally under 10%. Self-publishing suppliers will publish your book for free and take a small cut from 5% to 35% or more. But again, there will be no upfront costs to you, the author or small publisher, except for proofs.

Vanity presses charge you for the printing, the formatting, the editing, and all the rest. They are not the best resource for any of that. They are printing companies looking at you as a customer. They cost thousands of dollars, in almost every case—sometimes tens of thousands of dollars.

Kindle

To be honest, I used to start my e-book production with the Kindle version. The reason for that is that it is quite limited compared to EPUB capabilities. I have now changed that. Amazon offers a free app called Kindle Previewer 3.0. It will convert an ePUB to the Kindle format. That has given me better results [and allows me to start using nested styles again]. However, Kindle chews up your books pretty bad when uploading them through KDP. That might not be true if you own a Fire HD or better.

- It recognizes most basic text formatting, but not with anchored images: It's one of the reasons I am careful with anchored images for ebooks.

- Be careful with nested styles: It seems to retain them with few problems when converting an ePUB with embedded fonts through Previewer.

The CC ePUBs uploaded through KDP seem to be a little better now also. Proof carefully.

> It does a good job of retaining working hyperlinks, the TOC, and footnotes.

> **It also requires many more limitations to the graphics:** They cannot be larger than 127K and they cannot be taller than 500 pixels. This has supposedly changed recently (in 2015). But I have seen no evidence of it in my uploads. I would be very careful about adding larger images.

Calibre for conversions: Back in 2010 or so, I was using Calibre (a free download) to convert my ePUB version to the Kindle version. In 2012, Amazon quit accepting conversions from Calibre. However, you can open your ePUBs in Kindle Previewer [from Amazon} and it will convert it to a MOBI file. A direct upload of the ePUB in KDP worked the best last year. This year (2016), Kindle Previewer 3.0 seems to be the best option. Amazon upload procedures change all the time. Always proof your results carefully, and make any changes needed.

You can use Kindle Previewer to preview KF8 books for the Kindle Fire. But Amazon will reformat anything uploaded through KDP. If they were not so large and if they didn't sell so many books, I would consider them a second-rate supplier. But they are the 500# gorilla and they do sell a lot of books—more than half of the ebooks are sold by them, for example.

So far, Kindle remains straight, single-column HTML with no divs or anything that will really help the typography. Format 8 added HTML5 and CSS3 to the mix along with embedded fonts. The KFX format with its better typography is done to our books out of our control after our books are released.

Hopefully, by the next version of InDesign CC, we'll have some better tools, both from Adobe and from Amazon's Kindle Direct Publishing. However, Kindle has fallen behind in quality and in capabilities. I doubt Amazon will let that ride for long.

Payments

They do direct deposit of accrued royalties to your banking account every thirty days (with a 60 day delay)—with no minimum.

Gumroad & Ganxy

I have to thank Guy Kawasaki in *APE* for these suggestions. Gumroad and Ganxy are two companies which provide this service. I was using both. Lately I've forgotten about Ganxy. Through Gumroad I can sell an archive of my book containing DRM-free versions with fonts embedded: PDF, ePUB, and KF8.

Let your readers actually own your ebooks

Gumroad charges $.25 per download, plus 5%. So these options are usually the cheapest way to sell your books off your Website or blog. You can increase your income per book and give your readers a chance to actually own the book instead of leasing It. With Kindle, Nook, Kobo, and iBooks you are really only leasing your books. They can cut you off at any time.

Gumroad originally specialized in video streaming

So, they may have more use as video in ePUB3 becomes more common. I also sell quite a few font packages through them. It's a very good resource and they are working hard updating their marketing tools.

Zazzle

This is a giftware supplier using the same basic model as Lulu and the rest. They use 300 dpi PNGs. They sell a large variety of items (they claimed 250+ In 2012, but it's much more than that now).

Why am I listing it here? Because it is a very good resource for the production of companion gift items to your books. It's a marketing aid. You can produce promotional gifts to sell on your Website and at the table in back of your seminars.

Here's the spring 2011 list (they've added a lot since then):

- **Clothing:** Custom T-Shirts; Hoodies; Embroidered Polos; Embroidered Jackets; Shoes

- **Accessories:** Bags; Buttons; Hats; Keychains; Necklaces; Ties

- **Cards and Postage:** Envelopes; Greeting Cards; Invitations; Labels; Note Cards; Photo Cards; Postage; Postcards

- **Home and Pets:** Ornaments; Aprons; Calendars; Coasters; Mugs; Steins; Magnets; Pet Clothing; Photo Sculptures

- **More:** Skateboards; Bumper Stickers

- **Office Products:** Round Stickers; Stationery; 3 Ring Binders; Business Cards; Flyers; Letterhead; Mousepads; Travel Mugs; Rack Cards

- **Art and Posters:** Canvas Prints; Posters; Framed Prints; Photo Prints; Photo Enlargements; Cases; iPhone and iPad Cases

- **They are constantly adding items:** speakers, wood gift boxes with magnetic lids, trays, bath mats, shower curtains, flash drives, makeup mirrors, and much more. They are really pushing the envelope constantly.

They print from 300 dpi PNGs made in Photoshop. All reports are that the quality is good. The items I have seen were excellent. The prices are not cheap, but then they are on-demand with a minimum quantity of one. You set your royalties, as an add-on to their production costs.

Payments

Zazzle pays directly to your PayPal account, monthly (with a $25 minimum)—around the fifteenth for the previous month once the minimum is met. You do need a PayPal business account.

Opportunities outside America

I was discussing on Google+ with a young writer in the Netherlands. She mentioned that Smashwords is one of the best opportunities for her. Because Amazon does not have a bookstore in her country, she finds it much cheaper to buy her Kindle books through Smashwords—downloading the MOBI edition from them.

The main thing is to realize that globally you all have the opportunity to join the new self-publishing paradigm. If you want to sell in the American market, you need access to the iBookstore, Kobo, and Kindle. Smashwords can do that for you. As far as I know most places have access to Kindle KDP. You can probably upload your books to the iBookstore through iTunes no matter where you live. Kobo Writing Life is also widely available.

The main thing is to write and publish. All of us, nobodies that we are, have a place in this new self-publishing world. Step out and have fun!

It's a brand new ball game!

PART SEVEN:

Practical Christian Marketing

CHAPTER THIRTY

Why new authors & publishers need to read this

This is primarily advice for Christians, just so you know

I welcome all of you to read it, as you will find it helpful. But, you must understand many of these things do not work without a close personal relationship with the Messiah. It's a very different way of working than you find in the world.

Every day, as I go through my dozens or even hundreds of emails, I see posting after posting from new and first-time authors asking the same question.

What do I need to do to sell my book?

Why isn't my book selling? It's a sad question because so much bad or irrelevant advice is tossed at the new author—especially Christians. I want to help you clear the confusion.

You will hear all of this advice

- **You need an author platform**
- **You must build a following**

- **You must give away your books on Kindle**
- **You need to use other authors:** to help you promote yourself
- **You must have a Website**
- **You can't do it without a blog**
- **You need a FaceBook page**
- **Twitter is the only way to go**
- **Pinterest is better than Twitter for books**
- **GoodReads is your best bet**
- **Google+ is essential**
- **Linked-In is a must**
- **Some insist you still need MySpace**
- **Plus, there are dozens more...**

I am going to give you guidelines to help you determine what type of author you are, what kind of readership you have or will have, and what you are selling. Without that knowledge, picking any of the choices just listed is an exercise in frustration, unless you are very lucky. I don't believe in luck.

Now, if you are writing for a very popular genre (let's say erotic romance or revenge thrillers) almost any of the ten things listed will work quite well for you. But as Christians, appealing to the lusts of the flesh is not likely to help our calling. In fact those appeals put us in risk of being picked out as one of those Jesus said should have a millstone tied around their neck and tossed into the sea.

They will probably work for a popular genre like Christian Historical Romances. But if you're writing hard core prophetic or speculative fiction novels with a strong gospel message, most of that stuff will not work.

Small niche non-fiction has its own special problems, as do obscure biographies or history, minority persecution stories, testimonial reports of successful missions, and so on. Almost all books require a special strategy and you need to determine what it is before you write your book, if possible.

For most of you, it would seem to be too late, for your book is already written. But that is not true. The techniques I will share can enable you to re-market an existing book which is doing poorly and completely turn around its prospects.

It works for everyone else also

Who's this chapter for?

It's for Christian authors writing fiction and non-fiction who are boggled by the complexity of publishing and marketing your book. It's for new and unknown authors who need to cut through the intense competition with a plan to reach their specific readers. It's for self published authors frustrated by low sales. And it will certainly help those of you who are doing fairly well already.

Though many of these things will also help the person seeking to be published by a traditional publisher, that is not my focus. I've done that and I might be able to help a little, but the Lord let me know that I was wasting my time in that pursuit. The readers upon which He has me focused for most of my books are not huge in number nor easily found. You are a different person; and it is quite possible the Lord is asking you to find an agent and a publisher.

My focus is on do-it-yourself publishers. I didn't like to use the word self-publisher because that had traditionally been the term for authors who pay someone to publish your book. That type of self-publishing is also called Vanity Publishing. A vanity press will charge you thousands of money to print your book. Some may offer distribution help, but that costs thousands more. Plus, they are of no help in marketing. You need to carefully look at them, and RUN the other way.

I like to use the term DIY publishing because you can publish your book or someone else's book with little or no money while still offering your readers a professionally done book showing excellence and meeting genuine reader needs. The publisher's obligations are outside of the content of this book. But write me if you have any questions: david at radiqx dot com.

What's holding you back?

The blocks, in most cases, are preconceived notions of what it takes to sell a book, unrealistic assumptions, a ridiculous schedule, and the belief that it will all happen within a few weeks or months at most.

One of the worst expectations is the very common one which has you believing that you can take a simple Word document, upload it through an easy conversion process, and sell ebooks like crazy. That is wrong on so many levels it is hard to know where to begin.

Can I guarantee a million books sold?

Of course not! But I can give you the tools you need to sell your book online with reasonable expectations without spending a huge amount of money. I can give you a realistic shot at making your living from your books.

You are going to have to go through reality orientation and give up your Oprah interview fantasies and/or your spot on the Factor. For most of us that is not possible, necessary, or even desired. What is required is professionalism for your book production and a realistic examination of who is going to be attracted to your book. Determining who makes up your readership is initially an educated guess. This is updated by experience gained from talking with readers and seeing what they say when they review your book. But, you can always redo it until it works—with little or no financial penalty. It will take some time. The long term growth of steady income takes a while.

You can make a huge leap forward with a few simple steps

- Realize this is not rocket science.

- It is complex, but not particularly difficult.

- It will require the purchase of good tools—but that's always the case.

- There's not much room for stupidity.

- But if you are willing to learn and able to work, you can *get'er done.*

CHAPTER THIRTY-ONE

A note about my faith

Everything I write is based on the fact that I am a believer and Jesus is the center of my life. I'm assuming that this is true for you also. If not, these principles will work for you also. Please do not be offended by my beliefs. Many things change for us, as authors and publishers, because of these truths.

Many of the tools and techniques I read about book marketing involve sin: lying, false witness, and all the rest. My underlying operating principle for writing and publishing comes from these verses of scripture:

> Therefore, having this ministry by the mercy of God, we do not lose heart. We have renounced disgraceful, underhanded ways; we refuse to practice cunning or to tamper with God's word, but by the open statement of the truth we would commend ourselves to every man's conscience in the sight of God. [II CORINTHIANS 4:1-2 RSV]

I read a book a while back which suggested that I set up six separate Amazon accounts so I could write my own reviews, which are needed to increase sales for my books. That's lying, at best (disgraceful and underhanded are words which also come to mind). I can't do that or many of the myriad pieces of worldly advice you will hear as you look for methods and venues in which to share your book with your audience.

I will continue to trust God to provide those things necessary like reviews, likes, readers, and so on. We are different and live in a Kingdom with a King of power.

I am a bible teacher and a former teaching pastor as well as a professional graphic designer, typographer, and art director with 45 years experience. Now that I have my own company I am no longer forbidden to mention the blessings of working under the anointing of the Lord. I was forced to live under that constriction for several decades. The Lord blessed my efforts. But it is a real joy to be able to share how to work in the Kingdom.

Do you have a call?

If you aspire to be a Christian author working for the Kingdom, the first thing you must settle is your vision and the call of the Lord. If you're not called to this with a vision for your mission—*please **do something else***.

Ask Him. He'll make your path clear—if you seek Him for guidance. I realize that we all walk by faith and not by sight. However, if you are writing to get rich, famous, or any other worldly lust, repent now.

You cannot do this without His love, guidance, and anointing. Let me rephrase that. You certainly can do it—many do—but the results will not be good, either for you or for your readers. The Lord will not be pleased. So start your efforts with prayer and keep them bathed in prayer throughout your career as a writer.

We are teachers

Authors are teachers. Like it or not, readers will be affected. We are judged more strictly than normal because of this. The Lord told us this specifically through James.

> Let not many of you become teachers, my brethren, for you know that we who teach shall be judged with greater strictness.
> [JAMES 3:1 RSV]

This is a serious thing we are doing. We are attempting to use our God-given writing ability to affect change in our readers. Even if you are writing sheer escapist stories, you are responsible to make sure that you are telling the truth in love as you know it. Let them escape to a place of healing, regeneration, and spiritual growth.

- **Inspire them.**

- **Comfort them.**

If you are not a Christian...

As an author and designer, you have an obligation to "leave things better than when you found them" as we learned when hiking in the wilderness—way before I met the Lord. The world has enough hatred, bigotry, betrayal, temptation, and glorified evil. Marketing for those book types is very different.

Please do your best to lift up your readers, provide beauty and inspiration, and help them live better lives—even if it is just a bit of escapist entertainment. Your book is much more than that; or it certainly can and should be.

If you have spiritual questions, my wife and I will be happy to help. You can use the contact forms on my blogs: *The Skilled Workman* and *Reality Calling*. Or you can simply email me at: david at radiqx dot com.

CHAPTER THIRTY-TWO

What kind of writer are you?

Let's talk about a few common scenarios and see how they differ in marketing requirements. Most books have a unique readership unless you are doing formula books for popular genres. But even here there are differences between romances, historical romances, Biblical romances, redemptive romance, spirit-filled fantasy, and so on.

Are you new &/or unknown?

Unknown is the case for many, if not most of us. I consider myself unknown—even though I have been writing since 1994 and publishing books since 1995 with several dozen books. I write mainly to small niches, so that isn't surprising. But this is the reality for most of us—even if we are writing potentially mass market content.

But this does not narrow the categories enough. We really need to ask several more questions. Your answers may differ for each book. How do you categorize your book?

- **Fiction:** Popular genre like romances, thrillers, sci-fi, fantasy, or mysteries

- **Non-fiction:** Advice, testimonies, inspiration

- **Non-fiction:** Teaching, expert help, problem solving

- **Fiction:** Small niche genre like allegories, prophetic speculation; or technothrillers, historical military campaigns, epic fantasy, or action/adventures

- **Non-fiction:** Biblical teachings, devotions

There are many more. They each have a different marketing need and require you to do unique things. The market size changes for each. The reader location varies widely. The basic marketing advice will differ a lot.

Determining your target reader

I need to thank Jerry Jenkins for the focus of the next few paragraphs. He suggests you need to make a decision about your target readership before you write your first word. Because it is true that the identity, education, desires, and needs of your target reader are just as important as what you plan to say.

Here's a plan:

- **Think about demographics:** Who most likely needs your book? What is their age, skill level, education, lifestyle, maturity, religion? Determine as many of these things as possible.

- **Imagine one person who your perfect reader:** Is it a friend, colleague, client, student, associate, or apprentice?

- **As much as possible, write specifically to that person:** To quote Jerry, "Readers want to feel as if they are being addressed individually. Avoid phrases like "Some of you..." or "Many of you..." Rather, always address the reader simply as "You." That makes and keeps your book personal and gives your manuscript the best chance with a publisher."

When you understand the pains, specific needs, and desires of your readership you need to go to the next Level. Now it's time to meet those needs with a specific strategy. Now you have a book which might sell.

Who understands your market best?

For us as Christians, we have a unique answer. **The Lord knows our market.** More than that He knows who He wants to buy your book. In your overall marketing efforts, these readers are the ones who matter. But the Lord does not expect you to be silly and ignore the rest of the readers. He may know that your book will change the lives of a half dozen people out of the 500, 2000, or 35,000 copies you sell. It's likely He has several things going on with your book—including your ongoing character training.

So, we start with prayer

Yes, I've already mentioned this. What is our prayer? *"Lord, sell my book!"* Maybe a little. But the Lord would have you be involved in a larger part of your marketing than that. There are things He wants you to do. There are people you need to touch and influence. His main focus is building your character, pruning, and shaping so you can be more fruitful. Your readers need what you are offering.

Your goal in prayer is to find out what He sees in your book. You need to see and understand what His vision is. It really doesn't matter what you think. What He thinks counts. We must clean up our own lives to be fruitful.

> For who can know the Lord's thoughts? Who knows enough to teach him? But we understand these things, for we have the mind of Christ. [I CORINTHIANS 2:16 NLT]

We have the sure word of scripture that we have the mind of the Messiah. But God made this a walk of faith, not sight. Nevertheless he'll show us what He is doing and where he is headed—if we ask him.

> No longer do I call you slaves, for the slave does not know what his master is doing; but I have called you friends, for all things that I have heard from My Father I have made known to you. [JOHN 15:15 NASB]

But you know the way it works. You need to ask for wisdom. James tells us that. You need to understand what Jesus was saying to us when He said,

> "I tell you the truth, the Son can do nothing by himself. He does only what he sees the

Father doing. Whatever the Father does, the Son also does." [JOHN 5:19 NLT]

If that was true for Him, the man and god who showed us how to walk in the Spirit, it is certainly true for us. There was a real reason Jesus went out alone before dawn to talk things over with Dad. He needed to know what the Father was doing and how he (Jesus) should proceed in the coming day. I do too, and so do you.

You need to fit these questions in with your daily walk. My basic question in the morning is, "What are we doing today, Lord?" "What should I do first?" At least that's the basic question when I am doing what I need to be doing and seeking His face first every morning.

This is all about the normal Christian life. Our writing is part of the life, and we are doing it because He has asked us to do it. If not, our writing may well be merely self-help and cathartic therapy. There's nothing wrong with that, but it may also be true that the Lord does not want you sharing that stuff with other people.

Are you coming from a traditional publishing house?

Some of you already have books published traditionally. You need to remember that DIY publishing is a very different world. In this world, you are a new author just beginning. This is not bad. Inevitably you learned a lot in the publishing of those traditional books. You are breaking out on your own for good reasons. It is simply part of the new reality within which you now work.

This is a big change

Here's a comment from an author guest posting on the blog of a well-known agent. She was moving from a traditional house to DIY publishing:

> "I underestimated the thrill that comes with being in control – as well as the fear. I get to pick my cover! Set my own price! Make a special holiday edition for my friends and family and send it out tied up with a red bow! When I do something well, I feel like a rock star entrepreneurial author on

the cutting edge of the brave new world of publishing.

But book publishing is a detailed, complex enterprise requiring a range of skills completely different from writing a book. There are a thousand opportunities to screw up. Suddenly, it's not just my writing that's out there being judged, it's my eye for design, my sense of how readers behave, my business acumen. I used to wonder why it took traditional publishers nine months to produce a book. Now I get it; it's a lot of work."[1]

It will be a radical change if you leave the comfort of traditional publishing and move into the entrepreneurial world of self-publishing. One of the reasons you are making such a small royalty in a traditional house is the need to pay all the people who were doing what you will be doing now for yourself. You will earn those added royalties.

There are two basic areas to cover

For all of us in the new paradigm of true desktop publishing of books, we have things to do. They basically divide into two areas:

- **Building a social presence**
- **Developing a strong title, description and keywords:** improving your metadata

These two portions of our marketing efforts have different importance depending on what we are writing and to whom. As you continue to read this part of the book take notes so you can get a better handle on who you are, what your calling is, and who you are called to serve.

The Lord requires us to deal with the realities of life—proclaiming the good news to a sick and terrorized world. A story of true love discovered can really help a desperately lonely woman—if you let the Lord show you how. For authors bombarded by falsehoods and sinful techniques from our enemy (who uses them in a carnal world to entice readers controlled by the lusts of the flesh), a simple explanation like you find in this book can open

---

[1]   http://www.rachellegardner.com/2013/01/5-surprises-about-self-publishing/

your eyes to the glorious task which the Lord has set before you.

These things are truly important

You really do need to carefully place your book to be seen by those you are called to serve. You know our life is now endued with the power to actual help people. Jesus came that we might be set free to serve in love. Self-fulfillment is a result of His blessings as we follow the path He gives us to follow. It is not the reason we write but the result of our obedience to our call to write.

Your growth as a child of God is what will equip you to truly help your readers. You can do that with fiction or non-fiction. The key to excellence in Christian publishing is keeping your eye on the vision He gives.

Let's cover the social presence first:

CHAPTER THIRTY-THREE

Building a social presence

You should begin this process as soon as you have the basic idea for your new book. Even if you have an agent and a contract with a traditional publishing house, you need an active social presence online.

Actually, you should start this process as soon as you realize you intend to write a book and publish it. This process takes a long time. It is built up over months and years. I've been working on my social presence since 1996 and I feel like I'm just getting started.

It's a long term commitment: Any of the things we are about to cover take time and commitment. I'm currently putting in one to three hours a day to keep up with FaceBook, Pinterest, Twitter, Google+, Linked-In, forums, and so on. I manage most of it through email subscriptions. I have to deal with several hundred emails a day to keep up with FaceBook, Twitter, Pinterest, and the forums with which I'm involved.

The Author Platform misconception

You will certainly hear about the importance of the Author Platform (AP). You'll hear, *"You must build up your online presence until you have thousands of followers, likes, and so on. Then these thousands will buy tons of your books."* The whole concept is not really a lie, but it is certainly not portrayed in a real way.

Only two types of authors really need this type of author platform: spiritual leaders & subject experts.

The only other men and women with thousands of followers are best-selling authors and/or celebrities. In the Kingdom, celebrity is a burden, a temptation, and a responsibility. It is unlikely that you have that problem and I can barely imagine how I could help you deal with those issues. You may have a best-seller on your hands. That too is a source of temptation as well as a blessing.

In the secular world, Clive Cussler has almost 270,000 likes. Every book he puts out with the help of his various ghost writers is a New York Times bestseller. But the truth is that these followers do not buy books from his FaceBook page. They bought the books before they started following him. I had almost all the books he has written (a couple dozen anyway) and I'm not one of his Friends any more. I was, but it's boring. I loved his stories and characters, not him.

The purpose of an author platform is not to sell books

If you're a non-fiction writer, your platform can get you consulting gigs, speaking engagements, and lots of strokes. If you write historical fiction, you can share that history with your readers—thereby getting them more involved with you as a person and listening to you sharing the lessons of that event or period of time .

As a Christian your platform is a doorway to your ministry. You may be ministering to your readers, or some-one else entirely. If you are an expert writing non-fiction, your online social presence will enable you to share your wisdom with your readers and anyone else who is inter-ested in helping or who might be helped.

This so-called author platform may get people inter-ested in you as an author and you may sell a few books.

However, we are talking relatively few books sold in this manner. You may get a lot of strokes and warm fuzzies. It's not nearly as important as the second area we will cover in a bit: your metadata.

Before we go there, let's cover things which can build up an online social platform for you, your ideas, and your service to your readers.

Your own Website

In this day and age, you may do well to focus on your blog and make it your Website. This is what I have done with my main domain bergsland.org where I have *The Skilled Workman*, my professional blog. I have done the same with the Radiqx Press domain, radiqx.com, where I started *Reality Calling*, my spiritual blog.

I had a normal Website about font design and my font design books for the Hackberry Font Foundry, hackberry-fonts.com, but I decided it was a waste of time and money. I think I sold 2 or 3 fonts through it over the past two or three years compared with many hundreds sold through MyFonts.com and fonts.com. So I moved all of it's materials and resources to support my popular *Practical Font Design* books over to a set of pages on *The Skilled Workman*. I'm already getting more traffic there.

The reasons for these opinions are many.

- **Website design has become ridiculously complex:** This is getting worse rather than better. Because much content on the Web is interactively delivered from your server, providing custom content according to your needs [in the best cases], you need to be able to understand and write complex code. If we need this for our work, we will need to hire a pro. This costs thousands of dollars [unless you are a pro and writing about the process].

- **Website marketing is a specialized skill:** Usually we are talking about what is called SEO here [Search Engine Optimization]. You can learn the basics of SEO fairly quickly (and you'll need to do it for your metadata), but if you have major marketing needs, you will do better to hire a pro for this as well. WordPress blogs handle this reasonably well; and this is one of the main reasons I recommend them.

Websites need to updated constantly: Common wisdom tells us that your home page needs to be updated weekly or daily, if possible. If a reader comes back to your site and it looks like it did the last time, they'll quickly quit coming by the site to look. Using your blog for your home page solves this problem.

You have to learn how to code regardless: At a minimum, you'll need to learn HTML and CSS. There really is no good method of putting up a Website without understanding HTML and CSS. You'll probably need to know how to write PHP, Javascript, and more.

The bottom line is that a Website might be good, but it is very hard to monetize: It is very expensive to do well. Plus, it is very difficult to develop a site that people actually use without a great deal of invested effort, some genuine coding skill, and usually a fairly large staff.

As mentioned, I converted my two main sites to WordPress blogs. They are doing much better than the old Websites. But I am finding that, after many years of focusing on my websites, I really cut back. I had almost no reader involvement or personal interaction from my Websites; so I decided to focus my efforts on things that actually serve my readers and potential readers.

A blog or two

Blogging has become the de facto minimum within the social Web. You actually do need a blog or two or three. After all, it is meant for people like authors. We write. We like to write. And we are supposedly good at it. But there are some issues here also.

It takes a solid commitment: Like your Website, your blog is not going to be instantly popular (barring a miracle). As a result, you must start with a real dedication to your craft and a willingness to keep writing even when you see very few outward results.

* **It takes consistency:** You really need a schedule. It is possible that you will be one of those people who cannot help yourself and post new things all the time. But, even if you are, you need to make sure that you are consistent and keep your focus on your audience. I found I had two audiences: professional typography/font design/book design/DIY publishing and Christian writing/teaching. So, I have two blogs. Followers are difficult to find, and you need to keep your commitment in front of you at all times. You're in for the long haul. The followers eventually come.

* **It takes frequency:** You do not need to be crazy about this. But at least to start, you need a posting per week or more, at the same time & day, upon which your followers can rely.

* **It takes a new writing style:** Blog posts require shorter paragraphs, pithy statements, frequent lists, exceptional headlines, and more.

Your blog: headquarters of your online presence

I find that a blog functions as a very good headquarters for all my social presence. I post and then I tweet the posts, send them through FaceBook, add them to Linked-In group discussions, put a copy on my GoodReads page, add it to a question on christianwriters.com, email it to special friends, and so on—depending on the content of the post.

Socializing is transitory: Statuses, tweets, pluses, and the rest are momentary. In fact, they are so fleeting that some people spend a lot of time determining when to tweet. If you do not get them while they are on, they'll never see your tweets. Sharing out from your blog is close to distributing from a center of who you are and what you are about. In this online social world, a blog post is relatively permanent. Of course, not nearly as lasting as a book.

Blogging is very different from writing a book. People often do not read any further than the bottom of the page. They will not scroll up to see the rest of your amazing prose. Think excitement, joyful, and helpful—as well as intriguing and entertaining!

Blogs have a hard time getting traction if they are too diverse. You may want a personal expression blog and a book-specific blog. You want one to your niche. You want to include everything interesting to those in that small group of fellow travelers. One of my small niches is people who write in InDesign and typographers. My hope is that this is speaking to you. You may need several blogs if you write for several niches. But it can be a large time commitment.

However, they can be monetized well. Check out the bookdesigner.com to see how Joel did it. For me, I don't accept advertising so it's not an income source. My blogs are a service to my readers and a center for my various conceptualizations.

You need to talk in the language of the niche about specific group interests. I have a hard time with heathen speculative fiction groups, for example, because I don't play video games, read comics, or develop role-playing skills for D&D. In fact, I imagine that just writing D&D labels me as an outsider. As I recall, they have their own form of acronym.

The social sites

There are dozens, if not hundreds, of these sites. If you are not careful, they can consume all your time leaving you drained of creative time for writing. Pinterest, Squidoo, private FaceBook groups, Google+ Communities, Linked-In groups, hashtag groups on Twitter, dozens of forums for every interest group, and more—the list goes on and on.

However, all of these sites have followings or groups which might work very well for your niche. Pinterest for example, I use to help me visualize locations and cultures.

I also use it to meet and communicate with fellow typographers and type designers [though I may need to get into Behance to pursue that niche in any depth]. For me the advantage of Pinterest is that I can play with that in the evening while I'm relaxing with my wife watching the tube and talking. It doesn't require much attention or focus.

You need to find the mix which works for you. In the new millennium, the marketing of your books is up to you.

Here's a quote from one of Mike Shatzkin's posts[2]

He's talking about what publishers look for when assessing an author's online presence. But we can take is simply good advice.

- "**A robust author website:** to anchor an author's complete digital presence and act as the central hub and source of authoritative information on everything about the author, her books, her work, and life

- "**Complete author and book information:** at book cataloging and community sites like Goodreads and LibraryThing, as well as at all online retailers (especially an Amazon Author Central page)

- "**Google+:** to signal to Google who an author is, what she writes about, and all of the things connected to her

- "**The right social media mix:** which can vary – and evolve – depending on the author, the type of books she writes, and the interests and demographics of her audiences

- "**Mechanisms to collect, manage, and effectively use email addresses**

- "**Ongoing efforts to maintain accuracy and relevance across all of these**

- **Effective cross-promotion:** (across titles and authors)"

---

2 http://www.idealog.com/blog/comes-supporting-authors-marketing-efforts-no-publisher-right-yet/

By the way, Mike's blog offers us exceptional posts throughout the year from the traditional publishers' perspective. I highly recommend that you subscribe to his insight. You will find it very helpful.

http://www.idealog.com/blog/

Other useful blogs are:

Http://www.the bookdesigner.com

Joel Friedlander's blog is probably the best—also Jane Friedman's comes very close.

https://janefriedman.com/blog/

I'm not sure that it's a coincidence that Fried being a major part of their names is any commentary on the state of authors' brains as they deal with all these issues. But you decide. >chortle<

CHAPTER THIRTY-FOUR

The Social Sites

Everyone has their own mix, but here are the basic players. You need to find your readers and make friends with them, come to know them, understand them, and share their concerns.

FaceBook for fiction & niche building

We could add MySpace here—for musicians. This is a place to be more personal with your friends. However, you need to stay focused on your writing and the content of your writing. If you write about restoring classic tractors, it is unlikely your friends will be too excited about your latest find in French wine. But then, maybe you're writing about French tractors used by vintners in Bordeaux.

Because FaceBook is so focused on friends, it is not easy to use it for building readership and an audience. It can certainly be done, but it will take a skillful writer with a vastly entertaining wit and style. Your new friends are not interested in your need to sell. They want your insights, your help, and your wisdom.

You can have your blogs post to your FaceBook page. You can certainly post links to new finds in your field. You should share relevant info you find in your wanders on the Web. You can post about where you are speaking, signing books, leading tours, and all of that (but theat's not why they became your friend). Clive Cussler has nearly a quarter million followers and Tom Clancy was running almost 500,000 likes. But they are not doing much with it.

Check out your favorite authors and see how they do it. But be prepared for massive boredom. Most of them have little to say unless they are believers. If they are, you might find ministries they are involved with, prayer requests and maybe a prayer team, and all the things that are part of normal Christian living.

But mainly you need to find groups of readers who like the type of thing you are writing. The more focused the group, and the more it deals with content like yours, the more it will help you get your book known. Remember, the only real help is readers who like your work reviewing and sharing about your books. It's all about recommendations from friends. That's where most of us find many of the books we read and like.

Closed and secret groups

One of the best things about FaceBook are the closed groups and secret groups with people of similar interests. This is where I have some of my best online discussions, and get much of my support for my writing. Christian Indie Authors, Indie Christian Authors, & Iron Sharpens Iron are excellent groups for me among many more.

Twitter for your non-fiction niches

If you have a good non-fiction book and it is selling well, Twitter is the perfect place to develop as a resource for the readers and people of your niche. Do #hashtag searches to find people of like interests. If you have genuine knowledge, you can make yourself into an indispensable expert quite quickly or prove yourself to be an ignorant fool—been there too many times myself.

The main thing is to keep tightly focused. A Twitter feed is a great resource for the reader, but a very irritating waste of time if most of the tweets do not meet your need. You are not limited in the number of feeds you can have. Practicality limits how many you can realistically keep track of. The main thing is to keep your tweets useful and meaningful to your readers and your niche. They are not following your twitter feeds to get constant promos on your books. They are following you for free information, wisdom, and resources.

Pinterest is doing very well for authors and books

One of the surprising things that has emerged is that Pinterest is definitely the 2nd best [after FaceBook] for publishers and authors. I have boards for Christian books, book production, typography, writing ideas, locations, weapons, book reviews, and many more. I get more response there than anywhere outside FaceBook. But this is a site for people who love beautiful images. As an artist, that is part of who I am. As a writer, Pinterest is not so much help.

Linked-In Groups

This network seems to be more about employment and careers. As I work for myself now, I have very little use for this part of it. However, the groups can be very good sources of information and a way to make yourself known. I used the groups quite a bit for a while and still keep track of what they are doing. It's a good way to meet people in your niche. You'll be surprised. There is probably a group for your niche, maybe several of them.

GoodReads

You can easily become a GoodReads author. There's a link at the bottom of the home page called *author program*. It doesn't take very long to get set up. There's a lot here with groups, reviews, and so on. They have a print giveaway program which I have heard good things about. Again, it takes quite a bit of time, but you can meet readers like you can on few social sites. I've made more personal contact with other authors on GoodReads. Plus, I've found many good books and reviewed a few.

Specialized forums

I've been using christianwriters.com, for example. It's good to talk with peers. Almost every niche, career, activity, group has its own Website, FaceBook group, and/ or forum. But there are many.

My problem is that a forum is a very difficult type of communication if you do not know haw to use it. The basic step to take is simple.

Sign up for email notification of everything

This way you become part of the forum's overall conversation. Obviously, you want to find forums in which they talk about your interests. Don't fear being overwhelmed. You do not have to participate in every conversation. You only want to add a comment when you have something worthwhile to say. This is not a place for promotion, but a place for communication with like-minded people.

Your email list and newsletter

For ministries, many people I know tell me that this is their big money maker. It is used primarily for non-profit fundraising. It's not a good way to sell books. It's an excellent way to get people involved in your ministry. At this point, I don't even use one. If you have a good-sized list of readers addresses, give it a try.

A list is a strict taskmaster

Once you start an email newsletter, you are committed to a publication schedule. The first few newsletters are relatively easy to write. The difficulty comes in fifteen months or three years down the road. It's a long term commitment. Do start one unless you plan to do it.

For a resource, a company like MailChimp or Constant Comment is a great way to start off your newsletter. But even with the best software, there's a lot of writing involved in a useful newsletter your followers will look forward to receiving on a regular basis.

Find your own way

You need to budget your time and not waste it. There are ways to keep your time expenditures under control. Try things. If they become intrusive, cut back. Follow the lead of success and effectiveness along with the nudges of the Holy Spirit. If something doesn't work, drop it [unless the Lord orders you not to do that]. All of this is done in service to your King. However, this is a long-time commitment to your life as an author. Your readers and fans want and need a way to be in touch with you. It's up to you to provide that for them.

You are a writer. You need to be writing!

The most constant advice given to new authors who are worried about marketing their book is to get a second book out and a third. You cannot build on one book. You need multiple books and series—develop a body of work.

This is the difference in self-publishing. A traditional publisher will focus on one book and what it can sell in a month or two. A self-publisher is concerned with building a body of work for an on-going reader base.

The likelihood that your first book is even important to your writing career is low. Of course, there are exceptions. But, when I go back and look at my earlier books, it's very embarrassing. Even though these books have their followings so I cannot just delete them—my skill levels were so poor back then. The rule is that your work will be transformed by the books that sell enough to build a following. You have no idea which books they will be before you release them.

Build on your successes

When you find a book that seems more popular than usual, see if there are other books you could write that build on the popular book's success. But regardless keep writing. It takes a while to learn how to produce good work. You don't have your vision developed until you work out the details.

Make your novels into series. I just read an account from a young author where success, in terms of sales, didn't come until the fourth in the series. In fact, the author had dropped the whole thing and did something else for many years before she came back to writing.

Be prepared for surprises. Many of the books I have done had little response. The ones which succeeded surprised me. Over the years a body of work has emerged with nearly four dozen titles (many of which were simply junk). Right now I have six books in various states of writing and production. I'm truly amazed at where this all ended up. You will be also.

My writing income grows and solidifies every year. More and more my social presence grows and becomes more fruitful. I have met some wonderful people.

Have fun with it!

CHAPTER THIRTY-FIVE

What sells your books online

Simple answer: no one knows! They really don't. There are hundreds of books telling you how to sell your books. All anyone can do is give general guidelines. The only things which will actually sell many of your books are the personal recommendations of your readers to their friends and followers.

- **What should you do?**
- **How will you know what works?**

Conventional wisdom says that, for new and unknown authors, the social marketing tools and techniques we just covered briefly are essential. Building an Author Platform is key. But is this really true? As believers we know that reality is rarely what the world suggests. We need to be very careful lest we fall to the world's level.

Look at yourself and your book buying habits. *How do you find the books you read?* I used to find all of my new authors browsing in a brick and mortar store. That is no longer the case. I haven't found a new author in a bookstore for years. In fact, our local B&N doesn't even carry new Christian authors, let alone indies.

Where do I find new books?

- 💠 **Most of them are recommendations from online contacts**

- 💠 **I hear of books on TV shows.**

- 💠 **I read about interesting books in some of the RSS feeds and newsletters I get.**

- 💠 **I see things through Twitter, FaceBook, and all the rest.**

- 💠 **I find new books and new authors through the amazing recommendation engine developed by Amazon.**

Do you think they Google your book?

When researching, Google is a major tool. This is true for most people. Miranda Miller, on Search Engine Watch[3], December 17, 2012, reported that Google continues to grow coming closer and closer to the 70% mark. Bing is also growing with a bit over 25% of the search engine traffic. That only leaves 5%, supposedly, for everyone else. But this really only affects searches for general subject matter available for free online. This is important to those who primarily sell expertise on a specific subject. It is of little use for readers looking for new authors and new books, especially fiction.

How do they find your book?

As brick and mortar store profits go away, they usually only stock best sellers and authors with a following. For self-publishers, brick and mortar stores are usually not available. For unknown authors, even large online bookstores like Books-a-Million and CBD [the dominant Christian bookstore online and by catalog] will not list your work.

A necessary budget? Nope!

None of the traditional points of sale are available to unknown authors releasing their first book unless you invest quite a bit of money. I have built my career never charging and by only paying cash. I have a budget of zero.

3   http://searchenginewatch.com/article/2232359/Google-Takes-67-Search-Engine-Market-Share

So, the efforts I recommend don't cost money. What they take is perseverance and a willingness try new things.

The most popular search engine for books: Amazon

The reality of book sales for us, at this point, is that the most popular search engine for books—by far—is the one developed by Amazon on its site. No one else comes close their recommendations, also reads, and so on.

The reason Amazon sells so many books is not because Kindle is so wonderful. Remember they were dominating online sales of books way before Kindle was available. They so this because of service and price, but the main resource they have in this endeavor is their internal search and recommendation engine. They are in a league apart. Here's a quote from The Digital Reader, October 2015:

> "It's the first new look at the market that I have seen in...over a year, and it does not paint a heart-warming picture for those who hate Amazon. The report finds that Amazon can lay claim to 74% of the units sold in the US ebook market, and 71% of the dollars spent.

> "Something like 99% of consumer ebook sales are made through just five major ebook retailers. Amazon accounts for the majority of those sales, with iBooks coming in second with about 10% to 12% of sales.

> "Barnes & Noble has somehow managed to hold on to third place, with roughly 7% to 8%, followed by Kobo with 3% to 4% of sales. And rounding out the top five is Google Play Books, with 1% to 2% of the US ebook market."[4]

However, it differs for everyone. What we know for sure is that things continue to change rapidly in ebook sales. I know that the iBookstore and Kobo are virtually tied for 2nd. Google is 4th and Nook is virtually nothing. But all five only add up to 43% of my book sales, and only 63% of my ebook sales.

4   http://the-digital-reader.com/2015/10/09/amazon-has-an-even-bigger-share-of-the-ebook-market-than-we-thought-author-earnings-report/

So, what does this mean in practical terms?

How do you market your books online?

Some people, like Michael Alvear in *Making a Killing on Kindle*, [2012], would argue that only three things matter as far as book sales are concerned. That is his entire focus in his book. I must admit that he has compelling arguments. My experiences with social marketing lead me to believe that his view is probably closer to the truth for most of us than the conventional wisdom about building an Author Platform.

He argues that author platforms are a result of large sales and a huge readership. They don't produce those sales. His purpose is getting those sales.

His three that count are:

- 💜 **Your Book Title**
- 💜 **Your Description**
- 💜 **Your Keywords**

I must agree with him—at least for large-selling books. He dilutes this message later in the book by talking about things he does to maximize sales on Amazon, but he is almost exclusively focused on Kindle. I think that is a mistake.

No one dominates for long in this increasingly chaotic and changeable world. As believers, we know why this is true, and it has nothing to do with economic theories and particular companies—chaos breeds malleable people desperate for leadership from anyone who looks good.

What we need to do is glean wisdom from what we see, and allow the Holy Spirit to show us how to apply it to our situation. For me, Kindle sales are a major source of income. But they sell only a little more than a quarter of my books. Even if I include print books through Createspace, Amazon has only 54% of sales. I don't think the others will roll over & die any time soon. In fact, it is likely that someone will take Amazon's place.

Making your book discoverable

This is the importance of Michael's big three no matter who is selling your books. What will sell your book is the anointing of the Holy Spirit and the word of trusted friends. For some of you, the best place for sales is the table in the foyer where you are speaking with the smiling helpful person to handle it. This should be done professionally also—easy to find and see with good display help.

As we pray for the anointing and readers with a lot of friends, the best thing we can do is set up our book's title, description, and keywords so that people looking for what you are writing about can find the experience in your book easily. This is not difficult and becomes your bottomline tool for reader discovery.

In most cases, your readers are already searching for a book like yours. Your goal must be to learn their needs. Then you set up your metadata so a search for a book like yours leads them to your book at the top of the search results. This is not magic, as we shall see. It is stating the truth in love as it always is for us.

How do we help that to happen? First, of course, we seek inspiration from the Lord. With His guidance, we can use the two top search and recommendation engines in the world today to help us: Google and Amazon.

Using Google's keyword tools

One of the reasons Google is so dominant at this point in time is the statistical analysis available from the immense mass of data they are continuously harvesting about the usage habits of the entire online world. With over two thirds of the world's searches going through Google, they have really good statistics to help us in our research as we attempt to make our title, description, and keywords truly useful.

What they can give us is the number of times a keyword has been searched on a monthly basis. You get there by going to https://adwords.google.com/KeywordPlanner and you have to set up an AdWords account. You can search for any keywords, in any category, with powerful filters and so on. You can discover great information very quickly. And, you do not have to spend anything.

As you can see below, a search for book publishing shows an average of right around twelve hundred searches are made every month for book publishing. Adding InDesign gets it up to nearly 1500 per month. Like I said, it's a pretty small market. But adding desktop publishing to the mix get it up to nearly 8,000 searches a month.

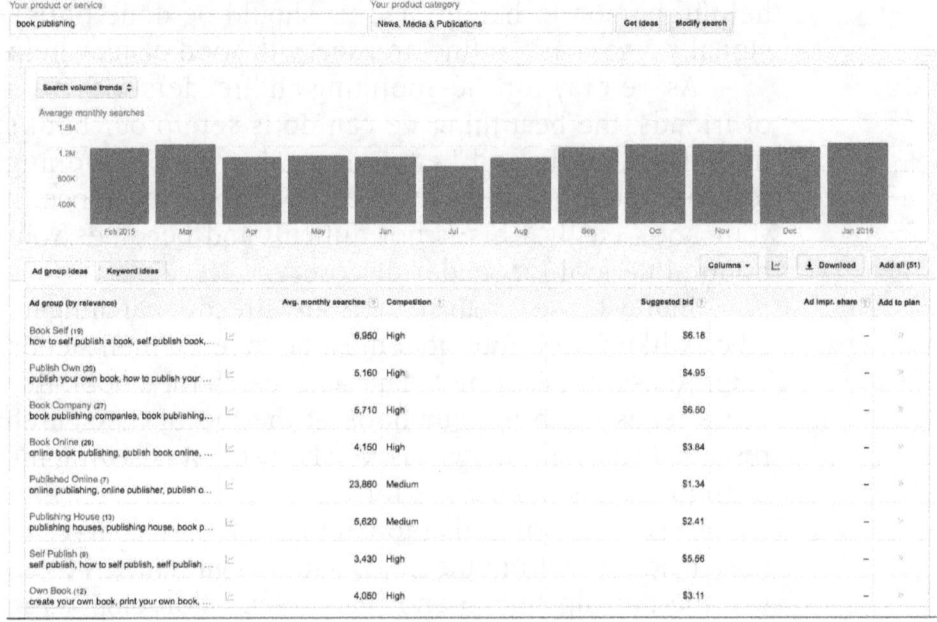

So, what can we do?

The fact of the matter is that if my book does not show up in the first two pages of a Google search, my potential readers will not find it. We want our book to end up high in the Google results. But I want to use an example of the data the AdWords tool gives us to help us as we pray for a title. It will also help us choose keywords. We also need to remember that Google really only helps for non-fiction. For fiction, most readers search on Amazon. For Christians, many would like to use CBD but their search engine is quite poor.

Some results for my marketing book

As I was picking a title for a book I did a couple of years ago (I hadn't yet written the description or decided on the seven keywords allowed by Kindle KDP), I found these phrases (among many others) which I thought were relevant to that book.

KEYWORD PHRASE	GLOBAL SEARCHES
Sell books	673,000
Marketing books	74,000
Market books	60,500
Sell books online	60,500
Marketing books online	2,400
Sell ebooks	27,100
Marketing ebooks	27,100
Books for Kindle	1,220,000
Christian guide	33,100
Books online	2,740,000
Self publisher	8,100
Self publishing	135,000

As you can see, there are massive differences between very similar word combinations. Look at the difference between self publisher and self publishing. I'll get nearly twenty times the hits using -ing instead of -er. I get nearly thirty times the hits using "sell books online" instead of "marketing books online". Just using sell instead of marketing gains me a lot more visibility.

Using Amazon's recommendation engine

The second place to look for naming and word use help is in Amazon itself. Here we are talking about the automatic recommendations which pop up as you start typing in your search for a book.

This works not nearly so well for those of us looking for Christian books. As you know, anyone can call their book Christian, and as far as Amazon is concerned Christian includes Mormons, Christian Scientists, even authors with Christian in their first or last names—like Christianson. **The problem is:** how do I let the readers know that my book is a technothriller which gives a strong example of genuine Christian living among the lies and sin of the intelligence community? Nevertheless Amazon does a very good job.

Below, you can see what happened when I started typing in Christian fantasy and before I got past fan you can see the categories which get attention.

Books ‡	Christian fan

s Deals   Sell

christian fantasy

christian fantasy fiction

christian fantasy books

christian fantasy adventure

christian fantasy fiction books

christian fantasy books for young adults

christian fantasy novel

christian fantasy kindle books

Amazon genre keywords

Another source of help is Amazon's listing of specific keywords for specific sub-genre books. In KDP help, search for "Categories with Keyword Requirements". This brings up a list of categories with keywords Kindle considers necessary for specific genre.

Amazon.com (US)

Biographies & Memoirs

Business & Money

Children's eBooks

Comics & Graphic Novels

Erotica

Health, Fitness, & Dieting

History

LGBT

Literature & Fiction

Mystery, Thriller, & Suspense

Religion & Spirituality

Romance

Science Fiction & Fantasy

Teen & Young Adult

Textbooks

Travel

For Science Fiction & Fantasy we see:

Category	Keywords
Fantasy Characters/Angels	angels
Fantasy Characters/Devils & Demons	demons
Fantasy Characters/Dragons	dragons
Fantasy Characters/Elves & Fae	elf, fae, fairies
Fantasy Characters/Ghosts	ghost, spirit
Fantasy Characters/Gods & Goddesses	deities, god, pantheon
Fantasy Characters/Psychics	psychic, telepathic
Fantasy Characters/Vampires	vampire
Fantasy Chara	shapeshifter
Fantasy Chara	witch, wizard, warlock, druid, shaman
Science Fiction	artificial intelligence
Science Fiction	aliens
Science Fiction	clones
Science Fiction	corporations
Science Fiction	mutants
Science Fiction	pirates, privateer, corsair
Science Fiction	psychics
Science Fiction	robots, androids
Science Fiction	horror
Science Fiction & Fantasy/Humor	humor

> Christian fantasy needs the keyword: god

Another help is the number of books in your category. Searching for "Guide to sell books online" pulls up nearly 2,000 competitors. Adding Christian to the title brings up nine books and no direct competition. That's good. I didn't find any more surprises, though I regularly am surprised at what Amazon comes up with. But we have not dealt with the real problem about these things. Look carefully and pray for wisdom.

An example

I published a book for a friend about creationism, specifically Roger Melquist's *The Young Earth*. He told me he had some direct competition, and he does. But his title still shows up on that first page of a young earth search as #12—with his competition at #1 and #2. But in a bible and science search, his book comes up on page 4 and his competition does not come up at all. For bible, science, and earth he is number one. For science & bible in the Kindle store, he is #7—his competition is missing.

Yet, he professes surprise that all he is selling is Kindle books (and now ebooks from other sources). In fact, for the Kindle store, his book is number three for young earth (and his main competitor is missing). The book is number one for bible, science, and earth. You begin to see how it works.

Google's recommendation engine works the same way. However, does this really give us meaningful, useful information? To a certain degree, yes—but not really.

We are still missing the core

All of these attempts to use the world's tools to get us information ignore several central issues:

- **We really have no idea who our market is:** If you are writing pink, fluffy Christian romances, some categories may be obvious—but, not really.

- **Popularity is meaningless:** The use of Amazon and Google can give us the popular results. But what does that have to do with our mission?

- **Using popular keywords and phrases to trick readers into trying your book is unethical:** In many cases, it may actually be sin—bearing false witness. Amazon may also cut you off.

We always need to go back to the original scripture I quoted at the beginning of this part of the book. I *have renounced disgraceful, underhanded ways; ...refuse to practice cunning or to tamper with God's word, but by the open statement of the truth...*

I will make my works known. The key to the whole thing is getting past your need to be popular. Jesus is not popular—not even in most churches today. The Gospel is especially offensive. By pursuing popularity to gain large sales we are severely compromising our mission. Large sales are the result of the Lord's blessing, or the enemy's. You have choices to make.

We have tools the world would covet

The only person who knows what will happen is the only person with the power to change things. He is also the person who can tell us what to do to mesh with His work in the world. The gifts of the Holy spirit are an immense help to our marketing efforts.

The Spirit can give us wisdom, knowledge, discernment, and anything else we might need to know about our book, its content, and its marketing. This is information which is simply not available to the heathen—oops, non-Christian—authors and publishers.

We can't offend, you know: Balderdash! Our very existence is offensive to all non-believers unless the Lord gives us favor. On the other hand, He can certainly enable us to reach those He wants to touch through our writing. That's our personal calling. We are not called to save the world. That's already been done. Jesus accomplished that perfectly. We are called to listen to and obey the voice of the Lord when He speaks to us.

Nothing more & nothing less!

Remember, in John 5, the Lord himself tells us that in the incarnation He could only follow the Father's leading. If that was true for Jesus, you better believe it is true for us. To be fruitful, we must remain in the vine. Without the vine, we can do nothing. Jesus said that!

The title

Nevertheless, this is very important. Both Google and Amazon rank books higher if the keyword being searched for is actually in the title. In this case, *Book Publishing With InDesign CC*, should work well, especially when adding the sub-title: *Using Desktop Publishing Power To Self-Publish Your Book*.

I have many of those keywords in my subtitle. There is quite a bit of evidence which shows that keywords in subtitles are very effective.

Descriptions

Michael strongly takes the position that the description must be a writer's tour de force, covering all bases and compelling the prospective reader to realize that he or she would be a fool at least or maybe just stupid to not buy and read your book. That sounds really good, but I don't believe we really have that much power to control readership—but offending readers is not good.

I find that Michael's approach is uncomfortable and irritating to read. It works for him, but I don't want people to think of me as they think of Michael.

I see a middle ground here. Rachael Ayala on a guest post at *TheBookDesigner* said the following:

> Fiction readers are looking for excitement or escape. Your job as a writer of fiction is to promise the reader an excellent emotional experience. The first impression may be the only one you'll get. Your cover must be worth a second look, and your summary has to grab and spark curiosity. Story problem, dilemma, and question begging to be answered—the big "what if." Short and sweet. Internet attention span is only a few simple sentences long.[5]

This fits much better with my experience. Though it is true that I usually read the entire description and I'm disappointed if it doesn't cover much (proving Michael's point for some people), many are only going to glance at what shows up—which is Rachael's point. My advice is to make sure that the "short and sweet" version is in the first couple of sentences—make the long one for others. Write it directly to your specific audience. Change it as you get more information.

Basically this revolves around the whole idea of advertising and marketing from the world's point of view. The world would have us believe without advertising we are without hope. The truth is that advertising and marketing are only necessary as a last ditch effort to stave off bankruptcy and/or liquidation. For example, you can look at the companies advertising the heaviest in a blitzkrieg campaign and almost know for certain that they are in trouble. That's normally the case.

The Christian presents himself or herself with the plain statement of the truth in Love. We do it without embellishing (lying) or distorting the truth. We leave the results in the hand of the One we serve.

On the other hand, we are not to be stupid. So we take what the distributors request seriously, like Amazon,

---

5   http://www.thebookdesigner.com/2013/01/fiction-marketing/

B&N, Kobo, the iBookstore, and so on. As believers, we know what we say is important. Our words express the true attitude of our heart. Don't try to trick readers into buying your books. If they hate it, you've got a bad review. We pray for the anointing. We ask for wisdom, and then we do the best we can without fear.

The description is very important!

Research your competition

You are looking for ideas to help you connect with your readers. You are trying to make a spiritual connection with them, meeting their needs, giving them good, solid reasons to buy your book.

For fiction it is much more emotional. You need to express what need in your reader will be satisfied by your book. Is it true love, the ability to help, heal, or protect? You're writing this for your Lord to help your readers see something important. What is that important thing you need to mention?

As you get ready to write your description remember Rachael's three clear points, for sure. But there are many more questions you might need to answer for the prospective reader. This varies a lot between fiction and non-fiction as well as the various niches. Even after you publish, look at the competition, solicit reader opinions, check out your reviews, and the adjust your description accordingly.

Fiction:

First you need to decide which is more important: the plot or the characters? They're both important, but political and military thriller lean much more heavily on the plot than romances do. Mysteries are all about characters, aren't they?

- **What is the major issue, catastrophe, or central conflict?**
- **Who are the main characters?**
- **What are their dreams, plans, or mission?**
- **What is their purpose?**

- What is the trigger for the disaster?
- What's the hook?
- Who or what are the biggest problems faced by the main character?
- Why does it matter?
- What's the core of the story?
- Where does it happen?
- What is the major motivation which causes the story to progress and develop?

Nonfiction How-To:

Here we have the same basic problems but much of the drama is missing. It is up to you to add that excitement to the process or report. You are explaining how you know what the reader's problem is and that you have developed a solution which will solve both the problem and the issues surrounding it for said reader.

Put yourself in the reader's shoes

Try to remember how you felt when you were driven to solve the problem for yourself. Seek especially for the frustrations you experienced. You should be able to answer most, if not all, of the following questions:

- What problem do you solve for the reader?
- How will you do that?
- What are the underlying issues?
- What will happen, worst case, if the reader doesn't solve the problem?
- How does the reader benefit by buying the book?
- What's the promise or incentive?
- What're your qualifications as a writer/teacher?
- How can you demonstrate you empathize with the reader's frustrations, fears, and trials?
- Have you identified the things which keep people from realizing their goals?

- ❧ What will they learn that they don't know already?

- ❧ What are your readers currently doing wrong that buying your book will correct?

- ❧ Have you given clear and real examples about actual people?

- ❧ Have you written in the language of your readers, solving real problems?

It's not written in stone

Finally, in this new digital world, you can always change, rearrange, upgrade, and rewrite. Usually there's no penalty. In fact, for an on-demand book or ebook the only things you cannot change are the trim size and the type of book [hard cover, paperback, and so on]. For an ebook, anything goes. But, even for print, you can change the title, layout, size, and anything else if you are willing to publish a new book with a new ISBN.

You can leave both of them available so you can see which book sells better. It may well be that different titles and covers speak to different audiences and niches. I hear regular testimonies from authors who talk about how much their sales went up after they reworked a cover, changed a keyword or rewrote a description to fit with new information about their readers and what they hoped for in their book.

Keywords

We've basically dealt with this already. Pick the ones which should help you the most—especially if you have some good ones which are not covered by your title. Lulu gives you five, KDP takes seven, and the rest all differ. NookPress [Nook] gives you a certain amount of words. Do the best you can.

Then as the book starts selling keep trying to get a feel for when, why, and who. A comment on a blog, tweet, or FaceBook posting can give you superior ideas you'd never thought of. Watch your competition—especially their titles. After a month or six weeks try one or two different ones and see if it changes your sales at all. These things change continuously throughout the life of your book.

Keep it fluid

One of the real benefits to the new on-demand self-publishing paradigm is that updates are allowed and easy to accomplish. If you get a new leading on who your readers are and who the Lord wants you to target, you can change the keywords, description, and anything else very quickly. I had to make a major upgrade to one of my books earlier this week. It took me a half hour to make the changes in the basic documents for print and ePUB. Once they were complete, uploading the changes to the various suppliers took about two hours. The changes were live on all the sites within a couple of hours more. Everything was updated in less than a day. Even if you can't change everything [the size for instance is tied to a specific ISBN], even a new size can be used if you re-release the book as a new book under that new size. It will take a little longer [maybe an extra day] to get the print version approved. But still it's not a big deal. As mentioned, you can even leave both of the titles published to see which one sells better.

CHAPTER THIRTY-SIX

Pricing strategies

You will get a lot of advice about this. Start with prayer and ask the Lord what you should charge. Check out your competition to see what they are getting. If you have big name competition, yours will probably need to be cheaper. However, you do not want to give it away. They'll never respect you in the morning.

For ebooks: There is a general ballpark figure in the publishing world for unknown DIY publishers. It at least gives you some input for a starting price. It assumes a "real" book of hundreds of pages.

Fiction: $2.99

Non-fiction: $4.99

But if everyone else is getting $12.99, you may not sell a thing unless you are $8.99 or a hair more. Mainly, this is just a starting place. After six weeks or so, start adjusting the price up or down a dollar at a time until you find the place where quantity and income are maximized. Make this adjustment every four weeks until you have the best price. Obviously, for your fourth or fifth book you'll have a much better idea of what works.

For print: base your price on the competition as long as you make some profit. If you are in a popular subject area competing against traditionally printed books from large publishers, you may not be able to match their price. Just do the best you can. Cut your profits, if necessary (and if it helps sales). Remember five books at $2.50 beats one book at $10.00.

In this arena, they do not know if you are self-published in many cases. You will be putting your own publishing house logo on the book. So you will not have pressure to strongly cut your prices. But do not get greedy either. You will not make as much profit as you do with ebooks. It costs real money to print books. The suppliers will give you a minimum price to meet costs and you simply adjust that up or down like before.

The large retail discount

Now that Amazon is giving away their extended distribution we are all having to deal with retail pricing. If you can't give 50% off or so, no retailer will touch your book. For many of us (me included) this has meant that the price of my printed books has gone up. Even so, royalties of $5 or so result in a royalty of less than a dollar for distributed books.

This is nothing new. Retailers normally require a 100% markup to stay in business. You might want to advertise the wholesale price at Createspace. Your readers can save a lot of money and you can make more.

For example, I released a book called *How To Teach The Bible* a couple years ago. I started it at $4.99. Sales were slow. I changed it to $.99 and sales improved a lot. After a couple of months, I upped the price to $1.99 and sales stayed at the same level. Several months later, I raised the price again to $2.99. Sales are still good. I do not believe any future increases will help, so I'll leave it at $2.99.

The Free Book Deal

Many authors believe this is what turned the corner for them. This may or may not be true. It may have been true in the past and no longer works. You do need to be prepared to provide free review copies to people. Giving away your non-fiction teaching has some ground in that you were given freely, so you can freely give. On the other hand, a workman is worthy of his hire. There is nothing wrong with expecting people to pay for your work.

Over the years, I have gone many ways on this—both with my fine art and my writings. I have found that people who do not pay for your work normally do not care about it. We are offering something of value when we strive to make a book which will change the lives of our readers. Even if we are offering escapist fluff, we are compelled to write truth.

Giving a book away will not help you at all unless the book truly has worth. This is what you need to strive for. If your only goal is sales quantity and massive income, it is likely you need to do some serious prayer and get your priorities in order. There is nothing wrong with selling a lot of books. There is a problem if that becomes your goal and the focus of your life.

THE ENTIRE BOOK FOR FREE?

Giving someone an entire ebook for free, especially for unknown authors, gives the potential buyer zero incentive to buy your book. Why pay for something (by an unknown author) that's completely free, especially in this economy? Some authors think doing this will generate lots of press (it won't - too many authors have done it before so only well-known authors get big press for this now). Others think giving away their book will increase their readership and help sales of future books. Yeah, this might happen...but people who download free files...aren't usually the type of readers that appreciate artists enough to promote them, or even to follow them and buy their future books. Kind readers, the type that tell their friends about their favorites, want to help authors so they can continue their craft.[6]

Though this attitude has a lot of truth in it, I know as a reader that free books help me find new authors. But, any book under $3 does that for me. I do value the books I actually purchase in most cases. But my case is compromised by the fact I'm a book reviewer.

---

6   http://writersweekly.com/the_latest_from_
angelahoycom/005949_03242010.html

Improving your visibility on Amazon's lists

The basic argument is that massive downloads can boost you to a place on Amazon where the book is internally marketed by Amazon. The problem is that only a genre like romance normally has that level of downloads. You need to give away thousands of books to have any real effect on your book's visibility.

For most of us, a few hundred is the best we can hope for—and they more closely represent lost sales than a marketing opportunity. On FaceBook a group called Christian Indie Authors has many practitioners of this art if you feel ready to proceed in that direction. They can give you a lot of experienced advice and help.

Deceptive practices

One of the real issues for us as believers are current marketing practices which can get us in trouble spiritually. One of the most common is the mass "like" swap. You cannot do this as far as I can tell without bearing false witness. The idea is that a large group of authors go to everyone on the group list and click on the Like button.

How can you like someone you've never talked to, interacted with, or read? It's a lie to say I like you or your books if I've never read any of them. This is especially true if you are writing in a genre I do not like and do not read.

All of this comes under what I was talking about as I began this part of the book [II CORINTHIANS 4: 1&2]. I refuse to practice worldly, underhanded methods of marketing my books. I won't risk removing myself from the Lord's blessing of the book. Mainly, it's a horrible witness to other believing authors as well as to my readers.

We are held to a higher standard

Our writing career is held not only to Biblical standards but to the higher standards of a Christian teacher. If we want the Lord to bless our efforts, we need to talk to Him about it, follow His lead, and work toward the vision He gives you. The type of book you write is between you and the Lord.

Colophon:

This book has been written in my small office at the back of our 132 year old [1881], two-story framed home in southern Minnesota—Mankato to be specific: It is a beautiful old section of this small city with streets lined with large, mature trees, brick and framed two and three story homes, near the bottom of the large (200–300 foot) bluffs lining the Minnesota River valley in this area. This is part of the view through the window next to my built-in desk. Actually it's the view last month. I'll show you the view a month from now on the next page.

I have a 21.5" late 2013 iMac running El Capitan with 16gb ram, an old Epson scanner, and cable modem access to the Web. I'm using Adobe's InDesign CC 2015 for this book, plus Photoshop and Illustrator.

For the fonts, I designed the basic fonts used in this book in FontLab 5. My most recent fonts have been designed for my new book on font design, *Practical Font Design With FontLab 5*. The serif faces are from the four-font Librum family and the headers are from the companion four-font family I designed for Librum: Librum Sans. The large heads are done in Bream, the a two-font display version of Librum. For ePUBs, I have a five font Librum E family with only the ASCII characters.

I produced all the graphics as well, though there are several royalty-free photos scattered in the book. The captures were mainly done with OSX's shortcut and Snapz Pro X, though I used Grab for timed captures.

As usual, it has been great fun putting this book together for you. I pray it's helpful for you in your work.

Today, it's nearly sixty in early April and spring is coming in a month or so.

Saturday, April 5, 2016 • Mankato, Minnesota

A extensive index

Symbols

A

B

My online presence

Bergsland DESIGN Since 1967

This is my primary graphic design site focused upon font design, book design, and typography. It includes my font design efforts, Hackberry Font Foundry, and all my book design and typography work through my blog:

The Skilled Workman

This blog has been the focus of my book design and typography work since the mid-1990s. http://bergsland.org Since 2009, when writing and publishing became my full-time work, this Website/blog has been the center of the design portion of my work.

Reality Calling

This Website/blog has become the outlet and expression of my Christian ministry. It is focused upon supporting Christian authors of fiction and non-fiction. Much of the site is about book reviews of Christian speculative fiction.

In addition, it is the home of Radiqx Press, a Christian publishing house. We are accepting manuscripts at this time.

Social media links

Facebook: https://www.facebook.com/radiqxpress
Twitter: I use @davidbergsland for Bergsland Design and @radiqxpress for Radiqx Press.
Pinterest: https://www.pinterest.com/radiqxpress/
Google+: https://plus.google.com/+DavidBergsland/posts

www.ingramcontent.com/pod-product-compliance
Lightning Source LLC
Chambersburg PA
CBHW080648190526
45169CB00006B/2029